Society Explained

Society Explained

An Introduction to Sociology

Nathan Rousseau

ROWMAN & LITTLEFIELD
Lanham • Boulder • New York • Toronto • Plymouth, UK

Published by Rowman & Littlefield
4501 Forbes Boulevard, Suite 200, Lanham, Maryland 20706
www.rowman.com

10 Thornbury Road, Plymouth PL6 7PP, United Kingdom

British Library Cataloguing in Publication Information Available

Library of Congress Cataloging-in-Publication Data
Rousseau, Nathan, 1957–
Society explained : an introduction to sociology / Nathan Rousseau.
pages cm
Includes bibliographical references and index.
ISBN 978-1-4422-0710-3 (cloth : alk. paper)—ISBN 978-1-4422-0711-0 (pbk. : alk. paper)—ISBN
978-1-4422-0712-7 (electronic)
1. Sociology. I. Title.
HM585.R677 2014
301—dc23
2013048231

∞ ™ The paper used in this publication meets the minimum requirements of American
National Standard for Information Sciences Permanence of Paper for Printed Library
Materials, ANSI/NISO Z39.48-1992.

Printed in the United States of America

Contents

Introduction

Welcome to the wonderful world of sociology! This book presents a holistic view of society using concepts from sociology and other fields of study in order to help you, the reader, better understand yourself and the social world around you. I hope this explains the ambitious title of the book. I do not believe that a single source can tell a person everything about a subject area, and if you are using your critical thinking skills, you are aware of this, as well. However, this book puts forward an interdisciplinary framework for understanding that seemingly abstract phenomenon called *society*. After you finish reading this book, my hope is that you will feel confident in using this framework to explain society for yourself.

I earned my degree in sociology in 1993 from the University of Oregon. I was studying to become a psychologist, but I found that field too limiting. At that time, psychologists were not sufficiently addressing the social conditions that affect what goes on inside the mind of the individual. Today, there are several areas where sociologists and psychologists meet in their understanding of human behavior (e.g., social cognition, constructivism, social epidemiology, and social neuroscience).

I remember telling my parents that I was going to change fields, from psychology to sociology, and they were a little upset; they weren't exactly sure what sociologists do. Actually, the field is vast, and sociologists work at universities, research institutes, hospitals, government, and industry. I would say that the reason why people know so much more about psychology than sociology is because American culture has always celebrated the myth of individualism. Psychology fits well into American mythology. I say *mythology* because myth always contains elements of both truth and exaggeration, and while there is some truth to American ideas concerning individualism, it is also wildly exaggerated. This topic will be discussed in detail later in the book, but for now I would just ask the reader to consider that individual achievement always feels more rewarding when others know about it.

Another reason why psychology is more widely known than sociology is because during World War II, military and business leaders discovered that psychological testing could be very useful for predicting behavior and placing people in jobs. Psychology boomed after the war. There is a really good, thought-provoking book written by psychologist James Hillman and journalist Michael Ventura called *We've Had a Hundred Years of Psychotherapy— And the World's Getting Worse.* The book is basically about how people need to take greater responsibility for the consequences of their actions on others and on what the authors refer to as the *world's soul.* Becoming more accountable requires taking a close look at one's assumptions. One popularly held assumption is that self-reflection can inform people about the underlying causes of their feelings and actions. There is no question that self-reflection can lead to self-insight; however reflection can also be self-serving and thereby be deceiving. Sometimes other people see you better than you see yourself. I believe that if there were an explosion of interest in sociology, like there was in psychology in the 1940s, people would better understand themselves, each other, and their society.

I decided to write this book after teaching sociology for many years and not feeling particularly happy with the book options for introducing people to the study of society. Reading a book is like having a conversation with another person. People write books, in part, because they have a lot on their mind, and they wish to share their thoughts with others. That is what I have done here, and I would like you, the reader, to engage in a conversation with me about a variety of social topics. We will discuss relationships, money, politics, religion, and other subjects. You may or may not agree with what I have written, but I would appreciate your giving the ideas presented here a fair hearing.

Authors regularly say that the books they have written are distinct from other books already published in the subject area. Indeed, in order to get a book published, an author has to convince a publisher that the presentation of their material is unique and will sell. I believe that this book actually delivers on that score. Textbooks have become a part of the corporate book world, and, with that, pressures to sell books have created an assembly line of texts that repeat a particular formula regarding what sociologists supposedly want people to know about sociology. The books are big, heavy, expensive, colorful, and sometimes they inadvertently make a thoroughly interesting subject boring. There are also a relatively large number of smaller and shorter books that introduce readers to sociology, but they tend to follow the same basic formula of the bigger texts.

This book is different in a number of ways from what has become the standard formula. Most authors of sociological books discuss concepts and theories in order to educate readers about society; in this book, I discuss society in order to educate readers about the usefulness of sociology. Moreover, I do not limit the discussion of society to sociological concepts and theories; society is a complex phenomenon and multiple fields of study, like anthropology, social psychology, political science, and economics, have made important contributions to understanding social behavior and society. As a result, as I discuss various facets of society, I refer to concepts and theories from whatever field of study that I believe best explains that aspect of social behavior or society.

August Comte, the individual who coined the term *sociology*, envisioned sociology as a field of study encompassing other social sciences. In more recent years sociologist C. Wright Mills (1972, p. 24) expressed a comparable view: "[T]he sociological tradition contains the best statements of the full promise of the social sciences as a whole . . . ." This book is consistent with that vision, and I believe that it results in a more meaningful understanding of how society works and what role each person plays in making society what it is.

Another difference between this book and many others is its application of what sociologists call the *sociological imagination*. C. Wright Mills introduced the concept with the publication of a book bearing that title. In developing the concept of the sociological imagination, Mills wanted to inspire people to investigate how social and historical factors impinge upon their personal lives. Discussion of this concept has become nearly obligatory in books introducing readers to sociology. The problem, though, is that the standard treatment of the concept in many books is to say something like, "we should all develop our sociological imaginations and change the system," and then to proceed by giving scant attention to history. In this way, neither personal (psychological) nor social (institutional) factors are contextualized, and this undermines the ability to develop and use the sociological imagination as I believe Mills intended. Mills's concepts are often used today in ways that, unfortunately, made him suspect by the standards of other sociologists in his own day and contributed to his becoming an intellectual outsider.

In order to develop one's sociological imagination, a person must become familiarized with history, particularly how past events shape contemporary assumptions and practices. In this book, I give a lot of attention to the historical development of social practices and their associated psychological assumptions, particularly in the chapters on politics and religion. If there is any shortcoming to my presentation of information, it is that I do not get into the debate raging in some academic circles about what constitutes history. I concur (as I believe many sociologists would) with the following statements made by historian George M. Marsden:

[D]eep-seated cultural patterns, ideals, values, and assumptions exert a subtle and often unrecognized influence on everyone in that culture. To the extent that these influences remain unconscious we are controlled by them . . . . So, as the analyst brings unconscious psychological factors into consciousness by tracing their roots . . . , the historian brings cultural patterns, ideals, values, and assumptions to consciousness by tracing them back to their historical origins. If only the present is considered, current political and social patterns, as well as general cultural ideals, often appear to have a certain inevitability about them. Once it is seen, however, how these patterns or ideals developed, who first formulated them, what preceded them, and what were the alternatives, they lose that illusion of inevitability and it is possible . . . to understand them better. (cited in Noll, Marsden, & Hatch 1989, p. 147)

For those readers who are new to sociology, I believe that you will find the presentation of the material in this book to be challenging but accessible, as well as interesting and relevant. For those readers who are already familiar with sociology, I hope that you will find the presentation of the material to be both novel and informative.

FORMAT OF THE BOOK

Chapter 1 introduces the reader to some of the historical factors and personalities that contributed to the rise of sociology in the nineteenth century. The chapter includes a discussion of the sociological perspective. Learning to think like a sociologist involves realizing that sociology is a social science with a particular way of assessing the world. Truly acquiring a sociological perspective requires being open to thinking about familiar things in ways that may be unfamiliar or uncomfortable. In order to see society through the eyes of a sociologist, you must first be fitted with sociological lenses. Vision through these lenses will enable you to see that human beings are social creatures and that even when we assume that we are free or alone, we are not. The chapter includes some discussion of the social glue that holds individuals and society together.

Each chapter builds on the ideas of the preceding chapters. Chapter 2 adds greater detail about the sociological perspective. The chapter discusses how and why Americans value individualism and the benefits and costs of recognizing the importance of the person but not the significance of social bonds. Many people see the individual and society as distinct entities, but intricate connections bind the two, even when social factors are at odds with the interests of individuals within the society. This chapter discusses the various social layers that connect individuals and society. It shows how individuals are connected through social networks and how different social institutions are connected and make up what is called the social structure of society. Given that individuals and society are interconnected, people have more power to effect changes in society than they usually realize. This chapter ends with a discussion on social inequality and change.

Chapter 3 takes a close look at culture, subcultures, and stereotypes, and challenges readers to examine their assumptions and biases regarding other people. Stereotyping not only leads to the disservice of others, it leads to a disservice of self because it is a relatively thoughtless way of assessing another and a circumstance—an inclination or social habit that undermines the potential of the situation. This chapter also takes a closer look at the various ingredients—such as language, norms, and values—that make up the social glue that holds American culture together. For example, the chapter shows how America's value of individualism is maintained. The chapter concludes with a discussion about the liberties and challenges presented by postmodern values.

Each of the preceding chapters has mentioned the importance of social-ization, and chapter 4 discusses three overlapping types of socialization: primary socialization, which occurs from birth to about the age of five; secondary socialization, which follows from primary and may continue throughout life; and consumer socialization, which became more important and influential over the course of the twentieth century. The chapter includes a discussion on cognitive development and examines the roles of play and imagination in human growth and development. Other sociologists have ex-plored the interconnections among play, imagination, and socialization, but the topic gets short shrift in most books that are intended to introduce readers to sociology. In this chapter, there is room to play! Given that the United States is the world's capitalism capital, production, marketing, and consump-tion are central themes in the lives of most Americans. More and more people today define their identity, and judge others, in terms of their consu-mer habits. Because of its importance, the final section of this chapter fo-cuses on how people are socialized into consumerism, and the impact this has on the person, relationships, and culture.

Chapter 5 delves into American politics, ideology, and money. The his-torical section of the chapter reviews how the nation's founders were able to put their differences to the side in order to create a new government. Many of the debates that occur today among liberals and conservatives date back to the birth of the country, so learning about how previous generations of politi-cal leaders with different worldviews were able to keep the government running may be instructive. This chapter includes a discussion about the origins of liberalism and conservatism, what these ideologies originally re-ferred to, and how they evolved to take on their present meaning. The chapter also includes a discussion about money and politics—specifically, how changes in economic conditions and politics led to the formation of a world-wide economy or globalization, how globalization has influenced the nature of work in the United States, and how contemporary working conditions create opportunities for some and continuous challenges for most. The final section of the chapter discusses the role of money in politics, as well as how today's ideological divide between the extremes in both major political parties contributes to inefficiency and corruption.

The main focus of chapter 6 is on the significant and shifting roles of the family in individual and social life. Readers will learn that the concern about the decline of "family values" in America is very old—the Puritan settlers expressed concern about it! Debates over high divorce rates, legal abortions, birth out of wedlock, and latchkey kids also go back many years in American history. The family has always been a flexible economic unit, adjusting to changing environmental and social conditions. The early settlers of the United States usually shared a one-room house, and everyone had a job to do in order to make their agrarian economy work. Industrialization reflected a new economy and a changing society, and, in terms of the family, these changes created a clear separation of roles associated with work and home. By the end of the nineteenth century, industrialization and other factors unique to American culture contributed to making the United States the world's leader in terms of both marriage and divorce rates. These trends would continue to the present time with the exception of the 1950s, when, for a number of reasons that will be discussed, getting married and having children was very popular. The chapter includes a detailed discussion about how modern social trends affect individual decision making regarding work and relationships. The chapter's final section on the meaning of love is another distinguishing feature of this introductory book on the study of society.

Chapter 7 discusses the ongoing importance of religion for individuals and society. Many intellectuals over the past hundred years or so have argued that religion is on the decline; however, a look around the world shows that religion today is alive and well. According to surveys, the United States is the most religious nation in the industrialized world. The United States is also the most diverse nation in the world. As it turns out, these two factors have much in common. Because the United States is founded on the separation of church and state and the culture insists on religious tolerance, a wide variety of religious groups have taken root and blossomed in the country. This chapter discusses the religious beliefs of the founders of the nation, the Great Awakenings that influenced American culture, the relationship between capitalism and religion, the difference between religion and spirituality, and the long-running squabble between religious liberals and religious conservatives.

The final chapter of the book is on education and social change. The chapter discusses the role of education in society as both a means to socialization as well as to innovation. As a source of socialization, education preserves social order and works against innovation. While education also can be a source of change and innovation, change doesn't always mean innovation, just as the accumulation of facts does not necessarily translate into becoming knowledgeable. Social change is only possible when a sufficient number of people or a critical mass is in agreement at the same time about an issue and they have the means to communicate with each other and direct their collective energy into an identifiable movement. Social change may be abrupt or gradual, and it can result from natural factors (such as the impact of a tremendous storm on a community) and from human-made factors (such as the impact of computer technology on social relations). The chapter notes that while many things change over time, some things never seem to change; for example, as fast as technology can go today, people can only absorb so much information at a time.

ACKNOWLEDGMENTS

When I began working on this project, the acquisitions editor was Alan McClare. We had spoken on a number of occasions about this project and an earlier book idea. We never met in person, but we enjoyed such an easy rapport that I felt I had a sense of the man. One month after we last spoke, I learned that he had suddenly died. I felt a sense of loss, even though we never met face-to-face. This book is, in part, dedicated to his memory.

When Sarah Stanton stepped in as the acquisitions editor, she asked me to resubmit my proposal for this book. I wasn't sure what would happen next. Fortunately, she supported this book project. It has been about three years since I first resubmitted my proposal to Sarah, and in this time, I have come to appreciate her support and patience. Writing a book is a lot of work, and everything always seems to take longer than it should—especially if you are a perfectionist.

The ideas expressed throughout this book come from years of reading, teaching, and reflecting on the conversations I have had with people, either through their books or in person, about individual and social life. My appreciation of social history and the world of ideas, which are apparent throughout this book, were impressed upon me during my years at the University of Oregon, and in particular, through many conversations with Professors Benton Johnson and Richard Chaney.

Finally, I would like to acknowledge the members of my family. As I am concluding the writing of this book, my son Malcolm is 11, and although I have tried to not let work interfere with play, my preoccupation with deadlines has sometimes precluded playfulness. Creating this book's cover drawings with him was really fun, though; thank you, Malcolm! He and my wife, Sonya, have been of great support to me during this lengthy process. Sonya is not only very smart, she is also a wonderful sounding board and editor. I have learned a great deal from her, not only about relationships and life, but about writing, as well.

Chapter One

Observing Social Life

In the introduction of this book, I noted that American culture places greater value on the subject matter of psychology—the individual—than the subject matter of sociology—interdependence, or more specifically the relationships among individuals and institutions. The subject matter of psychology seems more relevant to our personal lives. The circumstances and events that occur in our lives appear to us to be caused by our individual choices. Moreover, psychology's subject matter (the individual) is tangible and therefore requires less abstract thought than is necessary to grasp the basic subject matter of sociology (interdependence). Nevertheless, with a little effort, we can learn how to observe social life.

Learning to think sociologically requires, first of all, knowledge about where to look for interdependence. In this book the terms *interdependence*, *social life*, and *social glue* are used interchangeably. Rather than assuming that the thoughts that run through your mind are derived from you, reflect on the possibility that "your" thoughts are acquired—that your thoughts are not derived from you, but rather acquired by you from others.

Interdependence is reflected in the "oughts" and "shoulds" that run through our individual minds every day. These "oughts" and "shoulds" are learned, and we depend on them to serve as a basis upon which to make our individual choices and to gauge our individual behaviors as "suitable" or "appropriate." For example, interdependence is evident in turn-taking behavior and speech. If people did not coordinate their actions, individuals would routinely run into each other, and if people did not take turns when speaking, communication would be nearly impossible.

Social life can also be observed by paying attention to the rituals surrounding socially valued objects and ideals. Most Americans believe that it is important to stand for the playing of the national anthem and to show respect for the American flag. Standing and showing respect for the song and flag are ritualistic behaviors that are learned. The song and the flag are objects that we have learned to give special value, and we have learned that these objects represent the ideal of freedom. Many of the objects and ideals that we hold dear are special because of what they represent to us in relation to others. An object may hold value because it is part of a family's history, because it is rare (which usually raises the status of the object both in terms of desirability and economic value), or because it stands for an ideal. But in all of these instances, the value is determined as a reflection of social life.

SOCIAL BASIS OF FREEDOM: THE CASE OF THE UNABOMBER

An important ideal in American social life is freedom. Living in the United States we are bombarded—by our parents, friends, educators, politicians, and journalists—with the idea that we are free. When Americans think about freedom, interdependence is usually far from their minds. After all, most of us regard freedom as the ability to do as we individually wish. But the many "oughts" and "shoulds" that daily run through our minds and social interactions clearly show that we do not simply act as we wish. In fact, freedom is both made possible and limited by interdependence. The social glue that makes freedom possible is dramatically illustrated by one of the most exhaustive and expensive manhunts ever conducted by the FBI.

Theodore John Kaczynski was born in 1942 in Chicago, Illinois. He excelled academically, particularly in math. In 1967, Kaczynski won an award for writing the best dissertation in mathematics at the University of Michigan. He was hired right out of graduate school by the University of California, Berkeley and, at the age twenty-five, became the youngest professor ever hired there. However, Kaczynski quit his position as assistant professor of mathematics in 1969, and two years later built himself a cabin in a remote area in Montana where he devoted himself to a reclusive, self-sufficient existence.

Though Kaczynski attempted to seclude himself from modern civilization, development still encroached upon his life. He decided to take matters into his own hands, gave up on the possibility of peaceable social reform, and began advocating revolution, by force if necessary, against the industrialized system. Kaczynski's motivation for revolution against the "industrial system" is revealed in an essay that he wrote called "Industrial Society and Its Future" (or what became known in the press as the "Unabomber Manifesto"). In the paper, Kaczynski states,

> The Industrial Revolution and its consequences have been a disaster for the human race. They have greatly increased the life-expectancy of those of us who live in "advanced" countries, but they have destabilized society, have

made life unfulfilling, have subjected human beings to indignities, have led to widespread psychological suffering . . . and have inflicted severe damage on the natural world. The continued development of technology will worsen the situation. (1995, p. 1)

Kaczynski writes that the type of revolution that he is advocating, which may include violence, is not really against governments, "but the economic and technological basis of the present society" (1995, p. 1). In 1978 he manufactured a bomb and mailed it to an engineering professor at Northwestern University. In 1979 he placed a bomb in the cargo hold of an American Airlines plane; fortunately the bomb was found before it exploded. After the airplane incident the FBI got involved in the case and gave it the code name UNABOM for UNiversity and Airline BOMber. Theodore or Ted Kaczynski would become known in the popular press as the Unabomber.

Labeling the Unabomber a domestic terrorist, the FBI launched a massive investigation to discover his or her identity and whereabouts. Between 1978 and his arrest in 1996, Kaczynski sent sixteen bombs to targets that caused three deaths and twenty-three injuries. The FBI captured Ted Kaczynski at his cabin in Montana after being tipped off by David Kaczynski, Ted's brother, who suspected his sibling's culpability in committing these notorious crimes. Ted Kaczynski is currently serving a life sentence at a federal supermax facility in Colorado. Supermax prisons house those individuals who are considered to be the most dangerous to society.

Ted Kaczynski chose to reject the society of which he himself was a product. His abilities to reason, write, and build things were the result of learning from others. When he chose to live as a recluse, the skills, words, and ideas that he acquired in response to his social life went with him. We are made human by our early experiences with others. We learn our language and develop skills in relation to others. This process of developing our capacities for human expression through social relationships is called *socialization*. Ted Kaczynski may have lived alone, but he was enveloped in thoughts about, and inspired by, others.

The case of Ted Kaczynski shows, among other things, that self-reliance does not guarantee freedom. How do people acquire freedom? Freedom only has meaning when one becomes conscious of the idea of freedom, and one acquires an awareness of freedom only through relationship with other self-conscious beings. Can you recall the first time an adult asked you, "What do you want to be when you grow up?" The question itself reflects an appreciation of individual differences. In contrast, in many traditional societies, if you are born female it is assumed that your role in society will be that of mother, and the choice of not having children or postponing the role of motherhood in order to first secure a career does not arise. The question of a future societal role presupposes a certain level of autonomy among people. Individual differences can be valued only in an environment that already assumes a certain degree of autonomy. Autonomy itself is not only a function of exercising individual will. Indeed, if each person tried to exercise their individual wills without restrictions, social order would collapse into social chaos. Freedom arises from the construction of, and adherence to, a certain type of interdependence.

By society's standards, Ted Kaczynski crossed the line of appropriate behavior, violating an important "should": thou shall not kill. The exercise of autonomy among a group of people is not simply a product of each doing as he or she pleases, but is the result of each member of a group learning to abide by certain restraints on behavior. The French sociologist Émile Durkheim referred to this type of constraint as *negative solidarity*. According to Durkheim, "[T]he system of order . . . arises, not from competition, but purely from abstention. [T]he rules relating to 'real' rights and personal relationships . . . form a definite system whose function is not to link together different parts of society, but on the contrary to detach them from one another, and mark out clearly the barriers separating them" ([1933] 1984, p.75).

Negative solidarity is a socially recognized practice of self-control. Because it represents a constraint on behavior, the type of solidarity that it produces is negative: it reflects what people have agreed to not do. Negative solidarity arises under circumstances where people realize that their concerns may be best met by not engaging in certain behaviors. Individuals lining up at a movie theater to see a film are engaging in negative solidarity. The alternative would be a chaotic dash to the entrance. By not rushing to be first in the theater, individuals are exercising restraint, and this permits for a smooth flow.

Durkheim adds ([1933] 1984, p.75), "Negative solidarity is only possible where another kind is present, positive in nature . . . ." Positive solidarity reflects the liberties that people feel they have the right to exercise in their relationships with others. After waiting in an orderly manner at the theater, people would feel a little cheated if they could not get in, and they would feel that their individual rights were being violated if the theater refused to accept their money (even though their money is the same as everyone else's) or refused to sell popcorn to them for no apparent reason. Note that the ability of the individual to engage in a particular behavior is contingent upon mutual agreement.

A woman's right to vote was won by a group of women who worked tirelessly to convince male lawmakers that it was in the best interests of the nation to support that right and to impose laws to prosecute those who would attempt to obstruct that right. When civil rights legislation was passed in the 1960s, the National Guard served to restrain those opposed to school desegregation. Today, those who exercise their right to vote or to frequent whatever establishment they choose, assume a liberty that had to be won, and those who, for whatever reason, may be against certain groups having these rights, must assume self-restraint.

Durkheim noted, many years before the civil rights movement, that " . . . for a man to acknowledge that others have rights, not only as a matter of logic, but as one of daily living, he must have agreed to limit his own" ([1933] 1984, p.75). The point is that individual freedom is not merely about doing as we please; the amount of freedom exercised by any individual in a group is determined by the consciously and unconsciously agreed upon coordinated actions of the group members.

The dynamic interplay between negative and positive solidarity represents the social glue that makes any amount of freedom possible. Without the interdependence that produces, maintains, and reinforces solidarity, freedom is nonexistent, limited, or reduced to chaos. Kaczynski's actions of violating negative solidarity made many people fearful of opening their mail (thereby limiting an assumed freedom). Such infringement created the social need for an organized search for the perpetrator. The principles of negative and positive solidarity, and the freedoms associated with them, could be restored only by forcefully restraining the actions of the violator.

The reason why individuals have difficulty recognizing the medium that their liberties depend upon is that, as people have acquired and demanded more freedoms, the actual bonds holding people together have decreased in number and become more difficult to perceive. The development of modern civilization coincides with the demise of absolutes made by absolute leaders, and the rise of political, religious, and family practices reflective of, and conducive to, individual decision making. The greatest bond holding us together may be our mutual interest in supporting individual decision making. Our learning to value individual differences has overshadowed our learning to value interdependence.

HISTORICAL OVERVIEW OF THE SCIENCE OF SOCIETY

The rise of the study of society coincided with a series of historical events that focused thought among keen observers of social life on how individuals working in groups form, maintain, and change the social conditions under which they live. Pointing to the moment in time when a train of thought originates is a somewhat arbitrary process, but many social scientists agree that in the Western world, a fundamental shift in thinking about individualism, social relations, and the distribution of power in society occurred during a period of time known as the Enlightenment.

From roughly 1600 to 1800, a wide-ranging number of thinkers took advantage of the relatively new technology of printing in order to write down and disseminate their ideas. The Enlightenment was not a coordinated social movement, but rather a dialogue held by a number of commentators about individualism, power, social relations, religion, education, and other matters. This dialogue resulted in more and more people questioning the limits they felt were being imposed upon them by the controlling institutions of the day. The thinking of Isaac Newton in the natural sciences, John Locke on rights in civil society, Voltaire on social reform, and others stimulated new thinking about freedom and the capacity of human beings to bring greater order and justice into the world. The thoughts that culminated in the period known as the Enlightenment contributed to the rise of systematic inquiry and the revolutions for freedom that occurred first in England, then in America, and, shortly afterward, in France.

As innovative ideas in physics gave birth to the systematic study of the natural world, philosophers and reformers set forth to study the world of humankind systematically. The social world was changing in dramatic ways due to the rise of industrialization, capitalism, innovations in science, and the revolutions for freedom. French philosopher August Comte (1798–1857) argued that a science of society was needed in order to observe and describe the social developments taking place in a systematic manner. Originally calling this new field of inquiry *social physics*, Comte later replaced that label with the one he coined: *sociology*.

Though Comte's influence in the development of sociology, and social science in general, is clear, the pioneering works of Emile Durkheim (1858–1917), Karl Marx (1818–1883), Max Weber (1864–1920), and Georg Simmel (1858–1918) solidified sociology as an academic discipline. Durkheim taught the first course in sociology. Marx was one of the earliest thinkers to develop an economic theory of social change. Weber wrote on a number of sociological topics such as the relationship between religion and economy and the rise of bureaucracies. He also wrote the first encyclopedic book on sociology, nearly 1500 pages in length, entitled *Economy and Society* ([1954] 1978). Simmel, along with Weber, established the first sociological society or scholarly group devoted to the explication of sociological themes. Simmel developed a series of fascinating arguments concerning the nature of social interaction. Sociology emerged as a legitimate field of study as intellectuals began to recognize that, through systematic inquiry, one could acquire a clearer understanding of the factors that shape social life.

The seminal works of Durkheim, Marx, Weber, and Simmel show how factors, both external to and between individuals, profoundly affect the choices that individuals make. For example, by examining suicide rates in different cities in Europe, Durkheim was able to explain why suicide was more likely in some places than in others. He showed that the underlying factor explaining suicide rates is not depression, but rather the degree to which people feel connected to each other. In communities where social bonds are strong, an individual is much less likely to take his or her own life.

Marx explicated how those with wealth shape the priorities of everyone in a culture. In contemporary terms, a person with wealth has a much easier time gaining access to media to promote particular ideas or products. Paying a celebrity to commercialize the message or product can enhance widespread appeal even more. Consider Nike without the star athletes of today.

Weber coined the term *social action* to explain how people adjust their behaviors to each other. For example, in the morning as you prepare for your day, you are very likely to take into consideration what your schedule entails and who you are likely to see. Choices will differ depending upon whether your day will include hanging out with your best friend, going out on a lunch date, going for a job interview, or attending a family gathering. In each case, we orient our individual behavior in different ways in order to meet social expectations.

Simmel pointed out how the number of members in a group influences each of the participants. A group of two involves greater expectations upon each member in order for the group to continue than does a group of three or four. However, with greater expectations usually come more opportunities to establish meaningful interpersonal bonds. In general, the larger the size of the group, the easier it is to avoid feeling a sense of responsibility for the maintenance of the group; yet simultaneously, the bigger the group, the more readily the feeling of personal insignificance arises.

THE SOCIOLOGICAL PERSPECTIVE

The field of sociology has come a long way since the influential works of the founders were written. Sociological theories and methodologies have become much more detailed, varied, and rigorous in describing the factors that influence social life. In fact, the insights of the founders have been refined into what is called the *sociological perspective* of society. Perhaps no one expressed this perspective more powerfully, and thereby contributed more to popularizing it, than C. Wright Mills (1916–1962).

Mills was an American sociologist who, in the 1950s, asked readers to consider how obstacles to achieving one's goals, that appear to be personal shortcomings, can actually stem from political and economic conditions that reflect ongoing historical trends. For example, if one person fails to achieve his or her goals and another succeeds, we are likely to attribute a lack of initiative to the first person and characterize the second person as ambitious or persevering. While Mills did not argue against initiative and perseverance, he did say that political and economic conditions are ultimately the determining factors in whether or not an individual succeeds in achieving his or her goals. Despite advances in civil rights, even today, for women and African Americans in the United States, no amount of hard work is likely to result in equal pay with Caucasian men for doing the same type of work. In general, when the economy in a society is continuously unstable (even if the government is stable), hard work, initiative, and perseverance may be needed on the part of the individual just to make ends meet. Mills noted that "men [and women] do not usually define the troubles they endure in terms of historical change and institutional contradiction. The well-being they enjoy, they do not usually impute to the big ups and downs of the societies in which they live" (1972, p. 3).

Mills referred to the ability to see how social and historical factors affect the individual as the *sociological imagination*. The basic idea is to use your imagination to get out of your own personal frame of reference and then to use critical thinking skills in order to evaluate the social conditions that affect your perspective as well as the perspective of others. Mills added, "The first fruit of this imagination . . . is the idea that the individual can understand his own experience and gauge his own fate only by locating himself within his [time] period, that he can know his own chances in life only by becoming aware of those of all individuals in his circumstances" (1972, p. 5).

By practicing getting outside the frame of reference that you have learned and come to assume, you catch glimpses of social life (without the taken-for-granted elements that create personal bias) that gradually fit together into a picture of how society works. This evolving picture of the dynamic phenomenon called society constitutes the sociological perspective.

The sociological perspective does not lift the burden of responsibility upon the individual for improving his or her life, but it does point out the political, economic, and other social factors that may make achieving this goal difficult. Having a sociological perspective reveals that, as individuals become aware of the social obstacles that undermine their individual success, they can reduce or remove these barriers by working together. The issue of unequal pay for equal work is most likely a remnant of the long history of discrimination in American society. The progress that has been made in reducing discrimination in society is due to the efforts of persons who came together in order to change the social conditions that hampered their individual efforts.

A part of the difficulty associated with acquiring a sociological perspective is that even though we are much more likely to attribute situational causes to our own failings, we tend to attribute personal causes to the failings of others. When we fail, we usually add context to explain the failure, and ultimately we may attribute more of the blame to circumstances than to ourselves. However, when others fail, we usually do not apply the same standard and attribute their failings to personal causes, such as insufficient initiative and drive. This tendency was first identified by the social psychologist Fritz Heider in 1958, and it has been subsequently described by social psychologists as the *fundamental attribution error* (see, for example, Kahneman, Slovic, & Tversky 2007, p. 135).

Living in a society that places significantly more value on the individual than on interdependence most likely enhances the seeming naturalness of underestimating the impact of situational factors in attributing cause to the behavior of others. This is why developing a sociological perspective by using the sociological imagination is so important: It is a means to seeing outside of ourselves. Thinking in these terms is challenging on many levels, yet from the very beginning sociologists have stressed the importance of understanding how social factors impinge upon individual decision making.

ASSUMPTIONS OF THE SOCIOLOGICAL PERSPECTIVE

There are three key assumptions underlying the sociological perspective of society. The first assumption is that human beings are social animals. Our growth and development as individual human beings is contingent upon social conditions and relationships. The second assumption is that individuals working in groups create, maintain, and change the social factors that govern their lives. The third assumption is that, although social patterns (i.e., customs, forms of exchange, etc.) are established by the coordination of individual efforts, over time these social practices are experienced as obligatory. Let us review each of these assumptions.

Some people find it difficult imagining themselves to be animals. But like all mammals, a person who does not eat and drink dies. Like all mammals, there is only one way to further the species. Human beings have spun many tales about what happens after death, but the empirical evidence is out on any of these stories and theories save one: When the heart stops, life stops. Human beings have also expressed many tales and theories regarding love, but real life suggests that love is not necessary for marriage, nor is love necessary for producing a child. What distinguishes us from other mammals is our capacity to reason and imagine. It is probably our ability to imagine that makes it difficult to remember sometimes that, despite our capacity to reason, we are still animals.

Not all animals are social, but human beings are a particularly sociable species (even though we are also the most prone to kill our own kind). According to many sociologists, anthropologists, and evolutionary psychologists, this heightened capacity to organize our behavior in groups has had a tremendous impact on our ability to survive and thrive as a species. Our social nature is clearly evident in the mother-infant relationship. Human infants are among the most helpless creatures born into existence. Most other mammals are walking shortly after birth. A human infant cannot even turn itself over, and it takes months before a baby can hold up its own head. Without constant and enduring care, a human baby cannot survive.

The rate of brain development and the capacity to coordinate the body are tied to survival and longevity. Most mammals live shorter lives than humans, and all mammals depend upon specific physical qualities to enhance the likelihood of their survival. Our survival depends more on our capacity to reason than on our physical capabilities. There are animals in nature that can defeat a human being in every physical capacity (i.e., strength, speed, etc.), but no other animal possesses our capacity to reason.

Our ability to reason is tied to our facility for communication. We reason via words. Babies learn to formulate their babblings into the sounds that they hear, and they learn which sounds will get them what they need and want. Our ability to thrive as a species stems from our capacity to engage in complex communication and reasoning. However, the processes involved require additional time for the human brain to develop. Unlike other mammals, human beings develop neurologically more after birth than before. Rapid brain development during the first year of life facilitates the acquisition of language. The intricate and subtle ways in which human beings communicate is perpetuated by the mother-infant relationship, and this relationship reflects and continues the human proclivity for sociability.

Learning to formulate sounds into speech also comes with a value system. Human infants internalize the worldview of their parents before they have the critical faculties necessary to examine and evaluate what they are being taught. What we learn from our parents in the first few years of life serves as the foundation upon which we evaluate subsequent learning. This process is called *primary socialization* (see chapter four for a detailed discussion on socialization). Our parents, of course, learned what they know through the same means, and so what young children learn from their parents is a version of the world that the parents themselves were taught. Generally speaking, parents are the cultural agents who carry the primary responsibility for *socializing* or instilling into their children the ways of society. Through sociability, an infant's inborn talents and temperament are molded to fit the opportunities that are available to him or her.

One of the goals of childhood is to learn how to fit in with others, and one of the goals of parenthood is to teach a child how to fit in with others. Skills and behaviors that parents believe will help their child fit in and be successful are emphasized and rewarded, while socially unacceptable behaviors are discouraged. A child born with the gift of jumping high and having excellent eye-hand coordination finds his or her skills being channeled quite differently depending upon time and place. Recall the sociological imagination and how social and historical factors shape the lives of individuals. Individuals born with the skills of a Michael Jordan or a Cheryl Miller could not have found success playing basketball had they come along before James Naismith, civil rights legislation, and Title IX.

We are social beings who desire the company of others. In the process of being with others we learn about the world around us, we learn about ourselves, we learn how to interact, and we learn how to fit our inborn talents and skills into the existing milieu. Our individual sociability perpetuates society and society reflects our individual sociability.

SUMMARIZING THE SOCIOLOGICAL PERSPECTIVE

Pulling together the key assumptions of the sociological perspective and the discussion that preceded it, we can summarize the material that has been presented in this chapter so far in the following way: Our sociability or social orientation manifests itself at the individual level as interdependence, and at the societal level this interdependence is the social glue that holds society together. The social glue consists of a series of mutually agreed-upon beliefs and associated behaviors. Consider where our individual beliefs come from. We learn our religious orientation from our parents—we learn from our parents whether or not we should pray and to whom we should direct our prayers—God, Allah, Krishna, and so forth. We learn from our parents a political orientation—in most cases if your parents vote Republican, you vote Republican. At some point in your life you may desire to try on beliefs that are congruent with some of your peers, perhaps in direct opposition to the beliefs of your parents. But note that doing something in opposition points out how fundamental the original learning is to your way of thinking. If you decide to try on "conservative" beliefs because of your peer group and because your parents have "liberal" beliefs, you are still not thinking independently from others.

You and I are born into a social world already in motion—our birth changes our family, but our family expects us to get with its program. You may have dreams of getting into a career and shaping an industry; however, in most cases, the impact that an industry or company will have on you will be greater than your impact is on it.

The society that we create through our interdependence is experienced by each individual as an external force—sometimes threatening and sometimes comforting—but the power behind this force is nothing other than our inherent sociability. When this sociability is violated—either from without, as was the case with the 9/11/2001 attacks orchestrated by Osama bin Laden, or from within, as was the case with Ted Kaczynski—our interdependent voice demands action, and then representative agents from society apply themselves to removing who or what appears to threaten the established order. Ted Kaczynski, though a product of society, had to be removed from society because his actions diluted the social glue holding society together. He must have posed a serious risk, for he was sent to a prison that utilizes the highest level of security available.

HOW INDIVIDUALS MAINTAIN AND CHANGE SOCIETY

At this point it may seem as though sociologists believe that the individual is powerless against the weight imposed by the collective desire to preserve social stability. While it is the case that established beliefs and customs feel obligatory, every belief and custom has an origin, undergoes modification, and may lose credibility. The social world is not exempt from change. The extension of civil rights to more and more people is an example. The social world is made up of individuals engaged in *social interactions*. These interactions form social groups, which form the institutions of society. *Social institutions* include economy, political system, education, religion, and the military. Once formed, social institutions take on a life of their own—they tend to endure beyond the years of the individuals, who, at any given time, comprise them. However, because individuals create social institutions and maintain them through their interactions, they may also change them via their interactions. Sociologist Peter L. Berger (1963) referred to this process as the *paradox of social existence*. Essentially, as society creates us, we create society.

People cannot change the beliefs and practices of society until they recognize how their habits and routines perpetuate the beliefs and practices of society. We may be told over and over again that we are free. At the same time we may be told many times over what we can and cannot do. Many of us simply sidestep this contradiction, never reconciling a lingering belief in personal freedom with experiences that place limits on our actions due to what is expected of us or what is viewed as realistic for us. A key sociological insight from the sociological perspective is that people cannot determine how free they are until they can see how their socialization has influenced their way of thinking and feeling.

By using the sociological imagination, we learn to see beyond the social beliefs and practices that seem obligatory and come to the realization that their imposition is partly due to our complicity; because we are social animals, we usually take the path of least resistance. "Going with the flow" (of society) perpetuates society. Often this is not such a bad thing, but when it is, a sociological imagination can allow you to step outside of the world of the obligatory and envision other possibilities.

While one person cannot change a society, many persons working together can and do change a society. When a critical mass of people envisions another possibility for their society (whether or not they are aware of using the sociological imagination), change happens. The leaders of change, such as Martin Luther King, do not single-handedly alter the beliefs and practices of society. A leader is a focal point for a group. Without a group there can be no leader.

USING *YOUR* SOCIOLOGICAL IMAGINATION

Acquiring a sociological perspective entails learning to observe and evaluate social phenomena in a detached way. This is a more difficult task to achieve than it may sound. Acquiring a sociological perspective means, for example, observing and explaining the religious beliefs of a group while disregarding biases that may be a product of your own religious socialization, or focusing on the impact of an oil crisis in your own nation while disregarding biased assumptions about foreign governments.

It is always easier to assume that what we know and are accustomed to is better than or more in the right than a position that is new and foreign to us. This is referred to as *ethnocentrism*. While ethnocentric beliefs underlie many people's sense of pride in their country and faith, it is also the source of much of the conflict in the world. Acquiring a sociological perspective means becoming aware of individual biases and learning to see past them in order to observe the self in a realistic way and to envision the social world using the widest possible lens.

Seeing yourself in a realistic way begins by recognizing that many of your beliefs do not come from you, but have been taught to you, including the belief that you are an individual detached from the influence of others. Seeing yourself in a realistic way also includes recognizing that as people influence you, you influence people. It is like the saying, "failing to choose is a choice." As social beings, we influence each other. As conscious social beings, our social world is as good or as bad as how responsible we are in the choices that we make in regards to others. Taking responsibility for our actions includes seeing how our actions affect others. Ted Kaczynski was not a responsible person; he could have made other choices that would have communicated his concerns about society without destroying other people's lives.

In modern democratic societies, leaders behave as responsibly or as corruptly as the population permits. Leaders reflect both the interests and the actions of the group they represent. If people generally feel that their leaders are corrupt, then the likelihood is great that the routine actions of the majority of people (including perhaps you, the reader), contain a relatively high frequency of dishonesty and theft in their daily relations with others. The level of responsibility taken by individuals in a society reflects how responsible or corrupt that society is.

HOW FREE ARE WE?

In telling the story of Ted Kaczynski I am also revealing something about myself. In 1993 the search for the Unabomber was national news. I had heard about the FBI's investigation of an unidentified person who had been sending bombs through the mail. The story became personal, however, when one day I received a phone call from an FBI agent. He asked if I could meet with him in about a week. While he would not tell me over the phone about the purpose of our meeting, I agreed to see him. That evening I called my parents and discovered that an FBI agent had already spoken with them. The agent had asked my parents to describe what they knew about my daily activities. I felt a little uneasy about the whole thing even though I knew that I had nothing to hide.

A week went by and the agent came to my home, which at that time was in Portland, Oregon. The first thing that he said to me, after "hello," was something along the lines of, "You were hard to track down." At that time in my life I was moving my way up the West Coast, from San Diego to Portland, because of school or work. From a relatively thick file of papers he pulled out a picture of the man who, at the time, they believed might be the Unabomber.

The Unabomber left clues in his bombs (with the intent of confusing the search for him), and in one of the bombs there appeared the name, Nathan R. In their exhaustive search for the Unabomber, the FBI proceeded to look up every Nathan R. in the country and to correlate them with a likely age-range, level of individual achievement, and physical location.

One parallel that I had with the Unabomber was that I had lived in the areas from which some of the bombs had been mailed. The agent proceeded to tell me details about my recent past that even I had forgotten—like old addresses and phone numbers. He seemed to know where I had been living and with whom I had been associating for at least the past ten years. He was very polite, and after about an hour of talking he appeared to be assured that I was not the person the FBI was seeking.

About a year after the meeting, when I was visiting friends and family in Maryland, I decided that I wanted to get a copy of the file that the FBI had on me and see if it included information in it besides previous addresses and the names of family members and friends. The FBI offered a fascinating tour of its facility in Washington, D.C., at that time, and so after I took the tour, I completed a form associated with the Freedom of Information Act in order to get a copy of my file. About a month later I received a letter in the mail from the FBI. It was a short letter that said that there was no file. On the one hand I was relieved to think that I was deemed too insignificant to warrant an FBI file; on the other hand, I had seen an actual file that seemed to have a whole lot of information about my background.

On the subject of freedom, like so many other things, we are of two minds. We tell ourselves that we are free. Yes, we are free to quit that job that we hate, but—and here is the other side—we can't quit because we need the money. We tell ourselves that we are free to choose to come and go as we please, but this is a choice that few people make because it is impractical or has the potential for too many negative repercussions. We tell ourselves that we live in a free society, and yet the phrase about the futility of fighting against bureaucracy—"go fight city hall"—is commonly understood by the time we reach adulthood.

The processes that make the world go round are subtle, sometimes contrary to what we would expect or hope for, but it is only by bringing what is subtle to the light of day that we can begin to make more accurate judgments about right and wrong and what constitutes freedom. Our individual experiences can serve to either guide us or blind us in making accurate judgments about ourselves and others. The sociological perspective can serve as a powerful tool in making such fine distinctions.

FOR FURTHER READING

Berger, P. L. (1963). *Invitation to sociology: A humanistic perspective.* New York: Anchor. Classic introduction, a little dated, but good introduction and not too difficult.

Elias, N. (1978). *What is sociology?* New York: Columbia University Press. Thoughtful and not too difficult introduction.

Lessing, D. (2001). *Prisons we choose to live inside.* New York: HarperCollins Publishers. Literary writer's astute observations on social life.

Lukes, S. (1985). *Emile Durkheim: His life and work.* Palo Alto, CA: Stanford University Press. The biography.

McLellan, D. (1973). *Karl Marx: His life and thought.* New York: Harper & Row. One of the best biographies.

Mills, C. W. (1972). *The sociological imagination.* New York: Oxford University Press. Classic in the field of sociology, not too difficult.

Morrison, K. (2006). *Marx, Durkheim, Weber: Formation of modern social thought.* Thousand Oaks, CA: Sage Publications. Very good text introducing the thought of the founders.

Sears, A. (2008). *A good book, in theory: A guide to theoretical thinking.* Toronto, ON: University of Toronto Press. Very readable introduction to thinking sociologically.

Wolff, J. (2002). *Why read Marx today?* New York: Oxford University Press. Very readable introduction to the thought of Marx.

Chapter Two

Individuals and the Structure of Society

How powerful is socialization in influencing how we understand ourselves, others, and reality? One of the benefits of acquiring a sociological perspective is that it lifts you out of your cultural milieu, which allows you to observe who and what you are apart from so many of the cultural influences that we all assume are reflections of ourselves.

Do you recall your first experience of being self-aware? Within the first few years of life we become increasingly conscious of ourselves as independent beings in the world. With this awareness comes the recognition of our agency—that we can have an impact on the world around us. What also comes with this awareness is the dimly lit recognition of our terminality. I do not recall if this was my first experience of self-awareness, but I vividly recall sitting up in my stroller, looking around at the street, curb, and trees near my parents' New York City apartment, and thinking to myself, "Enjoy your life; it will not last forever." This thought has remained with me in such a way that I periodically pause from my routine and take stock of my life.

We human beings are social, meaning-making animals who continuously conjure up beliefs that give us a sense of purpose as we live and die on a ball of rock that is spinning around in a space too large to contemplate.

In a powerful book called *The Denial of Death*, author Ernest Becker observes, "[S]ociety is . . . a symbolic action system, a structure of statuses and roles, customs and rules for behavior, designed to serve as a vehicle for earthly heroism. . . . [S]ociety is a hopeful belief and protest that science, money and goods make man count for more than any other animal" (1973, pp. 4–5).

Each of us takes from society yarn (ideas and products) from which we weave individually meaningful lives. Perhaps the most difficult thread to see that we take from society is the significance we give to our individual uniqueness. The desire to live is instinctual—all creatures possess it—but only human beings, and specifically, only human beings in the modern Western world, attach ultimate significance to being a unique personality. While there is value in celebrating each person's uniqueness, the inability of each of us to celebrate the uniqueness of the more than six billion individuals living on this planet necessitates a great many illusions, for instance: that I count for more than others; that I am more deserving or less deserving than others; that people get what they deserve; that what I have acquired is solely due to my individual efforts; or that the measure of a man or woman may be determined by what they possess.

The fact of the matter is that our sense of feeling special and unique stems from the encouragement of others. Displaying a talent feels all the more special when there is an audience. The belief that we are born alone, die alone, and that the toys acquired in-between are the products of our individual efforts may be the most heroic and grandiose effort at achieving personal meaning ever devised by a culture. We are born into the arms of others, our death is another's loss, and all the things acquired over a lifetime are due to the efforts of countless people all attempting to thrive. Individuals do not create themselves. American society has produced and continues to nurture the illusion that it is heroic to accomplish all tasks on one's own. As a result, individuals growing up in this culture tend to believe that their strivings are accomplished independently of others, and in the process they deny the social bonds that support them.

Perhaps it is because the reality of death is always somewhere in the back of my mind that I appreciate both my distinctiveness and my ultimate insignificance. And perhaps this is why I have always yearned to be more like other people. It may be because I have felt like an "outsider" from as long ago as I can remember that I have acquired an appreciation of how much people are alike. I admit that it is ironic to be discussing individualism as a social creation, and then to be discussing my uniqueness. Of the term *outsider*, philosopher Colin Wilson says,

> For the Outsider, the world into which he has been born is always a world without values. Compared to his own appetite for a purpose and direction, the way most men live is not living at all; it is drifting. This is the Outsider's wretchedness, for all men have a herd instinct that leads them to believe that what the majority does must be right. Unless he can evolve a set of values that will correspond to his own higher intensity of purpose, he may as well throw himself under a bus, for he will always be an outcast. (1963, p.155)

I believe the root of my dilemma may be that socialization didn't quite "take" for me. Although I had some friends, I grew up feeling relatively detached from family and school, yearning for the day when I would be grown-up and left alone. Being "apart" from society in that way has helped me to be able to look at society dispassionately, a skill that has been very useful to me as a sociologist. Part of the value of taking a look at society in that way affords you the opportunity to see society freshly, anew, and to consider for yourself who you are and where you fit into society.

We tend to think that we make our choices independently of others; that what we want for ourselves is the product of individual taste; that what we think of as sexy reflects our personal desires. Our preferences in music and sport reflect not only individual tendencies, but cultural tendencies as well: our preference for rap vs. classical music, soccer vs. football, Volkswagen vs. Ford, voluptuous vs. skinny, the amount of money deemed necessary to take care of our basic needs. All reflect our peer group and social class—in essence, our cultural upbringing. What would it feel like to be African American and not like rap and modern R&B or be a working-class Caucasian male and prefer opera to rock 'n' roll and golf to football? It strikes me that an individual living under these circumstances might very well feel like an outsider.

According to sociologists Peter Berger and Thomas Luckmann (1967, p. 163), *successful socialization* requires a certain degree of symmetry or fit between one's preferences and one's circumstances. Successful socialization is reflected by a consistency between what we want and need and what our circumstances provide and encourage. When we reject our family's values, our peer group's tastes and interests, our culture's definition of success, then there is an asymmetric relationship between our individual preferences and our circumstances. If and when this conflict arises, the adjustments that we make reflect and reinforce our degree of successful socialization. Berger and Luckmann add,

> [T]otally successful socialization is anthropologically impossible. Totally un-successful socialization is, at the very least, very rare . . . . Our analysis must, therefore, be concerned with gradations on a continuum . . . . The possibility of "individualism" is directly linked to the possibility of unsuccessful socialization. We have argued that unsuccessful socialization opens up the question of "who am I?" In the social-structural context in which unsuccessful socialization becomes so recognized, the same question arises for the *successfully* socialized individual by virtue of his reflection about the unsuccessfully so-cialized. (1967, pp. 163–171)

In one sense we are all individuals occupying a unique place in the world. On the other hand, our individual tendencies are molded by the culture and the times in which we live. The tension between the preferences of the individual and the collective interests of the culture creates a continuum upon which each of us stand. For most of us, for most of the time, "going with the flow" is the easiest and best option. The more we find ourselves making this choice—going along with the actions and beliefs of our parents, friends, bosses, political and religious leaders that we do not really think about or fundamentally understand or agree with—the more must we find ourselves on the side of the continuum reflecting successful socialization.

By contrast, individualism is the product of relatively unsuccessful socialization. This is the case because the asymmetry between individual preferences and social circumstances creates a problem for the self regarding how to fit in and find one's niche. The problem of fit stimulates a great deal of self-reflection. The time engaged in self-reflection takes time away from being engaged with others, and this further increases the chances of *unsuccessful socialization*.

In the United States, where there is a lot of cultural diversity and the notion of individual achievement is idealized, the environment seems ripe for creating many unsuccessfully socialized people. Is the United States a nation of individuals? Many people would probably respond in the affirmative without understanding that individualism is, in itself, a product of a type of social relationship. In attempting to answer the question "Who am I?" the unsuccessfully socialized tend to exclude from their self-examination that it is society that has created this question for them in the first place and that their motivation for seeking an answer to this question is being driven by a deeply held desire to fit into that society. The unsuccessfully socialized may believe in the abstract notion of a society of individuals, but if they do, it is because their self-examination is blocking out the recognition that human beings are inherently social creatures. Their self-awareness is limited by a deficient social-awareness. The successfully socialized may be equally inclined to agree with the statement that the United States is a society of individuals because they are confronted by the exploits of the unsuccessfully socialized that sometimes cause them grief and at other times lift them out of the mundane.

Berger and Luckmann note that "psychologies produce a reality, which, in turn, serves as the basis for their verification" (1967, p. 178). How we think about ourselves is learned, and how we think about ourselves represents the psychological lens through which we interpret our personal experiences. Our personal experiences are interpreted through a psychological vocabulary provided by our particular culture. For example, a person who hears voices that no one else hears may interpret the experience—due to cultural circumstances—as one of being possessed, divine, or delusional. A person who constantly contemplates may be viewed as thoughtful, inspired, or neurotic. A person who is deathly ill may seek out the assistance of a spiritual healer who may attempt to remove an evil spirit, or a team of medically licensed physicians who may attempt to remove a cancer, or the person may seek the assistance of no one and allow the illness to take its course.

The psychology that we learn is a belief system that provides us with a means of organizing and interpreting our private thoughts. Psychologies are so intimately tied to our identity that we tend to interpret them as extensions of our temperament, when in fact the psychology that we learn organizes and interprets our temperament. In the United States, the cultural belief system regarding the self is one of individuation: we are supposed to emphasize our differences. In this environment, successful socialization means learning how to be different from others, and unsuccessful socialization means learning how to accept yourself, apart from others. In both cases, there is the failure to recognize that the psychological motivation driving us to prove our uniqueness or to prove that we can get along without others is a product of the cultural belief system regarding the self.

In my situation of being unsuccessfully socialized I came to the conclusion that my uniqueness was neither a blessing nor a handicap, nothing to be emphasized or minimized, not a reason to love myself or hate myself or others, but rather a reflection of the way things appear to me to be. With this realization, I came to see that all of the energy people invest in proving their uniqueness or their acceptability to others, or proving to themselves that they are okay even if the world doesn't understand them, is a terrible distraction from simply being. The energy we invest in proving ourselves typically involves denying important aspects of who and what we are, as well as denying how important others are in our lives. The cultural belief system that seems to celebrate the self often times functions to wound the self and culture by stressing a type of individualism that depends upon denying the social bonds that support the self and culture. How are self and society connected? The next section addresses this and related questions.

SOCIALIZATION AND THE MICRO-MACRO CONNECTION

Sociology, the systematic study of society, is theoretically and methodologically divided between *micro* and *macro* levels of investigation.

Micro-level sociologists examine person-to-person relationships. They differ from psychologists in that micro-level sociologists examine the behavior that is created and maintained by the interaction of group members while psychologists focus on the internal psychological dynamics operating within each member. A person seeing a psychologist for family problems may be encouraged to focus on his or her feelings in relation to the other family members. A person seeing a sociologically oriented therapist (i.e., social worker) would be encouraged to focus on the roles that each family member plays, including the client, in creating and maintaining problems within the family.

Macro-level sociologists examine issues at the level of institutions. For example, a macro-level sociologist interested in studying the family would not be interested in person-to-person issues within families, but rather in how changes in one or more institutions affect changes in the social institution of the family. Many macro-level sociologists conduct research that examines how changes in the social institution of the economy affect families. For example, it may come as no surprise to you that divorce rates increase during difficult or unstable economic periods of time.

A recent and growing body of research within sociology and psychology draws attention to how micro-level and macro-level factors may be linked. Socialization is the linchpin that connects the micro- and macro-levels of social life. We will begin at the micro-level and build up to the macro-level. In the process I think that you will see how self and society are intimately connected.

As we noted in the previous chapter, human beings are inherently social. Max Weber used the term *social action* to describe how people orient their language and behavior in terms of others. For example, everyone has a morning ritual. My morning ritual includes having breakfast, brushing my teeth, taking a shower, getting dressed, and brushing my hair. When you and I look at ourselves in the mirror in the morning we may think to ourselves, "Well, how do I look?" But this question masks why we are asking that question in the first place. When we address ourselves in the mirror before we begin our day, we are doing so in order to see if we look the way we want others to see us that day. Whether we are aware of it or not, we are orienting our actions in regard to others. Individuals are concerned on a regular basis about other people's reactions to them. When we disregard others' reactions to us, we are typically very conscious of them and may experience feelings of defiance. Social action evinces that human beings are intrinsically social.

As another illustration, let's say that you are walking on a narrow path and you see someone approaching you. Each of you will more than likely move out of each other's way so that both of you may continue on your way. In acknowledging the other and altering our actions because of another, we are engaging in social action. We can also engage in social action with someone who is not physically present or who may even be deceased. When we engage in an action due to the recollection of a loved one, we are orienting our behavior in terms of another who is not there.

Social action begins the process of social interaction that, if repeated over and over by more and more people, acquires the status of a social institution. Through repeated interactions, patterns of social behavior become organized and implicitly or explicitly prescribed. In other words, socially organized behavior repeated over and over in time gives rise to the social institutions that represent the pillars of a society. Institutions create the social structure through which individuals live out their lives.

Social institutions emerge around problems that require organized procedures and collective actions for their resolution. All societies, whether they
are simple or complex, small or large, display predictable social patterns of
behavior in the raising of children (institutions of family and education), in
the maintenance and enforcement of order (political systems or polity), in its
system of trade (economy), in forming some type of order in regard to defense and safety (military), in treating the sick (health care or medicine), in
forming answers to questions that defy everyday reasoning (religion), in its
mode and dissemination of ideas (communications or media), in organizing
and formalizing leisure activities (sports), and so forth.

The social actions and interactions of one or two generations may become
the institutionalized way of doing and believing for subsequent generations.
Once established as a social institution, a social pattern of acting, feeling, and
thinking becomes perceived as being obligatory. People tend to experience
institutions as unalterable, yet intangible, forces of influence. The social
pressure that individuals feel in relation to social institutions typically stems
from the fact that the social institutions' history predates anyone living, that
their reach throughout society is pervasive, and that their power is diffused
through the decision making of many individuals who depend upon their
continuing existence.

Social institutions are created and maintained by people, yet it is their
history, size, impersonality, and projected power that give people the sense
that institutions somehow have a life of their own. In one sense this really is
the case. Social institutions require people, but typically not specific persons
(unless it is a time of crisis, in which case persons with specific qualities may
be necessary). Social institutions tend to endure even though the individuals
who comprise them at any given time come and go. It is this enduring
impersonality that not only preserves an institution, but also an entire society.
A society can endure even though individuals come into being and pass
away. However, if a critical mass of individuals loses a sense of respect and
awe for institutions, the institutions and the society that is supported by the
institutions will crumble.

We tend not to think in these terms, but when we think about the future
and what we, and perhaps our children, can contribute to the future, we are
thinking in terms of the well-being of the group to which we are a member.
Such thinking displays how we have internalized a way of thinking that
ultimately concerns not our own longevity, but the endurance of our society.
To the extent to which social institutions socialize into their members a
feeling of responsibility for the future of society, the society, general speaking, has succeeded in extending its own life.

Our desire to be a part of society through the roles that we play, our
familiarity with historically important people, and participation in socially
significant events ultimately serves to perpetuate society. Consider, for ex-

ample, going to a sporting event. Let's say that after getting your hot dog and soft drink and climbing up the steps to your $50.00 seats, you hear an announcement over the loud speakers that all should rise for the playing of the national anthem. If you are like most people, you will stand regardless of how much you may want to sit down. Why will you stand? Because you say to yourself that it is the right thing to do and if you do not stand you will feel the stares of everyone around you. If you do sit down and people do stare, their social pressure constitutes what sociologists call a *negative sanction* (a form of punishment for violating a norm). By fulfilling our role (standing during a particular song), we participate in a social ritual or norm that reinforces an ethnocentric pattern of social behavior that perpetuates social order and society. Most people will not only stand, but will sing "The Star Spangled Banner" (which they have learned by heart).

In an important sense, a society is perpetuated through ethnocentrism or the belief that an acquired social custom is the best. By fulfilling our role we are also participating in a group action that conveys to others a positive sense of regard. Positive acknowledgment to and from others for following a norm is what sociologists call a *positive sanction*. Being acknowledged by others is a type of reward that usually serves to reinforce the behavior.

Roles are individually prescribed behaviors for a given set of social arrangements. Once we, and others, are comfortable with how we perform in a role—say as student or employee—we may attempt to make the role our own or increasingly display our temperament within that role. People do this every day—just observe the roles of mother, father, and teacher. They each come with prescribed behaviors, yet we can witness a great deal of flexibility in how individuals carry out these roles (within the socially agreed upon parameters). While roles manifest order and channel the expression of our individual needs and wants in socially defined, appropriate ways, roles ultimately constrain behavior. Innovation and originality come from individual or group deviation from a role or norm rather than its fulfillment.

Roles create and are created by social organization. Social institutions are perpetuated by their organization in society, or more specifically, by the roles that individuals play within this organization. Sociologically speaking, religion is an institution that is perpetuated by various organizations (churches, mosques, and temples), and these organizations are maintained by individuals who carry out specific tasks associated with their roles, which serve to perpetuate their respective organizations and the institutions of religion in society. Education is an institution that is perpetuated by the organization of schools, which, in turn, is maintained by individuals fulfilling the roles of administrators and educators. The economy is organized by a banking system and the banking system is maintained by individuals who have a personal and collective interest in carrying out specific duties associated with their roles.

Institutional interdependence contributes to the coherent structure of society. Social institutions tend to convey similar values, thereby giving individuals a coherent worldview that orients their past, present, and future. For example, the interdependent and dynamic relationships among the social institutions of society suggest a pattern that our individual lives take in regard to age and particular type of involvement in society (preschool; elementary, middle, and high schools; college; marriage; work; procreation; retirement; etc.). During times of war, political, economic, military, and religious leaders tend to convey messages in support of whatever the government is trying to accomplish (i.e., "support the troops"). An individual's sense of purpose and the avoidance of social unrest are derived from a social climate where institutions articulate and perpetuate similar values. The articulation of similar values among the social institutions of society also serves to reinforce their seemingly impenetrable and unchangeable quality.

Our desire for order, familiarity with the norms of society, and ethnocentric beliefs make social institutions resistant to change—even if such change is beneficial. For example, the diffusion of the right to vote in this country occurred slowly because of institutionalized resistance based upon the traditional norm that only men of property could vote disinterestedly or in terms of what was in the best interests of the nation. While social change can occur rapidly, such as during times of crisis or revolution, most change in society occurs over a period of generations.

The arrangements and types of institutions that make up a society reflect that society's unique history and cultural development. Every society has its own way of doing things and its own sense of what is meaningful; this is reflected in the institutions, organizations, and roles that maintain a society. For example, some societies have a Christian institutional basis while others have an Islamic basis. Some societies have a stronger secular institutional basis than religious basis. Some societies are socialist while others are capitalist. Societies vary in how the institution comprising the political system is organized in terms of its relation to religion. In some societies there is separation of these institutions while in others there is not. There are also differences among societies in how the economy is related to other institutions. In some societies religious and economic values are kept separate while in other societies the distinction is not clear-cut. In some societies there is predominantly one national pastime, such as soccer, while in other societies multiple sporting activities receive national attention. Depending upon institutional arrangements, people growing up in one society will come to appreciate certain holidays while being uninformed about holidays that people in another society recognize with equal passion. The unique arrangement among the social institutions of a society comprises what sociologists call the *social structure of a society*. The distinctive structure of a society also reflects the unique *culture* or what may be likened to the personality or character of a society. In terms of an analogy, consider a painting—every color and stroke (institution) adds character (culture) to the work of art (society).

Figure 2.1 presents one way of visualizing the social structure of a society. Each circle represents one of six institutions that may comprise a society (such as government, economy, military, media, religion, and family). The lines connecting each circle represent the fact that social institutions are connected to, or affect, one another. Changes in the economy effect changes in other institutions, such as family. The presence or absence of particular institutions, as well as the dominance of one institution over another, affects the structure or shape as well as the culture or personality of society.

Figure 2.1 depicts a pluralistic society; no single institution dominates. In actual societies institutions are organized hierarchically, with some institutions wielding more power and influence than others. I distinguish institutional strength by using the terms *hard* and *soft*: a hard institution is one that tends to dominate over a soft institution. Depending upon whether a society is predominately religious or secular for example, the religious or political institutions will loom larger than the other institutions. An example of the social structure of society being dominated by political and economic institutions, such as in the United States, is depicted in Figure 2.1A. In the United States, the political and economic institutions are relatively hard while the institutions of family and religion are relatively soft; family and religion tend to adjust to changes in politics and the economy more than vice versa. Figure 2.1B depicts the structure of society where religious and political institutions tend to be hard or dominant, such as in Iran.

We are born into a society already in motion. Our individual relationship to society is like a child's relationship to a merry-go-round: A child approaches it with music already playing, animals already named and decorated, and mostly the child just wants to hop on board. When children approach a merry-go-round, they do not inquire about why a given style of music is being played and why certain animals are represented; all they know is that the merry-go-round looks fun and worth trying. The point is this: The child represents any child living at any time and in any place, and the merry-go-round represents the social structure of society. What you and I know as fun and real are a product of the norms and values of our culture at that time and place.

The behaviors that we learn in order to get onto the merry-go-round, such as waiting our turn in line and getting on only after it stops, exemplify some of the norms of society. We learn how to behave from others in order to participate in social activities. Social arrangements usually operate smoothly when people follow the prescribed behaviors of a given situation or the social norm of a given circumstance.

Why do we usually abide by social norms? First, it is usually all we know about how to be in a given situation. Second, by following the norm we

Diagram 1

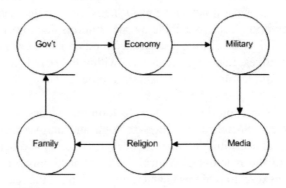

Diagram 1A

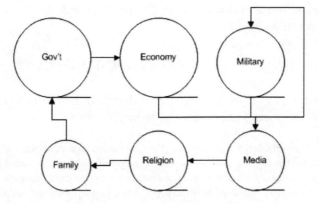

Diagram 1B

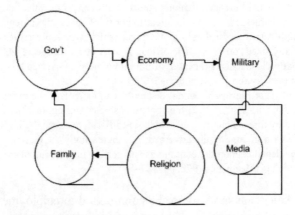

Figure 2.1.   Visualizing Structure of Society

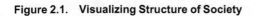

increase our chances of getting whatever it is that we want (even if it is not when we want it). Our participation in social roles reinforces the existing social order while allowing us to get—or perpetuating the belief that in this way we can get—what it is that we want (i.e., a ride on the merry-go-round, money, recognition, etc.). We abide by social norms due to personal choice, sanctions (positive or negative pressure from others), and our lack of awareness of alternatives. Learning social roles within the social structure of society is like a child learning how to behave in order to get a ride on the merry-go-round.

We have been exploring how socialization establishes the link between self and society. Socialization filters through and defines the roles, social organization, and institutions that connect the micro-sociological world of individuals to the macro-sociological world of institutions and to society itself. In the next section of this chapter, we will look at the rise of bureaucracies in society and then move quickly into the topic of social networks. The discussion on social networks will make plain how individuals are linked to the structure of society.

SOCIETY: ROLES, NETWORKS, AND INSTITUTIONS

Max Weber was a very astute observer of the rise of bureaucracies in modern society. Weber states in *Economy and Society*:

> Once fully established, bureaucracy is among those social structures which are the hardest to destroy. Bureaucracy is the means of transforming social action into rationally organized action. Therefore, as an instrument of rationally organizing authority relations, bureaucracy . . . is a power instrument of the first order . . . . Where administration has been completely bureaucratized, the resulting system of domination is practically indestructible.
>
> The individual bureaucrat cannot squirm out of the apparatus into which he has been harnessed. . . . In the great majority of cases [the bureaucrat] is only a small cog in a ceaselessly moving mechanism which prescribes to him an essentially fixed route . . . . The official is entrusted with specialized tasks, and normally the mechanism cannot be put into motion or arrested by him, but only from the very top.
>
> The ruled for their part, cannot dispense with or replace the bureaucratic apparatus once it exists . . . . If the apparatus stops working, or if its work is interrupted by force, chaos results, which it is difficult to master by improvised replacements from among the governed. . . . Increasingly the material fate of the masses depends upon the continuous and correct functioning of ever more bureaucratic organizations. (1978, pp. 987–88)

While most Americans have some choice in regard to employment, sources of information, where to live, what brand of consumer product to purchase, and so forth, we nevertheless live in and through institutions that entail complex bureaucracies. Most of us are born and raised in families that depend upon bureaucracies to gain access to what we consider to be necessary for living—food, clothing, shelter, education, employment, transportation—all of which are made available to us by a series of networks. Today, many sociologists approach the study of roles, bureaucracies, and institutions through the study of networks.

Many of us come from private, single family homes, and it can be difficult to remember that we are not isolated entities; we are not alone. My wife and I lived in relative isolation during the first few years of our marriage. We moved around quite a lot and did not have much of an opportunity to make close friends locally. Wherever we lived, we were hundreds of miles from our nearest relatives. And yet, when my son was born, my sister flew down to see us and bought us a beautiful crib as a gift. We received cards and letters and gifts from many people we knew from all over the United States. The entire experience was very heartwarming, and of course, it had very much to do with others.

Fortunately, we live in an age where communicating with others at great distances is easy, changing the nature of what is possible for social networks. Our family and friends already knew that my wife was expecting, but after the delivery we sent out announcements by mail, sent out pictures using the Internet, and spoke to a lot of people on the telephone. In order to be in contact with all of these people, all I had to do was write a letter, compose an e-mail message, or talk on the telephone. The ease and convenience of using these forms of communication was made possible by many, many people who I have never met and will probably never know personally. The people who made the paper and pen that I wrote with; delivered each and every letter; developed the technology necessary for and manufacture of the camera, computer, and telephone; and developed and maintained the Internet created the networks of communication that made maintaining these social ties possible.

The processes that enable communication and trade are part of a massive exchange network. In order to participate in these networks, people exchange their time, labor, or money. I am a teacher/researcher at a university. My relationship with the university came about as a result of a lengthy interview process. I earned tenure at the university by gaining respect and appreciation from both students and colleagues, and by demonstrating the ability to publish in my areas of interest. The students in my classes are there to learn and earn a degree in order to work, earn money—in essence, in order to become legitimate members of the exchange network that we call our economy. (Throughout the remainder of this chapter I use the somewhat redundant expression *exchange network* in order to emphasize that the exchange of information, goods, labor, or money is the central purpose of networks.)

Most students are able to attend college because of the financial support they receive from their parents as well as from scholarships and grants (supported by private and public donations), and from state and federal government loans (supported by tax dollars). Money for education from private and public sources is available because Americans generally agree that a college education is a worthwhile investment in the youth and for the future of the nation. The billions of dollars that are exchanged every year in order to keep the institution of education possible involves the coordinated efforts of many people who do not know each other personally; students are aided to attend college by people they do not know and people finance the education of students they do not know. Education is facilitated by a massive, impersonal exchange network; its size and impersonality give rise to the illusion that achievement is solely an individual accomplishment.

The books that I write feed into a network known as the publishing industry. There are so many people involved in that industry alone, that I cannot even begin to count their numbers—from editor, to typesetter, to publicist, and then to the bookstores, which have their own armies of people to sell books to customers in order to stay in business. Of course, I haven't even addressed the relationship between the publishing industry and the paper mills, the paper mills and the timber industry, and the relationship between the timber industry, environmentalists, and government regulators. Finally, you get this book, you read it, and perhaps you get a brilliant idea that you subsequently develop. You call this idea your own, and to some degree it is. Yet in this long process that I have just described, something essential is usually missed: Personal experiences are routinely and intimately tied to many exchange networks.

Generally, *networks* can be described as a series of personal and impersonal interactions that link together the interests of many people. Economy and media are distinct institutions that are enlivened and connected by people fulfilling roles in networks. Stated otherwise, the networks that give life to institutions and society itself are due to the many individuals who interact in the process of fulfilling their social roles. In the spirit of one of the founders of sociology, Emile Durkheim, who likened society to a living organism, we may say that networks represent the vital bloodstream that enriches the organs (institutions) of a living being (society). Durkheim would add that, as a person is more than the sum of its cellular parts, so a society is more than the individual parts that make it up.

The social interactions that make up exchange networks enable participants to achieve results that individuals working alone could not achieve. A highway system, a city skyline, potable water, a sports event—none of these could exist without the coordinated activities of individuals. John D. Rockefeller (Standard Oil), Sam Walton (Walmart), Bill Gates (Microsoft), and Oprah Winfrey are examples of intelligent people who were at the right place at the right time in terms of getting the most out of their exchange networks. No one builds an empire on his/her own.

While economic interests pervade the array of networks making up society, the impact of social values is subtly, though equally, just as pervasive and powerful. Living in the United States, individuals take for granted the expectation that others treat us decently and with a certain amount of respect (of course, this is the case in many countries, but it was not always the case in most countries, including the United States, and it is still not the case in some nations). Why do we as individuals feel this way? Running through our personal and impersonal networks are values that we have acquired during socialization that reflect democratic, republican, and religious principles.

The ideals of the American political system are not displayed in Washington, D.C., nor for that matter by our government's foreign policy; they are displayed in our willingness to wait in line at the entrance of a movie theater, to say "Excuse me" when we bump into another individual at a crowded market, to follow a protocol when we are in an auto accident, to abide by standards in a trade, and to provide assistance to individuals (whom we may not know personally) whose lives have been shattered by a hurricane, tornado, or terrorist attack. Most of us engage in such behaviors because we have been socialized to participate with others in exchange networks that emphasize democratic (individual liberty) and republican (mutual respect) principles. We grant to each other and expect from each other a certain amount of decency and respect not simply because each individual realizes some self-interest in such behaviors, but because it represents a standard, a baseline, that runs through the networks of society, and it offers to individuals and their families some semblance of political stability and economic predictability.

It is not the leader of a nation who provides his or her fellow citizens with a sense of political continuity and protection against violation of political principles. In fact, a leader can choose to disregard established principles. Political integrity is maintained or perverted by the nature of the relationships or exchange networks that make up political decision making. Political leaders, as well as the leaders of any social institution, may engage with impunity in lying and stealing so long as the individuals who comprise their networks engage in such behaviors. As we noted in the previous chapter, a corrupt system reflects a corrupt populace. How individuals act out their roles has a ripple effect that influences the efficiency and integrity of entire networks and possibly society itself.

While the relationship between political and economic networks sometimes undermines individual and collective expressions of fairness, the synergy among political, economic, religious, and educational networks, ultimately serves to invigorate demands for justice. When government-generated relief to developing nations is relatively lean, donations from individuals and NGOs (non-governmental organizations) reflect our response to others who are suffering. The government of the United States does not have a very strong record of protecting its youngest citizens, the children. However, some individuals and NGOs in the United States are able to galvanize the public to act on the behalf of children. The ability to stir up outrage among the public in cases of child abuse, whether occurring in families or in private organizations (such as day care centers), reflects the public's sense that such acts violate a deeply abiding principle. Ironically, it is another principle, our collectively acquired and reinforced interpretation of individualism—which fails to see itself as an outgrowth of a unique set of social circumstances— that limits institutional responses to the suffering and needs of children as a unique group of people.

The very notion of inalienable rights suggests a belief in principles that are at once individual and universal. The individual is justified in being respected because of mutual agreement to a set of guiding principles that transcend any given or single individual. Respect for the individual and for individual differences does not occur consistently among people, but the degree to which it does occur reflects mutual agreement to principles that belong to no one, but are expressed by the majority. Respect for the individual and their differences are a collective accomplishment.

To summarize, social interactions repeated over time create exchange networks that contribute to the rise and maintenance (as well as decline) of institutions. How individuals act out their roles while interacting in networks determines the state of an institution. The various networks that enliven institutions form society. A society is simultaneously immense and personal, abstract and concrete. A society reflects the collective sentiments and actions of those who comprise it. It reflects the interactions of people who may or may not know each other, and it reflects the interactions of people both alive and deceased (but kept alive in memory). Society always appears unalterable to the people who compose it, but the networks that make up a society are more malleable and tenuous than they seem.

In a popular science book called *Nexus*, author Mark Buchanan writes,

> For centuries scientists have been taking nature apart and analyzing its pieces in ever-increasing detail. By now it is hardly necessary to point out that this process of "reduction" can take understanding only so far. Learn all you want about the structure and properties of a single water molecule, for example, and you will still have no inkling that a collection of them will be a liquid at 1°C and a solid at [-]1°C. This abrupt change in state involves no alteration of the molecules themselves, but rather a transformation in the subtle organization of the network of their interactions. In an ecosystem or economy, the same distinction holds true. No amount of information at the level of the individual species or economic agent can hope to reveal the patterns of organization that make the collective function as it does. Today, the most fascinating and press-

ing problems almost invariably center on efforts to unravel the delicate and intricate organization of networks. (2003, p. 15)

A rough illustration of the networks that comprise a society is presented in Figure 2.2. Each point represents a person, while the lines represent the type of connection or relationship (direct or indirect) persons have to each other. Our position and the lines that connect them establish a series of networks that enable us to exchange ideas and commodities. These connections accurately depict society as an immense social matrix. This matrix represents another way to envision the structure of society. An indirect connection does not mean that there is no relationship, but only that the relationship is less apparent. People personalize many of these indirect or consciously abstract relationships: a privately owned professional sports club (i.e., the Los Angeles Dodgers or the Oakland Raiders) is "my team"; the president of the United States understands "my pain"; something you have acquired (like a car) or earned (like a degree) you feel you achieved independently of others.

So far, our discussion of Figure 2.2 has shown that society is a product of human interdependence; it is the culmination of direct and indirect relationships. Interdependence, however, does not mean equality of opportunity. Most Americans are socialized into believing that a level playing field exists with regard to working and achieving one's goals. The next section of this chapter takes a closer look at the social matrix as it is displayed in Figure 2.2 and explains the challenges involved in making equality of opportunity a societal goal.

THE PERSISTENCE OF INEQUALITY IN THE SOCIAL MATRIX

As we can see in Figure 2.2, indirect contacts are more frequent than direct contacts regardless of where one is located in the social matrix. Even though most relationships are indirect, order is maintained because of the pervasive need for relative stability in order to make the system of networks function. Direct relationships may be horizontal, vertical, or diagonal. Direct relationships reflect ongoing relations with specific persons (such as immediate family members and acquaintances through work, recreation, or religious affiliation). Vertical and diagonal relationships reflect differences in social standing. Relationships also tend to cluster, producing in-groups and out-groups. This clustering of individuals develops in response to the frequency of interactions, shared life experiences (which produce joint values and expectations), and a desire to make the macrocosm that is society seem more sensible and accessible through a shared sense of community (in essence, a microcosm of society).

In many if not most instances, clusters of people develop around income or wealth. Economic status determines the types of activities that people can

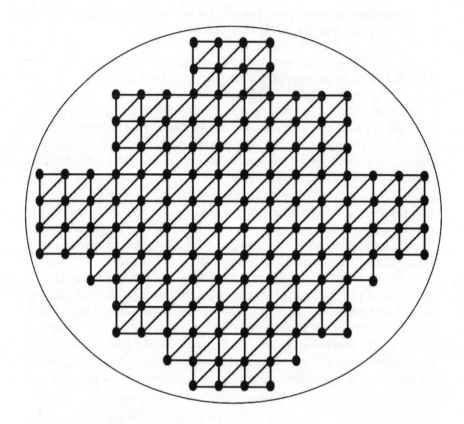

Figure 2.2. Networks of Society

afford. If your best friend of many years earns significantly less money than you do, you will probably not dine out together. If that friend cannot afford your recently acquired hobby of golfing, then you are likely to engage in your new favorite activity either alone or in the company of a new set of acquaintances or friends who can afford the equipment and greens fees. This produces a situation that is not unusual but is rarely expressed: economic differences create situations whereby people engage in their favorite activities without the company of their favorite people.

Where race, ethnicity, gender, and religion are tied to economic status, they become factors associated with the development of clusters of people. The result is typically what sociologists call a *subculture*. A subculture can be described as a group or cluster of people who share a common identity due to experiences recognized as unique to that group. The United States is the most diverse nation in the world. This means that the United States contains and recognizes more subcultures than any other society. While containing values, beliefs, and practices unique to their group, subcultures typically incorporate elements of the overarching culture into their way of life. For example, Americans living in a ghetto, barrio, and gated community may have dissimilar tastes in food, music, and recreation, but all share the vision of success rooted in the ideal of the American Dream.

The clustering of individuals around common life experiences also reflects the rarely articulated fact that those at the top can only understand life at the bottom in the abstract, and of course, vice versa. Buchanan makes note of the same point when he states that "the long-distance social shortcuts that make the world small are mostly invisible in our ordinary social lives. We can only see as far as those to whom we are directly linked" (2003, p. 55). Powerful people and those who are basically satisfied with their status have great difficulty imagining the motivations of a person who commits an illegal act because they are desperate to succeed but lack the support, resources, and skills necessary to do so. Conversely, people lacking in power typically cannot understand the pressures, responsibilities, and sacrifices associated with being an authority. Nevertheless, the decisions made by those occupying the top affect those below them more than the reverse.

The lower your position is in the social matrix, the more weight bears down upon you. In other words, more relationships need to be in transition in order for you to achieve vertical mobility or move up in the matrix. Figure 2.2 illustrates why this is the case. Changing one's location in the matrix is possible only if a position is vacated. Even when positions are "created" this is due to cuts coming from someplace else. Opportunity is based upon the exchange network and the social-economic cluster through which a person operates. If a person's socioeconomic cluster is near the bottom or in the middle, in order to increase her/his status, s/he is going to have to forge bonds with people s/he knows only indirectly, and this means that s/he is going to have to gain access to networks that s/he previously did not know existed.

Many years ago economic sociologist Mark Granovetter (1973) coined the phrase *strength of weak ties* to describe entry into such networks. Granovetter found that the best way in which people found out about jobs is through acquaintances and not one's social cluster. Granovetter reasoned that strong links or one's association with friends and family ultimately undermines the dissemination of information; the same people walk in the same circles, know of the same opportunities (or lack thereof), and grow tired of disseminating the same news to each other. Opportunities tend to arise from those weak links with people that we may not know very well, or do not know at all but are a friend of a friend who walks in a different circle or is surrounded by a different cluster of people.

If individuals are clustered around the top, then their chances of sinking to the bottom are much lower than for those who occupy the middle. This is not only because of wealth, but also because the network system creates a net of opportunity to catch familiars. A CEO who is fired from a major airline carrier is likely to become the executive administrator of the Department of Transportation or the American Automobile Association, or the president of a college. A senator or congressman who is not reelected can find another job in Washington working for a lobbyist and receive a better salary. In their study of networks between corporate boards, Gerald Davis, Mina Yoo, and Wayne E. Baker from the business school at the University of Michigan found that "corporate America is overseen by a network of individuals who—to a great extent—know each other or have acquaintances in common" (2003, p. 321). Reflecting on this state of affairs, Buchanan writes, "This implies that the boards of the major U.S. corporations are tied together socially into one immense web of corporate government" (2003, p. 117). Sociologists use the term *interlocking directorates* to describe the situation whereby the same people occupy seats on different boards.

The implication here is that the same people have influence in multiple places in society. As a result, people with new and innovative ideas may be blocked if the incumbent directorate sees them as threatening to the preservation (of the self-protecting) status quo. In other words, individuals acquire or maintain particular status positions in part because they demonstrate to others in the appropriate networks that they share a prevailing ideology. It is rare to see an individual acquire a position of power and then institute sweeping changes. A political leader will be hindered from taking steps that might affect lucrative but perhaps questionable activities among members of influential or powerful networks. Such actions reveal the tendency common throughout the social matrix: regardless of where we stand in the matrix, we seek to protect our position or to improve it.

Every cluster has its own net of opportunity to catch its familiars. At the bottom of the matrix there are streets in some areas that are perceived as being more dangerous than others depending on who you know. The circumstances are somewhat different at the top of the social matrix because those of lower status harbor contradictory views regarding the failings of the very successful. On the one hand, many enjoy seeing a winner occasionally fall. This is due to a number of factors, resentment not being the least of them. Yet, on the other hand, the activities and sometimes the exploits of the very successful often create the jobs that everyone below them needs.

The function of the law is to preserve order and stability. However, sometimes a violation of the law goes unchecked, and over time the violation itself can become a norm. Both economic and political networks seem to operate with a degree of mean-spirited arrogance and deceitfulness that is not even slightly condoned in any other realm of human activity.

In order to remain at the top, many public figures allow themselves to become the object of image-makers who produce a persona or fantasy person for public consumption. Once again, those lower in status have a contradictory view of those at the top. On the one hand, they expect their leaders to be somehow better than them, yet on the other hand, they expect their leaders to be humble about the qualities being projected onto them and to assert that no person is better than another. Of course, if a public figure contradicts the public image too often or cannot create a new persona out of the shadows of an image that has become tarnished or obsolete, then the image that once granted success now leads to demise.

Individuals with different points of view can come to occupy a position of power, but again, may exert little real change in how society functions. In some respects the networks comprising the highest positions of power may be likened to a row of chairs nailed to the floor with people coming and going as they temporarily take the reins of political and economic authority. Kevin Phillips, a long time observer of American politics and the economy, states,

> The history of the United States is full of money and wealth-related democrat-ization. Some were brief. A few stood the test of time and became pillars of American society. But . . . they have not, for more than brief periods or wave crests, notably changed the concentration of wealth in general or the concen-tration of financial assets in the hands of the top 1 percent. (2002, p. 368)

This helps to maintain the order and stability desired by the majority, but these circumstances sometimes hinder individual and cultural innovation. Social stagnation in the name of maintaining the status quo has hindered innovations in every human endeavor. There are perhaps no better examples than in the areas of developing networks for the global distribution of potable water, food, and medicine for preventable diseases, and in developing networks to energize a competitive market for clean and renewable sources of energy.

CHANGE NETWORKS, CHANGE SOCIETY

Changing the direction of a network or society itself requires the participation of many people. Oftentimes, those who recognize the need for change feel alone in having this perspective. Suppose that what stops one person from getting involved to make the world a better place is the thought, "I am just one person, what can I do? If everybody cared, then my time and effort would amount to something. But as things stand, it would be just a waste of my time." Understood in a social vacuum, this is a self-interested and ration-al response to a social problem. However, consider the possibility that this thought may be a contagion that runs through many networks. Understood in these terms, the scenario does not describe a state of affairs of self-interested and rational actors, but rather, a circumstance where individuals either feel inhibited to act because of their false reading of others or do not know how to proceed in following through on a course of action that would reflect their interests.

A part of what makes challenging the status quo (that a person is dependent upon) so difficult is that people are likely to be seduced into believing all sorts of illusions in order to justify continuing their participation in something they don't believe in or feel is downright harmful. Sometimes people rely on illusions in order to make themselves feel better about their lives. In a large and complex society, it is easy to fall prey to the illusion that we are alone in the world, alienated from others. *Alienation* is a misapprehension resulting from a system of networks that inadequately addresses how the whole functions. Alienation, however real it may seem in our minds, is due to network failure—individuals not being empowered enough to see the forest for the trees. Alienation is a product of a weak current operating through the system of networks that insufficiently amplifies how the whole functions.

The social failure to make plain how individual behavior and societal behavior are linked through networks, like a line of dominoes, produces a paradoxical result: On the one hand, isolation breeds self-reliance, yet on the other hand, self-reliance based upon false assumptions breeds false assumptions about self and others. When we look at ourselves in the mirror, a clear examination of what is being reflected back to us is obstructed by the misreading of our inherent relation to others. An illusion is created whereby people see only themselves reflected back in the mirror. This illusion prevents people from seeing the degree to which direct and indirect relationships affect our sense of self. A glance in the mirror often signifies concern about how we appear to others. A quick look at others usually concerns whether we are being noticed by others.

Popular science writer Matt Ridley states, "We are immersed so deeply in a sea of moral assumptions that it takes an effort to imagine a world without them. A world without obligations to reciprocate, deal fairly, and trust other people would be simply inconceivable" (1996, p. 143). Alienation is a treatable condition that requires amplification of the fact that the parts (individuals) and the whole (society) are connected by exchange networks. Networks are a product of many interactions. Alter the interactions and networks change, alter the networks, and society is changed.

FOR FURTHER READING

Buchanan, M. (2003). *Nexus: Small worlds and the groundbreaking theory of networks.* New York: W. W. Norton & Company. Very good in describing how networks function.

Elliott, A., & Lemert, C. (2006). *The new individualism: The emotional costs of globalization.* New York: Routledge. Thoughtful analysis of individualism in a complex world.

Gladwell, M. (2002). *The tipping point: How little things can make a big difference.* New York: Back Bay Books. Fun read on how one thing can lead to another.

McGrane, B. (1994). *The un-TV and the 10 mph car: Experiments in personal freedom and everyday life.* Fort Bragg, CA: The Small Press. Great exercises that stimulate an alternative view of self and society.

Shanahan, M. J., & Macmillan, R. (2008). *Biography and the sociological imagination: Contexts and contingencies.* New York: W. W. Norton & Company. Thoughtful analysis on the social construction of the life course and social change.

Chapter Three

Culture

The study of culture is of interest to sociologists, anthropologists, psychologists, linguists, and other professionals. We will explore some of the ideas from researchers in these different fields in order to build a reasonably comprehensive and clear picture of what culture is and what it does. Individual identity tends to be clearly linked to an individual's culture, so some of the information presented in this chapter may be emotionally difficult to take in and reflect upon seriously.

In the last chapter we discussed culture as the personality of society. The function of norms, which is to implicitly regulate how people behave under varying circumstances, as well as the role of culture, which is to reflect and perpetuate the meaning of things as defined by a people, are described eloquently by anthropologist David Schneider,

> [C]ulture constitutes a body of definitions, premises, statements, postulates, presumptions, propositions, and perceptions about the nature of the universe and man's [and woman's] place in it. Where norms tell the actor how to play the scene, culture tells the actor how the scene is set and what it all means. Where norms tell the actor how to behave in the presence of ghosts, gods, and human beings, culture tells the actors what ghosts, gods, and human beings are and what they are all about. (1973, p. 204)

For example, cultures vary in how they understand eternity and death. In some cultures death means an end, in others it suggests rebirth. Some cultures downplay the significance of death, while other cultures, exemplified by the Latin American tradition of the Day of the Dead, celebrate it. Most of us identify with the culture and subculture(s) into which we are born. Whatever our culture happens to be seems normal, natural, and right to us.

Every generation of parents socializes into their offspring the prevailing beliefs of their culture. In the United States we acquire the identity of "Americans," who value a particular form of capitalism and democracy because we have internalized or taken in as our own sentiments of our parents, teachers, and peers. The sentiments that are internalized via socialization are typically transformed by persons into individual goals. The expectations that shape us in childhood become the values and goals that we seek to live up to in adulthood. Cognitive anthropologist Roy D'Andrade states, "[I]n the cultural meaning system involving success, accomplishment may be rewarding both because it satisfies personal needs for recognition, achievement, and security, and because it represents the 'good' self" (1984, p. 98).

As noted above, we acquire a religious identity via the internalization of cultural beliefs. I remember sitting in a very nice park on a beautiful day in Philadelphia, and a mother and baby came and sat at a nearby bench. The mother gently raised the baby by her arms and started singing a song in praise of Jesus. She told her little girl that singing to Jesus is good because Jesus is good. I have a friend who is Hindu. She has a sanctuary in her home where she prays to a Hindu god. She sings to her little girl about the virtues of this god. I also know someone whose parents are professional philosophers. This person doesn't believe in a god at all. Reflecting on the lives of these three people, a thoughtful person would probably ponder, "What do the lives of these three people convey about the existence of a god? Is there one God, many, or none? Is one person right and the other two wrong? How do you ascertain who is right?"

When the child living in Philadelphia grows up she will probably be a Christian, and sing the praises of Jesus. When the little Hindu girl grows up she will probably worship a Hindu God. The person who does not believe in God, probably never will. Readers of this chapter who were born and raised in an "average" American Christian family may be inclined to respond, "The Christian woman in the park is right." If you have never seriously evaluated the beliefs that you have acquired through socialization and the collective sentiments of your culture, then how do you know who is right? As was noted in chapter one, sociologists use the term *ethnocentrism*, coined by American social scientist William Graham Sumner (1840–1910), to describe people who assume that their perspective is right and better simply because it is the way in which they were raised.

When I was a child, a boy I knew at school made fun of my family's religion. One day he made one comment too many, and we got into a fistfight. It wasn't the first fight that I would have with this boy over my religion. For some reason my family's faith bothered him, and it bothered me that he couldn't accept me for who and what I was. Each of us sought to defend our identity against a perceived threat. Many years ago sociologist W. I. Thomas (1863–1947) famously stated, "If men define situations as real, they are real in their consequences" (1928, p. 572). That which we define as real, we feel a need to defend: our sense of identity hangs in the balance.

Clearly, what we learn from our socialization colors how we see ourselves and others. Why is pink for girls and blue for boys? Do colors inherently convey gender differences? Does it mean something different to be born black in America versus being born black in Africa? Cultural definitions profoundly affect the meaning we attribute to our natural characteristics. Whatever we have been socialized to believe concerning who and what we are influences subsequent judgments about what is true and false. Moreover, we tend to defend our judgments rather than examine the sources upon which our judgments are made.

Cognitive psychologists use the expression *source monitoring* to refer to the process of referencing our recall while remembering. Marcia K. Johnson, Shahin Hashtroudi, and D. Stephen Lindsay observe, "Many source monitoring decisions are made rapidly and relatively nondeliberatively" (1993, p. 4). Present circumstances can dictate how we remember, and recollection of the source of a memory tends to be less clear than the information remembered. Even so, memories carry varying weights of influence. According to cognitive psychologists J. M. Keenan and S. D. Bailett, "[T]he crucial dimension underlying memory is not what the subject knows . . . but rather what the subject feels about what he knows" (1980, p. 668). Building an identity based upon selective judgment and recall can contribute to a sense of continuity, but accuracy may suffer.

The sociological challenge is to see how socialization biases your views of cultural beliefs and practices and to gain some mental distance from that socialization so that you can see culture in a more detached and objective way. Catching glimpses of our own ethnocentric points of view is often difficult because our identity is based, in part, on our biases. Taking the sociological challenge oftentimes feels threatening because it forces us out of our preexisting comfort zone and challenges us to examine anew both ourselves and how the world works. Examining our biases can reveal the subjective nature of our supposedly objective point of view.

The following sections include discussions on stereotyping and the postmodern impact of relativism on contemporary American society, respectively. As you will see, both of these topics lend themselves to taking the sociological challenge. While stereotyping on some level seems to be an inevitable part of many social interactions, it is ultimately maladaptive (Bargh & Chartrand 1999). We stereotype others when we are not truly engaged in the situation, the other, and ourselves. It is maladaptive in that stereotyped thoughts and behaviors anticipate what may be the case, rather than assessing what is the case and acting accordingly.

In terms of postmodernism, many of the world's technologically advanced societies abide by postmodern values. The core postmodern value is relativism. Yet, there are aspects of relativism that are also maladaptive. Many people find themselves having difficulty tolerating the beliefs of others, while at the same time espousing the importance of protecting their right to believe as they do.

CULTURE, SUBCULTURES, AND STEREOTYPES

Religion, race, and ethnicity are some of the main categories people use around the world to distinguish one culture from another. Cultural identification provides at least the following three things to most people: an individual sense of meaning and direction; a means of uniting individuals to a common identity and purpose; and an ethnocentric point of view that prevents people from seeing past language, dress, and ritual differences to understand that all groups of people basically have the same needs and emotions and want to maintain or acquire a secure existence. As was noted in chapter two, in the United States, where different groups of people share a common border, currency, and government, and where one group is constitutionally prohibited from dominating another, cultural distinctions constitute subcultures within the overarching culture of American society.

When I was a kid I had friend named Will. He and I played together a lot. One day I was hanging out with a couple of other friends and they asked me if the black kid, Will, was a friend of mine. After telling them that he and I were friends, they asked why I had him as a friend. I told them that he was fun. After that conversation I realized something about Will that I had never really gave much thought to—the fact that he was African American. I knew that he was black, but I never really thought about it; at least not until these other boys emphasized the fact of his color. I began to think that because these other boys made a little bit of a fuss about it, it must mean something. The conversation didn't change my friendship with Will, but I never saw him again the way I did before, through color-blind eyes. I realized that color meant something to people.

African American is one of many subcultures that exist in the United States. The term *subculture* denotes a culture within a culture. Asian American, Chicana/o, and even Irish American Roman Catholic and Irish American Protestant all represent subcultures within the diverse culture that is America. People used to refer to the United States as a "melting pot," where people from other lands would come and integrate themselves into the American way. Many Americans have come to recognize the value of retaining their cultural heritage. Acknowledging this, in recent years I have heard American culture being likened to a complex soup or stew that retains the flavors of its many ingredients.

Some Americans feel threatened by the rise of groups that want to retain and display their traditional heritage. The argument seems to be about whether people coming to the United States should or should not adopt the American way of living, talking, and thinking. The underlying problem here is that there is not one way to be an American. A brief look at regional differences makes this apparent.

At the risk of overgeneralizing and being accused of stereotyping others, I believe that it is fair to say that different regions of the country—North, South, Midwest, Southwest, and West Coast—reflect the different values of those who have settled there. A person can tell immediately that the different regions of the country reflect different subcultures by listening to the regional accents when people talk, by observing how people dress (a cowboy hat and boots will either make you feel right at home or like a fish out of water), and by noting the types of food that are regionally popular (i.e., lobster in the Northeast, hush puppies and grits in the South, and Tex-Mex in the Southwest). The Northeast reflects a basically urban and liberal tradition; the South, a basically rural, conservative, and Baptist tradition; the Northern Midwest, a Lutheran and urban and rural mix. The Southwest reflects traditions that are rural, Latino, and Catholic; and the West Coast reflects a rural and urban mix with libertarian tendencies. The American way varies depending upon where in the country you happen to live.

Nothing has brought this home to me more than the fact that depending upon where I have lived—Maryland, California, Indiana, Oregon, New Mexico, and Florida—the same ideas that I have expressed have been interpreted in different ways. A "conservative" point of view in urban Oregon is a "liberal" perspective in urban Florida. The apparent lesson from this, though I disagree with it, is that the meaning and value of an idea is not derived from the merits of the idea itself, but rather from the location in which it is expressed.

While ethnocentric attachment to traditions that represent a culture or subculture can be the source of pride and inspiration, such attachment also can be the source of misunderstanding and conflict. There is little question that tensions between subcultures within American society have been an ongoing problem. (Most societies have to deal with this issue in one form or another.) One way to get a handle on this problem is by gaining an understanding of why people stereotype others. The approach we will take to understand stereotyping will proceed from the intra- and interpersonal or micro-level to the institutional or macro-level.

Imagine walking into a kitchen where chocolate chip cookies have just been baked. The room is filled with the aroma of chocolate and there are two bowls on the kitchen table, one with cookies and the other with radishes. If you are like most people, you will be more interested in the cookies than the radishes. However, what if you are told that you cannot eat the cookies, but you can eat the radishes? Would you be interested in eating the radishes under these conditions? Due to the sight and smell of the chocolate chip cookies, interest in eating radishes, even if you like them, would be compromised.

What I have just described happened in a laboratory setting. Roy Baumeister et al. (1998) conducted this experiment in order to demonstrate what they call *ego depletion*. Subjects entered a room filled with the smell of freshly baked cookies and one group was told that they could eat from the bowl of cookies while the other group could only eat from the bowl of radishes. These subjects then completed two questionnaires and were instructed to solve a puzzle that had been prepared so as to be impossible to complete. Not too surprisingly, the subjects whose desire to eat cookies had been frustrated, the radish group, quit sooner on the frustrating puzzle. Baumeister and his colleagues concluded "that an initial act of resisting temptation impaired subsequent persistence at a spatial puzzle task" (1998, p. 1256). In another experiment, Mark Muraven and his colleagues (1998) found that regulating a display of emotion lowered an individual's stamina in performing a physical task.

People must attend to many internal and external events each and every day. In order to deal with this much information, the mind must decide what should be given attention and priority. When the mind tries to take on too much at once, its resources are depleted. As Muraven and Baumeister (2000) point out, coping with stress often leads to a breakdown in willpower. Depletion of mental and emotional resources can also occur from anticipating a situation that will require self-control. For example, worrying about passing a test can use up the energy that is required to take the test. Baumeister et al. (1998, p. 1263) conclude,

> The ego depletion findings . . . suggest that exerting control uses a scarce and precious resource, and the self may learn early on to conserve that resource. Assuming that the self is the controller . . . , it is not surprising that controlled processes should be confined to a relatively small part of everyday functioning, because they are costly. Responding in a controlled (as opposed to automatic) fashion would cause ego depletion and leave the self potentially unable to respond to a subsequent emergency.

Many cognitive psychologists and sociologists have come to the conclusion that information processing occurs either automatically or deliberatively (for a review, see DiMaggio 1997). In fact, it would appear that much more information than previously recognized is processed preconsciously or automatically without our awareness.

What if I told you that you could increase your performance on a test if you thought about the attributes associated with a teacher before taking the test? Would you believe me? Social psychologists Ap Dijksterhuis and Ad van Knippenberg (1998) tested this hypothesis and found that randomly assigned subjects who created a list of the behaviors, lifestyle, and appearance attributes of the "typical" professor performed better on a task involving questions from the game Trivial Pursuit than subjects who were asked to create such a list describing a secretary and better than subjects not asked to create a list at all. The experiment was to see if priming subjects in different ways would affect their performance on a task. K. S. Lashley (1951) was the first researcher to use the term *priming* to describe the process of suggesting a thought in order to prepare the body for action. Dijksterhuis and van Knippenberg also found that when randomly assigned subjects were primed with the stereotype of "dumb jock," they performed worst of all on the same task.

Researchers do not believe that a person can be primed to do anything, but they do believe that once a perception and a behavior have been linked repeatedly, the perception sets off an automatic response. Cognitive psychologists John Bargh, Mark Chen, and Lara Burrows (1996) conducted a series of experiments to test the automaticity of stereotyped beliefs and behaviors. In one experiment subjects were asked to complete a scrambled-sentence task containing words stereotyping the elderly; references to slowness were not included. Another group of subjects completed a scrambled-sentence task that did not have age-specific terms. After completing the task, the time that it took subjects to walk from the lab to the elevator down the hallway was clocked. In this experiment, and in a replication of the experiment, subjects in the elderly primed condition had a slower walking speed.

In a more dramatic experiment, Bargh, Chen, and Burrows (1996) asked subjects to work on a computerized visual task. The non-African American subjects were divided into two groups; one group was subliminally flashed a picture of a young African American male face and the other group was subliminally flashed a picture of a young Caucasian male face. On the 130th trial the subjects were told that a computer error had occurred and that they would have to complete the entire task again. A hidden camera recorded the reactions of the subjects. The subjects' reactions on film were then coded and rated for level of hostility. According to Bargh and his colleagues, statistical analysis revealed "that participants primed with photographs of African American faces behaved in a more hostile fashion compared to participants primed with Caucasian faces" (1996, p. 239).

Cognitive psychologists Russell Fazio et al. (1995) have conducted similar experiments but have observed somewhat different results. Fazio and his colleagues identified three types of individuals: (1) persons who do not experience automatic activation of a negative evaluation; (2) individuals who do experience automatic activation of a negative evaluation, but are motivated to counter that reaction; and, (3) persons who appear to have no misgivings about their experiencing such negativity and expressing it. Patricia Devine, who also identified this second type, explains,

> There is strong evidence that stereotypes are well established in children's memories before children develop the cognitive ability and flexibility to question or critically evaluate the stereotype's validity or acceptability. As a result, personal beliefs are necessarily newer cognitive structures. An additional consequence of this developmental sequence is that stereotypes have a longer history of activation and are therefore likely to be more accessible than are personal beliefs. (1989, p. 7)

Judging people by category is something that all people do. According to cognitive sociologist Eviatar Zerubavel (1991), categorizing is a human universal, though the nature of the categories constructed varies among groups. People categorize because they must; there is only so much information that the human mind can process at a time. Categorizing facilitates automatic information processing. In a sense, the real issue is socialization and the ongoing misreading of social situations by persons socialized in different cultures and subcultures.

J. Nicole Shelton and Jennifer Richeson (2005) conducted a study involving African American and Caucasian subjects. The subjects were told that the study concerned friendship formation and that they would be introduced to another individual and engage in a brief "get-to-know-you" interaction. Subjects were provided with background information and a picture of the individual they were about to meet. White subjects were given information about an African American and black subjects were given information about a Caucasian. After reviewing the biographical information and before the interaction (which never actually took place), the subjects were asked if they were interested in getting to know the other person. According to Shelton and Richeson,

> The results revealed that both White and Black participants were more concerned with being rejected by the out-group individual than they were disinterested in interacting with this person. In contrast, both White and Black participants believed that the out-group individual was less concerned about being rejected than they were. . . . [B]oth White and Black participants felt they were more interested in having the interaction. . . . Conversely, White and Black participants believed they were marginally more concerned with being rejected. (2005, pp. 99–100)

When a member of an out-group doesn't make the first move toward interaction, it is interpreted by the other person as a lack of interest. In the other person's mind, s/he is thinking something like, "I would be interested in being friendly if they showed an interest, but they don't, so why should I?" Given that the mind prefers to function automatically in order to shore up its resources, and given that people do not like rejection, this kind of response makes a certain amount of sense; however, this is also the intrapersonal dynamic that perpetuates stereotyping. Because we lack access to the thoughts of others, we can only infer another person's motivations. However, given our own motivations, like wanting to see ourselves in a positive light, we do not always see how our own motivations bias our thinking. A perfect example of this is what cognitive psychologists call *the illusion of transparency* (Miller & McFarland 1987). The illusion of transparency refers to overestimating how apparent our internal states are to others. This bias is present whenever people expect others to "read their mind." As Thomas Gilovich, Victoria H. Medvec, and Kenneth Savitsky state, this bias is also present when "[i]ndividuals mistake the true source of others' calm exteriors not only because they fail to appreciate that others have attempted to conceal their feelings . . . but also because they may underestimate their own ability to do so" (1998, p. 343). If both parties fear rejection for whatever reason, be it African American and a Caucasian, a female and male, or young and old, they are both likely to conceal their fear and wait for the other to initiate a dialogue, and both go away feeling that they were more interested in conversing than the other. By focusing on our reactions to others, we tend to not see how our actions and reactions are a part of the reactions and actions of others.

George Herbert Mead (1863–1931), the founder of American sociological social psychology, was one of the key figures who paved the way for the systematic study of social interaction, and in doing so, helped to expand the focus of attention from the intrapersonal to the interpersonal. According to Mead, what goes on in the mind of one person is a consequence of what goes on between persons. How we act in regard to others serves as a stimulus that produces a reaction in others. If individuals believe that the world is against them, then they are likely to interact with others in a rude manner, and people will respond accordingly. If they believe that others do not like them, then they are likely to not engage others in conversation, and others will respond accordingly. Others do not have the information that is going on in each individual's mind. As a complicating factor, people strive to conserve deliberative problem-solving for pressing issues. The result is that people tend to treat each other at face value—with the potential of creating circumstances that the actors themselves do not want. The dilemma is expressed well by David Hamilton, Steven J. Sherman, and Catherine M. Ruvolo:

> Because each person in an interaction is a perceiver, each has the ability to "create" the behavior that he or she expects from the other. However, each person is also the target of the other's expectancies, and his or her behavior will be affected by the expectancies held by the other. Thus, two people can interact in such a way as to bring to reality the mental image that each one has of the other. (1990, p. 52)

By committing the fundamental attribution error (as discussed in chapter one) of attributing disposition rather than circumstance (of which one is a part) to another's behavior, individuals participate in creating a reality that they may not want. We are once again at W. I. Thomas's famous statement: "If men define situations as real, they are real in their consequences."

Why do some people approach the world as though it were against them? We can identify at least three reasons. First, one or two bad encounters early in life can generate a lifetime of expectancies that perpetuate bad encounters. American sociologist Robert K. Merton (1910–2003) coined the expression *self-fulfilling prophecy* to describe such circumstances. A self-fulfilling prophecy is a process whereby a belief or an expectation affects the way a person or a group behaves and as a result guides the outcome of a situation. Second, some people who personally may never have had bad encounters with people from another culture or subculture may know others who have. Finally, some people may approach the world as though it were against them because of their culture's historical actions toward their own subculture.

Why do some people have no misgivings when stereotyping others? Once again, one or two bad encounters can generate a lifetime of bad encounters. Second, stereotyping and prejudice are learned, and once they are learned it requires deliberative effort to replace the preexisting belief. Third, because people want to see themselves in a positive light, they are not inclined to look for biases in their own thoughts and beliefs, and if any biases are discovered, people will try to either eliminate them or accept them as inevitable (Pronin, Lin, & Ross, 2002). The biggest problem with bias is that one rarely notices it as it is occurring in social interaction. A fourth factor explaining why some people stereotype others pertains to self-fulfilling prophecy. Hamilton, Sherman, and Ruvolo note, "Following the behavioral confirmation of an expectancy, a perceiver is likely to subscribe to his or her beliefs even more . . . . The perceiver not only believes the expectancy about the target person . . . but also may regard this 'confirmation' as 'evidence' that the stereotype about the target person is accurate" (1990, p. 52).

A person who has already acquired a stereotypical belief about another group is likely to behave towards a member of that group in a way that confirms their expectation (of course, not realizing the role that they have played in creating the circumstance), and once the expectation is confirmed, this is interpreted as evidence for the perpetuation of their stereotyped belief. Bargh, Chen and Burrows state, "If the automatic activation of a stereotype by the physical features (including speech accent, skin color, gender, and age-related features) of another person causes the perceiver him- or herself to behave in line with the stereotype first, the perceiver's own initial behavior to the target could well produce similar behavior in the stereotyped individual" (1996, p. 241).

Note here that if a perceiver believes that a person will behave or express an attitude in a certain way, the perceiver may mimic or initiate an interaction based upon an expectation that may or may not reflect the target person. It is not the case that all Muslims hate Americans, that all women want to have children, or that all African Americans are athletically inclined. But if perceivers approach a person who is a member of one or more of these groups with an expectation based upon the target person's group membership, then they are likely to initiate a conversation that may reflect their own view of the world and not the target person's view. Conversely, when perceivers from an exploited group meet a target person from the exploitive group, they may initiate an interaction that reflects their own view of the world and not the target person's view. In both cases, a dialogue quickly descends into a monologue, making mutual understanding impossible.

Given that people tend to be blind to their own biases and to the impact they have in shaping social interactions, it is little wonder that stereotyped beliefs endure. To address the larger issue of how stereotyping is perpetuated culturally, it is necessary to expand the discussion from the micro-level to the macro-level. Psychologist R. L. Schanck examined the religious and social attitudes of people living in the community of "Elm Hollow." Schanck engaged community members in various ways, including playing cards, drinking, and smoking. However, community residents expressed publically their near unanimous support of the local church's prohibition against engaging in these activities. Schanck's survey revealed that the majority of the residents privately assumed that everyone else supported these prohibitions more than they themselves (1932).

Schanck's research was one of the earliest demonstrations of what social psychologist Floyd Allport (1890–1978) called *pluralistic ignorance*. According to Dale Miller and Deborah Prentice, "Even when people have previously repudiated a public norm they previously supported, they may continue to act in public as they always have . . . . [P]luralistic ignorance serves as a brake on social change. Social practices will stay in place long after they have lost private support, because people do not recognize that their personal shift in attitude is shared by others" (1994, p. 543).

Pluralistic ignorance undermines personal, social, and cultural development. Individuals may suppose that they are unique in that only they get it. Because individuals feel inhibited or fearful to discuss what they each privately sense, these same individuals reinforce a cultural climate of conformity that suppresses the realization of their true wants and interests. Finally, pluralistic ignorance hinders the pace of change in areas that truly matter to people (e.g., civil rights, clean air and water, basic health care).

The sociological challenge here is to examine the personal and social categories we think in, assess their origin or source, and then evaluate whether these categories either contribute to a world that we want or to a world that we find objectionable. Hamilton, Sherman, and Ruvolo note that targets with a high degree of certainty in their self-concept were not influenced by a perceiver's expectancies about them, and targets who were made aware of a perceiver's negative expectancy were successful in modifying the perceiver's perceptions of them. Similarly, if the perceiver anticipates working with the target person or is motivated to form an accurate impression of the target, an initial expectancy has less directive effect on the perceiver's behavior, decreasing the likelihood of confirmatory [stereotypic] behavior from the target. (1990, p. 53)

Learning about what and how we think can facilitate taking responsibility for personal and social change. Implicit here is the realization that positive social change also requires that individuals have some understanding of what they share in common with others. This is the general theme of the next section.

COMMON CULTURE AND ITS DISCONTENTS

In a letter to a colleague, Sigmund Freud wrote, "My self-analysis is still interrupted. I have now seen why, I can only analyze myself with objectively acquired knowledge as if I were a stranger; self-analysis is really impossible, otherwise there would be no illness" (quoted in Gurevitch 1990, p. 302). In this quote Freud is not only saying that if self-analysis were possible, there would be no illness, he is also pointing out another one of the fundamental paradoxes of being human: on the one hand, each person is conscious of being separate and distinct from another; yet, on the other hand, without others, distinctiveness has little meaning. Terms like *separate, different, distinct*, and *individual* retain their meaning only in relation to something or someone else. Freud ([1922] 1975) begins a famous essay entitled, "Group Psychology and the Analysis of the Ego," by stating, "[O]nly rarely, and under certain exceptional conditions is individual psychology in a position to disregard the relations of this individual to others. . . . [F]rom the very first individual psychology . . . is at the same time social psychology as well."

No two human beings look alike (excepting identical twins). Without even taking into consideration variances in size, weight, and shape, the enormous range of diversity among human beings is apparent by looking at individual faces. Yet, our self-concept is an amalgam of personal attributes and cultural categories. All people fill their personal tank from the same cultural watering hole. In other words, individual diversity is tied to cultural development.

Many years ago Emile Durkheim pointed out that individualism is a product of the complexity of society. While there have been claims, counterclaims, and revisions of Durkheim's argument (such as anthropologist Claude Levi-Straus's observation that so-called "primitive" societies possess sophisticated ways of doing and understanding things), there is little disagreement among scholars that the recognition of individual freedom as a cultural value is associated with population growth, capitalism, and democratization. In other words, where populations, capitalism, and democracy have flourished, so have calls for the recognition and acceptance of individual freedoms (see, for example, Dahl 2000). Yet, once in place, individual freedom can undermine people's ability to see that the exercise of individual rights stem from a widely accepted set of cultural conditions. For example, there is wide agreement among Americans of the following norms: the right to privacy, the right to pursue any legal means of acquiring a livelihood, the right to a fair trial, the right to vote "the bums out" and the right to vote in individuals who make the best, long-term interests of the nation their priority.

The inability to see our widely shared norms also stems from the fact that associated with the value of individual freedom in the United States is the assumption of an atomistic view of the self. This means that we tend to think of ourselves as islands onto ourselves—each individual is an island in a vast sea and each of us chooses to believe what we wish on our own. While I value my individual freedoms, I also realize that freedom is an interdependent phenomenon. Consider the economy: It is composed of millions of people engaged in work. But each individual's work is dependent upon other people's work for the entire system to function. An individual may have a great singing voice, and she may have the individual freedom to sing whenever she wishes, but if she wants to sing on television, then she is going to need the assistance of others; airing a television show involves the coordinated efforts of many people.

The ability to act on our thoughts and feelings requires what we have previously referred to as the coordination of positive and negative solidarity (see chapter one). It used to be the case that women were denied the right to vote and African Americans were denied access to certain institutions. Positive solidarity reflects positive freedoms, such as the right to do as you please, and it functions in tandem with negative solidarity, which reflects negative freedoms or restrictions that protect freedom. In order for women to vote and African Americans to eat at whatever restaurant they choose (a *positive freedom*), others who desired to restrict these activities had to be restrained (a *negative freedom*). Once a particular negative freedom becomes a habit or norm, people tend to take it for granted that a given behavior by others is acceptable. The bottom line is that people are not simply free to do as they please. Freedom requires mutual agreement to a set of conditions that basically involve taking turns. Freedom—like separate, different, and individual—has little meaning without others.

SYMBOLIC MEANING SYSTEMS

Symbolic meaning systems, such as language, norms, and values are among the essential ingredients giving shape to culture and forming the glue that holds a society together. Let's briefly explore these three important components of culture.

Human beings are meaning-making animals. We apply simple-to-complex meanings to sounds, gestures, and objects. This ability constitutes human language—the most sophisticated form of exchange known. Language and thinking go hand in hand. We think in words. The more intricate verbal and nonverbal interactions in a collective become, the more complex the culture becomes. Indeed, a culture can develop to the point where the inhabitants completely fail to recognize themselves as social animals. Consider what would happen to you if you stopped eating and drinking. Like any other animal you would wither away and die. Consider a human infant: A baby boy or girl would perish without assistance. Moreover, without caregivers, human babies would not learn how to cultivate their ability for complex language. The words that we use to describe our thoughts and feelings are learned from others. Language is one of the ways in which human beings pass their culture along from one generation to the next.

A major breakthrough in our understanding of language was made by Ferdinand de Saussure (1857–1913) in his description of language as a formal system of signs, the study of which is called *semiotics*. Signs are made up of a signifier and the signified. A signifier is the form of a word and the signified is the concept conveyed by the word. For example, *chair* is a sign composed of signifier (the letters used in composing the word) and signified (the word conveys a consistent conceptual meaning). When we use the expression, "pull up a chair" we know what is meant because the word *chair* is a sign that conveys a consistent meaning: the word alludes to what de Saussure called a *referent* or the object that we typically use for sitting. The signified represents the concept of chair, while the referent is the object itself.

A sound acquires the status of a sign when it conveys mutual meaning. Like signs, images and objects can convey mutual meaning. A symbol is a gesture or object that conveys a commonly understood meaning. Gesturing with one or two fingers has specific meanings within and between cultures. Signs and symbols form the means of communication in culture. Anthropologist Michael Silverstein states, "To say of social behavior that it is meaningful implies necessarily that it is communicative, that is, that the behavior is a complex of signs that signal, or stand for, something in some respect" (1973, p. 12).

Every form of communication that gives shape to a culture also conveys how that culture uniquely understands the world. When a language dies out, its way of understanding the world dies also. A language is preserved by an underlying code or grammar that people, within a given culture, understand and perpetuate. Sometimes college students ask me, "Why is it important to distinguish terms like *there*, *their*, and *they're*? You get the idea, right?" My response is that these terms convey different meanings, and so long as we have a written language, maintaining these differences is important. If words break down, if a word's spelling is reduced to individual whim, mutual understanding necessarily breaks down, and eventually, so does culture.

Norms are also important for preserving culture. Norms are the unwritten rules which guide human interaction and reflect the "personality" of a culture. Sociologist Harold Garfinkel's breaching experiments—based on an approach that he called *ethnomethodology* or the study of culturally given norms—ingeniously demonstrate how social norms influence everyday interactions. An example of a breach of a culturally given norm is to respond to a request for a phone number with the answer, "7239-973" or "72-399-73." Try it. People usually react by displaying a facial configuration indicating confusion. This reaction is due to the fact that people are used to exchanging phone numbers in terms of a three- and four-digit sequence. In one experiment (see Heritage 1984, p. 80), Garfinkel instructed research assistants to engage in conversation with people, and to answer in ways that violate the norm. For example, when the subject would ask, "How are you?" the experimenter would say, "How am I in regard to what?"

Engaging in these experiments can be quite fun, if risky. You can observe the social norm of elevator behavior by just observing what people do and where they focus their eyes while in the elevator. But let us say that you want to demonstrate empirically that such behavior is a commonly learned social norm. The easiest way to prove it would be to stand unnecessarily close to someone in the elevator and focus your attention on that person. You could also try singing and dancing while in the elevator in order to get the results you want—people would let you know verbally or nonverbally that you are not behaving according to the unwritten rule (the norm) of elevator behavior.

The cultural relativity of social norms, language, and what is considered to be normal, natural, and right strike many initially as disturbing. However, with time and effort you can come to a greater appreciation of what you have learned as normal and right by considering it within a wider context. By placing your assumptions about yourself, others, and the world in the context of other cultural beliefs and assumptions, you can acquire greater insight into the limitations of your assumptions, and, utilizing insights from this wider perspective, develop a deeper understanding of yourself and a better appreciation of others.

Our understanding of right and wrong, good and bad, are based upon a series of guiding principles that we learn from our significant others (i.e., parents, teachers, and other role models, etc.). Our guiding principles are our *values*. While most people tend to think of values solely in personal terms, values are also learned. Individuals weigh and choose the values from culture that reflect their personal interests and attributes. Values are learned psychological tools that assist people in navigating through complex circumstances. How adults act on their values produces a cultural value system that is internalized by the subsequent generation of youth.

Living by our own values is difficult. A person's or a culture's values may be gauged most accurately by observing and assessing actions rather than words. For instance, many students begin college by claiming that they value learning. However, as soon as they encounter ideas that are new and unfamiliar to them, they immediately reject the new ideas without seriously considering them and embrace their preexisting way of thinking. Students sometimes attempt to navigate their entire college career by actively avoiding teachers who encourage them to think about things in ways that are different from their own. While such students may say to themselves and to others that they value learning, what they demonstrate in their behavior is that they value the familiar. Unfortunately, people don't really learn if they encounter only ideas that are already familiar to them. The same phenomenon can be observed in how people acquire their information. Many people choose a particular news source for getting information—not because it provides the most up-to-date or the most accurate news, but because it frames the world in a way that fits with what they want to believe.

The inconsistency between expressed values and behavior can be observed among nations just as much as among individuals—after all, a nation is composed of interacting individuals. Throughout history and even today, many of the same nations that exhort the values of compassion and nonviolence resort to violent means in order to have their interests met.

In the United States, one of the principal values is individual freedom. Throughout its history, Americans have been leery of institutions, both public and private, that seem to threaten their freedoms. Yet most Americans depend upon bureaucratic intrusions into their personal lives when it comes to securing their property and health. Personally, I cannot imagine a modern society that would require each citizen to figure out on their own how to get decent health care, education, and home protection. Imagine insurance companies and government regulators saying, "The American people should not have big business and the government intrude into their personal lives, therefore, we are eliminating all food subsidies, subsidies on gas prices, public funding for schools, free access to legal defense, insurance against the possibility of natural disasters, and private as well as public revenue streams for health care. If you want these services, utilize your individual freedom to secure them." The inconsistency here about valuing freedom stems from the failure to recognize that the right to do as we please is tied to turn-taking restrictions.

Freedom is one of a number of core values that the majority of Americans acknowledge irrespective of subculture. Let's review some of the other guiding principles of American culture. Americans value the capitalistic system of trade. Freedom undergirds both democracy and capitalism, though unrestrained capitalism can undermine freedom for the majority (as evidenced by the "robber barons" or businessmen who acquired tremendous wealth and influence through questionable or illegal means in the late nineteenth and late twentieth centuries).

Americans value diversity—the United States is a multicultural society, the most heterogeneous society in the world. Nearly any and every type of food in the world can be found and eaten in the United States. Nearly any language spoken in the world can be heard as you sit and eat in a restaurant. I can still remember living in San Francisco on a street where, on Friday nights, I could hear punk rockers blasting their music from one end of the street, on Saturday afternoons, I could hear Latin music and see break dancing going on in the middle of the street, and on Sunday mornings I could hear gospel music coming from the African American church at the other end of the street.

Americans value technology: We frequently depend upon technologies to solve our individual and collective problems. People meet each other through technology, remain connected to each other through technology, learn about the world through technology, and build, destroy, and repair things through technology.

The United States is a youth-oriented society; the nation was born a relatively short time ago, and it has always been driven by the ideal of progress and youthful energy. We tend to value youth and impulse over age and wisdom.

Americans value affluence: Success is determined by the acquisition and display of goods. We are willing to work hard in order to consume. Many of our interactions are oriented around consumer goods. Consider what you reflect upon, what you desire, what you talk about with family and friends—the focus tends to be on relationships, power, and/or consumer goods that you either have or want. The guiding principles or values that drive the emphasis that we, as Americans, place on democratic freedom, capitalistic exchange, diversity, youth culture, technology, and affluence serve to connect disparate groups and individuals to form a singular and unique American culture.

Anthropologist David Schneider notes, "Culture places disparate parts of the social system together into a meaningful whole. Put another way, it forms the unifying principle(s) for the total system by providing a set of symbols and meanings to which each part of that system is related" (1973, p. 204). If disparate groups or subcultures cannot acquire and maintain an overarching system of meaning from the overall culture, the consequence is division, tension, and possibly conflict. The guiding principles that keep American culture together are, paradoxically, the principles that cause great tensions.

While freedom is at the heart of capitalism and democracy, as noted above, unrestrained capitalism can undermine freedom and therefore democracy. Longtime democracy theorist Robert Dahl states, "Although not all countries with market economies are democratic, all democratic countries have market economies. Capitalism generally produces affluence, and so democracy and prosperity have tended to go hand-in-hand. However, capitalism also generates inequalities, and so it presents challenges to a democratic government" (2000, p. 58). Reconciling freedom with the fact of enduring inequities based upon social class has been a long-term source of stress.

Being the most diverse nation in the world also produces tensions. Groups vary in their practices, dress, language, celebration of holidays, and so forth. People living in a free society must find the means of respecting or at least tolerating differences that they may not understand. The alternative is to stereotype others, be the object of a stereotype, and fuel tensions that weaken society.

There are additional and more subtle sources of strain on American culture pertaining to what we value that threaten our individual and collective well-being. The United States is the largest market in the world (even though it does not have the largest population). Americans are consumers in what economist John Kenneth Galbraith, over fifty years ago, famously referred to as an *affluent society*. The United States is inundated with goods, and most Americans have their basic needs met. The level of poverty here is not as severe as in the developing countries of the world. Nevertheless, there is sufficient evidence to show that the accumulation of goods does not make a person happy (Easterbrook 2003; Myers 1993). Once needs are fulfilled, people can come to depend upon material goods to satisfy their wants. In an affluent society there is an endless supply of new things to want, so satisfaction can become elusive.

A part of the problem is that people adapt rather quickly to whatever they acquire: something desired and acquired today becomes just another thing on the shelf tomorrow, two weeks, or a month later. *Adaptation-level theory* (Helson 1964) points out that people acclimate to varying conditions and stimuli; once we adapt to the new condition or to possessing the new object, it becomes routine. The literature suggests that relationships make people happier than goods (Easterbrook; Myers), but in an affluent society, the effort to acquire goods can displace the effort needed to maintain relationships.

People born and raised in the United States tend to have a hard time getting their head around the fact that the value we place on individualism is learned. Every person values his/her life, but cultures vary on a continuum from individualist to collectivist. People living in collectivist cultures place greater emphasis on social bonds than people living in individualist cultures.

America's youth do not experience the same level of pressure that young people living in collectivist nations feel to refrain from actions that might embarrass the family name in the eyes of others.

A number of paradoxical consequences arise from the failure to recognize that the emphasis Americans place on individualism is learned. First, people may try so hard to distinguish themselves from others that they warp themselves into persons they themselves do not recognize. Second, many people rely on fashion to distinguish themselves, but since most people buy their goods from the same sources, they wind up looking alike. Third, many people in the West do not recognize that their sense of self was fashioned by historical events such as the Protestant Reformation (1517–1648) and the eighteenth-century movement known as Romanticism. Romanticist writers and poets (such as Johann Wolfgang von Goethe and Friedrich Holderlin) emphasized the solitary individual, the person who had the courage to abide by his/her feelings even against the crowd, to look within oneself in order to discover one's real self. Doesn't this sound familiar? This idea—that we must each search inside ourselves to discover our real self and to find our link to the spiritual world—took root and blossomed in America.

One of the unintended consequences of the psychological focus inward has been a split in the personality between an inner or real or spiritual self and an outer or social self. While it is fairly common today for people to refer to themselves as having different selves, many people fail to realize that this too is a product of historical circumstances. There are pros and cons to this historically driven psychological change.

The focus inward initially produced a reaction that called for greater tolerance and liberty outwardly. The social revolutions for freedom marched side by side with the inner revolution for freedom. However, as freedoms and technology increased the pace of change, more and more individuals felt it impossible to keep up. The consequence was a widening gulf between the inner self and the outer self, with people focusing more and more on the inner at the expense of the outer. The disconnection between the inner and outer was to produce the illusion of multiple selves and with it the illusion that the "inner" self can "grow" without simultaneously developing the "outer" self—that the self can "grow" without being whole.

Consider that if it is necessary for each of us to go inside ourselves in order to discover our real selves, then who are we when our focus is not on ourselves? Are we any less real? We cannot escape responsibility for our actions. This is just another example of an atomistic view of the self.

Under the present circumstances, people tend to feel responsible for themselves, but not responsible for how their actions contribute to forming the type of society that each of them must live in. On one level this is understandable—the wider the social circle, the less visible and definite is our influence. Nevertheless, society is a product of our individual actions in toto. While individuals' beliefs and values can and often do influence behavior, it is also often the case that individuals' beliefs and values about themselves and others do not reflect how they actually behave. Society reflects the behavior of the individuals who compose it and not necessarily the ideas and expressed values of the people who compose it. The wider the gulf between perceived and actual behavior among a populace, the more disconnected the members of the populace are from taking responsibility for the society that they collectively sustain.

CULTURE AND THE POSTMODERN TWIST

These splits within ourselves and between ourselves and society are symptomatic of what many scholars refer to as *postmodernism*. Social history can be roughly divided into three stages. The premodern period in Western civilization was a time when knowledge was based upon religious principles. With the rise of the movement known as the Enlightenment (beginning in the mid-1600s), people increasingly became more inclined to put their trust in science and technology rather than in religion to solve personal and social problems. This was the dawn of the modern era. The modern era gradually eroded over the course of the twentieth century (some scholars argue that its influence ended much earlier) as more and more people lost faith in science and religion. Many social theorists noted that by the late-twentieth-century modern values had become either exhausted or replaced. Bellah et al. (1985) observed that religious ideas were becoming increasingly idiosyncratic. Zygmunt Bauman (2000) described contemporary values as "liquid" in order to point out how transitory beliefs were becoming. Some social scientists also noted that the rise of fundamentalist religions and megachurches during this same period represented a backlash against these postmodern trends (Christiano, Swatos, & Kivisto 2008; Noll et al. 1989). Yet, during the latter part of the twentieth century and into the twenty-first century, more and more people felt that the only place they could put their trust was in themselves.

Many events triggered the transformation to postmodernity. From 1945 onward, there were revolutionary developments in defense (nuclear weapons), science (space exploration), civil rights (for minorities and women), international relations (the ascendency of the United States onto the world's stage, the collapse of the Soviet Union, the rise of China as an international powerhouse), globalization, technology (the microchip, fiber optics), and in biology (the birth control pill, mapping the human genome, cloning, stem cells). All of these factors contributed to making the world a much smaller and more tenuous place. These factors also contributed to a growing sense among many people that stability could be found—if at all—only within oneself.

The revolution in telecommunications has exposed more and more people to cultural ideas and practices that they have no mental category for other than "foreign and strange." As the world has been getting smaller, information overload more common, and more of the burden for processing ideas placed upon the individual, the individual has had no place to go other than inward in order to feel a sense of stability and security. The result is a world of relative beliefs and practices, where each person can believe as s/he pleases, yet at the same time, can never feel that the environment in which s/he lives is predictable and safe. We want to be ourselves, and yet we have difficulty understanding why it is so hard finding another with whom we can feel at home. The problem is that the more we differentiate ourselves from others, the more difficult it becomes to find agreement with others on more than one or two principles.

The postmodern twist is that we each want to define our own values, but we want our values to stand for what values stood for before postmodernism: values representative of the "Truth." An environment that protects the individual's right to believe as s/he wishes, also produces an environment where no one's individual beliefs are better than any others'. This is relativism. In many ways, modern people live between two cultural worlds—the postmodern world where all beliefs (that don't harm others) are acceptable, and the world before postmodernism, where beliefs and values represented absolutes (i.e., truth, heaven, God). Today, people want to believe as they like, but desperately want at least one other person to acknowledge their beliefs as the Truth (which makes sense, of course, because we are social animals).

With the turn inward, people engage in more introspection. Yet, introspection too has its illusions. Pronin, Gilovich, and Ross state,

> [W]e tend to treat our own introspections as something of a gold standard in assessing. . . whether our judgments have been tainted by bias. By contrast, we treat the introspections of other actors as merely another source of plausible hypotheses—to be accepted or rejected as a function of their plausibility in light of what we know . . . . We refer to this asymmetry as the introspection *illusion* because the faith people have in the validity of their own introspections is misplaced. Although people can report accurately on the *contents* of their thoughts. . . the psychological processes and the true determinants of their behavior are often inaccessible to introspection. (2004, p. 784)

Pronin, Gilovich, and Ross (p. 790) add that people might be willing to admit that their views are affected by their religion, ethnicity, or socioeconomic status, but that they are likely to add that in their own case, their religion, ethnicity or socioeconomic status has added to their understanding and those who don't see things as they do lack sufficient understanding.

Another twist to postmodernity is that the turn inward and the suspicion of the world outward is a collective phenomenon. How we see ourselves and others is a product of many social interactions, and these interactions produce a social order that is experienced as real by the individuals who compose it. The fluidity of meaning and the flight inward represent reactions (that may or may not last) to cultural conditions.

Cultures change as a result of the introduction of new technologies, immigration of people with unique customs, war, dramatic shifts in the economy, the rise of new leaders, and other factors. Changes in culture usually occur when a large segment of the population experiences a shift in attitude and behavior and a leader is able to articulate this shift nationwide. As was stated in chapter one, in a general sense, cultural change is due to the paradox of social existence; that is, as a society shapes individuals, individuals shape society. Because of the introduction of novel ideas and practices into social interactions that may spread, culture is never a completely static or unchanging social phenomenon. Culture is a reflection of the ongoing collective interactions among the individuals who compose a society.

FOR FURTHER READING

Bellah, R., Madsen, R., Sullivan, W. M., Swidler, A., & Tipton, S. M. (1985). *Habits of the heart: Individualism and commitment in American life*. New York: Harper & Row. A classic exploration of individualism and community in America.

Berlin, I. (1990). *Four essays on liberty*. New York: Oxford University Press. Classic essays on freedom.

Dahl, R. (2000). *On democracy*. New Haven, CT: Yale University Press. Thoughtful and easy to read book on democracy by an expert in the field.

Eagleton, T. (2000). *The idea of culture*. Malden, MA: Blackwell Publishers. Challenging and worthwhile read on culture.

Geertz, C. (1973). *The interpretation of cultures: Selected essays*. New York: Basic Books. Classic essays on culture by a prominent anthropologist.

Gladwell, M. (2005). *Blink: The power of thinking without thinking*. New York: Little, Brown and Company. Reader-friendly on a subtle topic.

Chapter Four

Socialization and Imagination

I was born in New York City to parents with little more than high school educations struggling to live out the American Dream. Some of my most vivid memories as a small child are from events that occurred at my grandmother's apartment. She lived in a large, old building in Brooklyn. When we visited, I would sometimes pretend that I was a detective and wander around the building looking for clues and hiding from bad guys. Other times I would go down into the basement and imagine that there were monsters lurking about. Occasionally, I would scare myself and race out of the basement as fast as I could.

My grandmother (my mother's mother) was from Ukraine and came to the United States when she was a child around the turn of the twentieth century. She was a superstitious woman and engaged in rituals that, through a child's eyes, seemed mysterious to me. For example, when she heard a dog barking or howling after dark, she would take a glass and set it upside down in the windowsill. She told me that it would keep away evil spirits. It was partly due to her that I came to appreciate the places that my imagination would take me.

While it is true that each of us is born with a unique arrangement of dispositions, skills, and physical characteristics, these are interpreted and molded by others and by ourselves in a context defined by place and time. I incorporated some of the beliefs of my grandmother, but most of them were discarded because I was a boy growing up in urban America and not a girl growing up in rural Eastern Europe. One of the main goals of youth is to acquire the skills necessary to participate in our world.

We have already explored the concept of socialization, but we will now take a more in-depth look at this process. In this chapter we will discuss three overlapping types of socialization. *Primary* and *secondary socialization* are

not merely types of socialization, but from the perspective of many sociologists, psychologists, and anthropologists, represent the fundamental stages of
enculturation (e.g., acquiring the ways and beliefs of one's culture). *Consumer socialization* is a special case of socialization that has rapidly developed
since the beginning of the twentieth century, and its impact is a hotly debated
topic among sociologists, psychologists, economists, and business leaders.

Like so many other topics in sociology, socialization is a complex area of
investigation not only because it is multifaceted but also because it is difficult to separate our own experiences from the topic. It is tempting to quickly
assume that we understand socialization based upon our own experiences of
being socialized. Even professionals in the sciences sometimes confuse personal interest with disinterested assessment of the topic. For example, it is
not uncommon to read books on socialization written by sociologists who
ignore the important contributions that have been made by developmental
psychologists in furthering our understanding of socialization. Conversely,
many books on socialization written by psychologists ignore the contributions made by sociologists.

An ongoing "chicken and egg" battle among professionals has been
whether a unique sense of self emerges as a product of socialization (sociologists usually support this position) or whether human beings inherently possess a unique sense of self (psychologists typically maintain this position).
Such a debate overshadows the real possibility that self and other continuously define each other. In this way human beings may be understood as
innately possessing a unique sense of self, though psychological and social
pressures, due to time and place, profoundly influence how an individual's
sense of self is expressed. Singer and Singer echo the same idea when they
state: "Whatever babies may bring with them at birth will be molded and
tempered by the behavior of those entrusted with their welfare" (1990, p. 62).
The point that I want to emphasize here is that there are many subtleties
involved in grasping concepts such as socialization.

As in the last chapter, this chapter takes a look at the contributions made
by individuals, regardless of their field of training, who have furthered our
understanding of the topic at hand. Finally, in this chapter I will argue that
cultural historian Johann Huizinga was probably right to suggest that the
fundamental activity of culture is playing (see his classic, *Homo Ludens*,
1955), but that he fell short in his study of play by paying scant attention to
the role of imagination in shaping individual and cultural development. As
we discuss the three types of socialization in this chapter, we will also address the important role of the imagination in contributing to the progression
or regression of humankind.

Sociologists typically divide socialization into two stages. Primary socialization occurs approximately from birth to age five. Secondary socialization
begins when a child emerges from the home and progressively becomes

ensconced in relationships outside of the immediate family. Secondary socialization is a process that can occur throughout one's life, as long as a person continues to integrate new information and modify previously learned information. In this next section, we will discuss the phases of primary socialization.

PRIMARY SOCIALIZATION

Human babies are among the most helpless of creatures. Most creatures are born with enough physical skills to at least give them a fighting chance at survival. Without caregivers to feed them and clean them, human infants would die. As was stated in chapter one, the survival of the human species depends upon our *sociability*. Up until eight weeks (sometimes longer), caregivers spend much of their time trying to stabilize and regulate an infant's sleep and feeding cycles. Newborns can neither sit up nor lift up their own head, but lying on their back, they can turn their head from left to right. Newborns will turn their head when they catch the scent of their mother's milk. They will also turn their head in the direction of a television that is airing a program.

At around six to eight weeks, babies begin to show more direct eye contact, smile more frequently, and generally become more responsive. A two-month-old can recognize his/her mother's face, voice, and touch. Psychologist Colwyn Trevarthen notes, "A totally blind baby can orient face and eyes toward a mother's voice, centering on her so well that the blindness can go undetected" (1993, p. 135). A great deal of social interaction is taking place at this time, though neither the infant nor the harried caregiver may recognize it. Psychologist Daniel Stern refers to this social interaction as *emergent relatedness* (1984, p. 67). It is also around this time that infants begin to coo or engage in what psychologist Mary Catherine Bateson (1975) refers to as *protoconversation*. Bateson's point is that cooing and smiling reflects an active form of communicating—there is a prelanguage dialogue going on between baby and caregiver. Rather than the baby being seen as merely a passive recipient of attention, Bateson and other researchers believe that infant and caregiver are mutually engaged.

Consider the following question: why do adults typically talk to babies in a raised and exaggerated pitch? According to Daniel Stern, "The social presence of an infant elicits variations in adult behavior that are best suited to the infant's innate perceptual biases; for example, infants prefer sounds of a higher pitch, such as are achieved in 'baby talk'" (p. 73). Without thinking about it, we talk to babies a certain way because we sense, and rightly so, that they respond to us when we do. Moreover, such "baby talk" appears to be universal: a comparison of the utterances of a mother and infant speaking in

Mandarin Chinese is the same (in terms of tone, pitch, and cadence) as a mother and infant speaking in English (Trevarthen, p. 136).

At about six months, interactions that were previously limited to "baby talk" and exaggerated facial expressions now include objects or baby toys. As Singer and Singer note, "the earliest form of play is simple handling or tasting and mouthing, followed by . . . functionally correct play, such as pushing a toy car or making a small plastic horse gallop along the floor" (1990, p. 122). Development within the first year of life occurs very rapidly. In fact, within the first year of life, the human brain develops faster than prior to birth. A newborn may be inherently prepared to learn to grasp, walk, and talk, but it is human contact that facilitates the process and makes actual what is inherently possible. The significant others (i.e., parents or caregivers) provide an infant with the physical sustenance necessary to survive and the psychological sustenance necessary to become members of society.

After six months of age, a baby increasingly observes his or her caregiver's behavior and attaches meaning to the caregiver's gestures and words through repetition and context. A caregiver points to an object and repeatedly says, "This is a chair, can you say *chair*?" As the sign becomes associated with the referent (see chapter three) the baby will externalize the significant symbol *chair*. Human beings are meaning-making creatures—we label an object with a sound and give that sound meaning. The sound and configuration of letters making *chair* are socially agreed-upon representations of the object to be used for sitting.

Significant symbols (i.e., language) constitute the means by which a culture reproduces itself (since members continually die). Through language babies internalize their parents' understanding of the social world, and when they are able, they will externalize or vocalize back to their parents the words they have internalized and learned. A key point here is that the caregiver can make any sound, say *table*, and associate it with the object used for sitting. Infants are capable of making any of the sounds that eventually become molded into one or more of the languages spoken on the planet. Whatever the primary caregiver says during this phase of socialization constitutes reality for the developing child.

In the course of primary socialization a baby uncritically internalizes the values and understanding of the world expressed by their significant others. During the preschool years, children learn over 14,000 new words—approximately nine words a day (Singer & Singer 1990, 58).

As young children acquire a language and the dexterity to manipulate objects or toys independently, they come to realize that the relationships they have with objects and with others are meaningful. Their ability to manipulate blocks shows them that they can accomplish things on their own. Singer and Singer state, "The early play of an eighteen-month-old, which may be functionally appropriate to an object (using a spoon to feed a doll), may later change to symbolic play (a stick can represent the spoon when the child feeds the doll)" (1990, p. 59). Separating thoughts and actions from objects establishes the basis for a child's emerging imagination and sets the stage for *pretense* or fantasy play.

There are competing views on the role of fantasy play in human development and socialization. Jean Piaget (1896–1980), one of the most influential cognitive development theorists of the twentieth century, argued that pretend play was a temporary stage of cognitive development—emerging around the age of two and declining by the age of six as more logically based thinking appears. He also argued that pretense does not accommodate to reality, but rather distorts it. At approximately the same time that Piaget was developing his ideas another psychologist by the name of Lev Vygotsky (1896–1934) was formulating a different theory of cognitive development. For example, Vygotsky states:

> The imaginary situation of any form of play already contains rules of behavior, although it may not be a game with formulated rules laid down in advance. The child imagines himself to be the mother and the doll to be the child, so he must obey the rules of maternal behavior. . . . [A] case where two sisters, aged five and seven, said to each other, "Let's play sisters." They were playing at reality. In certain cases, I have found it easy to elicit such play in children. It is very easy, for example, to have a child play at being a child while the mother is playing the role of mother, that is, playing at what is actually true. The vital difference . . . is that the child in playing tries to be what she thinks a sister should be. In life the child behaves without thinking that she is her sister's sister. In the game of sisters playing at "sisters," however, they are both concerned with displaying their sisterhood; the fact that two sisters decided to play sisters induces them both to acquire rules of behavior. (1978, p. 94)

According to Vygotsky, pretense does not distort reality, but rather incorporates it into play. A child playing at being a parent or a sibling is aware of the role of parent and sibling and in play attempts to act out that role as they understand it. Vygotsky also notes that pretense appears at about the age of two, but he does not see it as a temporary, prelogical form of cognitive development.

In a fascinating article, Alan Leslie argues that "Pretend play is one of the earliest manifestations of the ability to characterize and manipulate one's own and others' cognitive relations to information. This ability . . . will eventually include characterizing relations such as believing, expecting, and hoping . . . " (1987, p. 422). Contemporary research seems to side with Vygotsky in that the use of imagination in pretend play reflects the beginning of the cognitive capacity to entertain alternative scenarios in one's mind—in other words, it represents the emergence of flexible and abstract thinking.

We can observe an evolution in the growth and development of a human being through the development of play: from playing with a single object at the age of six months to the stacking of blocks at about twelve months, to engaging in symbolic play at eighteen months, to the development of pretense at two years, to the development of elaborate fantasy play at three years. This process involves social interaction, the internalization of words, the capacity to think abstractly, and the ability to take the role of others, all in a format that is relatively safe—play. Play enables children to practice reality in a safe way. Developmental psychologist Paul Harris observes:

> Richard, aged 24 months, and his sister were playing trains. Richard's sister pointed out that the train had got stuck and asked him to get some more petrol. Richard pretended to put some petrol in, making a suitable "Ssss" sound as he did so. His sister then "noticed" that the petrol was leaking and told him to put it in at a different place. Richard had no difficulty in realizing that his sister was referring to make-believe petrol . . . . He responded to her request with relevant gestures and vocalizations. She, in her turn, understood what he was doing but she spotted a further problem—the leakage of the petrol. This example illustrates how successful collaborative pretend play can scarcely be construed as withdrawal from the external world. . . . [J]oint pretense calls for mutual comprehension and accommodation of one partner to the other as they construct a make-believe episode. (2000, p. 9)

This example demonstrates that children must have some sense of what is real before they engage in pretense. It shows how pretend play teaches children how to be social: pretense with another requires verbal and behavioral turn taking. It also shows how imagination is used to contemplate problems and their resolution. Play provides practice in the *inhibition of taking action*. Turn-taking requires the coordination of verbal or behavioral activities. Such coordination requires thinking or engaging in mental imagery, before acting. Inhibition of taking action facilitates self-regulation and problem solving, and it decreases impulsiveness.

Two factors that interfere with the development of pretense are real-life stressors and television (Fein 1981). Again, children do not engage in pretense to escape from reality, but to learn about real life in a safe way. If real life is anxiety-ridden, play is inhibited. Because television is not truly interactive and cannot respond to a child's unique set of needs and temperament, it does not cultivate the social skills that pretense promotes. Moreover, because of its strong draw on attention, children will limit their own play time in order to watch television (Paley 2004).

As pretend play begins to fade between the ages of five and six, it is replaced by an interest in games. Many of the skills that children have acquired in play will now be used to enhance their physical and social dexterity. They are now acquiring significant others besides their parents and siblings.

SECONDARY SOCIALIZATION

When a child's social world begins to expand and s/he is subject to non-family members' interpretations of the world, then the process of secondary socialization begins, and it may continue for the rest of a person's life. Peers and teachers are the significant others during the early stages of secondary socialization. It is important to realize that school is primarily a societal instrument for inculcating youth into a common way of thinking. Children from unique family circumstances come together, they exchange words and beliefs they have acquired from their parents, and teachers guide this exchange while adding information that the culture deems important.

Secondary socialization adds to or modifies what has been learned during primary socialization. However, what is learned during secondary socialization rarely replaces what has been learned during primary socialization. For example, an individual may grow up to become a beauty queen and rocket scientist, yet if her parents treated her poorly during the formative years of primary socialization, she will likely always harbor doubts about her looks and ability. She may say things to herself like, "Others don't really see me for what I am." Because the messages of primary socialization come first, they tend to be experienced deeply and feel very familiar, however untrue they may be. Nevertheless, secondary socialization can profoundly influence or modify previously acquired beliefs and behavior. A couple of examples should make this discussion less abstract.

Let us say that a husband and wife have a little boy named Tommy, but that they secretly wished for a child that they could have named Tammy. The parents like to dress baby Tommy in frilly pink clothing. As a baby, Tommy has not yet learned that colors are gendered—that, typically, pink is for girls and blue is for boys. Let's say that Tommy is now six years old and is ready to begin first grade. Tommy gets dressed in his prettiest pink outfit. It is very possible that Tommy's first day of school may not go very well. The problem is that the other children have probably learned that some colors are gendered, and his wearing pink is inconsistent with what they have learned. Things that are inconsistent with previously acquired knowledge tend to make people, regardless of their age, feel uncomfortable. Some of the boys in Tommy's class may translate this uncomfortable feeling into verbal or physical abuse toward our poor boy in pink. What will Tommy say to his parents about his first day of school besides the fact that he doesn't like it? He will probably tell his parents that he doesn't want to go to school in frilly pink clothes.

The significant others in Tommy's life have grown to include peers. Their reaction to Tommy will influence how he thinks and acts. Secondary socialization is modifying Tommy's understanding of clothes and colors: they are not value neutral; people, regardless of age, tend to label each other based on what they wear. In a sense, clothing is a form of language in that it holds symbolic meaning for people (e.g., consider the impact of a uniform on social perceptions and behavior).

Let us consider another example of secondary socialization modifying primary socialization. Suppose that your parents have always enjoyed your jokes and have always told you that you are a very funny person. In all likelihood, you are going to consider yourself to be a funny person. Let's say that as an adult you make up a joke that you think is hilarious, and you tell it to a woman as a way to "break the ice" and become acquainted. However, rather than finding the joke funny, she finds it insulting and walks away. At this point, you might think to yourself, "There is nothing bad about the joke, she is just hypersensitive." In order to prove to yourself that it is the woman and not the joke, you proceed to tell it to some of your best friends. But to your surprise, their reaction to the joke is something like, "That is really stupid."

At this point, a little doubt may be creeping into the back of your mind about how good you really are at making up and telling jokes. Perhaps your parents laugh at your jokes because they love you or feel sorry for you, not because the jokes are funny. If you really think about it, qualities such as funniness and attractiveness really are in the "eyes of the beholder." Others' reactions to us inform us of the merits of our skills and looks. If for whatever reason you believe that you are funny or attractive, and you rarely receive reactions from others to confirm this, then eventually you are going to reevaluate the qualities that you have always assumed you have.

In our culture it is taken for granted as a truism that we know ourselves better than anyone else knows us. In certain respects this is the case; no one can tell you precisely what you are thinking or feeling at any given moment. However, when you are in the midst of feeling moody, down, or angry, who usually recognizes it first—you or a loved one? When you buy an expensive outfit that you feel makes you look outstanding, and a loved one or best friend, whose brutal honesty you depend on, says it does nothing to enhance your appearance, whose view are you going to trust—your view as reflected in the mirror or their view of you?

In many respects others are mirrors. This point was made over a century ago by sociologist Charles Cooley (1864–1929). He noted that human beings from an early age look to others for cues or information about themselves. Cooley referred to this social behavior as the *looking-glass self* because the individual learns about him/her-self by looking to others (Cooley, 1902, p.

152). In a sense, we are all mirrors to each other and there are many instances where others see us more clearly than we see ourselves.

Secondary socialization also influences the transition from fantasy play to games. Early on in secondary socialization, fantasy play recedes and is replaced by an interest in games. This transition is due to cognitive development, and no less significantly, increasing external pressures from parents, teachers, and peers, and internal psychological pressure to display behaviors that seem grown-up.

According to Vygotsky, the transition from play to games marks a progression in the child's ability to regulate his/her own behavior in accordance with abstract rules. While there are rules involved in play, the rules are always open to negotiation and play may proceed as long as there is an agreed-upon sequence of events. In games, rules are not subject to negotiation and their violation is subject to predictable consequences. Games build on the lessons learned in play in regard to regulating one's own emotions and behavior. By engaging in games, children acquire an implicit understanding of their role as well as the role of others in maintaining social organization.

The transition from play to games marks the child's unwitting and enthusiastic entry into a set of social norms. As social animals we want to become members of a group, and as self-conscious animals, group membership gives our identity structure and some sense of direction.

Vygotsky was not the only researcher at the time to theorize about the importance of play in human development. George Herbert Mead developed a number of parallel theories while pursuing his interest in social interaction. According to Mead, in the transition from play to games a child comes to see him/her-self as part of a greater whole or what he called the *generalized other*. In order to participate in a game, each child must be willing to inhibit certain actions that would violate a rule and must be willing to engage in certain actions that perpetuate the game. For example, Mead states, "In the game everyone wants the pitcher to throw the ball; it is the attitude of the group that calls on the particular individual to do a particular thing. There is thus a universe of discourse . . . . When the child can take the attitude of the entire group, he can come back to himself the same way and thus come to have self-consciousness" (2006, p. 17).

While Vygotsky and Mead both recognized the importance of play and interaction in human development, they approached the connections among play, interaction, and development from different theoretical points of view. Vygotsky advanced a historical-cultural psychology, while Mead advanced an influential form of micro-sociology. In the quote in which Mead uses the term, *everyone*, and the expression, *attitude of the group*, he is referring to the generalized other or the norms of the group. *Norms* are established and maintained by "a universe of discourse," which means that group members agree on a set way of doing things.

When a child leaves play and enters into games s/he learns how to be a member of an organized group, and as part of the group, s/he learns more about him/her-self. This is what Mead means when he states, "When the child can take the attitude of the entire group, he can come back to himself" (2006, p. 17). Like the concept of the looking-glass self, Mead stresses that we come to learn about ourselves by observing how others react to us. In the quote, Mead refers to a pitcher. How does a person know if s/he is good at pitching? Of course, by how well *others respond* to his/her pitching. We learn about ourselves by our participation in groups and we maintain groups by our participation. Mead notes, "In the game we get an organized other, a generalized other, which is found in the nature of the child itself, and finds its expression in the immediate experience of the child" (2006, p. 13).

From interacting with the immediate family, to playing a game with friends in the neighborhood, to attending school—each represents a larger concentric circle that a child is socialized into and that represents and maintains the generalized other that is society. Some examples of the generalized other in context should make the concept less abstract.

Consider two friends, Alf and Bee, walking down a long hallway. If their friendship is more than incidental or at the level of acquaintances, then they are significant others to each other. Now, consider Alf and Bee passing two other people, Cid and Dee, who are leaning up against the wall in the hallway and having an intimate conversation. Cid and Dee are significant others to each other. Let us say that these two couples do not know each other. As long as Cid and Dee do not interrupt Alf and Bee, and vice versa, each couple is engaged in being a part of the generalized other.

There is a protocol to be followed when we see others that we do not know. The protocol or social norm is that we do not engage people that we do not know unless we have a good reason and a way of making our introduction cordial (otherwise, it tends to be perceived as intrusive). Let us say that as Alf and Bee are passing Cid and Dee in the hallway, Bee unintentionally pushes Alf into Dee. Now the two couples know each other, and depending upon how they handle the situation, they may become significant others to each other in either a good or bad way. If Alf's shoulder lands on Dee's jaw and breaks it, then the significant relationship that will ensue will not be a good one. On the other hand, if Alf's lips meet Dee's and there is electricity, and Cid and Bee look at each other and there is instant chemistry, then the significant relationships that will result will be quite different. There are many possible scenarios. The point is that we are always a significant other to some and a member of the generalized other to most.

Abiding by social norms, even when we are the stranger in a crowd, connects us to a group. (If you have any doubt about this, all you need do is violate an accepted norm—in a sense break the web of cohesion that produces social order—and you will quickly become the object of attention, though not necessarily the kind of attention you may want).

During secondary socialization a child may be exposed to different views of gender roles, patriotism, and God. Reevaluating beliefs stemming from socialization is very likely to happen as a result of traveling. Spending some time in a Buddhist country, where little emphasis is placed upon God and Heaven, may make a fundamentalist Christian reexamine the belief that everyone who does not believe as they do is destined for eternal damnation. Spending some time in Boston, then New York City, and then Jacksonville, Florida, can help us realize that people are socialized into talking a certain way. Secondary socialization sometimes challenges us, but such challenges cultivate growth.

SOCIALIZATION AND LIFE STORIES

Primary and secondary socialization instills in each generation the stories that preserve families, cultures, and civilizations. As meaning-making animals, we depend upon stories, whether oral or written, to give us a sense of continuity. Such stories or *narratives* constitute the conceptual grid of society. When I state that we are born into a world already in motion, I mean in part that we acquire the stories of our culture, and these stories give us a grid upon which to direct our lives. Narratives are story lines that enable people to get their bearings and a sense of direction. Narratives are configured with a beginning, middle, and end. Psychologist Donald Polkinghorne, building on the work of philosopher Paul Ricoeur, states,

> Narrative configuration takes place through the process of emplotment (Ricoeur, 1983/1984). Emplotment is a procedure that configures temporal elements into a whole by "grasping them together" and directing them toward a conclusion or ending. Emplotment transforms a list or sequence of disconnected events into a unified story with a point or theme. . . . Emplotment is the means by which narrators weave together the complex of events into a single story. Through its operation, the historical and social contexts in which events take place exert influence in the understanding of the story. The synthesizing function of the plot provides narrators and storytellers a means to draw together information about physical laws, personal dispositions and character, responses to actions, and the processes of deliberation in reaching decisions. (1991, p. 141)

Emplotment is the process of using story lines to make sense out of the events that occur in our lives. People tend to perpetuate cultural story lines in order to give their lives a sense of purpose. For example, an individual pursuing a career in business gets into an auto accident, comes close to dying, eventually leaves the hospital permanently disabled but with a whole new perspec-

tive: He dedicates his life to "witnessing." Before the accident, this individual's life story was about the cultural theme of being a self-made businessman.
After the accident, he references the self-soothing cultural cliché, "This must
have happened for a reason," and even though the cliché does not really
explain why things happen as they do, it nevertheless provides him with
emotional relief. It tells him that his life plans have not been turned upside
down, that the universe still makes sense, and that the whole thing is not just
the result of negligence on the part of one of the drivers. He has embraced
another cultural narrative (whether it is in terms of Karma, Allah, or Jesus
Christ).

Emplotment provides a trajectory, linking the past, present, and future
into a consistent narrative. Narratives are always open to reconstruction, and
this enables individuals to twist and turn cultural narratives into forms that fit
their needs.

Narrative is a cognitive process that depends upon the imagination to
provide flexibility for a story line. Conversely, imagination depends upon
narrative to provide structure and direction for a story line. Cultural narratives are internalized as early as children are able to engage in fantasy play,
usually sometime in the child's second year. The earliest stories that children
are usually exposed to are nursery songs and rhymes, fairy tales, and contemporary stories for children, for example, "Twinkle, Twinkle Little Star,"
"Lullaby," "The Three Little Pigs," "Little Red Riding Hood," "Hansel and
Gretel," "Thomas the Train," "Bob the Builder," and "Rudolph the Red-
Nosed Reindeer." Children also learn about Santa Claus and the Tooth Fairy,
and eventually they learn the stories associated with their parents' religion,
race, ethnicity, gender, social class, and nationality: for example, "Jesus died
for our sins," "Moses led the 'Chosen People' to the promised land," "We
have always been the object of discrimination in this society," "As
Americans we have a God-given right to liberty." Stories such as these
become wedded to our identity, and once internalized, they guide our opinions, values, and behavior throughout our lives. As secondary socializing
events occur as we grow and acquire a wider range of experiences, some
stories are modified while others are replaced.

While we usually associate fantasy and imagination with childhood, and
rationality with adulthood, it may be more accurate to describe imagination
and rationality as two cognitive processes that people depend upon to gauge
decision making. Imagination appears to fulfill at least two vital functions:
(1) imagination allows children and adults to be creative (to contemplate or
do what they previously could not consider or carry out); imagination fuels
innovation, and (2) imagination provides us with escape, a break away from
boredom, tedium, pain, conflict, and the inevitability of death.

In a wonderful book called, *A Child's Work: The Importance of Fantasy
Play*, Vivian Gussin Paley states, "From the earliest 'pretend I'm the mama

and you're the baby,' play is the model for the life-long practice of trying out new ideas" (2004, p. 92). The stories that we learn in childhood fill the imagination with possibility, and everyday concrete life serves as the back-drop for practicing and potentially realizing these possibilities. As many psychologists, sociologists, and anthropologists have known for years, and as the examples in the following paragraphs demonstrate, make-believe does not fade away with age; rather, it "goes underground" or finds expression in socially acceptable ways.

Singer and Singer observe,

> As the child moves into adolescence, make-believe play certainly becomes a less prominent part of life, but it continues to be manifested in computer and video games and often in more formal school or after-school activities such as drama, ballet, or amateur filmmaking. But from adolescence on, most expres-sions of human playfulness and most continuing efforts at assimilating new experience occur in the private realm of thought. (1990, pp. 265–266)

The fantasies of childhood, and especially middle childhood, oftentimes be-come the daydreams of adulthood (Caughey 1984, p. 22; Singer & Singer 1990, p. 255). Such daydreams can include being wealthy and influential, being a professional athlete, well-known musician, war hero, or Nobel lau-reate. Most of an adult's daily mindful activities are consumed by what American pioneering psychologist, William James (1842–1910), called the *stream of consciousness* (1890). Throughout most of our day, our minds are not engaged in conscious rational planning and problem solving, but rather in expectations of what might happen or what one wants to see happen, reminis-cences of what might have been, rehashes of who said such and such and what they really meant. The stream is a continual flow of images and stories that blend imagination and reality. The stream operates below the level of conscious awareness (or the preconscious level of awareness), but is readily available to consciousness.

The sociologist Erving Goffman (1974) used the term *away* to describe the phenomenon of being physically but not mentally present. While engaged in a conversation our focus of attention may drift into an interaction that already took place, drift into preparing for an encounter yet to take place, or drift into an encounter that we wish were taking place with the person in front of us. All of these instances demonstrate *away* or absorption into the stream of consciousness. Wherever the mind goes, however, it is seldom alone; the images and stories that run through our minds are usually about social interactions, impression management, and fulfilling social goals.

Not all make-believe goes underground as we grow into adulthood. The pioneering sociologist Robert Park (1864–1944) used the term *moral regions* to describe places where like-minded people come together to express their "recreational passions" (Farberman 1980, p. 10). While children have playgrounds and amusement parks, and teens have arcades, game rooms, and musical concerts, adults have casinos, sports stadiums, shopping malls, and vacations. For example, while children play cops and robbers, fire chief, or princess, and teens play at their appearance, play sports, and play at dating, adults play "weekend cowboy"; trade in their suits for black leather and make the annual trek to Sturgis, South Dakota, for the bikers' rally (which has an approximate turnout rate of nearly a half-a-million people per year); or dress up in Elizabethan attire and attend a Renaissance Fair.

Based upon their five year ethnographic study, Belk and Costa (1998) describe the fantasy of reenacting the American frontier mountain man. From the 1820s through the 1830s, trapping animals for their fur—particularly beavers—were in high demand due to a booming market for top hats in Europe. About 3,000 men were involved in the Rocky Mountain fur trade (Belk & Costa, p. 220). As the new population of Americans moved westward, romanticized stories of the frontier grew in number and popularity. Contemporary accounts of the mountain man were portrayed in films such as *Jeremiah Johnson* (a favorite movie of mine from 1972) and the movie and television series called *The Life and Times of Grizzly Adams*, loosely based on the life of J. Capen "Grizzly" Adams (1812–1860). Belk and Costa attended thirteen rendezvous where mostly Caucasian men gather in mountain man garb and camp out in tepees and tents in the Rocky Mountain region for two to ten days. The men who gather at these rendezvous share a fantasy about the American frontier and collectively construct an alternative reality to modern life. According to Belk and Costa,

> The modern mountain man rendezvous as a fantastic consumption enclave is found to involve several key elements: participants' use of objects and actions to generate feelings of community involving a semimythical past, a concern for "authenticity" in recreating that past, and construction of a . . . time and place in which . . . adult play and rites of intensification and transformation can freely take place. (p. 219)

Like make-believe during childhood, these men put on costumes and act out a fantasy.

Children, like adults, know that make-believe is not real, and they can move in and out of the fantasy world they construct. It is important to remember that the belief in fantasy characters (such as Santa Claus and the Tooth Fairy) is usually encouraged by parents and American culture (Prentice, Manosevitz, & Hubbs 1978). According to Harris, "Children mostly live in the ordinary world and expect mundane causal principles to hold sway, but like adults, that does not prevent them from speculating and even hoping that it might be otherwise" (2000, p. 183). Indeed, in the case of Santa Claus, it is usually parents who are saddened more than children when the truth comes out (Anderson & Prentice 1994).

While children tend to get absorbed into playing on a more regular basis than adults, it is important to understand why this is the case: it is their way of learning about the real world in a safe way. Generally speaking, I would say that children engage in play in order to learn about the real world, while adults engage in play and fantasy in order to forget about the real world. Of course, creativity and learning can also occur in adult play and fantasy. Indeed, it is often remarked that science fiction is science that has not yet been discovered or invented. Make-believe is not unique to childhood; it occurs in one form or another throughout a person's life. Imagination is a vital part of human cognitive processing—it contributes to our ability as a species to adapt to different circumstances. Indeed, studies have shown fantasy play to be positively associated with verbal intelligence, mathematical readiness, perspective taking, concentration, and originality (Singer & Singer 1990, p. 136). By removing opportunities for play in childhood, we may be contributing to the development of adults who possess fewer coping skills and creative ways of navigating through a complex world. Indeed, it may be the case that as our intellectual ability to build technologies is progressing, our emotional capacity to deal with the consequences of technologies is regressing. The main difficulty with imagination is that where it stops and where rational processes begin is not always clear-cut, and as it will be made evident shortly, socialization can contribute to blurring the distinction.

In an experiment, Harris et al. showed two groups of children two large black boxes that were empty, and then asked one group of children to imagine that there was a rabbit in one of the boxes and they asked the second group to imagine that in one of the boxes there was a monster. The experimenters confirmed with both groups of children their understanding that the rabbit or monster was pretend. Each child was then left alone in the room with both boxes for two minutes. Harris elaborates:

> A video of the children's behavior during the experimenter's absence showed that almost half of the children opened one or both of the boxes. In doing so, they typically focused more on the box containing the imaginary creature. Apparently, children were curious about the pretend box. . . . [T]he experimenter returned and talked to the children about what they had done and thought while she was away. In particular, they were asked: "Were you sure there was nothing inside the box or did you wonder whether there was a bunny (monster) inside?" Half of the children insisted that they were sure that nothing was inside, but the remainder acknowledged that they did indeed wonder if there was a creature inside the box. Recall . . . the experimenter had asked children whether there was really a creature in the box, or whether they were just pretending. Almost all of them said that they were just pretending. Why then did a considerable proportion subsequently acknowledge that they wondered, while the experimenter was out of the room, whether the box contained the creature in question? (Harris 2000, pp. 175–176)

The first time that I read about this experiment, it reminded me of the time when I went to see a midnight showing of the classic horror movie *Night of the Living Dead* with a few of my friends. We were about twenty years of age, and this was my first viewing of the film. When I got home sometime between 2:00 and 3:00 in the morning, I could not fall asleep. I felt compelled to look once or twice behind every shadowy place in the house. Even after seeing the film, I did not really believe in zombies, but like the children who were asked to imagine a creature in an empty box, there was a part of me that could not shake the image in my mind after it had been placed there.

Paul Rozin, Linda Millman, and Carol Nemeroff (1986) observed a similar reaction when they asked a group of people (seventeen men and thirty-three women, from seventeen to fifty years in age) to consider drinking from a glass that they knew contained sugar water but was labeled as being the poison "sodium cyanide." In this experiment, subjects were presented with two empty bottles, sugar from a box of *Domino* sugar was poured into each bottle, subjects were then given two labels, one reading "Sucrose (sugar)" and the other "Sodium Cyanide." The subjects then placed one label on each bottle, and then asked from which bottle they would prefer to drink. Subjects, to a statistically significant degree, chose the bottle labeled "Sucrose (sugar)."

According to Harris, "the very act of imagining . . . infuses [our] appraisal of reality" (2000, p. 176). Young or old, the line between imagination and reality is not always clear. Moreover, the less clear we are about this distinction, the more likely we are to believe in direct mental-physical causality or that "thinking it, makes it real." For example, a child playing at being a great professional basketball player or a world-class golfer knows that s/he is not a superstar; however, with repeated infusions into the imagination from others and culture at large, a teenager or young adult can come to seriously believe that s/he will become the next star athlete even if the facts contradict the fantasy. As psychologist Penelope Vinden states,

> [W]hat we clearly know to be true concerning something does not necessarily dictate how we behave toward it. [P]retending something is the case is clearly not always the same as imagining something. One of the characteristics of pretense, both in the child and adult worlds, is that the pretender really does know that the pretense is not real, even if he or she is not always able to act that way. But a believed-in imagining is something that is clearly thought (by the one believing it) to be true or real. In fact, it is not thought of as an imagining at all, but as knowledge. (1998, p. 75)

The key concept in this quote is *believed-in imagining* or the belief in something as real that is not. For example, when we periodically harbor thoughts of others in our imagination, perhaps trying to discern their intentions, we can become swept away by a belief, an assumption made in our imagination that does not actually represent the others' intentions. When we engage in conversations with others that haven't happened yet, such as anticipating a discussion with a supervisor about salary, such anticipated conversations can convince us of consequences that have not happened.

As we grow and mature, we tend to accumulate experiences and the cognitive skills necessary to distinguish reality from fantasy. However, stressful conditions can undermine our cognitive acuity. The earnest belief in direct mental-physical causality and believed-in imaginings is much more likely to occur under conditions of duress, for example, when we are unemployed and low in resources or when we are very sick. Under these circumstances, people are much more likely to engage in wishful thinking or prayer, express a belief in destiny, or become convinced that there are supernatural entities representing good and evil operating in the world.

Social scientists have long observed the impact that strong emotions can have in blurring the lines between fact and fantasy. However, social scientists are still trying to ascertain the real impact that modern media, particularly television and advertising, have on people's ability to distinguish reality from fantasy. This is the topic of the final section of the chapter.

CONSUMER SOCIALIZATION

Let us recall the meaning of *socialization*; in brief it means teaching new members of society the beliefs and practices of that society. Socialization proceeds in two stages. Primary socialization occurs from birth and the main socializing agents or significant others at this time are usually parents. As a child's social world increases, secondary socializing agents come into play; now, peers and teachers also become significant others in a child's life. A child who celebrates the Jewish holiday of Hanukkah at home is introduced to Santa Claus, Christmas trees, and "Rudolph the Red Nosed Reindeer" through his/her widening circle of social interactions. A child who celebrates Christmas at home may come to the realization that Santa Claus is not real upon befriending a Jewish, Muslim, Buddhist, or Hindu child. Consumer socialization, a third type of socialization, has gained increasing influence, particularly in the United States, over the course of the twentieth century.

Consumer socialization is "the process by which young people acquire consumer-related thoughts and actions" (Stampfl, Moschis, & Lawton 1978, p. 12). Consumer socialization begins during primary socialization and proceeds throughout secondary socialization. Its impact is enormous in contributing to what contemporary citizens understand as being "an American." Indeed, consumer socialization has played a significant role in the transformation of Americans identifying themselves as consumers rather than as citizens. It is because of its remarkably powerful and pervasive influence on

personal identity and American culture that I have included consumer socialization in this chapter.

In order to truly appreciate its influence, I believe it is important to first
learn a little about the development of consumerism in American society.
Walter Lippmann, an astute journalist, was one of the earliest observers of
the changes taking place in American society due to innovations in technology and the growth of strong ties between industrial and political leaders. In
Lippmann's 1922 publication of a book entitled *Public Opinion* he
writes,"[H]uman culture is very largely the selection, the rearrangement, the
tracing of patterns upon, and the stylizing of, what William James called 'the
random irradiations and resettlements of our ideas'" (p. 16).

The discovery of society as a phenomenon to be studied gave rise to the
insight that culture is constructed by people, and the worldview created by
culture, which becomes "the pictures in our heads" (an expression used by
Lippmann) that reflect representations of reality rather than reality itself.
Lippmann also wrote:

> For the real environment is altogether too big, too complex, and too fleeting
> for direct acquaintance. We are not equipped to deal with so much subtlety, so
> much variety, so many permutations and combinations. And although we have
> to act in that environment, we have to reconstruct it on a simpler model before
> we can manage with it. To traverse the world men must have maps of the
> world. (p. 16)

Before the rise of widespread mobility, industrialization, and urban centers
many people took for granted that "the pictures in our heads" represented
their life experiences. The world that people lived in was smaller and less
diverse and so the cognitive "maps" (or schemata or schemas in contemporary terms) they used to traverse that world were simpler.

With the growing complexity of society came the realization that cultural
beliefs and the schemas they provided to individuals were concocted but
necessary. According to Benedict Anderson (2006), nation-states and nationalism arose as a way to create a common identity among peoples who had
little in common. As old social bonds deteriorated, ambitious and powerful
leaders called upon people to imagine and recognize social bonds based on
nationalism. People came to imagine having an association with strangers
living within the same geographical region. This trend continues to the
present time. Today, watching television enables people to imagine knowing
more than they actually do know about persons, populations, and conditions
that they have never encountered.

The image-makers have also changed over time. While in earlier times
religious and political leaders provided narrowly conceived schemas for people to live by, with the increasing sophistication of technologies and the
growing number of people desiring to express their uniqueness, the respon-

sibility for perpetuating these politically and market-driven trends, as well as crafting other cultural beliefs and schemas associated with modernity, went to specialists: pollsters, journalists, statisticians, and market researchers.

By the 1950s, several keen observers of society were writing with greater clarity and alarm than Lippmann had about the enveloping influences of commerce, media, and consumer values. David Riesman, Nathan Glazer, and Reuel Denney's *The Lonely Crowd* (1950) argued that the "American character" was changing from being "inner-directed" or independently minded and adventurous to being "other-directed" or conformist and comfort-driven. Vance Packard's *The Hidden Persuaders* (1957) publicized how advertisers were using psychological techniques in an attempt to manipulate people into buying products. Daniel Boorstin's *The Image* (1982) revealed that people were increasingly choosing fabrications of reality over reality itself because media images and advertising were successfully conveying how simulated environments could be more enjoyable and less boring than the real world.

Today, advertisements are a pervasive part of the American landscape. They saturate television, the Internet, public gatherings (such as sporting events), holidays, private affairs (for example, the preference for diamond engagement rings and the determination of what is considered sexy), and the clothes we wear, prominently labeled. Sociologist Michael Schudson observes: "Advertising . . . surrounds us and enters into us, so when we speak we may speak in or with reference to the language of advertising and when we see we may see through schemata that advertising has made salient for us" (1984, p. 210). The pervasiveness of advertising is evident, with the exception of periodic frustration, by our generally unresponsive reaction to its omnipresence. People focus on novelty and give little attention to that which they acclimate to.

Consumer socialization in the United States has evolved tremendously over the past three generations. As a result, people are socialized into consumerism as though it were always dominant. About three in four children have been to a store by the time they are six months of age (McNeal & Yeh 1993). Marketing professor Deborah Roedder John notes,

> For most children, their exposure to the marketplace comes as soon as they can be accommodated as a passenger in a shopping cart at the grocery store. From this vantage point, infants and toddlers are exposed to a variety of stimuli and experiences, including aisles of products, shoppers reading labels and making decisions, and the exchange of money and goods at the checkout counter. These experiences, aided by developing cognitive abilities that allow them to interpret and organize their experiences, result in an understanding of marketplace transactions. Children learn about the places where transactions take place (stores), the objects of transactions (products and brands), the procedures for enacting transactions (shopping scripts), and the value obtained in exchanging money for products (shopping skills and pricing). (1999, p. 192)

Marketing directly to children has increased dramatically in recent years—and with much success. Stampfl, Moschis, and Lawton maintain that "Children *are* consumers and therefore should be educated for this role as early as possible" (p. 26). What Stampfl, Moschis, and Lawton overlook is the fact that the United States is a consumer-driven society today, in part, because of consumer socialization. "Children *are* consumers" because they are socialized into this role early in their development. Many children recognize brands before they can read (John, p. 192).

Cele Otnes, Young Chan Kim, and Kyungseung Kim (1994) examined 344 letters to Santa Claus, written by children, obtained from the postal service. They found that each letter contained an average of 7.2 requests and that 51.6 percent of the requests were identified by brand name. Otnes, Kim, and Kim conclude that, "young 'consumers in training' are apparently highly aware of the importance of specifically requesting desired gifts by brand name" (p. 191). By the time children are eight years of age, they also may be making inferences about people based on the consumer products they use (Belk, Bahn, & Mayer, 1982).

Due to consumer socialization, many people's daily stream of consciousness is consumed by the acquisition of goods. A person's daily daydreams may be filled with thoughts such as these: How long must I wait before I have enough money to buy such and such, buyer's remorse, why did s/he buy me this instead of that, who's going to get what after the divorce or the funeral, or if I only had such-in-such I would get more attention, look better, feel better, and be happier. Consumer socialization not only educates people about products, but it also socializes people into a value system that makes the acquisition of disposable goods a central concern and an efficient means of sizing up oneself and others. Susan Fournier (1998) conducted in-depth interviews with people in order to better understand the relationship between consumer brands and personal identity. In one interview with a respondent identified as Vicki, Fournier notes,

> Vicki's brand behaviors are primarily reflective of the degree and depth to which she readily links brands with concepts of self. To Vicki, products and brands compose an efficient meaning-based communication system. And, Vicki is an active consumer of these symbols and signs. "God," she confesses, "I am every marketer's dream!" A child weaned on mass communication and MTV, Vicki is a master of advertising slogans and brand imagery. She is especially adept at constructing and announcing identities through brand symbols and believes that others rely on this communication system as well. (p. 357)

Besides going to stores, the other primary means of consumer socialization is television. Preschoolers watch an average of twenty-one hours of television per week while the average American family watches about twenty-eight hours of television a week (Singer & Singer 1990, p. 177). Children between the ages of nine and fourteen are exposed to some 40,000 commercials a year (Lindstrom & Seybold 2004, p. 23). Time once taken up by play and peer group activities has increasingly been replaced by watching television. George Gerbner, who has studied the relationship between television and culture for many years, notes, "Television viewing both shapes and is a stable part of lifestyles and outlooks. It links the individual to a larger if synthetic world, a world of television's own making" (1998, p. 180).The world of television is a consumer's dream, a world that blurs the distinction between fact and fantasy.

It is important to emphasize that television is primarily an instrument for marketing products; its secondary role is that of entertainment. Everything on television—the comedy, the music, the clothing, the sex, the violence, and the news—is utilized for the promotion and sale of goods. Television is also a powerful medium. Many people watch television longer than they would prefer and beyond their admitted level of enjoyment (Kubey & Csikszentmihalyi 2002). It is apparently so stimulating that some researchers have observed ten-week-old infants lying on their backs on the floor, turn their necks 180 degrees in order to peer at the lights and sounds of a television (Kubey & Csikszentmihalyi).

Consumer socialization perpetuates a consumer culture. However, the ideas that reinforce this culture are not seen as ideologies intended to perpetuate the culture. Consumer socialization prevents people from seeing consumer culture in an objective light. Consumer culture has transformed the relationship between person and object. Material objects have always served as representations or symbols of humankind's interests and activities (McCracken 1986; Belk 1988). What has changed is the direction of the relationship between person and object: where people (knowingly or unwittingly) once gave meaning to objects, objects and the stories that surround them now give meaning to people.

Does it matter if a ritual and a tradition is created by a religious body, political group, or marketing firm? Few Americans are aware that, because of their disdain for festivals, the Puritans of the American colonies were against the celebration of Christmas. In fact, they enacted a law in 1659 to punish people who "kept Christmas" (Barnett 1954, p. 3). Opposition to celebrating Christmas in the United States declined throughout the eighteenth and nineteenth centuries as people became more interested in its secular aspects (Barnett, p. 6). The establishment of December 25th as the legal holiday acknowledging Christmas Day occurred in all states and territories between 1836 and 1890 (Barnett, p. 19). The image of Santa Claus that most of us maintain in the back of our minds—a jolly and heavy-set fellow with a white beard—emerged between 1863 and 1886 (Belk 1987, p. 91). The image stems from the drawings of Thomas Nast, an important political cartoonist in his day.

The other secular image regarding Christmas that resonates with most people is Santa driving an eight-reindeer-drawn sleigh and coming into people's homes through their chimney late at night. This scenario was created by Clement Moore in his 1822 poem, "A Visit from St. Nicholas" (Belk, p. 87). Moore, however, did not come up with the idea of Rudolph the Red-Nosed Reindeer. The story of Rudolph was written in 1939 by Robert May who worked in advertising for Montgomery Ward & Company. May based the story of Rudolph on the existing tale of the ugly duckling (Barnett, p. 110). Rudolph the Red-Nosed Reindeer is ultimately the story of the American Dream—be yourself, work hard, and you will succeed—set within a Christmas motif.

Advertising has created rituals in other areas of our lives as well. N. W. Ayer & Son, the oldest advertising firm in the United States, introduced the idea of the diamond engagement ring with the slogan "A diamond is forever" in 1947 for DeBeers, the largest diamond company in the world. N. W. Ayer & Son also created the slogan "Be all you can be" for the Army in 1981.

An effective slogan is not just a sales pitch, but a symbol echoing cultural significance that resonates psychologically with people because of socialization: Rudolph is a poor kid who makes it big, "a diamond is forever" is everlasting love, "be all you can be" is "rugged individualism." As Otnes and Scott state, "All of the ways in which ads can affect rituals reaffirm the fact they are important socialization agents" (1996, p. 40).

Advertising is the engine behind consumer socialization and a great deal of what we consider culture. Advertising was devised as a means to keep pace with the increasing speed of the production of goods. New technologies facilitated industrial production creating the problem of keeping production at a fast and profitable level. Today, advertising is a multibillion dollar business. Some of the nation's most highly educated and gifted scientists, engineers, psychologists, writers, and artists work for marketing and advertising firms in order to create lifelike stories to sell products. Gerbner observes, "The storytelling process used to be handcrafted, homemade, and community inspired. Now it is the end result of a complex manufacturing and marketing process" (1998, p. 175). The subtle and dynamic relationship between advertising and culture was perhaps best described by Raymond Williams:

> In the last hundred years advertising has developed from the simple announcement of shopkeepers and the persuasive arts of a few marginal dealers into a major part of capitalist business organization. This is important enough, but the place of advertising in society goes far beyond this commercial context. . . . [Advertising] has passed the frontier of the selling of goods and services and has become involved with the teaching of social and personal values . . . . It is impossible to look at modern advertising without realizing that the material object being sold is never enough: this indeed is the crucial cultural quality of its modern forms. Beer would be enough for us, without the additional promise

that in drinking it we show ourselves to be manly, young at heart, or neighborly. A washing-machine would be a useful machine to wash clothes, rather than an indication that we are forward-looking or an object of envy to our neighbors. But if these associations sell beer and washing-machines . . . it is clear that we have a cultural pattern in which the objects are not enough but must be validated, if only in fantasy, by association with social and personal meanings . . . . The short description of the pattern we have is *magic*: a highly organized and professional system of magical inducements and satisfactions, functionally very similar to magical systems in simpler societies, but rather strangely coexistent with a highly developed scientific technology. (1997, pp. 184–185)

To confirm Williams' point, all one need do is cite from the marketing literature itself. For example, William Wells, in the opening essay entitled "Lectures and Dramas" to the edited book called *Cognitive and Affective Responses to Advertising*, states,

The distinguishing mark of a drama is that the viewer . . . is transported into an imaginary setting . . . . Like fairy tales, movies, novels, parables, and myths, television commercial dramas are stories about how the world works. . . . [A] television commercial drama can be very powerful . . . . The source of that power is the viewer's independent mind. From the viewer's point of view, conclusions drawn from dramas are "mine," while conclusions urged in lectures are "ideas that other people are trying to impose on me." (1989, p. 15)

Because appeals to the mind draw resistance, stories are a better way to reach consumers. On television, fictional ads are more persuasive than nonfictional ads (Deighton, Romer, & McQueen 1989).

Advertising sometimes combines images and ideas that contradict each other in order to break through the myriad commercial messages and get an emotional reaction. While the presentation of absurd images and ideas leads to a consideration of formerly unthought-of possibilities, it also blurs the distinction between fact and fantasy, and results in greater uncertainty about objective conditions and more frequent recourse to one's subjective emotions. When people's minds are overloaded with facts that do not seem to add up, they resort to their emotions. Arjun Chaudhuri in *Emotion and Reason in Consumer Behavior* asserts,

Emotions can never be wrong. Understanding and intellect can betray us and prove us wrong, but emotions are always true and real. There can be no doubt about the existence of feeling. This virtue has marketing applications. Consumers can be wrong about their beliefs about a product, but they can have no misconception about their emotional response to a product or advertisement. . . . [I]f we can generate feelings, these will be genuine and accurate and, thus, more resistant to competitive claims than a rational belief. (2006, p. 27)

It is not the case that "emotions can never be wrong," but rather that when the world appears incoherent, a person can rely only on emotions. However, dependence on emotions to ascertain what is real can lead to all sorts of magical beliefs. Through the presentation of fantasy on television, a person can acquire a view of love that is unrealistic and immature, a person can fall in "love" with an image, a person can acquire a view that there is only one "right look," a person may conclude that unless s/he becomes wealthy and famous s/he is nobody and that someone who is wealthy and famous is by definition "somebody." Today, people possess images in their minds that convey "blue collar," "CEO," "hip-hop," "hippie," "trophy wife," "sage," and these images come from the manifestation of our imaginations onto the screen. Hirschman and Thompson state, "Consumers' understandings of their identities are developed over the life course; often, cultural images and ideals become interwoven with self perceptions through fantasy and the media vehicles from which those fantasies derive" (1997, p. 54).

Consumer socialization, which grew out of secondary socialization, now influences both primary and secondary socialization in ways that make some people's lives a dream come true and makes most people's lives feel disjointed and rushed. Consumer socialization's response to those who live in their dreams is to offer them more dreams to buy, and its response to those who live beyond their means at an ever-accelerating pace is to distract them with ever-more-stimulating goods. Consumer socialization teaches people that happiness is a product of constant stimulation; it does not warn people that constant stimulation leads to exhaustion and boredom. Indeed, many people seek out the solution to boredom in that which causes it. Perhaps the greatest dream world that consumer socialization creates is that what people do for a living is somehow disconnected from how people live. We live within a social paradox: as we create society, society creates us.

CONCLUSION

Let us return to the idea of play and games. Play provides the building blocks through which children learn about real life. Participation in games refines a child's developing mental, physical, and social skills. When children get through puberty, the fantasies that once focused on toys and games become redirected toward identity, sex, and power. In adolescence, a young person experiments with appearance, with ideas, and with different roles. They ask themselves questions like: does this outfit make me look sexy? Will playing football get me noticed? If I can't get the love and attention I want from my folks for being good, can I get it from acting out? If I do all that I'm supposed to, will my dreams come true? Clothes are no longer just about not being naked in public, or distinguishing between rich and poor; they carry a range of symbolic meanings. A young person's manner of talking and walking, and style of dress, carry social and personal significance. In young adulthood, these fantasies of identity, sex, and power turn toward marriage, procreation, and a career. Clothing is now a uniform (a suit, a smock, overalls, an apron) and how you walk and talk plays a role in the types of doors that open before you. Yet, from childhood to adulthood it is always still playing dress-up—whether it is playing a fairy or goblin on Halloween, or playing at being goth or a jock in high school, or going through rush in college, or putting on a suit to go to the office in adulthood.

From childhood to adulthood it is always still about learning who you are and what you can do. The fantasies that exist throughout our lives are always, ultimately about identity, security, and love. Our wishes, expectations, and fears blend in with our notions of identity, security, and love, and from that, we fashion our own lives, and from that mix we collectively fashion a culture.

The silly uniforms portraying animals, Vikings, lightning, and what-not in professional sports; the fantasy leagues; the regalia with the goofy four-point hats worn by academics; the spectacle of Mardi Gras and Las Vegas; the absurd catwalk where women starve themselves in order to look like "beauties" who just stepped out of Auschwitz; the porn sites and phone lines where people simulate sex; the hostility that exists among people who need to prove that their god is better; the game of politics where "leaders" talk about freedom and opportunity and voters press a lever despite never getting the pellets promised during the campaign; and the business of advertising where "family" men and women contribute significantly to creating a world that they complain about at home—all of these illustrate that the real world is partly a manifestation of the human imagination.

Given the technology available to humankind today, we are more capable than ever before of making our fantasies tangible. However, adults are not like children who enhance their understanding of reality by playing. As people grow into adulthood and attempt to bury their fantasies, they lose a certain amount of control over themselves and the social world they collectively create and perpetuate. Caughey astutely notes,

> An examination of the imaginary relationships in one's fantasies, dreams, anticipations, and media involvements is a potentially rich source for increasing self-understanding. In part, one is learning here about the shape of one's own personality, but the process also reveals social and cultural influences. By paying attention to imaginary systems, the individual can increase significantly awareness of cultural conditioning. (p. 251)

By learning about how you are socialized and into what you are socialized, you can acquire a sociological perspective that gives you some distance from the social pressures that prevent you from seeing society and yourself in a more objective light.

FOR FURTHER READING

Caughey, J. L. (1984). *Imaginary social world: A cultural approach.* Lincoln: University of Nebraska Press. Insightful book on the role of imagination in human development and society.

De Graaf, J., Wann, D., & Naylor, T. H. (2001). *Affluenza: The all-consuming epidemic.* San Francisco: Berrett-Koehler Publishers. Fun read on a serious topic: shopping addiction.

Harris, P. L. (2000). *The work of the imagination.* Malden, MA: Blackwell Publishing. Very good book citing many studies on child development and imagination.

Paley, V. G. (2005). *A child's work: The importance of fantasy play.* Chicago, IL: The University of Chicago Press. Short, insightful, and easy to read book on child development and play.

Schudson, M. (1984). *Advertising, The uneasy persuasion: Its dubious impact on American society..* New York: Basic Books. Somewhat dated, but still relevant on key issues and well-balanced presentation on the effects of advertising in society.

Singer, D. G., & Singer, J. L. (1990). *The house of make-believe: Children's play and the developing imagination.* Cambridge, MA: Harvard University Press. Leaders in the field of child development for many years, this book reviews lots of studies in a clear and meaningful way.

Chapter Five

Values, Money, and Politics

"Demand integrity!" exhorts a popular bumper sticker, echoing the common belief that the system of politics is corrupt and politicians deceive. Yet it is important to keep in mind that every institution in society is comprised of people fulfilling roles. A politician is no more or less likely to resort to deception and corruption than his or her constituency. While politicians tend to represent the interests of a select few, they also represent the values as expressed in behavior by the majority. If most people lie in order to get ahead, so will politicians—and why shouldn't they? They are individuals, like everyone else, taking advantage of opportunities in order to get ahead. If the majority in a collective truly demanded integrity in their own lives, few politicians could afford to be disingenuous—they couldn't be and succeed in a representative democracy. The situation produces a vicious cycle because people are more willing to excuse their own indiscretions than those of others (identified in previous chapters as the fundamental attribution error), and this is especially the case in regard to individuals with power and status.

Do people really want to see integrity and authenticity in politics? The town hall format in presidential debates, where members of the audience directly pose questions to the candidates, would appear to be a spontaneous event—hence opportunities to see how candidates think on their feet. However, these corporate-sponsored, Commission on Presidential Debates (CPD) events are orchestrated to minimize spontaneity and maximize predictability—in other words, to present perfect performances. Commission officials want to orchestrate every aspect of the debates, including candidate participation, lighting, camera angle, height of the podiums, audience placement, selection and role of moderators, types of questions not to be asked, and time allowed for answering questions (Farah 2004, p. 20). Self-interest is the guiding principle: candidates desire to be seen in a positive light; CPD representatives want to keep their jobs by delivering a flawless product; the networks need a good show so even spontaneity is staged; moderators must play by the expressed rules in order to participate in this nationally televised event; and most viewers seem to respond more favorably to sound bites than to a candid presentation or exchange of ideas (this is one reason why debate formats have been reduced to 60-second, 30-second, and 10-second exchanges between candidates and why candidates practice their sound bites before the debates).

The collective pressure that viewers place on what a legitimate candidate should look and sound like instigates the desire among political and media officials to stage everything. At the same time, the staged performances reinforce the perceived legitimacy of the images viewers have come to expect. The medium of television itself seems to reinforce a preference for staged authenticity over the real deal. Without make-up and staging, people do not generally appear very polished on television.

This example also demonstrates at least three levels of social behavior. The first level is *individual behavior*. Every individual wittingly or unwittingly chooses how they are going to participate in social activities. The second level is that of *interpersonal relations*. Individual decision making is influenced by interpersonal contacts (e.g., individuals frequently engage in actions not because of preference but because of social pressure, whether it be due to wanting to impress or avoid ostracism). The third level is that of *collective behavior*. Interpersonal contacts culminate in a series of actions and judgments that do not necessarily reflect each person's preferences, but do reflect the net effect of these preferences combined.

In our society we emphasize the first level to such a degree that it tends to cloud our awareness of the influences of the other two levels. This emphasis on the person and the psychological in attempting to understand social behavior is due to socialization and the fact that insight into the first level is easier to obtain. However, the ability to see how one level affects another level grants greater insight into how, in fact, we are the system.

In this chapter we will be exploring the intersections of politics, money, self-interest, and deeply held, competing values in American society. We will examine the intersections of these four factors historically in order to create a basic foundation upon which to look at contemporary politics. By contextualizing our topic historically, a person can develop what some scholars call a *historical consciousness*, which is a valuable tool for gaining perspective on such a large and complex topic.

THE EARLY YEARS OF THE REPUBLIC

The first colonies to be established in North America looked very much like England in terms of the distribution of power. Even though there was a growing sense of egalitarianism, in the eighteenth century rich and poor alike viewed civilized society in terms of a hierarchy where everyone knew their place. Wealthy families in many of the colonies, like the nobility in England, actively sought to accrue estates that they could pass on to their heirs. Since land was the means to a livelihood and to life itself, possession of land was highly esteemed. Those with sprawling estates also dominated the political landscape. According to Pulitzer-prize winning historian Gordon Wood, "Dominant families everywhere monopolized political offices and passed them among themselves even through successive generations" (1991, p. 48). A servile existence was not limited to black slaves wrested from their native Africa; thousands of whites worked as indentured servants. Women's roles were very restricted, as they could not legitimately write and sign contracts, deal in property, file lawsuits, or contest wills. Even under these conditions, however, the notion of liberty was taking shape and being recognized in more circumstances.

Most of the founders of the United States of America accepted that their elevated status as financially independent individuals gave them the unique ability to see above the fray and make judgments in the best interests of the nation. At this time America was a republic and not a democracy with a full-fledged capitalist system. The idea of any and all people participating in government was anathema to most of the Founders' ways of thinking. They either perceived no discrepancy between patriarchal dependence and liberty or they chose to ignore it or manipulate it to their advantage. During his day, Thomas Jefferson perceived more acutely than most the tension that would continue to endure due to the discrepancy between liberty and patriarchal dependence. According to historian Joseph Ellis, "What . . . Jefferson understood intuitively, was that the very word 'aristocracy' had become an epithet in the political culture of postrevolutionary America. . . . [A] 'republican aristocracy' . . . violated the central premise of the revolutionary legacy— namely, that the people at large were the sovereign source of all political authority" (2001, p. 236).

Alexander Hamilton and Thomas Jefferson were two intellectually gifted individuals with rival visions of liberty and dependence. Hamilton, the first United States Secretary of the Treasury, expressed the more conservative point of view at the time when he argued that a strong federal government, a national banking system, and an ambitious merchant class were needed to conserve the nation. Conversely, Jefferson expressed the more liberal point of view at the time when he argued in favor of limited government, small businesses, and economic laissez-faire (a French phrase meaning "let alone"). These rival visions continue to this day. Nearly all Americans value liberty (the cause of liberalism), but people disagree about how to preserve its best elements, particularly in a democracy with a free enterprise system. (Conserving liberty with the stability of existing institutions in mind is the cause of conservatism.)

Jefferson and the other founders were profoundly influenced by the 1688 Glorious Revolution in England, a set of political principles that wrested power away from the Crown and strengthened the legitimacy of a governing body or Parliament. As John Locke explained it in *Two Treatises of Government* ([1690] 2010), human beings form political societies for their individual and collective good. Governments are the creation of rational beings who agree to set limits on their individual actions in order to abide by a common set of laws. These laws can be amended by subsequent legislative bodies, and if the government becomes autocratic, the people are released from their obligation to obey it. Government leaders do not get their authority from divine will. Revolutionary and subsequent American leaders would build on Locke's argument that individuals have a natural right to life, liberty, and property.

While the disparity between rich and poor was wide, immigrant populations poured into the colonies. America was an enormous land rich in natural resources. As the demand for goods rose due to the increased numbers of people, small farmers became more successful. More people saw opportunities to succeed due to the increasing division of labor. Growing economic independence led to increased interest in the political process. The number of contested elections grew over the course of the eighteenth century (Wood, p. 143). It was also during this time that religious revivalism, referred to as the Great Awakening, swept through the colonies. Protestant itinerant or wandering clergyman, George Whitefield, coming from England, stirred up unprecedentedly large congregations as he preached about faith, self-reliance, and opportunity. All of these forces—Locke's ideas on liberty, population growth, natural resources, and faith in the individual—came together to mold a culture based upon individual judgment, opportunity, and circumspection in regard to authority. Choice in the marketplace of ideas facilitated a language and consciousness of rights. As noted above, civic republicanism would give way to representative democracy and competitive markets (Moore 1994, p. 81).

After the Revolution, successful American merchants came to the realization that their political interests were not necessarily the interests of those with inherited wealth and political power. American gentry looked at politics as a patriarchal obligation; and this had them believe that their decision making was disinterested or not self-serving. Many among the new merchant class became active in politics plainly because of self-interest. Capitalist principles flourished alongside of Lockean principles of liberty. Wood states,

Government officials were no longer to play the role of umpire; they were no longer to stand above the competing interests of the marketplace and make disinterested, impartial judgments about what was good for the whole society. Elected officials were to bring the partial, local interests of the society, and sometimes even their own interests, right into the workings of government. Partisanship and parties became legitimate activities in politics. And all adult white males, regardless of their property holdings or their independence, were to have the right to vote. With these new ideas and practices came the greater participation of more ordinary people in politics. (p. 294)

Greater participation notwithstanding, the ideological beliefs that supported the American gentry's notion of disinterestedness survived as ideological beliefs that to this day sustain an American economic and political elite's notion of "knowing what's best for the American people" or self-righteously proclaiming—in a diverse nation of over six million inhabitants—"I know what the American people want."

MESSY DEMOCRACY

People rely on politicians to make laws in a manner that is relatively fair and effective. The problem is that the world has become very complicated, more people are involved in politics, more people have an economic stake in political outcomes, and more information travels faster than people can process. In such a world, a self-perpetuating cycle to the lowest denominator is produced by the antagonism among representatives from the two major political parties, the for-profit, bottom-line thinking that determines what media executives call *news*, and a misinformed electorate that too often confuses hearsay with facts. All of these factors contribute significantly to creating and maintaining a political system that few like. To begin the process of changing this cycle and perhaps making democracy less messy, it is important to decipher some of the politically-charged terms—like *liberal* and *conservative*—that are frequently bantered about in political discourse, and to understand how ideology is used to sway public opinion.

When young people refer to themselves as *progressive* or *conservative*, do they really understand what the label means? We acquire one of these labels from others, usually our parents. The process is sometimes referred to as *political socialization*, but generally speaking, we are referring to an aspect of secondary socialization. My parents were moderate Democrats from a moderately Democratic state. They usually voted for a Democrat, but not always; sometimes they voted for a Republican. My sister and I have carried on this voting tradition. We are not unusual in this regard; voting behavior tends to run in families. You, the reader, probably vote for people of the same party that your parents vote for—if your parents vote Republican then you probably do as well. And your parents probably vote for candidates of one of the two major parties because that is the way their parents voted. Consider the implication of this: People may not be voting for a candidate based upon an informed decision, but because of socialization and habit. As a result, people sometimes elect to office politicians who support legislation that undermines the voter's interests and well-being.

Being informed today has not been made simpler by technology. If people in the past lacked information because of the dearth of available resources, today people lack information in an attempt to insulate themselves from the overwhelming sea of available resources. Remember that people are cognitive misers: After a certain point, people do not want or cannot digest additional information.

Most Americans have some form of cable television, and with that, a multitude of channels. However, more channels do not necessarily translate into a more informed public. People tend to avoid watching news channels that may inform them of news that they don't want to hear, and they tune in to news shows that are programmed to meet their demographic. People select their news shows based upon the desire to see and hear information that conforms to how they want to see the world. This is not being informed, but rather, reinforcement of secondary socialization.

As we discussed earlier in this book, people organize information in their minds in terms of *schemas*. Schemas develop over time as a result of individual predisposition and socialization. The more a person depends upon schemas to make decisions, the less likely they are to think through new information; novel material is either internalized into an existing schema or it is rejected. Consider how you, the reader, are approaching the information being presented here. Are you rejecting the information as false or mere opinion because it does not conform to your preexisting worldview? Are you accepting it just because it does conform to your preexisting worldview? In either case, you are not really thinking, but going with the flow of your cognitive framework. The most pervasive ideologies are those that fit into preexisting schemas.

IDEOLOGY

Today, people throw around terms like *liberal* and *conservative* as though they have always had and continue to have a singular meaning. These terms represent different ideologies that have changed over time. The term *ideology* was first used by French philosopher Destutt de Tracy in order to develop a systematic understanding of ideas. He used the term in a positive sense. Karl Marx used the term to describe how people come to acquire a "false consciousness." In this sense, *ideology* refers to thinking that is not based upon independent judgment and is unsuspectingly conformist. Of course, it is the rare individual who truly thinks independently. A person's thoughts tend to be variations on what s/he has heard or seen others express. Our individual temperament and experience put a unique spin on a circulating theme. Since Marx, the term has acquired a relatively negative meaning and has come to describe beliefs that reflect political values and the distribution of power. An individual may think in terms of a singular overarching ideology or in terms of multiple ideologies that complement or contradict each other. In any case, the refusal to examine the ideology or ideologies a person depends on and lives by just makes their influence stronger. William Maddox and Stuart Lilie offer a reasonably detailed definition of the term:

> [A]n ideology may be said to be a set of interrelated ideas that purport both to explain how the political and social world works and to prescribe how that world should operate. . . . [A]n ideology includes three elements: (1) a more or less complex, systematic set of normative statements setting forth political and social values; (2) descriptive and analytical statements intended to elaborate on those political values and provide a guide for explaining and evaluating political events; and (3) prescriptions describing desired political, economic, or social conditions. The purpose of an ideology may be to provide a guide to action, to persuade others, to give legitimacy to a set of social structures, to engender passive acceptance of a set of social-political arrangements, or some mix of these purposes. (1984, p. 5)

LIBERALISM

People who are unaware of, or have a limited ability to articulate to themselves the underpinnings of, their political beliefs, nevertheless act on these beliefs. For example, many people assert that a liberal is someone who believes in big government, higher taxes, and social welfare programs, while a conservative is someone who believes in limited government, lower taxes, and corporate welfare programs. If you believe that government is part of the solution then you are a liberal, while if you believe that government is part of the problem then you are a conservative. This taxonomy is of recent origin, and an excurse into the history of liberalism and conservatism may cause you to give pause before throwing around these labels.

I have already introduced you to John Locke and stressed how important his ideas on liberty were in contributing to the fundamental formation of this nation. While Locke's ideas on liberty did not include all citizens (just citizens of property), his ideas were extended by Thomas Jefferson in the Declaration of Independence and by James Madison and others in the United States Constitution. Locke stressed limited government in furthering individual rights. This is the original intent of liberalism, as framed by John Locke, the founder of liberalism. Jefferson's statement that governments derive "their just powers from the consent of the governed" (cited in Kronenwetter 1984, p. 40) is a liberal idea, as is a government based upon a system of checks and balances (thereby limiting government power). Liberalism arose as a set of ideas to combat legislative authority based upon inheritance and favoritism. Wood points out that for people in the colonies, "Equality did not mean that everyone was in fact the same, but only that ordinary people . . . felt freer from aristocratic patronage and control than did common people elsewhere in the Western world" (p. 171). Though the founders did not apply liberal ideas to everyone, in time their ideals spread to all segments of the population.

Capitalism's link to liberalism is its reliance on individualism and contractual relations; the institutional arrangement is commonly called a *market economy* or a *free market*. The tenets of capitalism flourished relatively early in the development of the nation. According to historian T. H. Breen (2004, p. 19), American colonists "were the first to appreciate the extraordinary capacity" of commercial capitalism to bring about the opportunity for ordinary people to look aristocratic and to facilitate social relationships based upon trade and mutual interest. While the gentry did not appreciate competition with those lower on the economic rung, there was only so much they could do; commercial capitalism was helping the nation to grow in strength and size (Wood, p. 276).

Even though liberal ideas contributed significantly to the development of democracy and capitalism, it is important to emphasize that democratic and capitalist processes and goals can, and often do, clash. As Dahl states, "[A] highly favorable condition for democratic institutions is a market economy in which economic enterprises are mainly owned privately . . . . Yet the close association between democracy and market-capitalism conceals a paradox: a market-capitalist economy inevitably generates inequalities in the political resources to which different citizens have access" (2000, p. 158). This has been an ongoing problem for politically democratic and economically capitalist societies. The problem led to a split among liberal thinkers in the nineteenth century, and this divide has caused much confusion since then concerning the meaning of liberalism.

The modern-day confusion over what constitutes a liberal in America arose after a series of events following the Civil War. After the war, the nation's government ceased to uphold slavery for the South's moneyed class. Southern leaders who formerly believed in a strong federal government to maintain social order and the status quo now turned to state and local governments to protect their interests (Kronenwetter 1984, p. 50). Moreover, after the war the federal government subsidized industrial growth to an unprecedented degree and allowed formerly public resources to be privatized; this resulted in the proliferation of monopolies and less competition in the marketplace. As factories and cities grew—particularly in the North—so did abject poverty and the disparity between rich and poor. Northern leaders increasingly turned to the federal government to get assistance and to protect their interests. Growing dissatisfaction among the populace led to social unrest and social movements comprised of relatively poor people and intellectuals interested in wresting power away from government and corporate leaders.

From these movements in the late nineteenth century arose Populist (mostly in rural areas) and Progressive reformers (mostly in urban areas). Both movements expressed support for the liberal values of individualism and private property; both movements challenged political and corporate authority. But populists expressed a conservative interest in restoring conditions to an imagined, idyllic past while progressives expressed the new liberal vision for an enhanced role of the government in economic and social planning. With the Great Depression (beginning in October of 1929), the subsequent election of Franklin Roosevelt as president, and the implementation of Roosevelt's New Deal policies, progressives saw some of their new liberal proposals enacted into law. As part of the New Deal, the federal government implemented programs such as the Work Projects Administration (WPA), which provided jobs for many people who would build up the nation's infrastructure (there are many roads, bridges, parks, and schools still in use today across the country that were built at this time) and programs that have been maintained to this day: the Social Security System; the Federal Deposit Insurance Corporation (FDIC), which safeguards the money deposited by members in banks; and the Securities and Exchange Commission (SEC), which monitors the nation's stock and options exchanges. While Republicans opposed many New Deal policies in the 1930s, as the economy began to recover, "In the 1940s and 1950s the national leaders of both political parties generally accepted the fundamental economic premises of the New Deal, differing on methods rather than purposes." (Maddox & Lilie, p. 37). Indeed, from 1945 to 1973 the United States experienced the greatest economic growth in its history. (We will have a lot more to say about this later.) The key point here is that the Populist, and particularly the Progressive, movements reformulated liberal discourse.

While liberalism had traditionally meant limited government for the cause of liberty (classic liberalism was formulated as a rebuttal to monarchical rule), reformers (during the nineteenth century industrial revolutions in England and America) argued for some government intervention in the name of liberty. As the twentieth century proceeded, two liberal groups emerged: classic liberals and modern liberals. Some people argued that the New Deal represented the initial step toward transforming the United States into a socialist society. The cold war between the United States and the Soviet Union raised concern among some political and economic leaders that America could be overthrown from within. By mid-century, classic liberals would refer to themselves as conservatives, neoconservatives, or libertarians.

It has become routine for modern liberals to refer to themselves as progressives and for classic liberals to refer to themselves as conservatives or libertarians—ideological labels go in and out of fashion. However, when Americans run away from liberalism (whether classic or modern), they run away from their history, their tradition, and the values that they fundamentally share. Louis Hartz amplifies this idea: "Who was the real disciple of Jefferson, the man who wanted the Anti-Trust Act or the man who opposed it?" ([1955] 1991, p. 216). The Sherman Anti-Trust Act was passed in 1890 to limit the combination of business interests that could undermine competition (e.g., cartels, monopolies, oligarchies). Consider that at the time John D. Rockefeller's company Standard Oil monopolized oil refining worldwide. Now, if you are for liberty, competition, and a free market, what are you going to do with a business that becomes so successful that it limits competition? Whether or not you are for anti-trust legislation, your primary interest is preserving liberty. According to historian Joseph Ellis:

> It is truly humbling, perhaps even dispiriting, to realize that the historical debate over the revolutionary era and the early republic merely recapitulates the ideological debate conducted at the time, that historians have essentially been fighting the same battles, over and over again, that the members of the revolutionary generation fought originally among themselves. . . . [H]istorians have declared themselves Jeffersonians or Hamiltonians, committed individualists or dedicated nationalists, liberals or conservatives, then written accounts that favor one camp over the other, or that stigmatize one side . . . . [T]he awkward truth is that we have been chasing our own tails in an apparently endless cycle of partisan pleading. . . . [B]oth sides speak for the deepest impulses of the American Revolution. With the American Revolution . . . different factions came together in common cause to overthrow the reigning regime, then discovered in the aftermath of their triumph that they had fundamentally different and politically incompatible notions of what they intended. . . . [I]n the battle for supremacy, for the "true meaning" of the Revolution, neither side completely triumphed. . . . [T]he revolutionary generation found a way to contain the explosive energies of the debate in the form of an ongoing argument or dialogue that was eventually institutionalized and rendered safe by the creation of political parties. And the subsequent political history of the United States then became an oscillation between new versions of the old tension. (pp. 14–15)

Ongoing debates in politics are more often about how to achieve a goal rather than whether a particular goal should be achieved; this is because the dominant political parties are almost always arguing from different sides of the same point of view—the promotion of liberty. The result is debate, stalemate, compromise, and oscillation.

CONSERVATISM

Edmund Burke is generally credited with being the founder of modern conservatism. In his book, entitled *Reflections on the Revolution in France*, Burke articulated the concern that many people had in response to the French Revolution. America's revolution for liberty was significantly less violent than France's revolution. The economy in France was in bad shape due to poor fiscal management and rapid population growth. Heavy taxes on the middle class and poor and increasing hunger raised social tensions. King Louis XVI convened a meeting of representatives from the significant interest groups in hopes of coming up with a plan that would diffuse social pressures. Representatives of the common people who advocated for reform sat to the left of the king while representatives of the nobility who advocated against reform sat to the right of the king. It is here that the terms *left* and *right* came to be associated with liberalism and conservatism (Kronenwetter, p. 23). The meetings resulted in some progress, but not enough to silence the civil unrest. The king and his family were executed by guillotine. A radical faction took control of the government and proceeded to execute everyone in France that they believed posed a threat; nearly 20,000 people were killed during the "Reign of Terror" (Kronenwetter, p. 28). Order was restored in France in 1799 when Napoleon Bonaparte took control of the government through a military coup.

Burke was a British statesman and philosopher. He supported the cause of the American revolutionaries, but in the wake of the French Revolution, he gave voice to the limits of liberty. Burke was skeptical of the practical application of democracy. He, like many other British and American aristocrats—including many of the American founders—feared the "tyranny of the majority" or majority rule. Burke argued that social institutions are necessary to keep unrestrained liberty in check, that the maintenance of social traditions produced stability in society, and that the ideas of a single generation were inferior to the accumulated knowledge expressed through a society's traditions and institutions. Burke was not opposed to social change, but argued that change should proceed cautiously and continue to reflect social traditions. Finally, Burke argued that the government should limit its activities to preserving its revenue streams, established charters or corporations, and established religion; and to maintaining the peace through courts and the military. Burke's position concerning the limits of government, overlap with classic liberals, hence, the periodic alliance between conservatives and libertarians.

Burkean conservatism never had a strong and enduring following in America. Yet, one can clearly see elements of it throughout American history. Conservatism gained significant ground in the United States throughout the course of the twentieth century. Modern conservative American and British thinkers have elaborated on the conservative point of view. According to Frank Meyer, former senior editor of the conservative journal *National Review*, conservatism can be understood as

> a movement [which] arises historically when the unity and balance of a civilization are driven by revolutionary transformations of previously accepted norms . . . . Conservatism comes into being at such times as a movement of consciousness and action directed to recovering the tradition of the civilization. This is the essence of conservatism in all the forms it has assumed in different civilizations and under differing circumstances. (1968, p. 1)

Another twentieth century conservative, Russell Kirk, states that conservatives share some basic principles that date back to Edmund Burke (Love 2006, pp. 56–58). These principles include: (1) that social customs, rituals, and symbols are the sources of authority; and (2) that there is a hierarchy in every society, and that while people have equal rights, people do not have equal rights to equal things. Conservatives believe that people should work hard and accept existing inequalities with dignity because differences in station reflect the natural order and development of society (Love, p. 65). From a conservative point of view, governmental power should be used to guide people in terms of morals, but it should not attempt to counteract naturally occurring inequalities (Maddox & Lilie, p. 17).

The election of Ronald Reagan in 1980 was a turning point in regard to liberalism and conservatism in American politics; it marked a change in direction from modern liberal policies (that began during Roosevelt's New Deal) to a combination of conservative and classic liberal or libertarian policies (that bore some resemblance to Roosevelt's predecessors Calvin Coolidge and Herbert Hoover). In the next section of this chapter, we will discuss the events that gave rise to this watershed. In order to establish the context for this discussion that is concise and inclusive of the multiple factors involved, we will begin with the state of the world following World War II.

THE RISE OF THE GLOBAL ECONOMY AND POLARIZATION

In the aftermath of the Second World War, the United States—due largely to its distance from Europe—was the single remaining industrial nation left intact. The United States experienced little competition in its production and selling of goods to nations ravaged by war and eager to rebuild their infrastructures. By helping the industrial West and East (such as England, France, Germany, and Japan) get back on their feet, the United States became the center of the economy for the "free world." As America's mass-production industries made 50 percent of the world's manufactured goods, family incomes soared, as did the number of consumer goods that American families could purchase (Madrick 1997, p. 58). From the late 1940s to the early 1960s family incomes doubled (Whitfield 1992, p. 70). Malls, fast food, dishwashers, cars, and televisions represent just a few of the conveniences that became available to more people. The credit card was launched in 1950 by the Diner's Club. American workers made 57 percent of the world's steel, 43 percent of the electricity, and 62 percent of the oil (Patterson 1996, p. 61). Between 1947 and 1973 the annual rate of economic growth was nearly 4 percent (Madrick, p. 34). According to historian James Patterson, "No comparable period of United States history witnessed so much economic and civil progress" (1996, p. vii).

Confidence, military might and capability, productivity, lack of competition, the rise of a consumer culture, and a people made more aware of each other, events, and products through consumer goods—all contributed to creating a spirit of the times, or zeitgeist, in America that seemed to confirm the idea of the American Dream. America had not only survived through a great depression and two world wars, but ultimately thrived to become the leader of the "free world." Patterson adds, "The baby boom that ensued was perhaps the most amazing social trend of the postwar era. The total number of babies born between 1946 and 1964 was 76.4 million, or almost two-fifths of the population in 1964 of 192 million" (p. 77).

The commander-in-chief through the 1950s was Dwight Eisenhower. A five-star general, he led successful military campaigns into France and Germany in 1944–1945. Eisenhower was a moderate Republican, and though he ended the two decades' old lock that the Democrats had on the White House, he continued the New Deal policies. Eisenhower also negotiated with China to end the Korean War and supported the development of nuclear weapons and the National Aeronautics and Space Administration (NASA) to compete with the Soviet Union. Eisenhower was not a religious man but acknowledged the value of religion. He was noted for saying, "Our government makes no sense unless it is founded on a deeply felt religious faith—and I don't care what it is" (Whitfield, p. 88). He believed that the American people preferred a president who attended church, and that religion could provide further contrast between the United States and the Soviet Union.

Many unforeseen consequences followed World War II. On the positive side, the war facilitated America's transition from depression to prosperity. On the negative side, it created what Eisenhower called the *military-industrial-complex*. Investment in the military was understandably large during the war, but afterward, even with cuts in the defense budget, investment in the military remained disproportionately high. In his farewell address in 1961, Eisenhower warned the nation of a military-sanctioned weapons industry that could threaten domestic stability—his address gave further legitimacy to the book written by sociologist C. Wright Mills years earlier, entitled *The Power*

Elite (1956), which described an alliance among military, corporate, and political leaders to control the federal budget.

With the economy growing at a record pace, low unemployment, and liberalism still the dominant ideology, the nation chose John Kennedy over Richard Nixon (Eisenhower's vice president) to be the next president. Kennedy increased military spending and sparred with the leader at that time of the Soviet Union, Nikita Khrushchev. Kennedy ordered an unsuccessful invasion of southern Cuba in an attempt to overthrow the communist government led by Fidel Castro. The conflict, called the Cuban Missile Crisis, came to a head when it became clear that the Soviets were assisting the Cuban government to build nuclear missiles. Nuclear war was averted when Kennedy and Khrushchev both backed down. Kennedy also expanded the United States commitment to Vietnam. Kennedy's youthful charisma made him popular and his assassination transformed his short presidency into myth.

Lyndon Johnson (Kennedy's vice president), completed Kennedy's term and solidly defeated the Republican candidate, Barry Goldwater in 1964. Prosperity in the 1960s exceeded the previous decade and unemployment hovered around 4 percent. Johnson had been an effective legislator, and as president he signed into law a number of significant pieces of legislation. Early on he signed onto a tax cut that had been supported by Kennedy. Despite arguments from some legislators that calling attention to inequality in America was subversively communist, Johnson, along with Special Assistant Sargent Shriver, proceeded to push for civil rights reform. In 1964 the Civil Rights Act was passed into law. The act prohibited discrimination or segregation at movie theaters, restaurants, hotels, hospitals, libraries, and in employment. The act was inclusive of race, sex, religion, and national origin. In 1965, Johnson signed into law Medicare and Medicaid (i.e., financial assistance for medical costs for those older than 65 or living in poverty, respectively). From the point of view of the members of the Johnson administration, their efforts reflected an interest in facilitating equality of opportunity and not, as some critics called it, equality of condition. According to Patterson,

> Neither Shriver nor Johnson intended their efforts to increase governmental spending on public assistance. Both hated the very idea of long-term welfare dependency and of costly governmental outlays for public aid. "Welfare," indeed, remained a dirty word in the lexicon of liberals as well as conservatives . . . . Johnson hoped that a "war" on poverty would provide the "opportunity" necessary to help people help themselves. The goal, Shriver said repeatedly, was to offer a "hand up, not a hand out." (p. 535)

Prosperity, a booming consumer culture, and civil rights reform raised expectations to unprecedented heights. Despite fear of the Soviets, the nuclear threat, and growing involvement in Vietnam (Johnson significantly increased the number of troops stationed there), many Americans increasingly believed that there was little that the United States could not do. Few were prepared for the urban riots that erupted in 1966 and 1967 or for the sometimes raging demonstrations that occurred in 1968 and 1969. Urban African American youth saw opportunities and prosperity occurring for others at a much faster pace than it was occurring for them. Racial tensions were already strained by the increasing migration of African Americans into predominantly Caucasian working-class neighborhoods (where they were not welcome). Student groups got involved in the civil unrest: Among them were student groups against the war in Vietnam (at this point in time the military was not voluntary but utilized the draft), student groups in support of the war effort and against many elements of civil rights reform, and student groups for women's rights. The riots and demonstrations, in turn, triggered a backlash, predominantly among conventional older Caucasians. As the 1960s came to a close, clear factions arose between and within the lines of race, gender, and age.

After several tumultuous years while serving in the White House, Johnson declined to run for reelection. The Republican Party chose Richard Nixon (again) to run for president. Nixon defeated Hubert Humphrey in 1968 by a slim margin. By this time generations of Southern Democrats who opposed "Northern aggression" and the elimination of slavery after the Civil War—and thereby opposed the Republican Party—were moving toward Republican identification. Johnson's prophesy after signing the Civil Rights Act in 1964 that Democrats had now "delivered the South to the Republican Party" proved to be accurate (Patterson, p. 560).

Nixon, like Eisenhower, was a moderate Republican. He signed legislation that became known as Title IX, which prohibited sexual discrimination in higher education (Title IX opened up unprecedented opportunities for women in competitive sports); he signed legislation that increased funding for the National Endowments for the Arts and Humanities; he signed into law the National Environmental Policy Act that created the Environmental Protection Agency (EPA); he signed into law the Occupational Safety and Health Act that created the Occupational Safety and Health Administration which issues safety standards in the workplace; he initially increased United States military efforts in Vietnam, but eventually signed a peace accord, which led to the communist North taking full control of the country; he also facilitated negotiations with China and the Soviet Union.

However, in a climate of continuing social unrest, Nixon could not negotiate his way past a scandal that would prevent him from completing his second term as president. High-level officials working to reelect Nixon in 1972 were caught attempting to tap the phones of the Democratic National Committee headquarters at the Watergate Hotel. White House tapes of phone calls (recorded by Nixon) revealed that Nixon had ordered the CIA to stop an

FBI probe into the incident. The president tried to use one federal agency against another to cover up a crime. In order to avoid impeachment, Nixon resigned; his vice president, Gerald Ford, became the next president.

The Watergate scandal had many consequences: it seriously tarnished the reputation of the Republican party for a short period of time; it added to the growing cynicism among the public of the role of government in society; it became a model of modern muckraking (some journalists would sensationalize corruption in order to sell the news); and perhaps most damaging of all, Watergate paved the way for future presidents to assemble allies to cover up corruption ostensibly to protect the legitimacy of the office, somehow justifying such corruption as being patriotic.

In the early 1970s Americans were still acclimating to a series of rapid shifts in cultural values and practices, but despite increased spending on domestic and international programs and ongoing criticism against the government, the foundations of the economy and the government seemed to be on solid ground.

A turning point in Americans' faith and optimism regarding the nation occurred around 1973. Before this time, people knew that there was corruption in government, but in 1973–1974 corruption at the highest levels in government was headline news. Before 1973, the United States had never felt defeated in war, but after Vietnam the victories achieved during the Second World War seemed long ago. Before 1973, people felt the effects of inflation creeping up in terms of their growing inability to purchase the latest consumer goods, but after this time a number of factors came together that put to a halt the greatest economic expansion in American history. Competition in the marketplace with other nations such as Germany and Japan heated up.

During the heyday years, Ford, Chrysler, and General Motors accounted for 80 percent of the autos sold in the United States (Madrick, p. 63). By the 1970s Japan was producing cars more quickly, inexpensively, and in more styles than United States auto manufacturers. American automakers were not keeping up with the competition. Already by 1971 the United States posted its first trade deficit since the Second World War (Madrick, p. 68).

At the same time, the baby boomers were entering into the job market in droves. In the 1950s and 1960s when the boomers were young and the economy was growing, there were fewer people in the job market and more money to go around. In the 1970s and thereafter, the trends would be in reverse: more people in the job market, slower economic growth, and less money.

Finally, the United States increasingly became dependent on foreign supplies of oil. The overseas market for oil was cheap and plentiful. However, in 1973 the Organization of Petroleum Exporting Countries (OPEC) flexed their political and economic muscles and dramatically increased the price of oil.

As the members of the boomer generation slowly replaced their parents in occupational positions of authority, they found it difficult to replicate and perpetuate the world they had known as children. Many boomers grew up feeling that private ownership of any number of consumer goods was obligatory and a sign of their freedom. Freedom in America no longer meant freedom from the tyranny of kings or the freedom to explore new frontiers; by the 1960s freedom meant, more than ever before, the right to purchase goods. As the twentieth century wore on, the ability of more and more Americans to exercise that right became increasingly difficult to achieve, and as the boomers looked to their leaders for guidance, their leaders blamed each other. Because the boom years of 1947–1973 were identified as the new norm rather than properly being identified as a product of a unique set of circumstances, the nation was left vulnerable to the capriciousness of an unknown future.

The success or failure of a president is usually judged on the state of the economy under his watch. Jimmy Carter, a Democrat, had defeated Ford in 1976. The Iran hostage crisis, along with a recession, seriously undermined Carter's bid for reelection.

Americans yearned for a reason to be proud of the nation. Ronald Reagan's persona provided that reason. He encouraged Americans to pull themselves up by their own bootstraps and he took on the Soviet Union—the world's other superpower. Reagan was a popular figure among conservatives, libertarians, and disaffected Democrats. Reagan spoke for libertarians and conservatives when he insisted that in order to get the economy moving, government involvement in the private sector had to be removed.

Reagan expanded Carter's policy of *deregulation*. During the recession under Carter, business leaders argued that government regulations were a chief factor in the constriction of the economy. Many of these regulations had been in place for decades and were intended to prevent monopolies from undercutting competition, innovation, and the public's interests. It is important to remember that free enterprise is based on the notion of competitive markets—competition among different companies is supposed to lead to product innovation, lower prices for consumers, and an environment of winners and losers (based upon who can balance most effectively costs and innovation). Carter cut back on government regulation of business, but, according to Reagan, not enough. Reagan deregulated one industry after another. As American businesses became less accountable to government regulations, some businesses prospered enormously while many others collapsed.

Reagan also increased spending on defense and cut spending on domestic programs. In order to stimulate business activity he cut taxes, particularly at the upper bracket, but consistently raised taxes marginally at the lower bracket. In the Cold War against the Soviets, Reagan supported the Strategic Defense Initiative (SDI), nicknamed "Star Wars." The theoretical goal of the expensive project was to protect the United States against nuclear missile strikes using a space-based defensive shield. In many respects the competitive military buildup between the Soviet Union and the United States in the 1980s was one of who could outlast the other economically in an arms race. As we all know, the Soviet Union lost the race. However, in order for the United States to pay for increased spending on defense while cutting taxes, the government had to borrow money, so the nation's debt ballooned. Reagan argued that debt could stimulate economic growth. (The fact is that borrowing money and investing it for a profitable return does make debt worthwhile, but if the money is being spent on items that immediately lose their value, then carrying debt is a burden.) Meanwhile, deregulation, growing competition with other nations, and increased demand from consumers for variety at low prices fueled downsizing, outsourcing, and offshoring.

In the 1970s firms were already cutting costs (in order to stay competitive) by reducing their operations in the United States and sometimes moving entirely to locations where setting up shop was inexpensive and workers more compliant and cheap. Electronics, clothing, and food production moved overseas as manufacturing plants appeared in countries such as South Korea, China, Vietnam, Indonesia, Bangladesh, India, Mexico, Guatemala, Nicaragua, and Ecuador. Ironically, consumer demand in the United States contributed to the erosion of manufacturing-based jobs in America.

Less skilled and educated American workers unwittingly added to the process of trading employment opportunities for the ability to buy more products at lower prices. If the prices were not low enough or if cash was in short supply, people worked longer hours if they could or they followed the example set by the government and took advantage of easily available credit and bank loans. In some cases the credit company owned the retail outlet, so when people paid interest on their purchase they were paying the same company over and over again for the same item. Frugality gave way to living in debt. By 1985 the United States had become a debtor nation for the first time since the end of World War I (Whitfield, p. 230). The process of accumulating debt would continue into the twenty-first century (with the exception of the Clinton administration's ability to cut spending and reduce the deficit in the 1990s).

Just for clarification, the United States deficit refers to how much money the federal government brings in minus what it spends per year. If expenses exceed revenues in a given year, then the government must borrow money to make up the difference: the money that is borrowed is a deficit. A running deficit produces debt, which is the overall amount of money owed. Now, if revenues exceed expenses in a particular year, then the government has a surplus, and the additional money can go toward paying down the debt.

As companies found that they could be more profitable by maintaining operations overseas, business leaders who saw record profits due to deregulation, tax cuts, and government bailouts did not invest their ballooning profits back into the nation, but rather used it to bolster lavish lifestyles. In the 1960s CEO salaries were about forty times the average worker's salary; by 2000 and afterward it was about four hundred times the average worker's salary. The disparity between rich and poor is wider in America than in any other industrialized country in the world. During Reagan's administration, the rich got richer and the poor got poorer, but many conservative and libertarian working-class people felt proud to be an American again. Unfortunately, this pride may have come at the expense of their interests. Delli Carpini and Keeter point out:

> Respondents [of the 1988 National Election Study] were asked what the federal government had done during the past eight years. The survey questions [referred] to the nature of government efforts in four important policy areas: federal spending on assistance to the poor, federal spending on public schools, government spending on defense, and federal efforts to improve and protect the environment. For each, the alternative responses were that government efforts or spending "increased," "stayed about the same," and "decreased." Eighty percent of voters correctly perceived that defense spending increased during the Reagan years. But only a quarter to a third of voters knew that federal efforts on behalf of the environment, the poor, and the schools had declined during this period. Indeed, of the 60 to 68 percent of voters who believed that federal aid in these three domestic policy areas should have increased, substantially less than half knew that it had not. Perhaps most strikingly, a sizeable minority of the voting public thought the federal government had increased spending on the environment, the poor, and schools and said they approved of that action. (1996, pp. 263–264)

The movement of American firms to other countries in the 1980s and 1990s accelerated the process of what we now call *globalization*. Generally speaking, the term refers to the merging of the economies of the many different nations of the world. During the postwar years, and particularly during the last thirty years of the twentieth century, the United States economy became one part of, and still a very important part of, an immense global marketplace. Specifically, improved relations among nations after the Second World War, growing sophistication in travel and telecommunications, and United States business and government encouragement gave rise to modern globalization. Globalization has many benefits, but an economic downturn in one nation can reverberate throughout the global marketplace and do harm to the economies of other nations. In October of 1987, after several years of economic growth, the global markets crashed, and with them, the stock market of the United States. The date is referred to as Black Monday because of its likeness to the stock market crash of 1929 called Black Tuesday (which led to the Great Depression). The economy was once again in recession, this time with an immense debt. If you want to get a sense of the times (Holly-

wood style), see films such as *Working Girl* or *Wall Street* (where the character Gordon Gekko proclaims to shareholders that "greed is good").

Irrespective of the economy, Reagan enjoyed much popularity; after he
left office there was some serious talk of adding his face to the four presidents carved into Mount Rushmore in South Dakota. Reagan's continuing
popularity and Democratic nominee Michael Dukakis's lackluster campaign
probably contributed to George H. W. Bush's (Reagan's vice president) major victory in 1988. Unfortunately, the economy took a serious downturn in
1990–1991. The savings and loan crisis that occurred during Bush's tenure
did not help. Deregulation of the banking system under Reagan contributed
to questionable investments by management in the savings and loan industry.
When many of these investments failed, the institutions failed and depositors
lost their money (which was federally guaranteed). The end result was a
multibillion dollar bailout paid for by taxpayers.

"It's the economy, stupid" was Bill Clinton's mantra in the 1992 presidential election. Signs repeating this phrase were posted around Clinton's
central campaign headquarters in order to remind staffers that what concerned Americans most was the state of the economy. Clinton could not
borrow money in order to manage the economy; Reagan had exhausted that
avenue. Clinton's approach in dealing with the economy was multifaceted.
Rather than continuing to lower taxes on the upper bracket and raising taxes
on the lower bracket, he increased taxes on the upper bracket and lowered
taxes for those in the middle. Clinton followed Reagan in maintaining deregulated markets and encouraging international trade. The rapid development
of personal technologies and the Internet at this time accelerated global communications, travel, and trade. The transformation of the United States economy from manufacturing to services (a change that became evident under
Reagan) also increased dramatically in the 1990s.

During the last quarter of the twentieth century the United States economy shifted from being the world's manufacturing superpower to being one of
the world's leading service economies. As United States companies engaged
in outsourcing and offshoring practices in order to keep up with the demand
for cheap goods, manufacturing-based jobs were replaced by service-based
jobs. Today the United States economy is not based upon making products,
but rather managing the trade of products or trade in services. Service jobs
include corporate executive officer (CEO), financial advisor, risk manager,
accountant, marketer, advertiser, lawyer, physician, engineer, architect, general contractor, plumber, mechanic, realtor, nurse, teacher, librarian, police
officer, salesclerk, telemarketer, receptionist, secretary, construction worker,
waiter/waitress, cashier, bus driver.

A service economy produces a greater number of higher paying jobs than
a manufacturing economy, but overall, it produces fewer jobs and typical pay
and benefits are significantly lower. A service economy depends upon an

educated and skilled workforce more than a manufacturing economy does. In fact, more Americans are pursuing a college degree than ever before. Earning a degree does not guarantee success, but it increases the likelihood of higher earnings over the course of one's working life.

Flexibility is the hallmark of today's economy—flexibility in terms of products, services, skills, and employment. As the demand for products and services that fit the individual consumer increases, the skills and employment opportunities shift more rapidly. This is another way of saying that as the division of labor becomes more complex, individuals must acquire more and more roles in order to keep up. Yet, of course, individuals create the division of labor as they place demands on each other. Most people should anticipate having several careers over the course of their working lives. Joseph Stiglitz, former economic advisor in the Clinton administration and Nobel Prize winner in economics states,

> During the nineties a new culture had developed, one in which firms focused on the bottom line—today's profits, not long-run profits—and took quick and decisive actions when they faced problems. Fire workers as soon as it is clear that you don't need them. You can always hire them back again later. Firm loyalty—either of workers to their firm or the firm to its workers—were values of a bygone era. . . . [W]ithin the Clinton administration, we had recognized that with the increased pace of innovation, there would be large changes in the labor market. We knew that the idea of a lifetime job was a thing of the past. We talked about "lifetime employability," not lifetime jobs; and of "lifetime learning," to enable individuals to move more easily from job to job. (2003, p. 183)

As manufacturing moved overseas in the 1980s and 1990s, many Americans took jobs in services with inadequate salaries. Many people became contingent workers—working as the opportunity arose for the same or multiple firms. Being a part of the contingent workforce became the latest incarnation of "rugged individualism."

The transformation of the economy from manufacturing to services contributed to the shift that was occurring in the distribution of incomes. Throughout the postwar period the differences between income groups shrank (money was increasingly being distributed more evenly). By the 1980s and afterward, this trend would be reversed, with more and more money being concentrated at the upper bracket.

While Clinton was president, the economy bounced back for a while, as had happened in the 1980s. Madrick states, "[T]here were stretches of several years in which the economy expanded. These spurts of growth were neither strong enough nor sustained enough to compensate sufficiently for the steep recessions that preceded them or the unusually slow growth [that followed them]" (p. 7). The uneven nature of these growth spurts also contributed to the disparity between income groups. Some of the people working in global finance, telecommunications, and arms sales made unprecedented amounts of money as real wages remained largely stagnant. The accumulation of debt helped to compensate for the unbalanced growth of the economy in the 1980s. The importation of inexpensive goods helped to compensate for the unbalanced growth of the economy in the 1990s.

In the 1990s average Americans had more money in their pockets, but they had fewer hours of leisure and they found that more money was needed to maintain their standard of living; buying lower-priced goods was the only way to keep up. Meanwhile, big business traveled around the world in search of lucrative markets and governments that did not concern themselves with sweatshops and slave labor. Most Americans didn't seem to care that their goods were being made by people slaving on the other side of the world; they had what they hungered for—goods that they could afford. If you, the reader, take a look at where your belongings are made, you are likely to find that they are manufactured in China, Bangladesh, Vietnam, Guatemala, or wherever else the cheapest labor can be found at the moment. Walmart's ability to be the "low price leader" is due to the immense volume of inexpensive products they import from China and the developing world. The importation of cheap goods from China ballooned in the 1990s as that nation received from us modernizing technologies in communications, manufacturing, and munitions. The 1990s involved increases in global trade, megamergers, downsizing, outsourcing, offshoring, and sweatshops. Stiglitz states,

> America's international economic policy was driven by a whole variety of special interests which saw the opportunity to use its increasing global dominance to force other countries to open up their markets to its goods on its terms. America's government was seizing the opportunities afforded by the new post-Cold War world, but in a narrow way, benefitting particular financial and corporate interests. (pp. 235–236)

As international business sought to reduce labor costs, often through subcontractors, some of these contractors achieved the lowest cost by using slave labor (Bales 1999, p. 236). Globalization involves trade among individuals who never formally meet and may be involved in multiple capital ventures. Global trade often involves little oversight or regulation. As the twentieth century came to a close, a growing number of American firms, such as Nike, Sears, and Levi Strauss, were implicated in operating sweatshops or worse (LaFeber 1999, p. 106). Today, children in India are forced to work under sweatshop conditions to make rugs for export. Teenage boys are kidnapped and forced to work in cocoa fields in the Ivory Coast to make chocolate available for the global market.

Clinton's favoring of economic values over democratic values is not unique; it is usually the choice of leaders, especially during periods of financial crisis. His approach to the economy, along with some of the political and technological changes that occurred in the 1990s, helped to reduce the debt that was incurred by the previous two administrations. Clinton's restraint on spending, tax reform, the establishment of trade relations that disproportionately favored the American consumer at the time, the ending of the Cold War (with the collapse of the Soviet Union in 1991), a decade without major military involvement (though the United States was involved in a number of regional conflicts), and the emergence of new technologies (which created new opportunities)—all contributed to turning the federal government's annual deficit into a surplus. By turning the annual deficit into a surplus, the United States was temporarily able to chip away at its debt.

When Clinton left office, his presidency was generally perceived as morally in the red (due to a sex scandal), but economically in the black. But the economic exuberance that occurred in the late 1990s burst shortly after Clinton left office. People in highly placed financial positions were inflating the value of technologies, taking many risks with other people's money, and sometimes downright scamming the public and the government. The technology bubble burst as the housing bubble would in 2008. The result of all of this was once again a false sense of real economic growth, and by 2001 America was back in recession.

George W. Bush inherited an economy with a surplus, but on a downturn. Bush narrowly defeated Clinton's vice president Al Gore in a hotly debated election. Gore ran an uninspiring campaign for the presidency, and Bush emphasized his strengths in comparison to Clinton. People were tired of Clinton's moral indiscretions and his doublespeak in defense of his actions. Bush presented himself as a plain-speaking Texan. Few people realized that plain speaking did not mean speaking plainly; Bush could be obscure without resorting to big words. Nor did people question the authenticity of a man who presented himself as a Texan, even though he was born and educated in New England. Bush's tenure as president would be defined by the choices he would make after the 9/11/2001 terrorist attack. The attack was financed by the Saudi Arabian millionaire Osama bin Laden. Bin Laden began organizing a group of fighters that became known as al-Qaeda (meaning base or scroll) during the conflict between Afghanistan and the Soviet Union in the late 1980s.

The attack on the United States on 9/11/2001 was, in part, a response to globalization. Numerous books by respected scholars, notably Samuel Huntington's *The Clash of Civilizations* (1996) and Benjamin Barber's *Jihad vs. McWorld* (1995), predicted increasing tensions between the developed and developing world, yet our leaders turned a blind eye to these growing tensions. When the attack came, most Americans reacted with complete shock when confronted by the national vulnerability the day's events highlighted. The promise of globalization—the merging of economic markets and greater ties politically—can be the means of astonishing achievement for the people of the world. But until globalization is understood as a "we" rather than a self-interested "us versus them," the astonishing events that have occurred so far may be a precursor to events still more troubling.

After 9/11, concern over another terrorist attack gave Bush the political clout to write out blank checks with the nation's money wherever he felt necessary. Eight years later, with a poorly managed war, a poorly managed approach to trade, and unsupported tax cuts, Americans found themselves once again in a recession and with a record level of debt, with China becoming America's largest creditor. Debt was nothing new to Bush; his handling of various business ventures (before becoming president) had led to economic decline (Lewis 2000, pp. 194–220).

A part of the mismanagement of the war in Iraq was the privatization of military personnel. For example, Blackwell Security (a private security firm) had a $1.2 billion contract with the United States government to supply personnel in Iraq. Stiglitz and Bilmes note, "In 2007, private security guards working for companies such as Blackwell and Dynacorp were earning up to $1,222 a day; this amounts to $445,000 a year. By contrast, an Army sergeant was earning $140 to $190 a day in pay and benefits, a total of $51,100 to $69,350 a year" (2008, p. 12).

Dependence on private firms was caused both by the political decision to overextend military capacity and the economic self-interests among some politicians. Halliburton, a defense contractor once headed by Bush's vice president Dick Cheney, received exclusive rights to rebuild Iraq (Stiglitz & Bilmes, pp. 13–15). Financial mismanagement in defense remains a problem (Stiglitz & Bilmes, pp. 19–20).

When Bush left office in 2008, his approval ratings were low even among Republicans. After years of war and a deep recession, people were hungry for change and hope. Barack Obama tapped into this desire, and in 2008 he became the first African American president of the United States. Obama inherited from Bush an economy so deep in recession that some people in the media and in politics have called it the Great Recession (in reference to the Great Depression of 1929). In order to spur the economy, Obama signed into law a stimulus package that greatly increased the national debt.

Concern over a $14 trillion debt and politics led to a libertarian movement called the Tea Party. The movement was funded principally by conservative multimillionaire David Koch. In 2010, so many Tea Party candidates were elected into office that they acquired an influential voice among Republicans in Congress. At the time of this writing, hostility between the members of the two political parties is venomous.

I cannot say what will happen in the future, but I can use the political history discussed here, and the economic history discussed in the next section, to present an intelligible description of the political and economic circumstances in which we find ourselves in the early years of the twenty-first century. In the next section, we will begin by taking a closer look at the economic trends of the past sixty years, and then examine whether or not the ideological battles between the Democratic and Republican parties reflect a deeply divided or polarized population.

ECONOMIC TRENDS

Political discourse today among many politicians, special interest groups, and some media analysts emphasizes either that liberalism is the source of America's problems or that conservatism is the basis of the nation's troubles. This political discourse can easily lead observers to believe that the United States is divided or polarized into conservative versus liberal ideologies; "red states" versus "blue states." As social scientists it is contingent upon us to determine whether or not this is the case. Liberalism is the essence of the nation's heritage, but the meaning of liberalism has changed over time. In order to gain a fresh perspective on today's political tensions, we have been working on acquiring a historical consciousness. We have examined our political history since World War II. In order to complete the picture, we will now examine our economic history since the Second World War.

Table 5.1 and Figure 5.1 display in two ways the same data on aggregate income dispersion from 1950 to 2010 along a continuum from the poorest fifth or bottom 20 percent of income earners to the wealthiest fifth or top 20 percent of income earners. The Census Bureau changed the way it reported income distributions in 1967, from families to households, to reflect the changing nature of family composition. The data presented here refers to the older measure of families in order to remain consistent with the period of time that is the focus of this chapter; this economic data coincides with the political history discussed in the previous section (World War II to the present time). The data, from the nonpartisan United States Census Bureau, allows one to see where and when the nation's income has been concentrated. The more the nation's income is concentrated in fewer areas, the greater the inequality.

Note that we are discussing income and not wealth. *Income* refers to money earned, while *wealth* refers to assets. Most Americans' biggest accessible asset is in private home ownership. Many Americans have few to no assets.

In 1950 the lowest fifth of the population received 4.5 percent of the share of the nation's income. In the same year, 42.7 percent of the nation's income went to the highest fifth. Nearly half of the dollars earned in 1950 went to the top 20 percent of the population. In one sense, there is nothing surprising about this finding; the highest fifth is at the top because they enjoy greater

Table 5.1.   Share of Aggregate Income Received by Each Fifth of Families, 1950 to 2010

Year	Lowest fifth	Second fifth	Middle fifth	Fourth fifth	Highest fifth
1950	4.5	12.0	17.4	23.4	42.7
1951	5.0	12.4	17.6	23.4	41.6
1952	4.9	12.3	17.4	23.4	41.9
1953	4.7	12.5	18.0	23.9	40.9
1954	4.5	12.1	17.7	23.9	41.8
1955	4.8	12.3	17.8	23.7	41.3
1956	5.0	12.5	17.9	23.7	41.0
1957	5.1	12.7	18.1	23.8	40.4
1958	5.0	12.5	18.0	23.9	40.6
1959	4.9	12.3	17.9	23.8	41.1
1960	4.8	12.2	17.8	24.0	41.3
1961	4.7	11.9	17.5	23.8	42.2
1962	5.0	12.1	17.6	24.0	41.3
1963	5.0	12.1	17.7	24.0	41.2
1964	5.1	12.0	17.7	24.0	41.2
1965	5.2	12.2	17.8	23.9	40.9
1966	5.6	12.4	17.8	23.8	40.5
1967	5.4	12.2	17.5	23.5	41.4
1968	5.6	12.4	17.7	23.7	40.5
1969	5.6	12.4	17.7	23.7	40.6
1970	5.4	12.2	17.6	23.8	40.9
1971	5.5	12.0	17.6	23.8	41.1
1972	5.5	11.9	17.5	23.9	41.4
1973	5.5	11.9	17.5	24.0	41.1
1974	5.7	12.0	17.6	24.1	40.6
1975	5.6	11.9	17.7	24.2	40.7
1976	5.6	11.9	17.7	24.2	40.7
1977	5.5	11.7	17.6	24.3	40.9
1978	5.4	11.7	17.6	24.2	41.1
1979	5.4	11.6	17.5	24.1	41.4
1980	5.3	11.6	17.6	24.4	41.1
1981	5.3	11.4	17.5	24.6	41.2
1982	5.0	11.3	17.2	24.4	42.2

1983	4.9	11.2	17.2	24.5	42.4
1984	4.8	11.1	17.1	24.5	42.5
1985	4.8	11.0	16.9	24.3	43.1
1986	4.7	10.9	16.9	24.1	43.4
1987	4.6	10.7	16.8	24.0	43.8
1988	4.6	10.7	16.7	24.0	44.0
1989	4.6	10.6	16.5	23.7	44.6
1990	4.6	10.8	16.6	23.8	44.3
1991	4.5	10.7	16.6	24.1	44.2
1992	4.3	10.5	16.5	24.0	44.7
1993	4.1	9.9	15.7	23.3	47.0
1994	4.2	10.0	15.7	23.3	46.9
1995	4.4	10.1	15.8	23.2	46.5
1996	4.2	10.0	15.8	23.1	46.8
1997	4.2	9.9	15.7	23.0	47.2
1998	4.2	9.9	15.7	23.0	47.3
1999	4.3	9.9	15.6	23.0	47.2
2000	4.3	9.8	15.4	22.7	47.7
2001	4.2	9.7	15.4	22.9	47.7
2002	4.2	9.7	15.5	23.0	47.6
2003	4.1	9.6	15.5	23.2	47.6
2004	4.0	9.6	15.4	23.0	47.9
2005	4.0	9.6	15.3	22.9	48.1
2006	4.0	9.5	15.1	22.9	48.5
2007	4.1	9.7	15.6	23.3	47.3
2008	4.0	9.6	15.5	23.1	47.8
2009	3.9	9.4	15.3	23.2	48.2
2010	3.8	9.5	15.4	23.5	47.8

Source: United States Census Bureau, http://www.census.gov/hhes/www/income/data/historical/inequality/index.html

earnings. The data becomes more meaningful when examined over time. Looking sixty years later, in 2010 the lowest fifth received 3.8 percent of the share of the nation's income, while 47.8 percent of the nation's income went to the highest fifth. The nation's dispersion of income is more unequal in 2010 than it was in 1950.

Looking at the second fifth or what may be termed the working class: In 1950 their share of the nation's income was 12 percent, while in 2010 it was

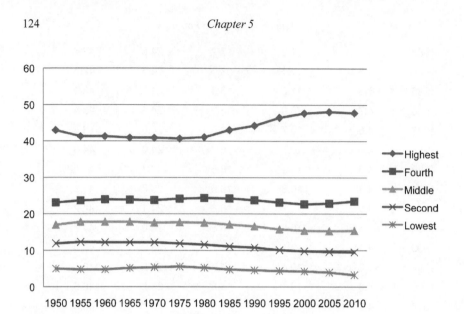

Figure 5.1.   Share of Aggregate Income Received by Each Fifth of Families in the United States, 1950–2010

9.5 percent. Regarding the middle or third fifth, in 1950 their share of the nation's income was 17.4 percent, while in 2010 it was 15.4 percent. Finally, let's look at the fourth fifth or what might be referred to as upper-middle class: Their share of the nation's income in 1950 was 23.4 percent, while in 2010 it was 23.5 percent. Clearly, over the span of those 60 years, the nation experienced growing income inequality, with earnings becoming concentrated at the top.

Let us now combine the economic data with the political events discussed above. The lowest fifth received a greater share of the nation's income from 1966 to 1981. During this period of time, Johnson, Nixon, Ford, and Carter were president. Both Johnson and Nixon instituted sweeping reforms, particularly in the area of civil rights. The next most activist president would be Reagan, who took office in 1980. The second, third, and fourth fifths received a greater share of the nation's income from the early 1950s to the late 1970s. As noted above, the greatest economic expansion in United States history occurred after World War II and throughout the 1950s and 1960s. The lower middle, solid middle, and upper middle classes benefitted the most from this expansion. During these boom years, the top fifth actually saw their share of the economic pie shrink. Their share was being spread around into the other fifths because of political decision making. This trend would be reversed in the 1980s and thereafter also because of political decision making. Since the 1980s the top fifth have seen their share of the economic pie

Table 5.2. Gini Ratios for Families, 1950 to 2010

Year	Gini Ratio	Year	Gini Ratio
1950	0.379	1981	0.369
1951	0.363	1982	0.380
1952	0.368	1983	0.382
1953	0.359	1984	0.383
1954	0.371	1985	0.389
1955	0.363	1986	0.392
1956	0.358	1987	0.393
1957	0.351	1988	0.395
1958	0.354	1989	0.401
1959	0.361	1990	0.396
1960	0.364	1991	0.397
1961	0.374	1992	0.404
1962	0.362	1993	0.429
1963	0.362	1994	0.426
1964	0.361	1995	0.421
1965	0.356	1996	0.425
1966	0.349	1997	0.429
1967	0.358	1998	0.430
1968	0.348	1999	0.429
1969	0.349	2000	0.433
1970	0.353	2001	0.435
1971	0.355	2002	0.434
1972	0.359	2003	0.436
1973	0.356	2004	0.438
1974	0.355	2005	0.440
1975	0.357	2006	0.444
1976	0.358	2007	0.432
1977	0.363	2008	0.438
1978	0.363	2009	0.443
1979	0.365	2010	0.440
1980	0.365		

Source: United States Census Bureau, http://www.census.gov/hhes/www/income/data/historical/inequality/index.html.

grow, while the remaining fifths have been stagnant or seen a decline in their share of the nation's income.

Another way to discuss the trend of inequality is in terms of what is called the *Gini* index. The Gini is an index of income concentration. Measured over time the Gini index reveals patterns of inequality across a distribution of incomes. Table 5.2 and Figure 5.2 show in two ways the same data of the Gini index from 1950 to 2010. A value of 0 suggests complete equality while a value of 1 suggests total inequality. During the postwar boom years, the trend shows a decline in income inequality (with the exception of 1959–1961), and a steady increase in income inequality beginning in the 1970s and thereafter. In terms of global comparisons with other capitalist nations, income inequality is greater in the United States than in the United Kingdom, France, Germany, Australia, Canada, Israel, Japan, South Korea, and Taiwan (Central Intelligence Agency 2013). Information gathered by the Census Bureau in 2006–2007 shows income inequality in the United States on par with Iran (slightly lower) and Philippines (slightly higher).

The overall picture from these data suggests that during the postwar boom years all income groups benefitted to some degree, but as the economy tightened, the dispersion of income became more concentrated at the top. This leads us to make the following two conclusions: (1) During good economic times, money is doled out more evenly across income groups, while during bad economic times money is consolidated within income groups that have power.

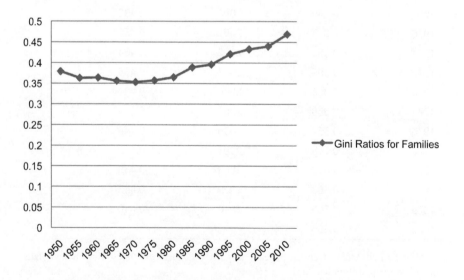

Figure 5.2. United States Gini Index, 1950–2010

Power can be defined simply as the ability to achieve one's will. The more power one has, the more freedom one has to carry out one's wishes. Power is tied to authority, organization, and wealth. A person without wealth and limited authority and networking has relatively little power. If you find yourself regularly responding to the wishes or demands of others, doing things or saying things that you would prefer not to, then you do not have power. Most people have some power in some circumstances, but people are usually more powerless than they like to admit. Most people do not have the power to determine their wages; many people feel powerless to get or change jobs, relocate to another community, place of residence, or determine when and if they will attend college. Some people are powerful enough to compel thousands, if not millions, to sacrifice their well-being and even their lives for an ideology or a paycheck.

The second conclusion follows from the first, but is more subtle in its implication: (2) A rich nation shares its prosperity; a struggling or poor nation engages in hoarding. Madrick (1997) states,

> Prosperity was the foundation of our best convictions as a nation, for what equality of opportunity meant in a rising economy was that with a lot of hard work most Americans could live a decent life. . . . As our material expectations are disappointed our new social, political, and religious movements become increasingly exclusionary, intolerant, and uncompromising, for now equality of opportunity implies sharing scarce resources (p. 133). . . . Once, equality meant that we could all get ahead. For too many of us, equality now means having to give something up. (p. 163)

While those in the majority or with power could see that all boats could rise without their losing out, those in the minority or without power were able to obtain a greater share of the nation's bounty. As the economy constricted in the 1970s and thereafter, sharing of resources declined. It seems that it is only during times of severe economic crisis or genuine prosperity that people with very limited resources have the chance to advance their interests. The postwar boom years seemed for many people to be the realization of the American Dream—that all people who applied themselves could become rich. In reality, the long view presented here reveals the durability of social class. Even granting the window of economic opportunity that was opened during the boom years, most income groups, and particularly those in the middle, experienced only marginal, temporary gains in their share of the nation's income. We may conclude that besides the fact that since the 1980s only the top 20 percent have seen their shares of the nation's income grow, another important pattern that is revealed by these data is the relative stagnation or stability of income groups; this stability reflects structured or institutionalized divisions in society.

ELITE POWER

For the past forty years G. William Domhoff has been researching the *power elite* (first discussed by Mills in the 1950s). According to Domhoff (2006), the power elite no longer includes military or political elites, but is solely composed of leaders in the corporate community, the top 1 percent of the upper bracket, and leaders in policy-planning organizations. Individuals from these groups form a powerful network that contributes to political candidates and lobbies government officials to support social and economic policies that represent their interests. What distinguishes this group is their access to leaders who establish public policy for the nation. Corporate leaders form an *interlocking directorate* (i.e., the same people sit on the board of directors for multiple organizations). This produces a uniformity of thought at the top level of many organizations.

The top 1 percent of the population owns nearly half of the nation's resources. They do not always agree on issues, but their influence is immense. David Koch transformed the libertarian Tea Party organization into a powerful group, while George Soros transformed the liberal MoveOn.org organization into a powerful group. Policy-planning groups include foundations, think tanks, political action committees (PACs), and 527s (i.e., advocacy groups that claim no party affiliation).

Most large sectors of the economy are represented by lobbying groups. Some of the most powerful lobbies represent the natural gas and oil industries, pharmaceutical companies, and the arms industry. If you have ever wondered why oil companies are subsidized by the federal government, the answer lies, in part, with the strength of their lobbyists to meet with and influence elected officials. Even when politicians pass legislation that seems to contradict the interests of powerful lobbyists, the implementation of the legislation may include conditions that minimize actual adjustments to existent policy. In this way, the status quo is maintained despite the trumpeting among politicians of new and improved legislation.

Many former members of the House of Representatives and the Senate, from both major political parties, work as lobbyists or advise a policy-planning group when they leave the government. They are a primary target to hire since a former member of a budget committee can have insider's information that can further the interests of a lobby or policy group.

Domhoff also argues that there is a certain type of mindfulness among the nation's elite; there is uniformity in terms of where they live, where their children go to school, the social clubs they join, the places they go to vacation, and the recognition of their influence. They share a respect for status, they tend to be conservative, and newcomers know that they must earn the trust and acceptance of the old guard. Zweigenhaft and Domhoff state, "The individuals in the power elite may come and go, and they may diversify in gender, ethnicity, and sexual orientation, but there is stability and continuity within the overall power structure" (1998, p. 180).

SOCIAL CLASS

Stratification is the term that sociologists use to describe social divisions in society. Every society divides people in certain ways. Societies can be stratified in terms of birthright, class, sex, race, or religion. *Social class* or status position, which is determined by income and wealth, is one of the primary ways in which societies organize divisions among people. American society has been traditionally stratified in terms of income and wealth, race, and sex. Of the three, income and wealth remain sources of divisiveness in American society that cannot be discussed constructively in public; attempts to do so typically digress into shallow rebuttals, like calling such discussion *class warfare*.

The social circles we live in are maintained by social institutions (family, economics, education, and so on) and these institutions infuse our lives with an ideology—a way of thinking about our circumstances—that is consistent with our class position. While belief in meritocracy (i.e., effort leads to success) cuts across class lines in the United States, people in different classes interpret merit in different and fairly predictable ways. At the risk of overgeneralizing, it is fairly common for a person from humble origins who acquires wealth to interpret the change in their circumstances in religious terms; they tend to refer to their change in circumstances as a "blessing." A middle-class person who acquires wealth tends to interpret their success in psychological terms; their change in circumstances is due to individual effort or "rugged individualism." The person who inherits wealth tends to interpret such circumstances as fortunate, but appropriate. Coming to terms with one's place in society includes accepting the ideologies consistent with one's class position.

Irrespective of the ways that people in different social classes interpret economic success, most Americans are inclined to believe that there are no clear class boundaries, and that those who succeed have earned it, and those who do not succeed have not earned it. Because of these beliefs, most Americans are inclined to pay homage to those who succeed and to believe that *vertical mobility*, or a major change in class position, is available to them. Upward social mobility and meritocracy are pervasively perpetuated ideologies—the lone hero in the community, school, business, or military who beats the odds against an unjust system; the actor, singer, athlete, or politician who rises to fame and wealth from humble origins. These themes are repeated daily in film, television shows, the news, and songs as an all-pervasive, institutionalized ideology.

Intragenerational (within a single generation) *mobility* to the top does happen, and there is certainly nothing wrong with it, but the point being made here is that it is portrayed in our culture as a norm, that anyone can do it, when in fact, what is portrayed by the media in stories and by celebrities and politicians in pep talks is the exception. Exceptional cases are displayed as the norm; this is the ideology of social mobility. The fact of the matter is that mobility is commonly *horizontal*, when most people change jobs their status remains relatively the same.

There is a counterargument to the interpretation of the data presented in these tables. The counterargument states that while the numbers of people in each class remain relatively static, the particular individuals who occupy each fifth do not remain static, there is continuous movement. However, if this argument were true, we would not see generations of men working as coal miners, we would not see political dynasties (i.e., Kennedy, Bush). The best argument in support of this point of view is reflected in *intergenerational social mobility*, particularly in the transformation of immigrant families. Many poor immigrants have come to the United States, and over a period of generations, have established themselves firmly in the middle class. Of course, there are many more instances of people coming to this country and remaining in poverty generation after generation.

Americans mostly accept the idea that our nation is "the land of opportunity." At various times in our history, and for certain groups of people during those times, America has been such a land. Compared to many other nations, past and present, the United States is a land of opportunity. However, the point should be made that the idea of opportunity is significantly larger than the reality. Indeed, a person of modest ability can succeed beyond the wildest dreams of a person of tremendous ability if the former has wealth and connections.

Education and Social Class

According to the Census Bureau, the poverty rate in 2010 was 15.1 percent, the highest rate since 1993. Living in a service economy requires people with technical training, critical-thinking skills, and financial sense. Consistent with living in a service economy, the Census Bureau reports that those with lower levels of education were more likely to experience downward economic movement than those with higher levels of education. Earning a college degree has become an important part of achieving horizontal mobility (i.e., increasing earnings and status, but not social class position).

In terms of education and stratification, two other factors are important. Family background is not only an important predictor of college attendance, but it is also an important predictor of college success. Young people whose parents are highly educated or affluent are more likely to be successful in college than young people attending college because of family pressure. There are several reasons for this:

1. Young people coming from homes that emphasized education are more likely to have acquired the skills necessary to succeed in college before they begin. These students feel comfortable in a college classroom and feel comfortable engaging in dialogue and debate with their professors.
2. Young people coming from affluent homes are more likely to have attended private school and received more personal guidance, and are more likely to pursue and receive guidance in college if they need it.
3. Young people coming from homes that have not stressed education and young people who have attended poor schools, may begin college but they may not really understand what the benefits of college are (besides getting a degree) and how to get them. Because they feel uncomfortable in the setting, they don't ask for what they need. The bigger issue though is that many young people with this kind of background drop out of school before college is even a possibility. And finally,
4. Because of the steady rise in college tuition, the inability of the dollar to keep up with the cost of living, and government cut-backs in aid for college, except student loans, even those who attend college but do not receive significant family support or grants will complete college and enter into the workforce with more debt than any group of college graduates in American history. In other words, even middle class young people who complete college will begin their careers economically behind those who did not need to depend upon loans. Over the long run, of course, middle class young people will come out ahead (compared to not attending college), but they will enter the job market in competition with those from other nations who can accept a lower wage, and in competition with those who will not have the burden of paying back a large debt even before they get started.

Gender and Race and Social Class

The information reported here on gender and race comes from the United States Census Bureau (http://www.census.gov/hhes/www/income/data/statistics/index.html). According to the data, as of 2009 female, full-time, year-round workers earned 77 percent as much as corresponding male, full-time, year-round workers. In 2009 median earnings for male workers was $47,127 while for female workers it was $36,278. Women have always outnumbered men in terms of those living in poverty. In terms of single-parenting and poverty, in 2009, 23.7 percent of male householders with children under eighteen years of age lived below poverty, while 38.5 percent of female householders with children under eighteen years of age lived below poverty. While single moms living below poverty continue to outnumber single fathers living below poverty, Census Bureau data reflects a decreasing trend for women and an increasing trend for men.

In 2009 Asian American households had the highest median income at $65,469, followed by Caucasian households at $54,461, Latino households at $38,039, and African American households at $32,584. The poverty rate for most groups of people has been increasing to a statistically significant degree since 2008. In 2009 Caucasians living below poverty was 9.4 percent, followed by Asian Americans at 12.5 percent, Latinos at 25.3 percent, and African Americans at 25.8 percent. In 2009 single Latina and single African American mothers made up the largest groups of families living below poverty—at 46.0 percent and 44.2 percent, respectively.

The data reflects a weakening economy affecting all groups of people, but especially single mothers and people of color. Much progress has been made since keeping these records began, but the fact that the poverty rate continues to climb (it is higher now than it was nearly twenty years ago), reinforces the claim made in this chapter that regardless of political party and ideology, the economy continues on a downward spiral. It also reinforces Domhoff's claim that, regardless of the growing diversity of those at the economic top, those at the economic bottom continue to be overrepresented by the same groups of minorities.

MYTH VERSUS REALITY

One of the reasons why I have presented the information in this chapter is to demonstrate that the belief in social mobility is basically a myth (i.e., a belief system based partly in reality and partly in fantasy). The data shows that class divisions are relatively stable over time. The United States was founded after successfully rebelling against a British government steeped in hierarchical traditions. In the remote wilds of America, if people could survive through the winters, find enough to eat, and keep the native population at bay, they were relatively free from government intrusion. As the population grew, the government offered incentives for people to move westward where the same conditions of remote, rural life once prevailed.

With the rise of industrialization in the late nineteenth century, some individuals acquired wealth that was unprecedented anywhere else in the world. It was around this time that the notion of "rags to riches" was born. In the late nineteenth century Horatio Alger wrote popular stories about youngsters who had gone from poverty to prosperity. The stories that he wrote were fictional; he himself came from a well-off family. Rags to riches is myth, it is a story partly based in reality (there have been individuals who have acquired great wealth in their lifetimes in the United States) and partly based in fantasy (anyone can achieve great wealth in the United States if they apply themselves).

The notion of rags to riches was transformed into the popular phrase "American Dream," by James Truslow Adams in his 1931 book, entitled *The Epic of America.* It was in this book that Adams wrote and solidified the notion that in America "life should be richer and fuller for everyone and opportunity remain open for all" ([1931] 2012, p. 308). Thomas Jefferson's words in the Declaration of Independence stating, "We hold these truths to be self-evident, that all men are created equal, that they are endowed by their Creator with certain unalienable Rights, that among these are Life, Liberty and the pursuit of Happiness," was fully transformed in the twentieth century from a statement about political rights into a statement of economic relations and possibilities. The postwar boom years were proof to many that the American Dream was real. For many people today, restoration of the boom years requires a return to the values that prevailed at that time. Yet, this too entails mythical thinking; the hands of time cannot be turned backward, and "the good old days" were not "the good old days" for many people who lived during the postwar boom years.

Anti-Catholic and anti-Semitic sentiments were strong in the 1940s and 1950s. At least 70 percent of Southern blacks lived in poverty in 1945 and all public accommodations, such as schools, parks, beaches, restaurants, hotels, rest rooms, and drinking fountains were segregated (Patterson, p. 23). Despite continuing challenges, African Americans as a group have achieved a lot since the 1960s, though because of ongoing challenges, they continue to be overrepresented in terms of unemployment.

In the 1950s, 75 percent of working women were in so-called "female" jobs, and medical schools, law schools, and many businesses maintained quotas limiting women (Patterson, p. 33). Single women usually could not get access to birth control devices (Patterson, p. 35). While women as a group have made great strides since the 1960s, they still have the status of a minority (because they possess less power in society than men), even though they narrowly outnumber men in the population.

In addition to civil rights issues, there was also the fact of the Cold War with the Soviet Union, Joseph McCarthy's interrogation and ruin of many innocent people (due to his overzealous mission to reveal a Communist threat within the United States), and the nuclear bomb scare that led many people to construct bomb shelters in their homes in the early 1960s.

POLITICAL POLARIZATION

The information presented here from nonpartisan sources suggests, in contradistinction to Republican leaders who pontificate about Reagan's economics and Democrats who boast of Clinton's economics, that neither party has been able to replicate the economic growth that occurred during the postwar boom years. Members of the two political parties have always been ideologically divided on important issues, but during the postwar boom years, many Democrats and Republicans could work together to produce legislation that would gain the support of the majority of lawmakers (Brady & Han 2006).

Core supporters from both political parties want their leaders to create an economic condition that neither party can reproduce. In order to get their votes, political leaders continue to promise what they remain unable to deliver. Because all political promises lead to only short-term economic gains, in order to maintain core voter support, political leaders have become more extravagant in their spending and campaign promises, and more virulent in how they portray their opposition. According to political scientists Nolan McCarty, Keith Poole, and Howard Rosenthal (2006, p. 184), "The most direct effect of polarization-induced gridlock is that public policy does not adjust to changing economic and demographic circumstances." Polarization-induced gridlock makes both of the major political parties inefficient.

The partisanship that we see today actually began in the late 1950s. In 1958, a new group of Democratic liberals was elected to the House. In order to increase the chances of getting their legislative agenda passed, they encouraged reform of the House rules (Sinclair 2006, p. 75). This strengthened the hand of the majority party and led to greater party cohesion (Sinclair, p. 85). The passage of the Civil Rights Act of 1964 and the Voting Rights Act of 1965 transformed politics in the South. In 1952, when voting was made difficult-to-impossible for African Americans, 79 percent of Caucasian Southerners were Democrats (Sinclair, p. 16). After 1965, many Southern Caucasians begrudgingly joined the party of Lincoln and many African Americans in the South and North identified with the Democrats. In turn, Southern conservative Democrats were replaced by either more conservative Republicans or more moderate Democrats (Sinclair, p. 19). As a result, each party became more homogeneous and divisions between the parties became clearer. As the Republican Party moved further to the right, the Democratic Party moved further to the left. When Republicans gained the majority in the House in 1994, they excluded Democrats the way in which they had been excluded.

Given that the majority party can now exclude the minority party from participating in the legislative process, winning the majority during elections is crucial. This has given rise to an unprecedented number of influential partisan grassroots organizations, think tanks, corporate lobbying groups, and media-driven political pundits. Activists and special interests are at the core of today's political polarization. While think tanks such as the Heritage Foundation, the American Enterprise Institute, and the Economic Policy Institute, began as independent organizations designed to conduct empirical research on policy and social issues, they have become part of the new party machines. The pharmaceutical industry and the energy industry (oil, gas, coal, and electricity) are just two of the many industries that spend more on marketing, including lobbying, than on research.

There is no doubt that cultural issues and the things we can accomplish today due to technological innovations tend to pivot people in different directions. Issues such as abortion, euthanasia, capital punishment, and humanity's role in climate change produce strong emotions and moral ambivalence for the majority of people, yet there are issues that most people, regardless of political persuasion, are not ambivalent about. And these include that government is inefficient and that too much power is concentrated in large companies (Fiorina, Abrams, & Pope 2011, p. 39). However, when it comes to these issues, political candidates offer voters little choice—they all say it is something that must be dealt with, yet they and the voters know that elected officials cannot bite the hands that feed their coffers. And so activists on both sides fuel discussion about what most people are morally ambivalent about, thereby widening the gulf between people, and say little about what most people agree is the problem with government and the economy. Political scientists Morris Fiorina, Samuel Abrams, and Jeremy Pope (p. 55) note, "In both red and blue states a solid majority of voters see themselves as positioned between two relatively extreme parties."

There are voting preferences based upon social class. The majority of lower income Americans, including born-again and evangelical Christians, vote for Democrats because their policy proposals include some provisions for redistributing the nation's resources (Gelman 2008, p. 19; McCarty, Poole, & Rosenthal, p. 101). Middle income Americans tend to split when it comes to voting Republican or Democrat (Gelman, p. 19). This split may reflect dissatisfaction among middle income voters about the effectiveness of either political party. Many wealthy people vote for Republicans because their policy proposals support their economic interests; however, this was not always the case. McCarty, Poole, and Rosenthal point out.

> Partisanship was, in fact, only weakly related to income in the period following World War II. In the presidential election years of 1956 and 1960, National Election Study respondents from the highest income quintile were hardly more likely to identify as a Republican than were respondents from the lowest quintile. In contrast, in the presidential election of 1992, 1996, and 2000 [and thereafter], respondents in the highest quintile were more than twice as likely to identify as Republican as were those in the lowest. . . . [T]he stratification of partisanship by income has grown steadily over the past forty years. (p. 73)

Not all upper bracket Americans are conservative and Republican. In states such as California, New York, Massachusetts, and Connecticut, wealthy people tend to be liberal and Democrat (Gelman, pp. 19, 167). The reason why it is important to know how wealthy people vote is because the greater the income, the more likely one is to vote (Gelman, p. 143). Hence, wealthy people constitute a small but influential group of voters. Moreover, they have more to give to their respective interest group or political party. Indeed, it is mostly wealthy Americans who are filling the coffers of their favored political organization.

The cultural shifts that began in the 1960s, the rule changes in Congress increasing partisanship, the weakening of the economy in the 1970s, the growing need for money to support the rising costs of running a political campaign, and the opportunities that arose for some due to the rise of the service and technology industries along with the rise of globalization—all contributed to creating a battleground upon which elites could strive to protect and further their own economic interests and promote their own ideological agenda. This last statement is not an indictment on the upper class, it is merely pointing out that wealthy individuals are using their resources to influence public policies in ways that maximize their narrow interests rather than the broad interests of the majority. Gelman sums it up well:

> The polarization on issues that has occurred in the electorate is not as strong as the divergence between the two parties in Congress. The relatively extreme ideologies of congress members—to be more precise, their consistency in issue positions—should not be a surprise because elected representatives are constrained by their political parties, interest groups, and funders in a way that voters are not. In between voters and politicians are political activists, who tend to have ideological positions that are more extreme . . . than the general population. (p. 125)

The battleground among elites is not occurring just in Washington, D.C., it is occurring over the airwaves twenty-four hours a day, seven days a week. Rather than describe the polarization between Democrats and Republicans or blue states and red states as a "culture war," I believe that it would be more accurate to describe it, using Barbara Sinclair's terminology, as a PR war (p. 288). Political activists and party leaders devote a lot of their resources to reaching the public, and particularly, energizing their respective base supporters.

MEDIA AND POLITICAL POLARIZATION

As a social scientist, I am sometimes asked, "What is the practical value of social research?" The effectiveness of research in sociology and psychology may be found readily in advertising and in the use of polls and focus groups. Politicians, business leaders, and special interest groups rely on techniques devised by social researchers to cultivate support for policies that further their respective interests. Both parties use focus groups or small discussion groups to test their political messages before making them public. Phrases such as "tax and spend," "hope and change," "flip-flop," and "job creators," are tested in small groups in order to discern what schema they tap into. If the message taps into a conservative schema or a liberal schema such that the message reverberates emotionally with the recipient, then this is the phrase that will be discussed at each party's morning briefing and then be disseminated by politicians when facing reporters and the public. Does testing messages for public consumption work? Exit polling after an election would suggest that they do. Ask a person why they voted for a particular candidate, and the chances are high that they will repeat the sound bite.

As we discussed earlier in this book, schemas organize incoming information into already established thought patterns. Schemas are domain specific so each one of us establishes a schema to organize our thoughts around politically based information. Politicians depend upon information derived from focus groups, media aides, and political activists in order to frame issues in ways that tap into a viewer's political schema. The reason why conservatives like Fox News and not MSNBC, and the reason why liberals like MSNBC and not Fox News, is because information is framed or presented in different ways that reinforce particular kinds of political schemas. If the audience is big enough, such framing increases media profits, confirms a perspective that regular viewers are already familiar and comfortable with, and creates spokespeople or leaders who represent the viewership. The problem with *media segmentation* (as this is called), is that it reinforces political polarization. Because of media segmentation, neither liberals nor conservatives are exposed to a perspective that would enable them to formulate an effective system of communication to confront the nation's problems.

The polarization of left versus right serves as a distraction for the displaced anger that most people share about their doubts concerning their own as well as the nation's economic future. Voters are not merely passive bystanders in the battle between activists on the extreme left and extreme right, yet, their apathetic response based upon exasperation, or their willingness to get sucked into the polarizing rhetoric, fuels the political stalemate and economic stagnation.

The media could serve as a conduit between the public and policy makers, but it is not set up to work this way. The media is set up to promote one-way conversations: from political and economic leaders and political pundits to the public. The public does not possess the means to communicate with itself (despite the promise of the Internet).

While the profit motive contributes to producing stunning sights and sounds, this same motive undermines the media's role to be the eyes, ears, and voice of the nation. The need to increase media share contributes to polarization in many ways. Most reporters today do not go out of their way to get information about a political story line; rather, they depend upon partisan think tanks to produce "an expert" who can be interviewed. The profit motive also prevents political candidates from getting free air time (though the government sold the airwaves to media conglomerates for significantly less than they needed to—due to lobbying), and this contributes significantly to the cost of running a campaign. And it is the cost of running for office that undercuts serious campaign finance reform.

CORRUPTION AND POLITICAL POLARIZATION

According to political scientist Susan Rose-Ackerman, "The distinctive incentives for corruption in democracies depend on the organization of electoral and legislative processes and on the methods of campaign finance. These factors may be intertwined" (1999, p. 127). The need for money to run for office or get reelected produces a constant search for money. Private partisan donors and special interest groups supply the dollars to pay for the expense of advertising. Alliances are formed between lawmakers who need money and wealthy partisan individuals and groups who can supply the capital if the lawmaker's ideological and economic agenda is consistent with their interests. Campaign finance is one of the key factors contributing to corruption among members of both political parties. Political scientist Robert Harris sums it up well:

> [I]n the United States it is clearly the formal duty of elected representatives to serve the people without fear or favor; equally clearly, in practice the political system works on rather different principles. . . . [C]ongressmen can effectively become advocates for powerful interests . . . . Hence emerge . . . "iron triangles" of congressional committees, civil servants and private interest groups. In such situations the symbiotic nature of political, bureaucratic and interest-group relations creates a collusive structure impermeable to external influence. (2003, p. 2)

Contemporary partisanship and polarization contribute to political corruption, which produces inefficiency, waste, and favoritism. When government is corrupt innovation is nearly impossible because the larger picture is overshadowed by short-term profitability. Corruption in government has always existed, but I would say that since Richard Nixon's resignation as president, it has gotten worse. This is not to say that Nixon is to be blamed for contemporary corruption—many people after him have made their own decisions.

However, his resignation was a national and international disgrace, and this most likely increased the felt need to cover up subsequent transgressions. Today, politicians seem to be accused on a regular basis of stealing, lying, or infidelity, but no one in politics or the media will come out and say that these actions are endemic in politics and in fact the way to advance one's position.

Even an uncorrupt politician and executive may be compelled to do business with a corrupt politician or executive in order to achieve seemingly worthwhile goals. Such alliances blur the distinction between legitimate practices and criminal activity. As corruption spreads through an institution it is difficult to stop: the uncorrupt become the deviants and are marginalized.

Corruption at the top becomes an example of how to reach the top and so corrupt practices work their way to lower-level operators. This then perpetuates a cycle of corruption that even the exceptional uncorrupt leader may be unable to change.

CONCLUSION

Society is what we as individuals, working together, make it. This is the moral lesson underlying Adam Smith's vision of the division of labor in society, outlined in his book, *The Wealth of Nations* ([1791] 2000), which inspired America's economic system. We, in our individual lives, participate in networks, which establish institutions, which create and sustain society. The consequences of our collective efforts (society) act back upon us through the same networks. These consequences may not reflect our individual actions and interests, but they do reflect the results of our collective actions and interests. The political and economic conditions in the United States reflect the actions or inactions of its people.

FOR FURTHER READING

Domhoff, G. W. (2006). *Who rules America? Power and politics, and social change* (5th ed.). New York: McGraw-Hill. A classic on elite power in the United States and very readable.

Fiorina, M. P., Abrams, S. J., & Pope, J. (2011). *Culture war: The myth of a polarized America* (3rd ed.). Boston, MA: Longman Publishing Group. Very thoughtful, data-based analysis on polarization.

Gelman, A. (2008). *Red state, blue state, rich state, poor state: Why Americans vote the way they do*. Princeton, NJ: Princeton University Press. Another thoughtful and accessible book on political polarization.

Kronenwetter, M. (1984). *Are you a liberal? Are you a conservative?* New York: F. Watts. A short, informative, and easy read about liberalism and conservatism.

LaFeber, W. (1999). *Michael Jordan and the new global capitalism*. New York: W. W. Norton. Interesting approach to learning about globalization.

Love, N. S. (2006). *Understanding dogmas and dreams: A text*. Washington, DC: CQ Press. Good overview of different political ideologies.

Madrick, J. G. (1997). *The end of affluence: The causes and consequences of America's economic dilemma*. New York: Random House. A little challenging, but one of the best books explaining the rise and fall of the United States economy after World War II.

McCarty, N., Poole, K., & Rosenthal, H. (2006). *Polarized America: The dance of ideology and unequal riches* (1st ed.). Cambridge, MA: The MIT Press. Another thoughtful and accessible book on political polarization.

Napoleoni, L. (2005). *Terror incorporated: Tracing the dollars behind the terror networks*. New York: Seven Stories Press. A little challenging, but well worth the read: a very good critical analysis on the war on terrorism.

Patterson, J. T. (1996). *Grand expectations: The United States, 1945–1974*. New York: Oxford University Press. Long, detailed, and informative book about mid-twentieth century America and its enduring impact.

Reichley, J. (1992). *The life of the parties: A history of American political parties*. New York: The Free Press. Long, detailed, and informative book about American politics.

Wood, G. (1991). *The radicalism of the American Revolution* (1st ed.). New York: Vintage Books. Excellent discussion on the ideas and people surrounding the American Revolution.

Chapter Six

Sex, Marriage, Family, and Community

Is there any purpose to having two sexes who oppose each other regularly on issues that concern both? Are these differences due to culture, biology, or a combination of these and other factors? How are intimate relationships connected to other types of relationships? These questions and related issues will be addressed in this chapter.

One of the key differences separating organisms into simplistic and complex functioning concerns reproduction. If you and I were single cell creatures or vegetative organisms, we would not be divided into males and females. However, many creatures are multicelled, complex organisms and two sexes are needed to carry all of the biological information required for reproduction. Most mammals are seasonal breeders—which means that they have sex only at certain times of the year and only for reproduction. Many animals mate with multiple partners, but some creatures mate with a single partner either for life or for extended periods of time. The latter is referred to as *pair-bonding* and it is found among many species of birds as well as human beings and some other primates.

According to anthropologist R. I. M. Dunbar, species that mate promiscuously or engage in sex without establishing a relationship and with multiple partners have smaller brains than pair-bonding species (2009, p. 566). Dunbar states, "[T]he pressures for close coordination on a daily basis for months or even years on end might seem to be more demanding cognitively than a one-off decision about mate quality" (p. 568). It appears to be the case that pair-bonding gives rise to more complex thinking, which facilitates self-consciousness within organisms and more complex forms of communication between organisms. Human beings and higher primates are unique sexually from the rest of the animal kingdom in that humans and bonobos, in particular, engage in sex for non-reproductive purposes on a regular basis. A part of humankind's complex social nature is its ability to choose to engage in sexual activity. Conscious selection represents perhaps the most complex form of mating.

Many animals engage in a series of rituals prior to mating, with some species of birds engaging in perhaps the most exaggerated of mating rituals. Human beings also engage in ritualistic behavior prior to mating—the culmination of these rituals usually being marriage. Anthropologist Helen Fisher points out that in order to attract attention from females, "Men tend to pitch and roll their shoulders, stretch, stand tall, and shift from foot to foot in a swaying motion" (1992, pp. 26–27). For their part, women "arch their backs, thrust out their bosoms, sway their hips, and strut." In the 1500s Catherine de Medici invented high-heeled shoes in order to produce the sexually attractive gait (Fisher, p. 27). Men swagger and women strut in order to get the opposite sex's attention. John Cacioppo and William Patrick point out, "Most neuroscientists now agree that, over a period of tens of thousands of years, it was the need to send and receive, interpret and relay increasingly complex social cues that drove the expansion of . . . the human brain . . . . [I]t was the need to deal with other people that, in large part, made us who and what we are today" (2008, p.11).

If you think about it, our early survival as human beings depended upon our ability to coordinate our activities—otherwise, we could not have thrived while other bigger, stronger, and faster creatures diminished. In addition to social neuroscientists, many psychologists, anthropologists, and sociologists are in agreement that social bonding may be at the heart of humanity's complex development. While people are self-interested beings, we are also self-sacrificing beings. Certainly, raising children often involves self-sacrifice. Human beings maintain relationships at multiple levels that are all interconnected: We maintain an inner dialogue with ourselves, we strive to maintain an intimate relationship, we are part of familial relationships, we are part of relationships involving large groups (e.g., local community, corporation, military, religious group), we are members of society, and many people maintain a relationship with a spiritual Other. In the following sections of this chapter, we will focus on intimate, familial, and large group relationships, respectively. These relationships will also be discussed in historical perspective in order to provide a context for a better understanding of contemporary society.

INTIMATE RELATIONSHIPS: SEX

If you think about sex rationally and objectively, it seems weird, yet most people feel, at least occasionally, a strong desire to engage in sex. Why? Built into a thriving species is a strong desire to survive, and the way a species survives is through sexual reproduction. Species have varying degrees of consciousness, and for higher primates and human beings, this has also led to engaging in sex for pleasurable or nonreproductive purposes. In human relationships, sexual attraction is an impetus for pair-bonding and can help to maintain relationships over time. It is very likely that the drive to survive and perpetuate the species led to the characteristics that we typically associate with maleness and femaleness.

We like to think that partner selection involves processes that are unique to each couple. While it is the case that people with compatible interests and temperaments tend to have enduring relationships (contrary to the notion that opposites attract), there are a number of factors that seem to be universal in terms of partner selection. Fisher notes that men tend to prefer women with smooth skin and who are wide-hipped: the former conveys health and the latter conveys fertility. Women tend to prefer men with a good complexion and who possess money and goods: the former suggests fitness and the latter suggests the ability to provide for children (1992, p. 47). Even though the conditions under which people live vary over time, these signals continue to influence our choices.

In addition to biological forces exerting pressure on sexual expression, cultural factors also play a crucial role. Throughout recorded history, sex has been controlled through customs and rules associated with marriage, adultery, and divorce. Control of sex means control over intimate desires and control over the distribution of available resources (the more people, the fewer resources available for each person). Customs and laws associated with marriage, adultery, and divorce are practiced in every culture in order to contain sex, reproduction, and the distribution of necessary resources. Issues surrounding sexual expression today have roots that extend back into history.

SEX IN AMERICAN HISTORY

The problem with looking back in time is that we tend to look back with a contemporary understanding of the past. To contemporary ears, the terms *Puritan* and *sex* convey contrasting meanings: someone who is pure is innocent of sex. However, we know that the Puritans were fruitful and multiplied so they must have been familiar with sex. Consider the size of homes in colonial America. Families usually slept in the same room. According to historians John D'Emilio and Estelle Freedman, "The small size of colonial dwellings allowed children quite early in their lives to hear or see sexual activity among adults" (1997, p. 17). Moreover, it was not exceptionally uncommon in the colonies for children to be conceived out of wedlock, or for women to be pregnant at marriage (Coontz 1992, p. 184).

Because colonial America was driven economically by agriculture—which involved lots of labor—the demand was great to produce large families. Women might raise seven or eight children (D'Emilio & Freedman, p. 14). The number of children who grew to adulthood, however, does not convey how often women might have become pregnant. Miscarriages and infant and child mortality reduced the number of live children considerably. In addition, there was always the risk of the mother's life during childbirth—nearly one birth in thirty resulted in the death of the mother (Mintz & Kellogg 1988, p. 13).

As the economy changed, so did the size of the family. Industrial growth drew many people away from farming and into urban factories. Once an asset, children were now an expense. Concerns about birth control grew in importance. By the mid-1800s information about contraceptives circulated far and wide (D'Emilio & Freedman, p. 59). Statutes against abortion did not appear until the 1860s, partly in response to their growing number and the dangerous methods used to induce them. Products used for abortions included calomel and turpentine, tea made from the tansy plant, or rusty-nail water (D'Emilio & Freedman, p. 63).

The reduced need for children facilitated a greater focus on sex for enjoyment. Men and women increasingly viewed sex as a means to personal pleasure apart from its utilitarian function of reproduction. New ideas about sex, love, and marriage gained momentum. Frances Wright was a "freethinker" who advocated that love, and not marriage, should be the precondition for sexual relations. Reformers in education began to stress the importance of sexual education. In 1929 Katharine B. Davis surveyed 2,200 women on sexuality. The vast majority of the participants stated using some form of contraception. In 1948 and 1953 Alfred Kinsey published his research on the sexuality of men and of women, respectively. D'Emilio and Freedman note,

> The study of the male revealed that masturbation and heterosexual petting were nearly universal, that almost ninety percent had engaged in premarital intercourse and half in extramarital sex, and that over a third of adult males had had homosexual experience. Virtually all males had established a regular sexual outlet by the age of fifteen. . . . Over three-fifths [of American women] had engaged in masturbation, ninety percent had participated in petting, half in premarital intercourse, and a quarter in extramarital affairs. (p. 286)

The Depression of the 1930s and the family-centered postwar economic boom years of the 1950s obscure the larger historical trend toward sexual expressiveness in American society. This trend was fueled by some of the very social forces that people like most about American society: liberty, individualism, and commercial growth. Those who paint the 1950s as a simpler and better time, obscure the fact that widely popular President Eisenhower was an ideological moderate, that supporting the growth in marriages was a booming economy that focused on the middle class, and that below the surface of "Happy Days" were deep anxieties about the Soviets, the rise of juvenile delinquency, and a growing number of people who wanted to exercise greater individual choice. "The pill" would not have become so widely popular after it was approved in 1960 if there had not already been a strong demand. During the 1950s the director of Planned Parenthood (established in 1942) estimated that "roughly 2,000 [abortions] a day, every day—are performed in the United States. And to the best of our knowledge most of them are performed on married women with families" (D'Emilio & Freedman, p. 253).

Throughout the 1950s and 1960s a gay and lesbian subculture was growing. "Coming out" among gays and lesbians in the 1970s was part of the trend toward exercising greater individual choice that emerged in the 1960s among heterosexuals. A key point here is that resistance among some groups of Americans to these trends is as old as these trends themselves and is a part of these trends: greater expressiveness in a tolerant society will produce a backlash because what some consider freedom others consider outrageousness. However, the overall trend is markedly toward greater individual expression.

The trend toward greater expressiveness, including sexuality, was aided significantly by industrialization and marketing. Rapid industrial production, which was solving problems associated with manufacturing, led to problems of consumption: Mass production can only be profitable if there are mass consumers. Advertising was created in the early years of the twentieth century to deal with this dilemma. Working with psychologists, industry leaders discovered that the best way to sell a product was to associate it with human desires such as achievement, relationships, and sex. If the objectification of the female body had not yet achieved prominence in society, this trend would certainly fuel it. D'Emilio and Freedman state,

> By using veiled nudes and seductive poses, advertising spread throughout the culture images designed to stimulate male erotic fantasies. More and more of life, it seemed, was intent on keeping Americans in a state of constant sexual excitement. And, as mainstream businesses and entrepreneurs routinely employed a sexual sell, they weakened the hold of nineteenth-century obscenity codes. (p. 279)

In order to solve a problem associated with industrial production, American society would be faced with a cultural contradiction that continues to reverberate and wreak havoc to this day. Herbert Hoover once famously said, "The business of America is business." America is celebrated as "the land of economic opportunity" and we usually consider the small entrepreneur who makes it big a hero. Yet some of these heroes use false portrayals of America's past in order to promote an ideology or to sell products. For example,

Rupert Murdoch's News Corporation, one of the largest media outlets in the world, uses terms like *tradition* and *conservative* interchangeably in order to sell a political ideology, yet also uses sex in its programming in order to sell products and maximize its media share.

There is nothing surprising about learning that a researcher once explained advertising's dilemma in the following way: "We are now confronted with the problem of permitting the average American to feel moral . . . . One of the basic problems of prosperity . . . is to demonstrate that the hedonistic approach to life is a moral, not an immoral one" (Coontz, p. 171). As the twentieth century progressed, each generation found itself increasingly in a culture that, on the one hand, displayed sex as a means to sell products and, on the other, taught that sex is a private and perhaps sinful activity. The message seems to be that as long as sex sells a product, it is a necessary evil, but discussing sex as a normal human act is an unnecessary evil. So, however explicit we become about sex, we are no closer to understanding and appreciating its value.

FAMILIAL RELATIONSHIPS AND MARRIAGE IN AMERICAN HISTORY

Families represent a core institution in every society, though the composition of families varies by culture and has varied over time. In the vast majority of societies, families are organized by marriage. And while marriage to more than one partner is legal in many cultures, most people around the world practice monogamy or partnership to one person at a time (Fisher 1992, p. 72). As noted above, pair-bonding is common among human beings.

As we explore what family means to us in society today, it is useful to remember that, until about 200 years ago, the idea of *family* was synonymous with *household*, not with blood ties. In other words, whoever happened to live under the same roof (including servants and farm laborers) constituted the family (Gottlieb 1993, p. 7). The household was the basic unit of production in society. Individuals were not considered fully adult until they were able to afford to marry and have a household of their own, often having to wait many years until they had accrued the necessary capital.

Then as now, parents and the young people in question wanted what was "best" when a marriage match was made. Marriages were often arranged, insofar as parents sought to maximize the status and stability of their offspring's future, as well as their own. The greater the possible gain from such a match, the more likely it was that arrangements were made without regard for personal sentiment; in such cases, people hoped that couples would learn to love each other over time after marriage rather than, as it is practiced today, fall in love and then marry (Mintz & Kellogg, p. 10; Gottlieb, p. 53).

During the colonial period in America, marriages were not tightly arranged by parents, but families did exert a strong influence to marry along class, religious, and racial lines.

Life during the colonial period was very difficult, mortality for infants was high, and life expectancy among adults was not long. Because of the difficulty in getting established, young men usually did not marry before the age of twenty-five and young women rarely before twenty (Mintz & Kellogg, p. 16). As a result the average length of marriage was less than twelve years (Coontz, p. 10). Outside of New England, and especially among the poor, not all couples who lived together were formally wed (Cherlin 2009, p. 50). Indeed, informal marriage was widespread outside of New England until the rise of the "freethinkers" who set in motion a reaction and a crackdown on the practice (Cherlin, pp. 53–54). Formally wed or not, families depended upon each other for their collective survival. Each family was an economic unit that traded in services based upon practical need. This is an important point to understand: historically and cross-culturally, marriage represents a contract devised to house sexual expression and the development of an economic unit (via children) that maintains the viability of the community. Ethnologist Donald Symons succinctly states,

> the human family . . . does not really exist apart from the larger social matrix that defines, creates, and maintains it. For the great majority of humanity—and possibly for all of it before modern times—marriage is not so much an alliance of two people but rather an alliance of families and larger networks of people . . . . Obligations and rights entailed by marriage vary among societies, but marriage is fundamentally a political, economic, and child-raising institution, based on a division of labor by sex and on economic cooperation between the spouses and among larger networks of kin. (1979, p. 121)

The notion of a family consisting only of a mother, father, and their children, set apart from the community, did not exist during the colonial period. Children were doled out to other families for extended periods of time by the age of seven to learn a trade, work as a servant, or attend a school (Mintz & Kellogg, p. 15). There were no boarding schools, orphanages, or retirement homes; raising and caring for children and those who lived into old age were part of the responsibilities of family, kin, or neighbors of the community (Cherlin, p. 40). There were no factories or corporations. Men did not leave the home to go to work; there was plenty of work to do in these agricultural communities. Women did not spend all of their time attending to what we would consider today to be housewife duties (cooking, cleaning, raising children); they also made products and participated in trade (Mintz & Kellogg 1988, p. 12). Moreover, families checked up on each other to make sure they were living by community standards—privacy within the home as we understand it today did not exist (Cherlin, p. 44; Coontz, p. 126; Gottlieb, p. 25).

Yet, despite this interdependence and mutual oversight, there were still some who lamented the decline of moral standards. Within forty years of settling in New England, "colonists feared that their families were disintegrating, that parents were growing ever more irresponsible, and that their children were losing respect for authority" (Mintz & Kellogg, p. 17). This phenomenon of the older generation lamenting social decline is a pattern that seems to repeat throughout history.

Husband and wife worked equally hard in order to maintain their domestic economy, but the laws legitimated male dominance—this was particularly evident in some communities in terms of a type of heritance called *primogeniture*, where property went to the eldest son and not to the mother upon the death of the father. However, as the colonies grew in size and the notion of independence spread, ideas about marriage changed. Population growth and density made land ownership more competitive, and this had the consequence of undermining the father's dominance: He had less land to pass on to his children and his children became more inclined to venture further from home in order to establish themselves (Mintz & Kellogg, pp. 18–19).

The more distance young people gained from their elders, the more they were exposed to different beliefs and practices; for instance, people began to talk more and more about love as a reason to marry. Moreover, as agrarian domestic economies in local communities were replaced by factories in cities, the roles of husbands and wives diverged. The husband was now leaving home to work and the formerly integrated worlds of private and public life split apart. The role of husband was to be increasingly defined as breadwinner and the role of wife was to be increasingly defined as homemaker. There were pros and cons to this split: while families gained in terms of privacy, they would increasingly lose the familial support system garnered from strong community bonds.

In classic Durkheimian terms, the division of labor in society gave rise to more specialized roles, and with this specialization came an increasing awareness of self. Couples increasingly recognized that mutual rights and the acknowledgment of differing emotional needs were a part of marriage. In time the "companionate marriage" would come to describe the ideal relationship. This ideal was defined by "mutual affection, sexual attraction, and equal rights" (Mintz & Kellogg, p. 115).

However, a number of factors worked against the realization of this ideal. First of all, men and women were now working in different domains and facing unique challenges—working in different worlds added to the complexity of effective dialogue. Second, equal rights did not really exist for women in both the private world at home and especially in the public world of employment. Finally, as love and sex became more of a reason to marry and men and women considered their own emotional needs more, differences between the sexual needs and wants of men and women came to the fore.

While both men and women sought greater satisfaction from sexual relations, the possibility of pregnancy always weighed more heavily upon women (D'Emilio & Freedman, p. 80). This contributed to a sexual double standard: as men and women sought to explore the pleasures of sexuality more, the moral burden and responsibility of dealing with one of the natural consequences of engaging in sex was placed squarely on the shoulders of women. (Because men do not carry the biological burden of pregnancy, they are generally less selective of partner and timing. These opposing interests play themselves out in most relationships, and unless women occupy positions of power and authority, norms and laws will side with the interests of men, and men will not see these social conditions as self-serving, but rather as "normal" and "natural." In other words, unless women can control the means of reproduction, their interests are compromised.)

All of these factors gave couples more options, but it also placed greater strains on couples. In the mid-nineteenth century, many states passed more permissive divorce laws. By 1889 the United States had the highest divorce rate in the world (Mintz & Kellogg, p. 109).

Even though industrial growth was tremendous at the beginning of the twentieth century, most of the wealth went to a minority of America's people. A dramatic rift between rich and poor emerged, and with this grew a large number of mothers into the workforce. Many poor mothers worked at night so they could care for their children during the day. In other cases, children might be left by themselves all day—over a century ago, newspaper articles were published warning of the harmful effects of what they called *"latchkey" kids* (Mintz & Kellogg, p. 162). While some people emphasized the positive side of these times: more rights, greater choice, and innovations in science and technology, others focused on the negative: the high rate of divorce and the growing frequency of premarital sex, illegitimacy, and adultery (Mintz & Kellogg, p. 131). During the early years of the twentieth century many bemoaned the decline of marriage and parents increasingly worried about the rebelliousness of youth (D'Emilio & Freedman, p. 198).

The Great Depression and World War II altered marriage and families in many ways. Shortly after the draft was instituted in 1940, many young couples got married before the husband went off to war. During the war, many women enjoyed the opportunity to work in areas formerly reserved for men. With millions of men serving in the military, an unprecedented number of unmarried and married women made up the labor force. When the war ended, the growing trend toward divorce seemed to resume where it had left off before the war. Throughout much of the decade of the 1940s the divorce rate climbed to a record level of one in four (Mintz & Kellogg, p. 171). However, as the 1940s ended and the 1950s began, a new sense of optimism emerged—buoyed by unprecedented economic growth. Coontz observes that "The 1950s suburban family . . . was subsidized . . . by government spending" (p. 76). The Federal Housing Authority and the GI Bill insured and regulated private loans at record low levels of interest to a record number of people (Coontz, p. 77). The government also subsidized new highway systems, sewer systems, and utility services to tend to the needs of the growing number of suburban families. Getting married was in style. The age at which men and women married dropped to twenty-two and twenty, respectively. And between older couples, who had delayed having children because of the war, and younger couples eager to start a family, there was an unprecedented baby boom. Wedding rings, which had become popular in the nineteenth century, were now being supplemented by the diamond engagement ring—a sign of the times of growing affluence and of the increasing influence of marketing and advertising into the private lives of people.

As the children of the boom age grew and the economy grew, more jobs were available than there were people to fill them. However, as more and more of the boomer generation began to enter the labor market, the ratio of jobs to people reversed. At the same time, people—young and old alike— were becoming accustomed to the trappings of suburban life. Throughout the 1960s and 70s, increasing numbers of women entered into the labor market, not only because they wanted to earn their own money and because many found the role of housewife unfulfilling, but also because two incomes were increasingly needed in order to maintain their desired standard of living. Something had to give, and Coontz hit it on the mark when she wrote that "young Americans preserved many trappings of the postwar *economic* dream by sacrificing many aspects of the postwar *family* dream" (p. 266).

By the late 1980s the divorce rate was the highest on record. It would eventually stabilize, but, at around 50 percent, it would be the highest in the world. Today, the United States has both the highest divorce rate and the highest marriage rate in the world: we marry faster and divorce faster than people elsewhere (Cherlin, p. 15). Second and third marriages are more likely to fail than first marriages (Cherlin, p. 18). And the growing number of couples living together or cohabitating are more likely to see the relationship fail than first marriages (Cherlin, p. 23). It turns out that the 1950s were a historical anomaly. The decade did not represent a new trend in marriage and community, but rather a temporary break from the historical movement of self-interest that would resume into the 1960s and thereafter.

LARGE GROUP RELATIONSHIPS: FAMILY, COMMUNITY, WORK, AND CHANGING VALUES

Both micro- and macro-sociological forces push and pull families in opposing directions. The evolving world of work has been one such force. The meaning of work has changed significantly for women over time. Prior to industrialization, women engaged in productive work, like their husbands, in order to keep their family economy together. Identity enhancement was also found within the family economy.

Industrialization split the roles of men and women and made the family dependent on the market. While family and work values once coincided, they increasingly split. When productive work was based on the family economy, men and women shared productive work goals. When family and work goals split, so did the values associated with work. When the family economy was replaced by work and family, the problem of reconciling the differential values associated with work and family was placed exclusively on women. Increasingly work done outside the home was viewed as more valuable than "housework."

In 1963, when Betty Friedan wrote about "the problem with no name" in her seminal book *The Feminine Mystique,* she was touching on the fact that Americans generally have a higher regard for economic values than family values. She helped to give voice to many who were wondering: Why should women feel content with being housewives if the cultural message is that work outside the home is what really constitutes productive work? Why should women not engage in productive work when throughout history they had?

Just as human beings are made to reproduce, they are made to produce or engage in productive work (however defined). People like to work when the work is to their liking (and liking one's work is almost always associated with receiving social acknowledgement). The tensions between needs for self-fulfillment and family/connection intensified as more and more women pursued work outside the home.

As the twentieth century drew to a close, the economic reality of the prosperous 1950s felt like a distant fantasy. More men and women competed to succeed in the marketplace, and more men and women felt stressed in their relationships. Even if a person values family more than work, the pressures associated with economic survival during difficult times lead to a basic cost/benefit analysis: regardless of cost, work provides a rather immediate extrinsic benefit—payment, while the benefits of home are intrinsic and usually not immediate; under duress, the benefits of work seem more compelling (despite its costs) than the benefits of home (with its costs). As a result, the divorce rate rocketed upward.

Other pressures appeared in unexpected packages. The introduction of products such as cell phones and personal computers not only provided more convenience, they also created more work, more time "on," and more time engaged with technologies rather than with other humans. Modern technologies are personalized technologies, so more people today spend time alone even if they do not feel alone because they are "plugged in." Being "on call" more of the time because of technology also means that our time and attention are scattered; we talk on the phone or text with someone while the person sitting right next to us does the same. Rather than seeking out others to connect to, and appreciating connection, we long for time to be apart from others and get a little "down" time. Personalized technologies—each person texting or talking on an individual device, or listening with headphones to a custom blend of music, or sitting alone in a room streaming video—remove an opportunity to learn about cooperation and other social skills and add to the strain of family relationships.

Finally, the trend of maximizing personal space and self-interest that has been occurring within families has also been occurring between families. For example, gated communities have created physical barriers separating one neighborhood from the next, delineating increasing gradients of insularity and exclusivity. In sum, as the twentieth century came to a close, there were many more centrifugal forces pulling families apart than centripetal forces pushing them together.

STRESS AND DISTRESS

The research on work-family conflict makes clear distinctions among internal and external stressors and distress (Story & Bradbury 2004; Randall & Bodenmann 2009). *Internal stressors* refer to stressful events that occur within families (e.g., differences of opinion), while *external stressors* refer to stressful events that spillover into family functioning (e.g., loss of a job). Couples tend to handle internal and external stressors somewhat differently, in part because they usually have more control in ameliorating the internal stressor. *Distress* refers to the negative reaction of the individual to the internal or external stressor. Because Americans place great value on individualism, a great deal of pressure is placed on persons to handle stressors over which they may have little control. Although people can control their level of distress to varying degrees, prolonged or chronic stress leads to *ego depletion* or wears down a person's cognitive strength. While most people respond with distress to finding work in a competitive marketplace, stress research suggests that anticipation of a stressful event, such as losing a job, may produce even greater distress (Sverke & Hellgran, 2002).

The biological substrate of the effects of chronic stress on health was described by neuroendocrinologist Bruce McEwen (2005) as *allostasis*. Ongoing stress taxes the body's ability to function normally or in homeostasis. Chronic hypertension, major depression, and chronic sleep deprivation are symptoms of allostasis. Researchers Nancy Adler and Alana Snibbe state,

> Exposure to acute and chronic stressors, including those associated with lower socioeconomic status elicits a cascade of cognitive, affective, and biological responses. These responses are often functional in the short run, but over time

may damage systems that regulate the body's stress response. . . . [Allostasis] is the cumulative wear and tear caused by repeated adaptations. (2003, p. 121)

Despite the profound growth in technology and inexpensive consumer goods since the 1970s, the ongoing changes in the job market since that time have been an external stressor for most American families. While political leaders such as Ronald Reagan have said, "Strong families are the foundation of society" (Coontz, p. 94), very few policies implemented into law have created safeguards to assist families in adjusting to the global economy or have served to cushion the fall of families that could not withstand the ongoing stress. Job loss and unemployment have been associated with child abuse, decreases in mental health, and marital and family dissolution. In particular, financial strain can produce a self-perpetuating negative pattern of interaction among couples (Vinokur, Price, & Caplan 1996). Psychologists Neil Jacobson, William Follette, and Debbie McDonald have observed that "events are particularly salient for distressed couples" (1982, p. 707)

Distressed partners react more strongly, both negatively and positively, to each other than non-distressed couples. Jacobson and his colleagues state: "In distressed relationships, a . . . negative event delivered by one spouse is more likely to be reciprocated in kind . . . . Thus, the reaction to negative events makes them 'distressing,' as much as does the mere occurrence of those events" (p. 712). Under duress, couples create a pattern of relating that repels each of them, and instead of recognizing that they are coproducing the interaction, they react to the interaction as though they are independent agents. Distressed couples are more likely to fall into the *illusion of transparency* or overestimate how apparent their internal states are to their partner, and they are more likely to commit the *fundamental attribution error*, mistaking a behavior associated with a situation for a personality trait. Of course couples experiencing major stressors are also likely to have low sexual desire and this generally contributes to dissatisfaction in the relationship (Bodenmann, Ledermann, & Bradbury 2007; Bodenmann et al. 2010).

In sum, while attempting to manage the level of distress as an individual, a person may lose the emotional and cognitive resources necessary to maintain the perspective that a relationship is a dynamic dyad. A relationship is not merely a partnership between agent Alice and agent Ben; it is also a group of two that is more or other than the sum of its parts: Alice without Ben and Ben without Alice cannot form a "we." This "we" is produced by an identification that is shared by each partner; and this identification is maintained by each partner's ongoing global evaluation of the relationship.

Couples maintain global and specific evaluations of each other and their relationship (McNulty & Karney 2001; Neff & Karney 2009). *Global evaluation* refers to a person's overall view of the other and their relationship. *Specific evaluation* refers to personal attributes of the other or particular

events that may occur on any given day. Specific evaluations tend to fluctu-
ate more frequently than global evaluations. If a couple has an argument,
their specific evaluation of the other and their relationship at the time will not
be positive, but as long as they are able to separate this specific evaluation
from their global evaluation (assuming that it is positive), the relationship
will endure. However, under duress, the ability to maintain the distinction
between specific and global evaluations becomes more difficult to maintain:
People become depleted of the emotional and cognitive resources necessary
to see the forest for the trees. As each partner reacts to the other's distressed
state, each is more likely to merge specific with global evaluations of the
other and the relationship. Research by psychologists Lisa Neff and Benjamin Karney aptly summarize the issue:

> Results revealed that at times when spouses were experiencing higher levels of
> stress than normal, they engaged in a less adaptive processing of daily relation-
> ship experiences, exhibiting a stronger covariance between their daily global
> satisfaction and their specific perceptions. Conversely, at times when stress
> was lower, these same individuals maintained a greater separation between
> their daily satisfaction and specific experiences. Thus, though person-centered
> variables . . . may predispose certain individuals toward a more adaptive
> processing of daily relationship experiences, these results speak to the impor-
> tance of recognizing how those general relationship skills may be constrained
> by changing situational factors found in the couples' environment. (2009, p.
> 446)

The value we place on individual and psychological problem-solving can
undercut our ability to problem-solve in a more all-inclusive way.

INSTITUTIONAL INFLUENCES ON INDIVIDUAL THINKING

Government programs to assist families date back to when pioneers and
ranchers were able to stake out claims of land because of federal land grants
(Coontz, p. 73). The government helped states to finance land-grant colleges,
which assisted families and the development of the West (Coontz, p. 74).
Suburbanization in the 1950s was aided by the GI Bill. Betty Friedan stopped
short of discussing the whole situation when she wrote about the "problem
with no name." The problem is not just about work in the home versus in the
marketplace; it is also about the definition of work itself and the values
associated with work, family, and community.

Freedom means little without independence and self-sufficiency, yet
when the family economy split into family and work, self-sufficiency became associated with wages and consumerism, and the trend toward valuing
work over family was established. Because personal identity is tied to usefulness and self-sufficiency, when productivity and self-support became tied to

work outside of the family, identity became tied to work outside of the home. Though the home is still sometimes viewed as a "haven in a heartless world," the marketplace has become *the* place for achieving recognition for identity enhancement. Carlson and Kacmar note that in regards to work-family conflicts, as people invest more of themselves in one domain, that domain becomes important to their self-image and affects both domains of work and family (2000, pp. 1034, 1037). Moreover, the less-valued domain is perceived to be the source of conflict, which heightens the perceived level of dissatisfaction in that domain. While the topic of "family values" is frequently addressed in the media, the ways in which work has trumped the family runs so deep that it is difficult to address sufficiently on television; it is subtly reflected in our priorities and how we think and talk about our individual and relational goals. This is not to say that people do not value their family; rather, work values take precedence in powerful yet understated ways.

Spending time in two or more "domains" can create *role conflict*. Perceptions and expectations at work may contradict those of one's home life. For example, an adult who tells a child to never tell a lie at home may engage in a great deal of "puffery" (e.g., this is the best product in the world; s/he offers the best service in America) at work. One way of keeping conflicting expectations and values from causing personal confusion is by *compartmentalizing* them in one's mind. The person engaged in the work role is separated from the same person engaged in the home role. In modern mass society, this commonly leads to the ironic situation in which the same people are unwittingly both the contributors and beneficiaries of living in a "heartless" world. Compartmentalizing may also lead people to minimize the consequences of their actions by rationalizing them as being necessary in order to receive a wage. Compartmentalizing one's life in order to avoid role conflict leads to another type of conflict; the effort required to keep separate the roles that the same person engages in can lead to the depletion of cognitive resources, meaning that one has less energy to deal with issues at home. For example, a person may expect to be left alone or not bothered at home because they can't get that at work, but this demonstrates that however compartmentalized their thinking may be, their work lives are spilling over into their home lives. Because work is viewed as a necessity and home a luxury, many people are going to put more of their energy into getting and keeping a job than in maintaining a family. Families adjust to changing working conditions, but unstable working conditions destabilize families. Moreover, in the past forty years roles in the home have changed in important ways that roles in the workplace have not. Roles at home have become more subject to negotiation, which has had the effect of making them both more egalitarian and ambiguous. Modern couples struggle to make sense of roles that have lost their meaning, and sometimes a clearly defined role at work just requires a lot less effort.

Compartmentalizing, which works better for the work role than the home role, is but one of the cognitive devices that people use today to cope with work-family conflicts. Because roles at work may be more clearly defined today than roles at home, this does not mean that a person's role will always be the same. Though a certain amount of variety is preferable, in today's workplace, a person's role or roles may change frequently. In today's service economy, it is important to have flexible skills and be open to change. While flexibility is a valuable cognitive style to possess, its spill-over effect in the home adds to the ambiguity that already exists there. Even though a certain amount of flexibility of mind is very adaptive for coping with changes in both the workplace and the home, it is ill-suited for coping with the idea of permanence. Sociologist Marlis Buchmann states,

> [I]ncreased flexibility . . . of life course patterns provides structural support for a logic of action oriented more toward the present than toward the future. The individual's time horizon tends to shorten, and there is a greater emphasis on immediacy. The present is perceived as the "here and now," rather than as an element in the movement from the past to the future. (1989, p. 77)

Continuous adaptation to change increases one's focus on the present, and though this can lead to a greater awareness of how present choices establish future possibilities, it can also merge specific and global evaluations of one's circumstances (which runs counter to maintaining long-term relations). *Flexibility*, like compartmentalizing, is a cognitive style that appears to be more adaptive in the workplace than in the home.

Another change in the workplace is the increasing requirement of managing displays of emotions in communication. For example, many service jobs require interactions with customers. In order to create an environment conducive to a positive or particular experience, or to simply make sure that a transaction runs smoothly, an employee may be required to receive training on not only what to say but how to say it; the display of a smile may be a minimum requirement. Arlie Russell Hochschild points out that the containment of negative emotions and the encouragement of courteous behavior is potentially very good, but the routine summoning up of emotions that a person doesn't feel can lead to a generalized detachment from feelings (1983, pp. 9–21). A person, who must smile all day as part of their work, may come home and not want to exercise those muscles any longer. However, the issue runs more deeply than this—emotional management can become a skill that is difficult to not turn to in private life; it may be easier to manipulate circumstances rather than be genuine, although under these circumstances, people may look at each other and wonder where are all the "real people"? Emotional management could be used to deepen one's self-understanding and understanding of oneself in relationship to others, but it is not used to achieve that aim under ordinary circumstances. *Managing emotions* is yet another cognitive style that works well in the workplace, but, once it is brought home, it may be used as a way to not get in touch with genuine feelings. Rather than adding clarity to interpersonal relationships it may also create a front that serves as a safe haven from loved ones. Sociologist Eva Illouz states,

> Instilling a panoply of procedures to manage emotions and to substitute for them adequate and standard speech patterns implies that emotions are increasingly . . . disentangled from concrete . . . actions and relationships. The precondition to "communication" is, paradoxically, the *suspension of one's emotional entanglements in a social relationship.* (2007, p. 38)

Alternatively, individuals could decide to forgo any use of emotional management after having employed it all day, with the expectation that loved ones can handle the unedited version of their emotional displays. All of these scenarios point to how a cognitive style used in the workplace can spill over and adversely affect relations in the home.

The "problem with no name" is the fact that, for most people, work conveys usefulness, yet the work itself is devoid of purpose for most people. Nevertheless, the workplace remains one of the few gathering places left where people can interact in person. Interactions follow prescribed guidelines in terms of roles, immediate gratifications tend to come more frequently at work than at home, and American culture emphasizes work as a paycheck and consumption. As a result, work is valued more than family; the values of work spill over into the family more than the values of family crossing over into work. Many people seek to escape from home in order to work—people will work on any day and any time.

Yet work does not provide what many dream of it providing. Women's wages continue to lag behind men's wages, and wages for minorities continue to lag behind the wages of Caucasians. Theodore Cohen adds, "Most men are not 'movers and shakers' but rather employees in jobs that deny them the opportunity to fully realize the American dream of success. Despite fairly widespread belief in the 'achievement ideology,' where hard work and ability yield success, most men fall short of their ultimate goals" (2001, p. 278).

The separation of work and home, the transformation of work from self-sufficiency and independence to wages and consumerism, conflated (with a lot of assistance from government officials, psychologists, marketers, and advertisers) consumption with personal identity. Modern capitalism is hardly conceivable without combining consumption and selfhood. About a hundred years ago Thorstein Veblen coined the term *conspicuous consumption* to describe the behavior of buying objects for the purpose of displaying income or wealth (Veblen, 1899). Credit allowed more people to engage in conspicuous consumption. What few people seem to realize, though, is how much conspicuous consumption ties personal identity to objects and orients values toward materialism. People who depend upon a wage in order to engage in conspicuous or *compensatory consumption* (i.e., consuming in order to take the edge off of disappointment) tend to have a materialistic attitude in terms of work and family: time for family is viewed as interfering with the fulfillment of material goals (Promislo et al. 2010, p. 939).

People may believe that spending many hours at work conveys a dedication to preserving their family, but what it actually conveys is a materialistic outlook on life, that their values are work oriented and not family oriented. People are working more and more not necessarily in order to achieve their own personal goals or to secure their family life; they are working more and more because they feel they have to and because on some level they want to. We, as a society, have a value system that is not family friendly.

The connection between work, family, and identity is also apparent when someone loses a job. A substantial body of research shows that job loss and unemployment have adverse effects on physical and mental health (Price, Choi, & Vinokur, p. 2002). Unemployment increases depression, which adds strain to a relationship. If one spouse is employed and the other is not, issues usually arise about equity or "carrying one's fair share of the load." The fact of the matter is that chronic stress is higher at the lower end of the socioeconomic scale (Turner, Wheaton, & Lloyd 1995). Hence, it is not surprising that, despite tabloid stories of celebrity divorces (which sometimes give people the false impression that break-ups are more common at the top of the economic scale), divorce rates appear to go up as incomes go down. It is unfortunate that in today's economy two salaries are needed for most people to maintain a consumption-oriented household of four. The irony is that a work- and consumption-driven household oftentimes destabilizes a family's ability to stay together and get ahead (Story & Bradbury).

The value system that drives today's focus on wages and consumption links money and goods to happiness. Richer people, on average, do report higher subjective well-being (Frey 2008, p. 27). This association is tied to the fact that richer people have greater access to the resources they can use to address both predictable and unanticipated problems. However, the relationship between money, goods, and happiness is one of diminishing returns. A recent study analyzing over 450,000 responses made by 1,000 individuals over time concluded that emotional well-being does increase with higher income, but only up to about $75,000—above which the benefit does not increase (Kahneman & Deaton 2010). Frey states, "[A]s people predict their well-being in the future when experiencing a higher material living standard, they mistakenly apply current aspirations . . . and expect to be happier, not realizing that their aspirations will adjust over time" (p. 41). People's aspirations acclimate to their income level. As a person's income increases, so do their interests in more expensive goods and services. Researchers refer to this process as *preference shift*. Bruno Frey reports that "the 'preference shift' through higher individual income is found to 'destroy' 60–80 percent of the expected welfare effect of an increase in income" (p. 38).The anticipated gains from an increase in income are absorbed by greater demands for more within about a year (Frey, p. 131). In a consumer society people are not inclined to evaluate how quickly they adapt to their consumption of goods. In a consumer society people are motivated to achieve immediate and extrinsic rewards at the expense of achieving long-term and intrinsic rewards.

In such a society people are not inclined to evaluate how nonconsumptive activities resist adaptation. For example, a person may have little time and energy left for relationships after investing a lot of time and energy in working and consuming the latest product. In this situation, a person has chosen work and consumption over time with others. This decision typically reflects a calculation that suggests that work and consumption will be more rewarding than time spent with others. However, when people resist the consumption-based calculation, they usually recall how intrinsically rewarding it is to be in the company of others they care about and others that care about them.

Happiness appears to be a by-product of two primary factors: physical well-being and social well-being. After health and social well-being, other factors such as status and behavioral confirmation play a supportive role in contributing to happiness (Frey, p. 5). Certainly, temperament also plays an important role in achieving happiness. However, the basic point here is that, despite the frequency of messages in popular culture and advertising that associate consumption with happiness, the research on happiness clearly shows that "those individuals who prize material goods more highly than other values in life tend to be substantially less happy" (Frey, p. 29). Past a certain point, self-interest undermines the well-being and happiness of the self. I refer to this phenomenon as the *suffering of self-interest*, and it is produced by valuing a distorted view of the self—a self that is more needful of products than of people. This constitutes one of the most insidious "externalities" of modern capitalism.

In many ways the United States is a great experiment in freedom. A part of that experiment in freedom is capitalism, and an important part of modern capitalism is marketing and advertising. Now, an experiment is only as useful as the analysis and implementation of its results. It seems very possible that taken to an extreme, capitalism, marketing, and advertising can blunt progress toward "life, liberty, and the pursuit of happiness." Human beings are social animals, yet the prevailing message today is that of *self-contained individualism*: Everything is to be done by the self and for the self.

This emphasis on individualism comes at a time in history, ironically, when human beings have never been more interdependent: We don't grow our own food, we don't make our own clothes, we don't build our own homes, and we don't educate our own children. The fact of the matter is that capitalism depends upon interdependence, but marketing research shows that the concept of "rugged individualism" best sells the products that we make interdependently. As a result, we live with a distorted view of ourselves as individuals, and we feel it, but we cannot articulate it to ourselves because it is not a part of the nation's consciousness and media-driven conversation about itself. This is part of the "problem with no name," and because it lacks a label it is treated with a wide range of medications—antidepressants, anti-anxiety drugs, sleep aids, drugs for attention deficit disorders and hyperactivity, and so on (Horwitz 2003; Putnam 2000; Cushman 1996).

THE CULTURE OF DIVORCE AND THE CULTURE OF INDIVIDUALISM

While the divorce rate continues to hover at around 50 percent, there are more and more people delaying marriage, cohabitating, or living alone. Economic pressures are an important contributor to this trend, but other factors are also at play, such as a culture of divorce and a culture of self-contained individualism. One of the consequences of a high rate of divorce is a larger number of children experiencing family breakup. A substantial body of research shows that "parental divorce increases the likelihood that their offspring will divorce" (Bradbury & Karney 2004, 869; Cherlin 150). As the pool of young people who have experienced their own parents' divorce increases, the number of people likely to divorce also goes up. In this way, divorce becomes more normative than taboo and a *culture of divorce* is created: However painful it may be, divorce becomes a more likely option than working through issues. In addition, stressors affect behaviors associated with coping, and if one or both partners have acquired feelings of intense vulnerability while in relationship, then when relations do get challenging or are undergoing change, partners are more likely to retreat from each other and exit rather than work together on their coping skills. Karney and Bradbury state, "[M]arried couples must adapt to a variety of stressful events . . . over the course of their lives. The capacity of a couple to adapt depends on the degree of stress they experience and the enduring vulnerabilities that each spouse brings to the marriage" (1995, p. 26).

While there are more and more people living alone or living in shared homes, married men and women enjoy better physical health, psychological well-being, and live longer because they have more social support and financial resources (Ross, Mirowsky, & Goldsteen 1990, pp. 1061–1065; Frey, p. 88). The unmarried experience more stressors than do the married, and a powerful yet understated stressor is social isolation (Aneshensel 1992, p. 34). "[S]ocial isolation has an impact on health comparable to the effect of high blood pressure, lack of exercise, obesity, or smoking . . . . [C]hronic feelings of isolation . . . accelerate the aging process" (Cacioppo & Patrick 2008, p. 5). The ideologies of "rugged individualism" and self-contained individualism, economic stressors, and a wide range of technological products that contribute to isolation (e.g., talking with someone who is not in your presence while ignoring those who are, or texting someone because you're not sure of what to say) all contribute to loneliness. The problem with loneliness is that the longer it lasts, the more difficult it is to get out of. Chronic loneliness leads to the erosion of whatever social skills a person may have acquired; it contributes to selfish behavior and it leads to a distorted view of others (Cacioppo & Patrick, pp. 161, 216). Loneliness contributes to a state of mind and affect that signals to others, "Stay away," and rather than seeing how you are pushing others away, you only see their reaction to you. Consider that if more and more people live this way, then their collective actions produce, ironically, an environment of increasing social isolation.

TECHNOLOGY AND THE DEMISE OF SOCIAL SKILLS

This trend toward increasing social isolation was documented in Robert Putnam's widely cited book entitled *Bowling Alone* (2000). According to Putnam community involvement has been declining at a rapid pace since the 1970s (p. 60). Economic insecurity, the trend toward temporary and flexible employment, the increase in divorce and cohabitation, individualized and isolating technologies, and the ideology of self-contained individualism—all conspire against civic and social engagement. Consider that more and more children are spending their time watching television or playing on a computer rather than playing together. Even if a group of children is watching television or playing a video game, the focus of attention is on the technology and not each other. This undercuts the development of social skills. "Adolescents spend more time alone than with family and friends" (Putnam, p. 264). Rather than talking to each other, young people and adults sit or walk together, each talking or texting with someone else.

The most popular form of entertainment today is television (Putnam, p. 222). Watching television requires minimal effort and it helps pass the time—an overstimulated population is also a population that is easily bored, and so a device that passes the time feels cathartic. However, "More television watching means less of virtually every form of civic participation and social involvement. . . . [H]eavy television viewers are . . . significantly less likely to belong to voluntary associations and to trust other people" (Putnam, pp. 228, 234). Television is at least mildly addictive, and so whatever tears us away from the screen is likely to be felt as an irritant (Kubey & Csikszentmihalyi 1990).

The Internet enables people to stay in contact with more people who may be spread apart, but it undermines reaching consensus on civic issues because only like-minded people are talking to each other. Modern technologies focus consciousness on the technology or what's on the technology, and so it distracts us from engagement with others. Television programming manipulates the signals that people depend upon to communicate in order to sell products and the Internet and texting undercut the acquisition, or the honing of social skills.

NATURALLY CONNECTED

In the 1980s neurophysiologist Giacomo Rizzolatti isolated a sensory system in the brain that he named *mirror neurons*. According to Rizzolatti and Craighero,

> Each time an individual sees an action done by another individual, neurons that represent that action are activated in the observer's premotor cortex. This automatically induced, motor representation of the observed action corresponds to that which is spontaneously generated during active action and whose outcome is known to the acting individual. Thus, the mirror system transforms visual information into knowledge. (2004, p. 172)

Mirror neurons stimulate resonance with others or create a sense of shared experience (Cacioppo & Patrick, pp. 154–155). For example, Chartrand and Bargh (1999) conducted an experiment where subjects were asked to choose pictures that they thought were very stimulating. Meanwhile, a confederate (i.e., a researcher pretending to be another subject) was also in the room completing the same task while deliberately either rubbing their nose or shaking their foot. It was found that the real subjects mimicked these behaviors of the confederates. If two people are facing each other and one crosses their arms, the other person is likely to do so (Cacioppo & Patrick, pp. 117–118). Why is the home team always more likely to win in a game of sport? It is not just due to familiarity with the environment, it is also due to the collective and coordinated cheers of the audience—athletes themselves will say that they feed off of the enthusiasm of the crowd. How is it possible for improvisational jazz to become music? People get into a mutual groove. When we observe another yawn or laugh we feel the urge to yawn or laugh. In an experiment by Bavelas et al. (1986), subjects mimicked the expression of pain upon observing a confederate seemingly drop a heavy object on their foot and grimacing. Mirror neurons not only stimulate imitative responses, they also provide a flexible coding of actions between persons that enables coordinated and complementary actions (Iacoboni 2009, p. 660).

Human beings have developed an elaborate system of social signaling, yet, I sometimes wonder if it is possible for people to lose this capacity. If people are overstimulated, stressed, or find that the signals they depend upon are being used for ulterior motives (like selling products), they may be more inclined to try to control their initial response to others and not respond. Economic problems only exacerbate the tendency of people to recoil. Putnam notes that "People . . . who feel financially strapped are much less engaged in all forms of social and community life" (p. 193). Moreover, children who have experienced the breakup of their families tend to have more behavior problems than children who have not had this experience (Cherlin, p. 22). Behavioral problems undercut the establishment of healthy relationships. While many people are engaged in self-help and support groups, membership in such groups tends to be fluid and the focus is usually on the individual (Putnam, pp. 151–152). The fluidity of relationships was one factor that prompted sociologist Zygmunt Bauman to use the word *fluid* to describe social conditions in modern society—people today, like fluids, are perpetually available and prone to change (Bauman 2000, p. 2).

Many years ago Emile Durkheim ([1897]1997) wrote about the importance of social integration for the health and welfare of individuals and communities. Today, Putnam writes,

> Countless studies document the link between society and psyche: people who have close friends and confidants, friendly neighbors, and supportive co-workers are less likely to experience sadness, loneliness, low self-esteem, and problems with eating and sleeping. Married people are consistently happier than people who are unattached, all else being equal. (p. 332)

Yet the factors that would make for happiness are undermined in multiple ways by the priorities we have established for ourselves in society. Our atomistic view of the self has been generalized into an atomistic view of the family. As each individual is viewed as an island unto himself or herself, families are also considered as separate units. However, one does not need to get into the issue of privacy to realize that what affects one family can have a domino effect on other families. For example, neighborhoods live or die by the number of families who lose their homes due to foreclosure. Self-interest taken to extremes undermines individual and collective well-being; it produces what I have called in this chapter the *suffering of self-interest.*

MODERN MARRIAGE

Before addressing the state of marriage in America today, I believe the reader is entitled to know a little about my own family situation. I married rather late in life. When my wife and I married, she was thirty-three and I was thirty-seven. We each had dated many people, and we each had engaged in cohabitation. This time around, we decided not to cohabitate, though we spent a lot of time at each other's homes. We married after about a year of dating, and we had a beautiful wedding without spending a tremendous amount of money.

My parents were married for many years and died a month apart from each other. My parents quarreled a lot, but they also had fun together. My wife's parents had divorced when she was a young teen. Our marriage has not always been easy, and there have been times when each of us has thought seriously of ending our marriage; however, after twenty years we are still together. Together with our one child, I believe that we are a happy family.

What is the state of marriage in America today? People, young and old, still value marriage (Cherlin, p. 136), but the ability to get established financially takes longer. This is due to the number of consumer goods deemed necessary to possess in order for people, generally speaking, to feel established. In addition, completing college is more important now than in the past, and once a person earns a degree it may be some years before enough money is earned to acquire the trappings of looking established. People are also living longer and may feel in less of a rush to form long-term relationships. People today enjoy greater control over reproduction and there is less of a stigma attached to having a child out of wedlock—both factors that ease the pressure to marry early. In the past, people worked out their lives while they were married, but conditions in many ways warranted it: People lived shorter lives and they needed to combine their efforts in order to survive. In today's climate, while being single (with or without children) comes with its own sets of economic and social challenges, the option of focusing on job and self may ultimately appear to be less daunting and more appealing than the realities faced while nurturing and managing a long-term relationship.

The family was once connected to networks and community associations. These ties helped to diffuse tensions within the family and thereby strengthened family bonds (Coontz, p. 120). The values of self-interest that are learned today and pervade America's institutions cannot serve as a basis for sustaining marriages and families.

As was noted early on in this chapter, marriage is but one institution among many in society, and it is affected by changes in other institutions. Throughout American history, marriage and families have fared better when other institutions have supported them. Organized religion would appear to be one of the institutions that no longer provides sufficient support to marriage and the family. While secular Americans are still more likely to divorce than Americans who espouse religious commitment, religious Americans have a higher divorce rate than religious people in other nations (Cherlin, p. 112). The divorce rate among Catholics, conservative Protestants, and mainline Protestants shows little variation (Cherlin, p. 111). The American South, which is known for advocating conservative religious values, includes six of the ten states with the highest divorce rates in the country (Cherlin, p. 14).

CONCLUSION AND SOME THOUGHTS ABOUT LOVE

A historical glance at the record of marriage and divorce in the United States reveals that like most things, it is cyclical. People have been lamenting the end of marriage for an extremely long time and yet most people, in the United States and throughout the world, marry at some point in their lives. Most people who divorce strive to remarry. I believe the cultural battles over issues affecting families, such as divorce, gay marriage, stay at home mothers versus working mothers, single parenting, abortion, and other issues, stem from a misguided approach to the meaning of human intimacy.

People today adapt their identity to the workforce: scheduling, multitasking, documenting constant "growth," thinking "more is better," assuming conversation is practical or utilitarian. It is this identity that then comes home and unwittingly wants to apply the same techniques that seem to be functional at work to relationships at home. Moreover, people unwittingly apply their work identity when thinking and talking about what is wrong with other people's families.

A work identity with a bureaucratic "let's get down to business" attitude seems absolutely necessary and applicable to most circumstances for most people because the supply of workers greatly outnumbers the supply of jobs in many fields. The battles over issues affecting the family concern, at bottom, an unwillingness to allocate limited resources into areas deemed private. However, I would argue that funding for services such as childcare, housing, healthcare for families, and education is a public issue. Battles over what constitutes a marriage, the legality of the right for a woman to choose her future, and what the "appropriate" role is for a mother (home or employment), divert attention away from the fact that limited opportunities and resources have people chewing out each other because they feel under constant pressure, they feel helpless to deal with the big issues, and the person who needs access to funds that I, too, need is a target that can be easily seen and too readily judged. So each person thinks, "Why can't other people think as logically as I do? I work hard and make sacrifices; why can't others? The problem is that people only think of themselves and what they want!" If enough people in society think this last point, it creates a self-fulfilling prophecy.

The first mistake people make when sizing up other people's family circumstances is assuming that they really understand those circumstances. The second mistake is in assuming that anyone's family operates according to the principles and procedures of a business. Routine may be the first thing a person wants when they come home because of a hectic day working at a job that is persistently asking for change, but routine eventually destroys love. Love is maintained by novelty. Marriage is an attempt to bottle that novelty. Divorce is the realization that that novelty cannot be bottled and the couple feels ill equipped to effect change.

Love is many things, but it is not logical—and neither is having children. Despite the recent popularity of "emotional intelligence," I would say that many people are too afraid to feel: too afraid of not making it, losing what one has gained, not finding love, losing love. And the technologies we employ to connect us, serve to distance us. Intimacy or human closeness cannot be easily scheduled, negotiated, or contracted. Intimacy involves another type of talk and another type of interaction. Romanticism also goes in cycles, and today, it is not faring well.

I would like to end this chapter in an unusual way; most books introducing readers to the study of sociology do not address the topic of love; however, in my view a discussion about marriage and the family is incomplete without some discussion about the meaning of love. Given our atomistic view of the self, it should come as no surprise that, as a culture we believe that love means something different to each person. What love means to me may not be what it means to another.

However, I suggest that implicit in the meaning of love is inclusivity. During adolescence, when young people are searching for identity, it is not unusual for young couples to define their relationship as "us against them." This is "love as exclusivity" and I suggest that it is an insufficient definition of the term. As Erich Fromm said many years ago in his classic essay, entitled *The Art of Loving*, "If a person loves only one other person and is indifferent to the rest of his fellow men [and women], his love is not love but a symbiotic attachment, or an enlarged egotism" (1974, p. 39). Too often people desire in their lover a person who can anticipate and fulfill their every desire. Not only is this an unrealistic expectation, it is not love, but, rather, narcissism. The point is that unless love is recognized as referring to some quality of humanness that transcends each person, then it cannot be love as we like to think of the term, but rather a projected sense of ourselves—in which case, a person can never find love in relationship. Love in relationship requires two people approaching each other, not two people projecting themselves onto the other and failing to recognize the distinctiveness of the other.

The notion of love as the recognition of the universal in the particular (i.e., the recognition of love as a principle derived from a meaningful and deeply caring relationship with another) has a history. Such a definition of love could not have come about without the growing recognition of the value of the person (Swidler 1980). It is this understanding of love that people cling to despite living in times of self-contained individualism. It is this understanding of love, therefore, that we will discuss.

To begin with, a person must recognize how fantasized lovers may have little basis in reality. Wishing that your lover acted like, or looked like a person in a movie or as described in a novel blurs the difference between fact and fantasy. A character in a story is a fiction, and even the person who looks and acts a certain way in a movie, does not really look that way and may not really act that way in person. People like fantasy lovers because they are projections of themselves, but this is egocentrism and not a loving relationship. It takes strength to feel, and it takes strength to be yourself in situations that make you nervous. Intimacy makes many people feel nervous; they feel that their "inner self" is on the line. So sometimes people project an image rather than be themselves. This feels safer than the alternative, but the alternative—being vulnerable with another—is what makes love powerful. Intimacy cannot be obtained by using a business model. Love-making is not fun or meaningful if it is reduced to impression management between two people. Love cannot endure if the relationship is between two people with self-serving ambitions who are willing to terminate relations rather than engage in genuine dialogue about uncomfortably personal issues.

I wonder if people living through times of media saturation, frequent divorces, and job instability ever feel really worthy of receiving and giving love. If not, intimate moments must feel more awkward today than ever before. The "sexual revolution" that occurred during the latter part of the twentieth century increased opportunities for women in the workplace, increased the range of acceptable behaviors for male and female social roles, and loosened norms about sex in the media. But American society still has difficulty articulating social policies that might encourage responsible birth control and family planning, and intimacy in the media is frequently portrayed as something only done by people in their twenties—and it is either of an awkward encounter, a passionate one-night stand, or something that leads to murder. If there were real-life alternative portrayals of learning about intimacy, these media versions would be counterbalanced. As things stand now, the sexual revolution and the technological revolution have merged into new ways of selling products and commodifying intimacy and have done little (with the possible exception of websites like eHarmony) to foster a culture where most people can enjoy doing what they report wanting to do—maintaining a long-term intimate relationship. The sexual revolution increased the acceptance of nudity and sexuality in the media, but it did not convey the fact that learning how to achieve and care for intimacy requires more effort than having sex.

Sociologist Ann Swidler points out some of the contradictions in modern American society that make expressive, long-term relationships difficult. Swidler states, "Modern moral ideals for the self, in particular . . . the demand for continuing growth and change in adulthood, clash head on with the traditional ideal of love as commitment" (p. 128). The demand to demonstrate continual growth and change in the workplace may lead people to not want to feel the need for ongoing growth and change at home; however, relationships minimally require adjustments and adaptations over time.

On the other hand, the ongoing demand for change in the workplace can become a mindset that people take wherever they go. People can come to seek change just for change, or come to assume in every instance that the "grass will be greener" elsewhere.

These factors undercut acquiring the skills necessary to obtain and maintain a mindset focused on commitment. While flexibility is important in the workplace and in the home, the temporary relationships we have today with jobs, people, and gadgets make the work of continually choosing commitment seem like a bigger and harder thing to do. The result is a social situation where more people go in and out of relationships quickly—each wishing to find something unwavering, but each unwittingly working together to produce relations that are informal and unstable.

In a nutshell, the breakdown of social supports from other institutions to sustain families makes choosing commitment to marriage more challenging for the individual. Each person wants a fulfilling life yet has fewer internal and external resources to achieve that goal; the result is more people living alone than ever before (Fisher, p. 305), and a seemingly greater dependence upon entertainment and pills as a way to cope (Putnam, p. 289).

Swidler (p. 137) also notes the contradictory messages in American culture about partnering with another and standing alone. On the one hand, people are encouraged, and deeply desire, to fall in love; on the other hand, people are encouraged to not depend upon anyone else. Love entails mutuality or interdependence. In other words, being a couple does not mean two autonomous individuals who engage in meeting on a regular basis, nor does it mean two individuals who have merged two identities into one. It does entail two individuals learning to communicate about how they each may develop as persons by seeing how they affect and are affected by another. Coupling involves making conscious and deliberate the cognitive, emotional, and behavioral dynamics that naturally and implicitly occur between persons engaged in relationship. A loving relationship involves each person preserving the self while being engaged for the well-being of the other. In this way, coupling or a union is created and maintained.

In many relationships people seek both reassurance and independence from their partner. These contradictory desires create conflict within the individual and for the couple. Human beings tend to react to one another. Healthy relationships are based upon the effective communication and exchange of real needs and realistic wants. Today, the dominant message from popular media, along with the convenience of technology, suggests that talking with a loved one about things that make one feel awkward, vulnerable, embarrassed, or dependent, is too much of a hassle and perhaps a statement that there is something wrong with the relationship or maybe that one is not sufficiently independent. Yet, it is the ability to feel strong in self while exposing one's weaknesses that demonstrates esteem.

Another cultural contradiction noted by Swidler (p. 139) is between sexual expression and sexual restraint. In a culture dominated by values of self-interest and flexibility, and the use of sex to sell products, gratification in sexual relations seems a top priority. Yet, sometimes old ideas die slowly, and so while people feel a desire to express themselves sexually, they simultaneously wonder or feel bad about the demise of long-term commitments. The result seems to be a preoccupation with sex and the inability to enjoy it with the same person for long. Sexual liberation, which held the promise of increasing sexual gratification for both partners and thereby deepening intimacy and emotional attachment, turned out to be less fun and more work than many people expected. Talking about sex rather than talking about having sex turned out to be two different things. Rather than working through issues with the same person, it increasingly seemed simpler to more and more people to move on. And in a culture that feels fast paced and sometimes overwhelmingly complex, stresses the importance of flexibility, and encourages immediate gratification, choosing the path of least resistance makes a certain amount of sense—even if one is ultimately alone.

With the increasing complexity of society and a greater emphasis of putting on fronts and engaging in rational dialogue, people have a harder time understanding acts that seem irrational. Unfortunately, the more rational people have become in some aspects of their lives, the more difficulty they have discussing and understanding the irrational aspects of their lives. Sex is not rational. It is ultimately about reproduction even if that is the last thing on the participants' minds. Marriage as an institution is, in part, about channeling sexual energy and making it meaningful and productive.

Marriage has never been an easy institution to maintain; it has always required external factors (other institutions) to support it or make it necessary (survival). Today, marriage has neither institutional support nor is it necessary for survival. Indeed, divorce may be even good for business—every "broken" home requires another shopping spree.

The current configuration of marriage and the family is metaphorically that of a team or a business. I would say that it is neither. Teams today are less about loyalty and more about competition; marriage and family is about cooperation. Businesses today are about self-interest, flexibility, and the financial bottom-line; marriage and the family are about mutual interest, commitment, and bloodline.

When marriage and the family ceased being independent and local economies and became dependent upon jobs within bureaucratic, corporate economies, there were a series of tradeoffs. The number of goods increased, ties to companies strengthened as ties to family members weakened, a sense of usefulness became tied to activities outside the home rather than activities associated with or supporting the home (irrespective of the fact that however much a company describes itself as a "family," a person can be replaced), and the values of corporate America seeped into the language and activities of family members.

Today, men and women, adults and teens, seek to maximize their interests within bureaucratic structures where they are always expendable, and boast of being an independent contractor within relationships that crave continuity.

Marriage is an old and always evolving institution. As other institutions change over time, so will marriage and the family—for better or for worse.

FOR FURTHER READING

Buscaglia, L. (1996). *Love: What life is all about.* New York: Ballantine Books. An easy book to read that offers a lot of food for thought about relationships and love.

Cherlin, A. J. (2009). *The marriage-go-round: The state of marriage and the family in America today.* New York: Alfred A. Knopf. A very readable and informative book about marriage and the family.

D'Emilio, J., & Freedman, E. B. (1997). *Intimate matters: A history of sexuality in America.* Chicago, IL: The University of Chicago Press. A readable and detailed account of sexuality and social change in American history.

Frey, B. S. (2008). *Happiness: A revolution in economics.* Cambridge, MA: The MIT Press. A not very technical book in economics about what makes people happy from a global perspective.

Fromm, E. (1974). *The art of loving.* New York: Harper & Row. A little dated, but still a readable and thought-provoking discussion about love and society.

Mintz, S., & Kellogg, S. (1988). *Domestic revolutions: A social history of American family life.* New York: The Free Press. A readable and detailed account of marriage and the family in American history.

Myers, D. G. (1993). *The pursuit of happiness: Discovering the pathway to fulfillment, well-being, and enduring personal joy.* New York: Quill. The subtitle is mostly puffery, but the book is very readable and offers valuable insights about what really makes for human happiness.

Neff, L. A., & Karney, B. R. (2009). Stress and reactivity to daily relationship experiences: How stress hinders adaptive processes in marriage. *Journal of Personality and Social Psychology, 97*(3), 435–450. A very informative and well-written journal article about the role of stress in relationships.

Sternberg, R. J. (1986). A triangular theory of love. *Psychological Review, 93*(2), 119–135. A thoughtful discussion about love and relationships from a cognitive psychologist's point of view.

Story, L. B., & Bradbury, T. N. (2004). Understanding marriage and stress: Essential questions and challenges. *Clinical Psychology Review, 23*(8), 1139–1162. Another very informative and well-written journal article about the role of stress in relationships.

Swidler, A. (1980). Love and adulthood in American culture. In N. J. Smelser & E. H. Erikson (Eds.), *Themes of work and love in adulthood* (pp. 120–147). Cambridge, MA: Harvard University Press. A very thoughtful essay about love and society.

Chapter Seven

Religion

I grew up in a home that was not very religious. My parents talked a little about God and fate, but it was never very detailed and it didn't seem to sway their daily decision making a whole lot. I was always very inquisitive about such matters, but adults usually told me to hush up when I asked questions like: What is God like? Where is heaven? If God is good and made people, then why are people sometimes mean?

Many factors and experiences influenced my thinking on these matters. For example, I remember in high school reading the following about truth by Mohandas Gandhi, "One cannot reach truth by untruthfulness. Truthful conduct alone can reach truth" (1983, pp. 306–307). "I will not sacrifice Truth and Non-violence even for the deliverance of my country or religion" (1983, p. 200). I found these insights both comforting and challenging. If you want to know the truth, you must be truthful and honest with yourself in all aspects of your life, including your thoughts and actions regarding power, money, and faith. In some ways it gave me a foundation upon which to explore many powerful themes.

Another influencing experience was a college philosophy course that I took in which the professor spent part of the term arguing against the existence of God and then asked the students in the class to find faults in his reasoning. I really learned a lot in that class about my own assumptions regarding religion. Both my master's thesis and doctoral dissertation were in the areas of religion (the former in the psychology of religion and the latter in the sociology of religion).

In this chapter, we will explore the role of religion in people's lives and discuss the diversity of religious organizations in the United States. We will then examine the history of religion in the United States in order to contextualize the present or give the reader a foundation upon which to think about religion in contemporary society. The final section of this chapter takes a look at why religion remains of vital importance in the lives of most people.

RELIGION AS AN INSTITUTION IN THE UNITED STATES

According to sociologist and Catholic priest Andrew M. Greeley, religion offers to people a sense of meaning and direction, it gives people a feeling of belonging, and it provides a connection between people and "[p]owers that are real . . . [and] frequently mystical and even ecstatic" (1985, p. 16). Religion deals with issues that transcend everyday experience (even if everyday experience is said to be a reflection of the transcendent).

Religion is of particular importance when it comes to grappling with the fundamental dilemmas of being human: Why am I here? Why do bad things happen? What happens when people die? In addressing these questions, religion offers a moral compass for behavior. People value religion because it addresses key concerns and because it instructs people on how to live. Religion enables people to feel that their lives have purpose and direction (even if they are unable to express it or see it clearly), and this creates a sense of empowerment (particularly during difficult or confusing times). When people lack the direction that others derive from religion, they seek it out in other social activities—such as making money or engaging in scientific discovery.

Our understanding of individual purpose and direction, regardless of religious or secular categorization, is a product of temperament, socialization, and the culture and time period in which we live. As Greeley states, "Religion . . . is learned and exercised within a community" (1985, p. 132). Regardless of religious or nonreligious orientation, individuals seek out like-minded people to confirm how they wish to see the world.

Like all social institutions, religion is a product of social action, organization, and institutionalization. Even though survey research consistently shows that the United States is the most religious country in the world among other modern, industrialized nations (Norris & Inglehart 2004; Bader, Mencken, & Baker 2010), religion is a soft institution in comparison to some of the others in American society. For example, while religious beliefs affect how people think about money and economic issues, the economy (which is a hard institution in modern America) has a greater impact on the institution of religion than religion has on the institution of the economy.

The Pew Research Center is a nonpartisan organization that provides data on a variety of social issues, including religion and public life. The following data summarizes a portion of the information on religion that may be found at their website (http://religions.pewforum.org/reports/#): Seventy-eight percent of Americans describe themselves as Christian; however, there is a lot of diversity within this broad categorization. Protestants may be generally divided into three main groups: evangelical churches, mainline churches, and historically African American churches. Among the differences that exist among these three groups is that evangelicals support proselytizing or seeking to convert others to their faith more than the other two groups; mainline Protestants place less emphasis on personal transformation and greater emphasis on social transformation than the other two groups; and the African American Protestant churches incorporate elements unique to their experience in America. Of these three groups, evangelical churches have the largest membership in the United States, with 26 percent of the adult population.

Within these three broad groups, there exist other Protestant groups called *sects* or *denominations*. Under the broad umbrella of evangelical Protestant churches are religious groups such as Baptists, Adventist, and Pentecostal/ Charismatics. Under the umbrella of mainline Protestant churches are religious groups such as Methodists, Congregationalists, and Anglican/Episcopalians. In recent years, evangelical churches have experienced growth in membership while mainline churches have experienced some decline. Baptists, followed by Methodists, make up the majority of Protestants in the United States.

Protestants retain majority status in the United States, however their predominance has dwindled to 51 percent of the population. Nearly 25 percent of the adult population is Catholic, and though they have lost members among native-born citizens in recent years, Catholicism among immigrant populations has made up for the difference. Immigration has also increased the number of Muslims and Hindus in the United States: 0.6 percent and 0.4 percent, respectively. Buddhists comprise 0.7 percent and they are primarily United States-born converts.

Because of the separation of church and state, many observers of religion in America refer to the religious landscape as a marketplace of competing faiths (Finke 1990; Moore 1994). Because the government does not favor any one religious organization, all religious organizations compete for membership in order to sustain themselves. This diversity of options also gives rise to religious experimentation; it is not uncommon for people to switch religious membership. About 44 percent of adults have either changed their religious affiliation, moved from being unassociated with a religion to being affiliated with a religion, or moved from being associated with a religion to being unaffiliated.

The biggest change in recent years concerning religion has been in the growth of the unaffiliated—from about 5 to 8 percent in the 1980s to about 16 percent today. The unaffiliated are comprised of more men than women, mostly between the ages of eighteen and twenty-nine, who describe their religion as "nothing in particular." Only a minority of the unaffiliated describe themselves as being atheists; most vary on a continuum from religion not being important, to religion being important but identification to a particular religion not important. The increase in the number of unaffiliated may be a part of the broader trend noted by social scientists, such as Robert Putnam, who study individual disengagement from social organizations. This trend may be also reflected in the growing number of people who identify them-selves as being "spiritual" rather than "religious." Identification with spiritu-ality typically signifies an individualized belief system—one that incorpo-rates elements from different faiths (referred to as *syncretism*) and weak ties to organized religion.

Religious groups and those unaffiliated with a particular faith are concen-trated in different regions of the country. The Northeast has the greatest number of Catholics and Jews (Jews make up 1.7 percent of the United States population). Evangelicals are well represented in the South, and the West has the largest number of unaffiliated people and Mormons (Mormons comprise 1.7 percent of the United States population). The Midwest reflects the nation-al distribution of evangelicals, mainline, Catholic, and people unaffiliated.

Finally, in terms of marriage, divorce, and faith, Hindus report the highest rate of marriage and the lowest rate of divorce. Members of historically African American churches report the lowest rate of marriage and the highest rate of divorce. Minimal differences exist between evangelical and mainline Protestants in terms of marriage and divorce rates. Marriage rates among Catholics, Mormons, Jews, and Muslims are either about the same or higher in comparison to Protestants, and divorce rates among Catholics, Mormons, Jews, and Muslims are lower in comparison to Protestants.

RELIGION AND THE PARANORMAL

According to survey research, a majority of Americans believe in the para-normal in one form or another (Bader, Mencken, & Baker, p. 129). By *paranormal* I mean phenomena that people see, hear, or experience that seem otherworldly and unexplainable by science. Religious background, educa-tion, income, and gender influence how people describe the paranormal. People who are attached to a religious tradition are inclined to describe paranormal activity in terms provided by their faith. According to Bader, Mencken, and Baker, "The person most likely to view the Earth as a spiritual battleground between good and evil is a conservative/traditionally religious person who is not faring well in the socioeconomic status system by conven-tional standards" (p. 175). People with more education, higher incomes, and who are not active members in a tradition that emphasizes evil are signifi-cantly less likely to believe in the personal embodiment of evil as Satan (Baker 2008). Evangelicals and those with less education and lower incomes are more likely to report extraordinary healings and hearing the voice of God than members of other religious groups as well as people who adhere to some form of personal spirituality (Bader, Mencken, & Baker, pp. 180–181). People who are skeptical of organized religion, yet describe themselves as being religious or spiritual, relate to the paranormal in different terms, such as belief in clairvoyance, personal auras, past lives, and so forth. Many people of varying traditions believe in spirits that guide or protect human beings. Many people of varying traditions as well as people who are not particularly religious or spiritual believe in fate or destiny. The bottom line is that most Americans believe in some form of paranormal activity, but how they categorize it is affected by temperament, religious socialization, and the culture and time in which they live.

UNITED STATES RELIGION IN GLOBAL PERSPECTIVE

Christianity is not only the majority religion in the United States, it has more members than any other faith worldwide. There are approximately five-hundred million Protestants and one billion Catholics worldwide, and there are more than one billion Muslims and more than one billion Hindus worldwide (Norris & Inglehart, p. 49). In their analysis of religion worldwide, Norris and Inglehart report

> In the agrarian societies, religiosity was strong and broadly distributed across most social groups . . . although . . . participation was indeed strongest among the least educated and poorest groups. In industrial societies, however, as secular orientations become more widespread, sharper social differences emerge among the residual religious population. Religiosity remains stronger in industrial societies among the more vulnerable populations. (p. 69)

As people become more secure in their lives, there is a general tendency to move away from collective and traditional religious practices. The trend is most evident in Western Europe (Norris & Inglehart, pp. 85–89), though this does not mean the demise of religion. People still want meaning in their lives, and in modern societies more and more people are seeking meaning in personalized spirituality—a trend most likely popularized as a latent effect of the Protestant Reformation (see below for elaboration).

Even though the United States is less religious than developing nations, it is one of the most religious among industrialized nations in terms of belief in God, prayer, and church attendance (Norris & Inglehart, pp. 70, 216). Social researchers have come up with a variety of theories to explain America's religious uniqueness. According to some social scientists it is America's free market of religion that encourages competition and innovation among religious organizations and this preserves interest in religion in the population (Finke; Moore). Other theorists point to the large number of immigrants with traditional religious beliefs and practices who continually flow into the United States (Pew Forum on Religion & Public Life, 2008). Still other theorists note that even in modern nations, religion tends to be stronger among vulnerable populations (Norris & Inglehart, p. 107). The gap in the distribution of resources in the United States is exceptionally wide and this may help to explain why the country continues to be exceptionally religious. It is probably safe to say that all three factors—religious free market, immigration, and insecurity—play a role in explaining America's unique position of being a highly religious and modern country.

SECULARIZATION

One of the many debates that exist among social scientists interested in religion is about *secularization* (i.e., whether or not religion is declining in society). Many social theorists in the nineteenth century believed that religion would eventually die out as science came to resolve age-old questions and technology came to ease human suffering. Today, we know that for every question science answers, new questions arise, and that technology can alleviate as well as cause suffering on a massive scale. Moreover, and as previously noted, a look around the world today shows that religion in its various guises has billions of adherents. All of this suggests to me that religion serves a purpose for humankind that science and technology cannot address.

There are three main social theories concerning secularization. One theory suggests that religion as an institution is weaker today than it used to be, and even though faith continues at the individual level, this cannot make up for the authoritative role that religion once had over large numbers of people (Bruce 2002). Another theory suggests that secularization is a self-limiting process, that at the point when religious organizations become well integrated with their surrounding social institutions, calls for the revival of old traditions or for the rise of new and innovative ideas and practices give rise to a resurgence in religious enthusiasm (Stark & Bainbridge 1985). Finally, a third theory suggests that changes over time in religious ideas and practices do not mean that religion is of less importance to people, and that there have always existed skeptics (Greeley).

I tend to agree with elements of all three theories: there always have been people who questioned the authenticity of religious beliefs, religions over time appear to make peace with other institutions and then some people want their faith to assert dominance over secular practices, and in many countries today, religion is less communal than it used to be and is more individualized.

Certainly one of the ways in which religion has gained attention in recent years is in terms of conflict between particular Muslim groups and the modern Western world. Many years ago psychologist Milton Rokeach (1965, pp. 9–12) called attention to what he called the *Paradoxes of Religious Belief*, such as the fact that the world's major religions are based upon scriptures supporting collaboration, and yet differences among these religions have often led to antagonism. In some respects, religion is born from conflict as human beings struggle to understand their place in the universe. Religion and spirituality are tied to identity so much, there is little wonder that conflict follows it around.

RELIGION IS INCLUSIVE AND EXCLUSIVE

Religious beliefs function to both integrate and exclude. If you believe that the greatest prophet in history was Mohammad, then you are going to be integrated into one group of believers, but excluded from the group of believers who profess Jesus Christ to be the most important religious figure in history. Even a single faith can serve to integrate and exclude. In the eighteenth and nineteenth centuries many Southern preachers and politicians used the Bible as a means to condone the enslavement of African Americans.

An atomistic view of faith can also lead to exclusionary behavior. The idea of faith as a "personal relationship with God" or some higher being masks some important issues. First of all, sociologically speaking, religion is an institution tied to other institutions in society. A person's religious orientation is tied to social history, economic condition, whether a society is heterogeneous or homogeneous, and other sociological factors. Second, the history of Judaism and Christianity reveals that early believers did not think of their faith in such personal terms. To have a personal relationship with anything requires possessing a vocabulary that focuses on the self, but *self-* as a prefix and the word *individualism* didn't even come into popular usage until the eighteenth century. I sometimes wonder if the phrase "personal relationship with God" is really a modern theology and psychology of self-interest. Third, the expression "personal Truth" is an oxymoron; a contradiction in terms like "jumbo shrimp." The Truth is the Truth because it is applicable universally. A Truth that applies to you, but not to me contradicts the definition of the term; perhaps the word *Truth* is antiquated. Nevertheless, many people are passionate about their religious beliefs, even though there are many views about the Truth.

Because of the separation of church and state in the United States people enjoy religious liberty. There are many pros and some cons to having religious freedom. An obvious pro is the freedom to choose our own place of worship. People often times select a place that presents God in a way that they want to hear or experience it. A con is that sometimes people make the presumption that they know God better than anyone else. This can lead to consequences that are aptly expressed by contemporary writer Anne Lamott, "You can safely assume that you've created God in your own image when it turns out that God hates all the same people you do" (1995, p. 22).

In order to create some space so that a degree of objectivity can be achieved, let's take a look at America's religious roots.

RELIGION IN AMERICAN HISTORY: BEFORE THE REVOLUTION

Where the appropriate place is to begin a discussion of American religious history is debatable. We will begin with Constantine and the Roman Empire and work our way quickly to the times of the American Revolution, and then gradually work our way to contemporary society. If there ever was an Age of Faith where Christianity dominated, it began with the conversion of Constantine I (272–337 C.E.), emperor of Rome, to Christianity, and continued until the fragmentation and collapse of the Western Roman Empire in the fifth century. The Empire survived for another thousand years as the Eastern Roman or Byzantine Empire, but its reach was far weaker, and European leaders found church-state relations increasingly problematic in terms of power and authority. Tensions increased when Pope Gregory VII (1015–1085) declared divine sovereignty over aristocratic authority.

When the German monk Martin Luther tacked his "Ninety-Five Theses" on the door of the church in Wittenberg, Germany in 1517, he did not expect that it would lead to war. What Luther attacked was the sale of indulgences (or the reduction of sins for the deceased) by religious authorities. Luther also translated the Bible from Latin into the vernacular or native language. Luther's actions set into motion the Protestant Reformation. One of the major changes brought on by the Reformation and the translation of the Bible into a variety of languages that more people could read was an increasing emphasis on the individual's interpretation and emotional experience of his or her faith.

At the time of the Reformation, Henry VIII was King of England. Henry had been loyal to the Catholic Church, but when he appealed for an annulment of his marriage to Catherine of Aragon so that he could marry Ann Boleyn, and Pope Clement VII refused, Henry cut ties with Rome and established the Protestant Church of England. When Henry died, his and Catherine's daughter Mary I became the Queen of England. She was Catholic and attempted to undo the Reformation that had occurred in England. Many Protestants were killed and many more fled the country. When Mary died of illness, her half-sister (Henry and Ann Boleyn's child) Elizabeth I acceded to the throne. Elizabeth restored the Protestant Church and England became the dominant Protestant power.

Not all Protestants were satisfied with the Queen's reforms; some believed that the church needed purification. This group acquired the name Puritan and they divided into Separatists (Baptists and Quakers) who believed that the only route to purity was separation from the Church of England and Non-Separatists (Presbyterians and Congregationalists) who believed that the church could be purified from within. The term *denomination* was introduced in the late seventeenth century as a way to describe these different Puritan groups.

England was interested in establishing settlements in America in order to acquire resources and to keep up with Spain, their main Catholic rival, which was already establishing itself as a force in the New World. The first English groups to found colonies in America were Anglicans or members of the Church of England in Virginia, a group of Separatist Puritans in Massachusetts (the Plymouth Colony), and a larger group of Non-Separatist Puritans in Massachusetts (the Massachusetts Bay Colony). Though the English colonies differed in many ways, they shared a belief in religious freedom. According to historian Frank Lambert, "From their past, the various English transplants brought with them a keen appreciation of the tensions running between church and state" (2006, p. 45).

Religious freedom in the colonies meant that people were free in private to interpret Scripture as they pleased; however, people were not at liberty to promote beliefs that varied too far from the Anglican Church in Virginia or the Congregational church in Massachusetts Bay. Catholics, Quakers, and Baptists were discriminated against in Virginia. Persistent preaching by non-Congregational Puritans, such as Quakers, could be punishable by death (Lambert, p. 92). The colonists forwarded religious freedom by showing greater tolerance of religious diversity; however, the testing of the limits of tolerance was not socially acceptable.

Before the Revolution, diverse Native American religions, African religions, Catholics, Jews, and a variety of Protestant faiths coexisted, though not harmoniously, in the New World. Nevertheless, America was on its way to becoming the most diverse nation in the world.

DEISM AND THE FOUNDERS OF AMERICA

George Washington, Thomas Jefferson, James Madison, James Monroe, George Mason, and Patrick Henry all grew up in the Anglican Church (named the Episcopal Church after the American Revolution). Benjamin Franklin and John Adams grew up in Puritan New England. Yet, all of these founding figures of America came to embrace Deism. Deism emerged as part of a new generation of ideas coming from the Enlightenment in the eighteenth century (though its roots go much further back in time). Enlightenment thinkers such as Francois-Marie Arouet (popularly known as Voltaire), Jean-Jacques Rousseau, Denis Diderot, Francis Bacon, Isaac Newton, and John Locke challenged the dominant social, political, religious, and scientific ideas at the time. While attending college at William and Mary or Harvard, many of the Founders learned about, and were deeply influenced by, Enlightenment thought. The basis of Enlightenment thought was the capacity of reason to address human concerns. This is why the Enlightenment period of time (about 1600–1800) is referred to as the Age of Reason.

Deism is revealed in the words of the Founders themselves. While George Washington valued organized religion, he was not a Christian in the conventional or orthodox sense. Bishop White, who was the pastor of the church that Washington attended, wrote, "I do not believe that any degree of recollection will bring to my mind any fact which would prove General Washington to have been a believer in the Christian revelation" (Holmes 2006, p. 163). Washington's speeches, letters, and public communications on religion routinely preferred using terms like "the Deity," "the Grand Architect," or "the Author of all Good" as opposed to terms like *Lord* or *Savior* (Holmes, p. 65). Deism acknowledges a supreme being, but not one that can be known personally. Deism stresses God as the creator of the natural world and suggests that an understanding of the natural world leads to a deeper understanding of humankind and of the forces of creation.

The second president of the United States, John Adams, was an anti-Trinitarian or what became known as a Unitarian. Unitarian beliefs that stem from the time before Christianity adopted the doctrine of the Trinity in the fourth century. Consistent with Deism, Adams stressed the ethical lessons that may be derived from religion. Adams said, "All sober inquirers after truth, ancient and modern, pagan and Christian, have declared that the happiness of man, as well as his dignity, consists in virtue" (quoted in Lambert, p. 246).

Thomas Jefferson, the author of the Declaration of Independence and third president of the United States, read the Bible, and even revised it to reflect what he saw best in it (commonly referred to as the *Jefferson Bible*). Jefferson held Jesus in high regard, but he did not think of Him as a Savior (Holmes, p. 83). Jefferson said, "I am a Christian in the only sense in which I believe Jesus wished any one to be; sincerely attached to his doctrines, in preference to all others; ascribing to himself every human excellence, and believing he never claimed any other" (quoted in Holmes, p. 83). Deism downplays supernaturalism, and views significant religious figures as role models of human moral excellence. Because of their views on liberty and ethics, many of the Founders did not have a high regard for dogmatic beliefs—religious or otherwise.

The Deist beliefs of the Founders are evident in the key documents of the United States: the Declaration of Independence and the Constitution. Contemporary historical and evangelical scholars, Mark Noll, Nathan Hatch, and George Marsden state, "The Declaration of Independence . . . is based on an appeal to 'self-evident' truths or 'laws of nature and nature's god.' The reference to God is vague and subordinated to natural laws . . . . The Bible is not mentioned or alluded to. The Constitution of 1787 says even less concerning a deity" (1989, pp. 130–131). The Founders were not antireligion or anti-Christian—many of them saw real value in religion—but their faith was rooted in Deist rather than orthodox or common folk-religious principles.

James Madison was the main force behind the forging of the Constitution. One of his major objectives was to get disparate partisans to agree on a common document that would solidify the new nation. In order to make this happen, Madison engineered a system whereby no one group could dominate. Favoring no one and giving freedom of speech to all caused competing interest groups to create their own system of checks and balances. From Enlightenment thinkers like John Locke, many of the Founders came to the conclusion that the best way to discern the truth is within an environment of liberty, rather than through a system of following the one with the loudest and most powerful voice, or through a system based upon blind obedience to traditional practices. In this regard, Jefferson said that "truth . . . will prevail if left to herself; that she is the proper and sufficient antagonist to error, and has nothing to fear from the conflict unless by human interposition disarmed of her natural weapons, free argument and debate..." (quoted in Lambert, p. 234). I believe that it is reasonable to say that many of the Founders were forward-looking rather than backward-looking men. A certain amount of determination and optimism is required to look ahead at what might be, rather than behind at what has been. However, it was not just many of the Founders who looked toward the future; a religious movement called the Great Awakening inspired a great many Americans. After describing the Great Awakening in the next section, we will examine all of the major social trends that came together to shape the religious foundation of the United States.

THE FIRST GREAT AWAKENING

At the beginning of the eighteenth century, Anglicanism was the dominant church in the mid-Atlantic Colonies, Congregationalism was the dominant church in New England, and in Rhode Island, New Jersey, and Pennsylvania, multiple denominations wrestled with each other for control (Lambert, p. 129). Regardless of region, local churches maintained a monopoly; no one could preach without permission from the local authorities. All of this would change with the Great Awakening.

From approximately the 1720s to the 1750s, Christian revivalism swept through the colonies. Itinerant or traveling preachers crisscrossed through the land, ignoring local parish boundaries, and stirred up crowds in the thousands about the spirit of Christ and the feeling of grace. The most influential preacher at the time was George Whitefield. Though he expressed an interest in theater in his early years, he wound up attending Oxford. There, he was influenced by a group of young Christian men, including John Wesley—the founder of Methodism (Moore, p. 41). Whitefield and other itinerant Methodist and Baptist preachers challenged the dominance of the Congregational Church in New England and especially made gains in the mid-Atlantic and Southern states where the Anglican Church was dominant. Traveling preachers went to where the people were, expressed the gospel in nondoctrinal and emotional terms, and provided hope and fun to people who were relatively isolated and vulnerable. This is the beginning of evangelicalism in America. Noll, Hatch, and Marsden state,

> The most important effect of the revival on the Revolutionary period . . . was the new model of leadership which it created. . . . [T]raveling evangelists . . . called for direct and responsible response from the people; they encouraged lay people to perform Christian services for themselves that were the traditional preserve of the clergy. Whitefield did not read his sermons like so many ministers did . . . . Rather, he used spontaneous extemporaneous forms of address. His speaking style drove home the implicit point that it was not formal education or a prestigious place in the community that mattered ultimately. It was rather the choice of the individual, the common person, for or against God. (p. 55)

Itinerant preachers added to a strand of thought that had already gained ground in Puritan New England. Strict Calvinists believed that people could neither determine nor alter their destiny. According to John Calvin's doctrine of predestination, people, by God's decree, were either saved or damned from birth and no action in this life could change that. Over time that idea softened. A Dutch Reformed pastor by the name of Jacobus Arminius (1560–1609) taught that salvation or condemnation were not foreordained. Subsequent reformers emphasized individual freedom and personal responsibility. This reformed approach came to be known as Arminianism. The emphasis placed on individual responsibility for salvation among Baptist, Methodist, and Puritan reformers all worked to spread notions of liberty.

The revivals also made religion more fun. People traveled to attend camp meetings not only for religion, but for social reasons—to meet with others, relax, and sometimes drink alcohol (Moore, p. 45). Revivalism was about religion, but it was also about entertainment. As this chapter will make plain, the connection between religion and fun comprises another social trend that will be of increasing importance in the development of religion in America.

THE WALL OF SEPARATION AND CIVIL RELIGION

With growing dissent against the dominant churches in New England and the mid-Atlantic and Southern states, pressures mounted toward religious pluralism. In a pluralist society, no one group has dominance over another, yet each group is free to exist. Though Baptist and Methodist leaders disagreed with Deist leaders on issues of faith, they were of like mind when it came to religious pluralism. In Jefferson's successful bid for the presidency, he quoted Baptist minister John Leland, "Let every man speak freely without fear, maintain the principles that he believes, worship according to his own faith, either one God, three Gods, no God, or twenty Gods: and let government protect him in so doing" (quoted in Lambert, p. 286).

Jefferson and many of the Founders were swayed by the writings of the British politicians John Trenchard and Thomas Gordon. In a collection of influential essays called *Cato's Letters*, published in 1755, Trenchard and Gordon argued that while governments may have power over the affairs of persons, governments cannot give voice to matters pertaining to God's relation to persons. While human beings are the cause of governments, human beings are not the cause of themselves; hence, on the issue of the latter, governments have or should have no say. As a result, there should exist a separation of church and state whereby no one church can dictate the kind of faith that all people must maintain. With support from Baptist and Methodist leaders, and eventually Anglican and Puritan politicians, American leaders came to the conclusion that religious enthusiasm and political power make dangerous bedfellows.

The separation of church and state was intended to achieve two functions: first, to prevent a religious group from having political power, which could then be used against other religious groups, and second, to prevent government itself from intruding on religious expression. Religion was not to dictate political decision making as government was not to dictate religious decision making. In the world today, Iran is an example of a modern society that does not separate government and religion.

Even though religious and political leaders differed on matters of faith, they shared a belief in what is usually called *civil religion* (Lambert, p. 282). The term was first used by the Enlightenment thinker Jean-Jacques Rousseau, and its meaning for the Founders was summed up in the Latin phrase, "*e pluribus unum*," which means, "one from many." The Founders believed that America represented a new order in government and for society. The foundation of this new order was liberty. The guarantee of the freedom of speech among disparate peoples would secure the promise of liberty. Civil religion reflects a belief that America has a special purpose in history, and that purpose is to model to the rest of the world what a free society looks like as well as promote the cause of freedom worldwide. ("Manifest Destiny," an offshoot of civil religion, was the ideological driving force of America's push westward.)

Abraham Lincoln's famous Gettysburg Address and Martin Luther King, Jr.'s "I Have a Dream" speech, exemplify civil religion in their blending of the themes of freedom, America, and God. The civil religion of America is a belief in God along with the right to personal liberty and expression. This God, which is expressed on American currency and in nationalist songs, is nonsectarian or not affiliated with a particular religious group; it refers to the Creator, however defined (thereby protecting freedom of speech and individual liberty). In this way people of different faiths can share in the nation's civil religion. The belief in civil religion, shared by the leaders of America's first generation, enabled them to see the importance of the separation of powers, including the separation of church and state. They were keenly aware of the fact that the association between religious enthusiasm and political power had led to divisiveness in both Europe and the American colonies.

In practical terms, civil religion has often been the ideological force behind America's involvement in foreign wars. People of different faiths join the United States military and are willing to fight together against another nation in part because they believe that the other nation is a threat to the free world, and America's mission, "under God," is to protect freedom in the world. The war against the Nazis, the Cold War against the Soviets, America's involvement in the War in Bosnia and Herzegovina in the 1990s, the invasion of Saddam Hussein's Iraq, are all examples of conflicts that the United States purportedly engaged in to protect liberty throughout the world. Civil religion was the ideological (not political or economic) force driving America's involvement in these conflicts.

RELIGION IN THE NINETEENTH CENTURY AND THE SECOND GREAT AWAKENING

Though the First Great Awakening raised many people's awareness about individual freedom, the religious fervor derived from the Awakening had subsided by the 1750s. The churches once again saw a decline in attendance. Certainly settling into life after the revolution in 1776 must have diverted a lot of people's attention and time. However, by 1801 there was a resurgence of revival camp meetings. One revival at that time at Cane Ridge, Kentucky was said to have included people crying, dancing, and falling into trances.

As Whitefield had been influential during the First Great Awakening, Charles Grandison Finney was influential during the Second Great Awakening. In the 1820s Finney codified a preaching style that would be emulated by subsequent revivalists. Finney encouraged preachers to use "practiced spontaneity" (Moore, p. 50). Finney said that people's attentions had to be diverted away from "worldly excitement," and the best way to do that was through stage acting, looking, pointing, and calling out people's names in the audience, and by engaging in self-promotion and advertising (Moore, pp. 50–51). According to Finney and others aware of America's growing commercial culture, audience enthusiasm could and should be created.

It was also during the Second Great Awakening that Christianity spread through the African American population of slaves in the South. Slavery in the South was a ruthless system that was defended because of its economic significance to the region. While some slaveholders feared that teaching slaves to read the Bible might lead to social unrest, others felt that it could be used to teach slaves that their "proper place" was in slavery. The slaves who converted to Christianity, though, heard a different message. Many could relate to Moses and the Exodus and to a God who loves all of His children equally. Over the course of the nineteenth century, African Americans would establish their own churches. These churches created opportunities for African Americans to acquire positions of leadership, provide mutual support, and become one of the few sources of hope that was uniquely theirs. By the end of the nineteenth century, many African Americans had become Baptists or Methodists in a way that reflected their African heritage and experience in America.

COMMERCIALIZATION OF RELIGION

By 1850 membership in the Methodist and Baptist churches had grown tremendously. As Arminianism replaced the last vestiges of the Calvinist orthodoxy of predestination, John Wesley's doctrine of sanctification spread with the revival movement. *Sanctification* refers to acquiring the feeling of grace. According to contemporary religious studies scholar John Prothero, "…the God-fearing faith of Calvinism yielded to the Jesus-loving faith of evangelicalism, and American religion became less intellectual and more enthusiastic" (2007, p. 46–47). Prothero's point is that religious observances, such as sermons, during the eighteenth century were based upon the explication of dogma that included phrases in Latin only the educated could understand— religious services that were more often solemn than joyous. Revivalist preachers during the first two Awakenings challenged this style, and gradually religious observances included self-disclosure, storytelling, entertaining anecdotes, therapeutic advice, and the means of acquiring personal and financial success.

As people's attentions shifted to the revivalist preachers, other church leaders felt compelled to change their approach. Because no one church was state sanctioned, churches had to compete for members in order to continue to exist. Sociologist Peter Berger describes the circumstances very well:

> The key characteristic of all pluralistic situations . . . is that the religious ex-
> monopolies can no longer take for granted the allegiance of their client popula-
> tions. Allegiance is voluntary and thus, by definition, less than certain. As a
> result, the religious tradition, which previously could be authoritatively im-
> posed, now has to be *marketed*. It must be "sold" to a clientele that is no longer
> constrained to "buy." The pluralistic situation is, above all, a *market situation*.
> In it, the religious institutions become marketing agencies and the religious
> traditions become consumer commodities. (1969, p. 138)

Even as the Puritans in the eighteenth century bemoaned what they considered to be the loss of religious seriousness among younger people, in general,
they separated the sacred from the secular. Before the nineteenth century
merchants did not assume that religious holidays were opportune times to
increase sales and make a lot of money (Schmidt 1995, p. 27). However, over
the course of the nineteenth century it would become increasingly difficult to
discern the difference between secular and sacred.

Concern about the commodification of religious observances is almost as
old as the observances themselves. Social critics and poets expressed concern
that the commercialization of religious holidays trivialized its emotional
underpinnings. However, supporters of the commercialization of religious
holidays outnumbered the critics and their views would ultimately prevail.

Ralph Waldo Emerson was one of the critics of commercialization. In the
nineteenth century, Emerson would come to represent another strand of
American religion and spirituality. Emerson was the chief spokesperson for
Transcendentalism. In many ways it reflected the Deism of the Founders.
Transcendentalists believed that each person's soul was connected to a universal soul. A thoughtful life entails cultivating one's qualities to reflect this
underlying bond. In a famous essay called "Circles," Emerson writes,

> St. Augustine described the nature of God as a circle whose centre was every-
> where, and its circumference nowhere. We are all our lifetime reading the
> copious sense of this first of forms. Our life is an apprenticeship to the truth,
> that around every circle another can be drawn; that there is no end in nature,
> but every end is a beginning . . . . The life of man is a self-evolving circle,
> which, from a ring imperceptibly small, rushes on all sides outward to new and
> larger circles, and that without end. The extent to which this generation of
> circles . . . will go, depends on the force or truth of the individual soul. (quoted
> in Geldard 2005, pp. 125–128)

Emerson, like many other American idealist thinkers of the nineteenth century, was influenced by the writings of Swedish scientist Emanuel Swedenborg
(Taylor 1999, p. 61). Swedenborg was a prolific writer on science and mysticism (e.g., the personal experience of other-worldly states or of a heightened
consciousness of reality). Swedenborg elaborated on the correspondence between the natural and supernatural worlds. Out of an interest in spirits and

metaphysics (e.g., the study of being and mind), there developed the Theosophical Society. Founded by Helena Blavatsky and others, Theosophy developed into an international organization that blended Eastern and Western spiritual traditions, and built up a large catalog of works in mysticism and metaphysics. Psychologist William James and novelist Aldous Huxley would carry some of the ideas developed by the Transcendentalists and Theosophists into the twentieth century. James's *The Varieties of Religious Experience* and Huxley's *The Perennial Philosophy* are classic books on comparative spirituality. Finally, another movement called New Thought, developed by Phineas Parkhurst Quimby and Warren Felt Evans, would become popular over the course of the nineteenth century and have an enduring impact on American culture. In *The Mental Cure* (1869), the first of his many books, Evans wrote that physical illness arises from wrong ideas. From Evans developed practices such as self-affirmations and guided mental imagery for treating illness. Some of the ideas stemming from this body of work would become highly popular through Norman Vincent Peale's book *The Power of Positive Thinking* (1952).

Regardless of a phenomenon's otherworldliness, people can find ways to market it. This would become evident in the years following the Civil War. As industrialization made productive capacity greater, the problem of making goods shifted to the problem of selling goods. Merchants increasingly saw opportunities to sell goods by advertising intensively around religious holidays. As they helped to popularize the holidays, they also changed them. For example, Easter was not widely celebrated as a religious holiday in the United States before the 1860s. The celebration of Easter became widespread shortly after it was apparent that many people liked the commercialization of Christmas—despite criticisms by social critics and poets (Schmidt, p. 195). Indeed, before the end of the nineteenth century people were already shopping for Christmas gifts right after Thanksgiving (Schmidt, p. 186). Some people were already wondering if Santa had become more important than Christ (Schmidt, p. 187). However, as some people bemoaned the loss of the "spirit of Christmas" or the "reason for the season," these very concerns were commodified as slogans on commercial products (Schmidt, pp. 188–189). For their part, religious entrepreneurs increasingly depended upon the same marketing techniques used in business—though merchants sometimes got their marketing strategies from the churches—to attract people to their particular religious organization.

Neither merchants nor preachers intended to transform the meaning of religious symbols and practices. In this way their actions may be described as having a latent or unforeseen effect (as opposed to a manifest or predicted effect). Nevertheless, over the course of the nineteenth century, economic and religious sentiments reinforced each other and, in many respects, became one and the same. For example, consider songs like "It Came Upon the

Midnight Clear" and "Joy to the World," both written in the 1840s, and "White Christmas" and "I'll Be Home for Christmas" both written in the 1940s. All of these wonderful songs conjure up warm or melancholic images and feelings. But when we hear or sing these songs, the feelings we get are fleeting and the images in our mind may have little to do with people we actually know, and may stem more from the commercialization of the holiday. The commercialization of symbols—religious and otherwise—changes what they signify or mean to people.

As churches acquired the tactics of industry and industry acquired the tactics of churches, tensions among various churches mounted about the implications of the Civil War. One key issue was about whether or not Scripture supported or condemned slavery. Religious liberals argued that slavery went against the spirit of Jesus's teachings. Many religious conservatives argued that the Bible condoned slavery. An argument frequently used among adherents of the Bible's legitimating of slavery was the story in Genesis of Noah's curse on his grandson Canaan (Finkelman 2003). In Genesis we read that Ham saw his father Noah asleep naked. When Noah awoke and learned of this, he cursed Ham's son Canaan, declaring that his descendants (who supposedly then settled in Africa) would serve the descendants of Noah's other sons, Shem (who supposedly settled in Asia) and Japheth (who supposedly settled in Europe). The tension over the religious legitimacy of slavery contributed to the growing importance among conservatives of the inerrancy or the literal word of the Bible (the underlying theological issue with political implications was whether the meaning of the teachings in the Bible remains always the same or changes with the times). Historian George M. Marsden notes, "The Bible condemned slavery only if one forsook the letter of the text for the alleged spirit. Committed to the letter of Scripture regarding slavery, southern conservatives were hardly in a position to play fast and loose with other passages that might be interpreted in the light of alleged modern progress" (1991, p. 173).

The ideological divide among the churches following the war would endure in various forms throughout the twentieth century. This divide would also mark historically "the great reversal" of the evangelical movement in the United States (Marsden, p. 30). Since the founding of the nation most evangelicals had been in favor of reform, but after the Civil War and into the twentieth century, a growing number of evangelicals sided against reform.

THIRD GREAT AWAKENING

After the Civil War, the number of small farmers dwindled as cities grew in size. Problems typically associated with urban life ballooned and an unprecedented division emerged between the very rich and the other classes in society (disillusioning many about the prospects for a better life). Industrialization and urbanization were not the only forces changing society; innovations in science and technology were also having an impact. In order to make sense of the changes taking place, men and women arose with novel explanations and solutions. This would give rise to the Third Great Awakening (about 1890–1920).

The Third Awakening reflected and reinforced the split in the churches. Generally speaking, it was led by two groups, right-wing or conservative evangelicals who emphasized individual behavior, economic laissez-faire, and inerrancy, and left-wing or liberal Protestants who emphasized collective action and the spirit of the Bible, particularly the message of the Golden Rule. The differences between these two groups were evident in their dissimilar reactions to the dramatic changes taking place in the world of work and the growing influence of scientific reasoning.

Dwight L. Moody held revival meetings from 1875–1885—in the years leading up to the Third Great Awakening. He was not an ordained minister, but he was a great showman, a supporter of industry, and well financed by wealthy business leaders. His message to the middle class and to the urban poor was that the free enterprise system works: Work hard, believe in Jesus as your savior, and sooner or later your prospects will improve. Historian R. Laurence Moore (p. 185) states about Moody: "As a shaper of popular/commercial culture he was as important a figure as P. T. Barnum. No one understood better than he did that religion had become a business in the nineteenth century and that success in religion depended on sound and innovative business practices."

However, it could be argued that of greater importance than Moody was William A. Sunday, a former baseball player turned revival preacher. Moody died in 1899, and Billy Sunday picked up where Moody left off. Sunday criticized what he called *modernist* trends in society and among liberal Protestants. Sunday was also critical of the liberal churches' involvement in social services and reform (Marsden, p. 31). Sunday's ministry, like Moody's, was well financed by wealthy industrialists. Indeed, Sunday was backed by names that are familiar to this day: John Rockefeller, Louis Swift, J. Ogden Armour, H. J. Heinz, and others (Moore, p. 187).

The industrialists, though not extremely religious themselves, saw in Moody and Sunday a pro-business message and a message of hope (the combination of which makes many people feel better and more inclined to accept the status quo). Religious conservatives viewed "modernist" trends as an encroachment upon religious truth; this would become evident in the 1925 trial of John Scopes, who was accused of violating Tennessee law by teaching evolution. From the right-wing perspective, industrialization was not a part of the "modernist" threat—free enterprise was part of the "Good News." This point of view would be played out in Bruce Barton's popular book, *The*

Man Nobody Knows ([1925] 1987). Barton's message combines free enterprise with salvation. For example, Barton discusses Jesus saying that He has
come "not to be ministered unto but to minister." In other words, Jesus as the
highest being must be servant to all other beings. Barton continues,

> Be a good servant and you will be great; be the best possible servant and you
> will occupy the highest possible place. A splendid speech but utterly impracti-
> cal . . . . That is just what most men thought century after century; and then,
> quite suddenly, great enterprises . . . woke up . . . . Free men, acting indepen-
> dently of government, pool their skills and money to aid other men . . . . The
> huge plants and financial strength of, say, an automobile manufacturer rest on
> the willingness and ability not only to provide for your safety, comfort and
> convenience but to feel –and convince you of it—a genuine concern for your
> pleasure in the product, your benefit from it. (pp. 89–90)

Religious liberals embraced science, particularly social science, as a means
of furthering the Gospel and realizing the "Kingdom of God on Earth."
Religious liberals had attacked the institution of slavery and now they were
supporting the new social sciences as well as social reform. From their perspective, social reform was part of the "Good News." A popular book at this
time was Charles Sheldon's novel, *In His Steps* (1896). The story concerns
members of a church who vowed not to do anything that they could not
imagine Jesus doing. Sheldon's book, from which was derived the phrase,
"WWJD?" ("What would Jesus do?"), reflected what left-wing Protestants
called the *Social Gospel*. The message of the Social Gospel was most clearly
expressed by Walter Rauschenbusch. He argued that religion was not only
about changing individuals, but also about changing the ways in which social
institutions demoralized individuals. None of this is to say that the Social
Gospel was opposed to corporate sponsorship; here, too, religion's continuing absorption into the marketplace was recognized (Moore, pp. 212–217).

Many significant figures contributed to facilitating different strands of the
Social Gospel, including Jane Addams and W. E. B. Du Bois. Jane Addams
was inspired by the work of other reformers and became a leader in the
movement for a woman's right to vote, and through her work at Hull House
(a place where poor people could receive aid) she raised social awareness
about the needs of poor woman and children, and the need to strengthen
communities. Addams was the first American woman to receive the Nobel
Peace Prize. Du Bois was the first African American to earn a doctorate at
Harvard and was one of the cofounders of the National Association for the
Advancement of Colored people (NAACP). He was an outspoken advocate
for civil rights and political representation at a time when the Klu Klux Klan
was strong and many African Americans were being terrorized by mob hang-
ings. Christian historian George Marsden notes that, "In the 1890s lynchings

of blacks in the South took place at an average rate of three per week" (1991, p. 47).

THE TWENTIETH CENTURY

At the beginning of the twentieth century two broad religious camps existed offering competing views for how people could cope with the problems of the times, eventually known as religious liberals and religious conservatives. Both groups put their own spin on the same social trends that were changing humankind's understanding of itself and its place in the universe—both groups also depended upon the same marketing techniques and technologies to get their message across.

As Bacon, Newton, and Locke had dramatically altered humankind's worldview in the eighteenth century and thereafter, Darwin, Freud, and Einstein had the same kind of effect in the twentieth century. The impact of Darwin's book *On the Origin of Species* (1859) cannot be understated. It influenced the natural sciences, the social sciences, philosophy, and religion. Many religious liberals at the time adopted the view of historian John Fiske that "[e]volution is God's way of doing things" (Marsden, p. 36). Religious conservatives, like Charles Hodge of Princeton Theological Seminary, saw evolution as a threat to the theological worldview. Evolution suggested a naturalistic worldview that eliminated the need for absolutes. The naturalistic notion of humanity's origins went too far. A real sticking point was the story of creation in Genesis. It was at this time that inerrancy became essential. Marsden notes,

> The most articulate of these conservative spokespersons were the theologians at the . . . seminary in Princeton. Carefully they defined what they took to be the church's traditional stance regarding the Bible. The text as originally inspired by the Holy Spirit, they insisted, was "absolutely errorless." This doctrine of "inerrancy" as it came to be known, was no invention of the late nineteenth century. Many Christians in the past had said or assumed much the same thing. But the fact that now some conservative Protestants were making biblical inerrancy a central doctrine, even sometimes virtually a test of faith, signaled the degree to which the new scientific and historical threats to the Bible were forcing everyone to shore up whatever he or she considered the most critical line of defense. (p. 37)

Around the same time that Hodge and others associated with the Princeton Theological Seminary were defending a theological worldview based upon the Bible, John Nelson Darby's notion of *dispensationalism* was catching on. Darby and his followers believed that the world was getting worse and that a time of tribulation was coming, and that ultimately Christ would triumph and establish His kingdom in Israel. Between 1910 and 1915 dispensationalist leaders published a twelve-volume paperback series called *The Fundamentals*. The series avowed their core beliefs, such as inerrancy, the divinity of Jesus, and the second coming. In 1920, a militant group of conservative evangelicals adopted the term *fundamentalist*, first used by Curtis Lee Laws, to describe their efforts. Fundamentalists described themselves as people willing to "battle" for the "Fundamentals" and wage a religious war against the "modernists" (Marsden, p. 57). Contemporary dispensationalists see the establishment of the state of Israel and conflicts in the Middle East as evidence of their beliefs.

The election of Franklin D. Roosevelt resulted in the enactment of the many proposals sought by religious liberals. The liberal agenda would now predominate for decades. Nevertheless, religious conservatives were developing the groundwork that would produce its dominance during the final decades of the twentieth century. During World War II evangelists sponsored a series of successful rallies across the country. These rallies produced a series of networks and organizations. One of the organizations to emerge was called Youth for Christ—its leader was Billy Graham. Graham went on to become one of the most influential revivalists of the twentieth century.

In the decade following the war, Americans found themselves clearly in the position of being the leader of the free world. The 1950s witnessed a time of unprecedented economic expansion and global dominance. The Founders' core belief in civil religion seemed evident: America was the world's beacon of freedom. This was a time of relative quiet between religious conservatives and religious liberals. Will Herberg's (1960) book, entitled *Protestant, Catholic, Jew*, seemed to sum up the times. There were three dominant religious groups with three different worldviews, yet they share in common a belief in America. Of course, it helps to have a bad guy to rally against, and in the 1950s the go-to bad guy was the Soviet Union. People in both countries feared nuclear war and so the Cold War ensued. In order to further demarcate the differences between the two nations, Eisenhower fully supported adding the phrase "under God" into the Pledge of Allegiance in 1954 and making "In God We Trust" the national motto in 1956.

The relative quiet of the 1950s gave way to its opposite in the 1960s. The following events probably conspired to produce the tumultuous decade: the near nuclear catastrophe between the United States and the Soviet Union over the status of Cuba in the early 1960s, the Supreme Court decisions in 1962 and 1963 that outlawed prayer and devotional Bible reading in the public schools, the assassination of President Kennedy, the signing of the Civil Right Act by President Lyndon Johnson, the campaign for women's rights, the insufficient number of jobs for the growing numbers of young people looking for work, the rapid influx of narcotics into the country, the assassinations of Robert Kennedy and Martin Luther King, Jr., and the controversy over America's involvement in Vietnam. Liberal churches and conservatives churches responded to these challenges in different ways. Many liberal church leaders marched with civil rights protestors, activities reflecting back to the times of the Social Gospel. Many conservative church leaders feared the erosion of social order, saw civil unrest as the realization of dispensationalist expectations, and rallied supporters around themes such as morality, traditional roles, and social control.

Behind the scenes of civil unrest an explosion in new forms of religious expression was occurring. Indeed, some social scientists refer to the period of about 1960 to 1990 as the Fourth Great Awakening (Fogel 2000; McLoughlin 1978). An example of this new religious and philosophical enthusiasm among liberals occurred at the Grace Cathedral in San Francisco in 1966. George Leonard, the West Coast editor of *Look* magazine, and psychologist Abraham Maslow spoke at the cathedral in honor of the opening of the San Francisco branch of the Esalen Institute. Leonard was one of a number of people who supported the opening of the Institute in 1961 in Big Sur, California. Esalen became one of the key learning centers for the burgeoning exploration in new religious expression (Taylor 1999, p. 238). Leonard expressed two countervailing sentiments held by many religious liberals at the time: "The life of every man—the heart of it—is pure and holy joy," and, "At a time when at last we have all the means at hand to end war, poverty, and racial insanity, the prophets of despair discover no vision large enough to lead men to the merely possible" (quoted in Taylor, p. 236). The themes among many religious liberals at the time stressed the importance of discovering one's spiritual center and developing it to its greatest potential, as well as applying the realization of this potential to solving large scale, age-old problems. In some respects it harkened back to the Transcendentalists and Theosophists, yet new technologies and America's appearance of invincibility created a larger vision of what seemed possible.

During the 1960s religious liberals engaged in many different religious practices, collectively referred to as New Age Spirituality. I believe the following four aspects of the religious liberalism expressed at this time could be reasonably argued to have been particularly important because of their enduring impact on American society:

1. President Johnson's signing of the Immigration and Nationality Act of 1965 eased restrictions on Asian immigration to the United States. One of the consequences of this change in law was an influx of Asian people, customs, ideas, and Asian religious teachers. As Theosophists stressed the importance of both Eastern and Western religious traditions in the nineteenth century, Eastern practices blossomed among Westerners in the twentieth century. Meditation, yoga, acupuncture, Asian herbal remedies, and a vast literature on ancient Asian and Indian religious beliefs and practices filled bookstores.

2. Eastern religious and philosophical ideas fed into the development of humanistic psychology. Psychologists such as Abraham Maslow, Carl Rog-

ers, and Viktor Frankl contributed to the development of this field of study. In many ways, they confirmed what religious liberals had been arguing all along: self-realization is contingent on social conditions or how one reacts to those conditions. Maslow's hierarchy of needs suggests that self-actualization, or the realization of one's full potential, is contingent upon satisfying one's basic physiological needs, safety needs, social needs, and esteem needs, respectively. This theory of human potential may now be found in left- and right-wing religious publications as well as in the business literature on success. Some people associated with humanistic psychology argued that there are different levels of consciousness and suggested the inducement of these alternative states in order to better understand the mind. This way of thinking gained some prominence through Aldous Huxley's book, entitled *The Doors of Perception.* The book describes Huxley's experiences and visions from ingesting a psychedelic or mind-altering substance. Huxley was not a druggie, but a learned man interested in mysticism. In the early 1960s, psychologists Timothy Leary and Richard Alpert conducted a series of experiments at Harvard University on the effects of psychedelic substances. Subsequently, Leary advocated psychedelics for therapeutic purposes, but his promotion of substances such as LSD ultimately served to enhance its use among teenagers for recreational purposes. Richard Alpert went on to explore spirituality in India and changed his name to Ram Dass.

3. In the 1960s many young people explored the religious traditions of America's indigenous peoples. Native Americans are comprised of many distinct cultures and languages; however, they share in common the belief that the planet and all of its beings, including humans, are part of the same spiritual world. While the Judeo-Christian tradition separates sacred and profane, spiritual and material, Native American religious traditions see continuity, so that the natural world is spiritual. The surge of interest in Native American traditions resulted in many young people learning to live more naturally, discovering the importance of caring for the planet, and participating in rituals like the sweat-lodge ceremony and a ceremony involving peyote, a psychedelic substance. The impact of learning about Native American as well as Eastern beliefs and practices continues to this day in the form of greater environmental awareness, better understanding of the mutual existence of all beings, use of herbs and alternative practices for health and healing, and the creation of entire new markets such as organic and natural products, health food stores and restaurants, alternative bookstores, healing centers, and spiritual retreats emphasizing Native or Eastern practices.

4. The fourth form of religious expression that I would like to mention is the movement around Martin Luther King, Jr. Like his father, King, Jr. was a Baptist minister. What was particularly special about King, besides his charisma, was his ability to articulate the cause of civil rights in terms of America's civil religion. As the leader of the civil rights movement in the 1960s,

much of what King called for, like desegregation, was considered by many at the time to be against the norm. King, as a sociologist, minister, and visionary, recognized that sometimes a norm is so unjust that the right thing to do is stake out the deviant or "maladjusted" position. In the following quote, King uses a variety of themes, including civil religion, to argue that conformity to social trends that maintain injustice is not the way of America's greatest religious and political leaders. King writes,

> In a sense all of us must live the well-adjusted life in order to avoid neurotic and schizophrenic personalities. But there are some things in our social system to which all of us ought to be maladjusted. I never intend to adjust myself to the viciousness of mob rule. I never intend to adjust myself to the inequalities of an economic system which takes necessities from the masses to give luxuries to the classes. I never intend to become adjusted to the madness of militarism . . . . It may be that the salvation of the world lies in the hands of the maladjusted. The challenge to us is to be maladjusted—as maladjusted . . . as Lincoln, who had the vision to see that this nation could not survive half slave and half free; as maladjusted as Jefferson, who in the midst of an age amazingly adjusted to slavery could cry out in words lifted to cosmic proportions: "All men are created equal, and are endowed by their Creator with certain unalienable rights, that among these are Life, Liberty, and the pursuit of Happiness"; as maladjusted as Jesus who could say to the men and women of his generation, "Love your enemies, bless them that curse you, do good to them that hate you, and pray for them that despitefully use you." (cited in Washington 1991, pp. 14-15)

While religious liberals received more media attention than religious conservatives during the 1960s, religious conservatives were nonetheless building on the networks they had established in the 1940s. Besides establishing a voice on the radio, evangelicals Rex Humbard and Oral Roberts began broadcasting on television in the 1950s. Roberts helped to popularize Pentecostalism, an evangelical movement that first began to grow after 1900 and emphasizes emotional exuberance, faith healing, and speaking in tongues (Marsden, pp. 42–43). However, the most popular evangelist in the 1950s and 1960s was Billy Graham; thousands of people attended his revival meetings.

By the 1970s conservative churches were outpacing their liberal competition on the airwaves and in the churches. While liberal churches were ambivalent about the side effects of modern technology and commercialism on the delivery of their religious message, evangelicals saw these as new avenues for promoting the gospel. Building on Moody's and Sunday's formula of being upbeat and presenting an image and message of success, televangelism, megachurches (defined as two thousand or more people attending worship services per week), and Christian schools grew in size and profits;

televangelism and megachurches became modern versions of the old revival camps.

By the early 1980s evangelist Jim Bakker had built a popular Christian resort and community, Heritage USA, in South Carolina, which boasted a shopping complex, timeshares, a Bible and evangelism school, cable TV network production studios, a water park, and recreational facilities. Bakker created an environment where like-minded Christians could submerge themselves in a Christian, middle-class world (Moore, p. 251). However, by the end of the 1980s, Bakker was embattled by sexual and financial scandals and Heritage USA was bankrupt.

Jerry Falwell cofounded the Moral Majority in 1979. Falwell's organization became a powerful means for social conservatives and right-wing religious groups to get their worldview on the political agenda. Conservative evangelicals thought that they had elected one of their own when Jimmy Carter, a Southerner and self-described "born-again" Christian, was elected president in 1976; their disappointment in Carter was a catalyst for organizing and looking in a new direction. When Ronald Reagan courted the evangelical vote, the Moral Majority backed Reagan and helped him to get into the White House in 1980. Once again, they thought they had elected one of their own, but it turned out that Reagan was more of a libertarian than a conservative Christian. By the late 1980s a lot of the enthusiasm that had helped Falwell's organization acquire some degree of prominence had eroded.

Pat Robertson's Christian Coalition would pick up where Falwell's Moral Majority left off. Robertson founded the Christian Broadcasting Network (CBN) in 1960 and built it into a multimillion dollar media empire. By 1986 Robertson had the resources to launch a campaign as the Republican nominee for the White House, but George H. W. Bush won the nomination and the White House in 1988. After the election, Robertson joined forces with a young organizer named Ralph Reed. Together, they developed an influential political lobby called the Christian Coalition. George W. Bush narrowly won the presidential election in 2000 with their support.

Throughout the 1980s, 1990s, and the first decade of the twenty-first century, organizations like the Christian Coalition tried to turn the United States into a Christian nation rather than a pluralistic one. Jerry Falwell often made comments like, "It is time for Americans to come back to the faith of their fathers, to the Bible of our fathers, and to the biblical principles that our fathers used as a premise for this nation's establishment" (quoted in Noll, Hatch, & Marsden, p. 126). Yet, the nation was founded on pluralistic principles—not antireligious, but not favoring any one religion. Noll, Hatch, and Marsden state,

Further incidental evidence of the founders' own views is the statement from a treaty with the Islamic nation of Tripoli in 1797. This treaty was negotiated under Washington, ratified by the Senate, and signed by President John Adams. The telling part is a description of religion in America: "As the government of the United States of America is not in any sense founded on the Christian Religion—as it has in itself no character of enmity against the laws, religion, or tranquility of Musselmen [i.e., Muslims] . . . , it is declared by the parties that no pretext arising from religious opinions shall ever produce an interruption of the harmony existing between the two countries." (p. 131)

The rise of conservative and fundamentalist religions toward the end of the twentieth century has been the subject of much analysis and debate among social scientists (Wuthnow 1988; Smith 2002). It may have been part of a Fourth Great Awakening—I would suggest from about 1960 to 2000. By 1970 the economy was weakening after decades of unprecedented growth, social roles were changing dramatically, a large youth culture was questioning religious and political authority; it was a time of great uncertainty—and for many people, uncertainty increases the desire for familiar and unambiguous answers. The United States was not alone in witnessing a surge in conservative faiths. Throughout the course of the twentieth century, many religions experienced decline in many countries. However, as the twentieth century came to a close, conservative, fundamentalist, and orthodox religious groups grew.

The rise of new technologies in communications and travel, the merging of international economies, the collapse of the Soviet Union, and the rather abrupt meeting of people from different cultures from around the planet—in a word, *globalization*—produced uncertainty around the world during the latter part of the twentieth century. As Wuthnow states, "Much of the . . . uncertainty in the economic and political realms may seem remote from the world of religious convictions—until it is remembered that . . . religion . . . connects closely with ethical, social, and inevitably economic and political concerns" (p. 321). Economist Laurence Iannaccone (1994), building on Dean Kelley's book, *Why Conservative Churches Are Growing* (1972), suggests that people who feel vulnerable during difficult times tend to want the restrictive structure that many conservative churches provide.

In addition to the rapid development of globalization that occurred during the latter part of the twentieth and into the twenty-first centuries, there also arose an increasing closeness between religious and political leaders on the two ends of the ideological spectrum, the effect of which was to drive people of faith in opposing directions. The effect fueled *polarization* (where groups have such extremely different worldviews that they can't work together to get things done for the national interest) rather than pluralism—what the Founders intended. In a climate of polarization, conflict replaces a sense of commonality.

Though the specific contents may vary, the core concerns of religious liberals and religious conservatives are very similar: the tendency to think more in terms of personal spiritual needs rather than in terms of religious organization and dogma, acquiring a secure life for themselves and their loved ones, and a belief system that is understandable, relevant, and entertaining. This has been the basic trend in religion throughout American history.

THE TWENTY-FIRST CENTURY

As Americans and the people of other nations have been adjusting to coexisting in a diverse and crowded world, new religious leaders have emerged to meet the needs and wants of people living through different circumstances. Among Christian evangelicals, Pastors Bill Hybels, Rick Warren, and Joel Osteen are among the most popular leaders in the United States and in the world today. Hybels (based in Illinois), Warren (California), and Osteen (Texas) lead megachurches that offer people, young and old, a wide range of programs and services. They do not demonize those who disagree with them, they call attention to "the power of positive thinking," and they promote the American Dream: Work hard and you will succeed. These pastors highlight how the revival meeting has been transformed into a market-driven spectacle and shopping mall.

Hybels, who got started in the 1970s, led the way in applying consumer-focused principles for increasing church membership (Einstein 2008, p. 103). Hybels asked himself the same questions that management expert Peter Drucker suggested to entrepreneurs attempting to grow their business: "What is our business? Who is our customer? What does the customer consider value?" (Einstein, p. 103). Applying a similar strategy, Rick Warren's ministry has outpaced Hybels's in membership, revenue, and influence. A key element of his success has been outreach and leading small groups for people with varying interests and needs, from physical fitness to support groups and recovery groups on a wide range of issues (Einstein, pp. 97–98). Finally, before taking over his father's position as pastor, Joel Osteen worked behind the scenes marketing the church. Today, Joel Osteen is a televangelist with the largest church membership in the United States. He fills stadiums when he goes on tour each year. Like other televangelists, Osteen's television show and tours also promote his latest book and other products.

Among religious liberals and spiritual people unaffiliated with a religious organization, there are inspirational speakers like Deepak Chopra, Wayne Dyer, and Eckhart Tolle. They also do not demonize those who disagree with them, and though the terminology may be a little different, it is also familiar:

They call attention to the power of right thinking, and promote the American Dream. Focus and you will succeed.

Born in India, Chopra is an American physician and leader in alternative medicine. He has authored many books on topics such as mind-body spirituality, and spirituality and success. With product names like "Unleash Your Potential," Chopra taps into some of the same themes expressed by Osteen, one of whose slogans is "Discover the champion in you." Chopra is also the cofounder of the Chopra Center in California, which provides a wide range of products and services—classes and programs on healing and wellness, spiritual awakening, yoga, meditation, aromatherapy, herbs, body lotions, music, and books.

Wayne Dyer holds a doctorate in educational counseling, is the author of many books on spirituality and achieving success (including *Manifest Your Destiny*), and his seminars are aired on public television (which also promotes his books and DVDs).

Eckhart Tolle, who was born in Germany, reports having an awakening that transformed his life. He discusses his life, his transformation, and spiritual teachings in his books, DVDs, and other products. The title of his first best-selling book, *The Power of Now*, is reminiscent of one of Osteen's popular books, *Your Best Life Now*.

BRANDING RELIGION

The beginning of the twenty-first century, in many ways, is reminiscent of the beginning of the twentieth: A minority of people own the majority of the nation's resources and possess unparalleled access to lawmakers, while a majority of people hustle to make a living, angrily divided about how best to respond to those who seem responsible for their sense of insecurity while clinging tightly to a range of hopeful, other-worldly beliefs. While conservative evangelicalism seems to be in ascendency in the early years of the twenty-first century, many indicators suggest that younger people are not as emotionally and intellectually attached to right-wing or left-wing ideologies and institutions. Indeed, younger people seem lax about the legitimacy of many existing institutions, religion included (Einstein, p. 194; Wuthnow, p. 88).

This makes a great deal of sense on multiple levels: (1) they have seen left-wing and right-wing agendas come and go and fail to achieve a stable social order: Each wing's failure is blamed on the other wing's agenda. (2) they have been raised to believe in themselves and in whatever feels right—while their parents struggled to find meaning in a world with multiple meanings, they embrace the notion of a self-made ecumenical faith and they are more likely to describe themselves as spiritual than religious, being more likely to believe in a higher power (like America's founding Deists) than a personalized God with white hair and a long beard. And, (3) they have been raised in a market-driven, media-saturated environment: There is nothing peculiar or necessarily meaningful about being promised anything and everything from anyone, including a commercialized God or higher power.

Religion in the twenty-first century is more about marketing than ever before, and it makes sense that it would be. Throughout the development of the United States, the nation has become more and more about business and industry. Since society is a product of the configuration of its institutions, religion and other institutions have had to adapt to the rising dominance of the economic institution. Max Weber noted this trend in his classic book, *The Protestant Ethic and the Spirit of Capitalism* ([1904] 2001) in which he discussed the rise of a calculating and acquisition-based mentality, or *rationalization*, spreading into all aspects of social life.

As there were manuals for growing the size of one's church a hundred years ago, there are many such manuals today. One contemporary book is Richard L. Reising's *ChurchMarketing 101* (2006). In today's crowded marketplace, Reising states, "As more and more churches use direct mail, billboards, Yellow Pages, newspapers, movie theaters, and the like, the allure of being 'the church that advertises' decreases because so many are doing it. What remains is an opportunity to differentiate yourself in the recipient's minds from any number of churches that are vying for people's mindshare" (p. 41). In order to do this, Reising suggests repetition in promotions and branding.

The notion of branding is ubiquitous in today's marketplace. Branding is about creating an image in the mind of the consumer of your product. In order to do this, stories are generated around a product, and the intent is for consumers to associate the story with the product. The story is usually about a fairly common human desire. What makes the product stand out is whether the story fits the product and somehow resonates with the consumer. Branding is intended to effect a predictable response in the consumer in relation to the product, and the consumer becomes "loyal" to the brand if s/he likes the predictable experience associated with the product.

Sociologist Roger Finke states, "[C]hurches must effectively market their religion to the people . . . . This forces religious organizations to provide a message and a messenger that appeal to the people. The messenger is now judged more by his personal appeal . . . and the message is judged by its application to the practical life of the parishioners" (p. 615). Church consultants urge pastors to incorporate multimedia technologies into their services and to adapt their sermons to the needs of the parishioners. Today, there are cowboy churches, country music churches, motorcycle churches, surfer churches, churches for people dramatically decorated by tattoos—all the product of niche-marketing (see, for example, Symonds, Grow, & Cady 2005).

On the surface, it would appear that evangelicals represent the largest religious group in the United States. However, elements of New Age spirituality have become so commonplace that it may not occur to people that what they are doing or saying was representative of a spiritual practice just a few decades ago. Components of New Age spirituality have been marketed for many years, and some of their elements are now a part of mainstream society (due, in part, to the successful activities of people such as Deepak Chopra, Joseph Campbell, and others). An example of the mainstream adaptation of New Age spirituality was when the blockbuster film series *Star Wars* used the expression "The Force" and many people knew what that referred to, or once they did, adopted the expression themselves. Consumer capitalism can turn anything, including dissent (religious or political) into a commercial venture.

Spiritual practices once associated with New Age are now typically referred to as mind, body, and spirit (Einstein, p. 199). Fitness centers, large companies, universities, and hospitals around the country utilize one or more of the following techniques to promote concentration, productivity, and health: yoga, tai chi (a form of focused movement), massage, Reiki (using one's hands over another person to increase life energy), acupuncture, aromatherapy, and guided imagery. Many people being treated with conventional methods for serious illnesses augment their treatment with one or more of these practices. Many large companies offer classes on stress management, conflict resolution, as well as heightening concentration and becoming more productive—basically techniques for focusing one's "energy" or practices associated with different forms of meditation.

The point is that aspects of what was once called New Age spirituality are now practiced by many people with different worldviews, wittingly or unwittingly, in mainstream America. There is actually nothing unusual about this. Religions go through a life cycle: Religious movements that are different from the norm eventually become more like the norm or become the norm as subsequent generations preserve the religion with their own set of needs and as the religion becomes established in its social environment. The alternative is the demise of the religion. Successful religions are those that eventually become a part of society.

According to religion professor Lake Lambert, "Mass media and corporate power have brought together evangelical Christians and New Age devotees in a way no ecumenical dialogue or council could have imagined" (2009, p. 83). The fact of the matter is that America employs some of its best minds to calculate ways to tap into people's hopes, desires, and fears—the stuff of imagination, magic, and religion. Yet, as marketer Margaret Mark and New Age writer Carol Pearson state, "For the first time in human history . . .

commercial messages are now taking the place of shared sacred stories" (2001, p. 359). Consider the ad campaign for Danner boots that reads, "The road to Nirvana is not paved" (cited in Mark & Pearson, p. 118). Consider the names of cars—*Quest, Pathfinder,* and *Soul*—which would make little sense in countries with a different set of religious assumptions. These names suit the American market in that they convey to us that our religious or spiritual journey may be more successful if we drive a *Pathfinder* or *Soul* than if we drive, say, an *Avenger* or *Edge*.

The bottom line is that more and more people practice their faith through the commodities they buy: prayer beads, spiritual or religious music on compact discs, religious or spiritual books, t-shirts with religious messages or images, lectures or sermons on DVD, inspirational calendars, and so on. People are meaning-making animals and we communicate with each other less and less in person and more and more through technology and media simulation. As theological professor Vincent J. Miller points out, "[M]eaning has remained a fundamental part of culture, but one that is situated within other cultural dynamics. The change is not in the content of beliefs but in the way in which they are disseminated, interpreted, and practiced" (2005, pp. 26–27). Imagine what Jesus or Moses looks like in your mind's eye, and then ask yourself where that image comes from. When I think about what Moses looks like, I picture Charlton Heston in Cecile B. DeMille's epic film *The Ten Commandments*.

People gravitate to different messages and traditions because of socialization and increasingly because "it feels right." Of course, that is what branding is all about—tapping into what feels right to the consumer and creating a story and an experience that involve the consumption of products. Church marketer Reising (p. 147) emphasizes the importance of providing an experience in order to sell the product (whether that product is a brand of coffee or a brand of church). According to Miller (p. 179), "Consumer culture forms [socializes] people in consumerist habits of use and interpretation, which believers, in turn, bring to their religious beliefs and practice." Let us take a look at some examples.

One of the reasons why religious services are boring unless they have nice visuals, lighting, and a message that people want to hear is because people spend more time watching images on a screen than engaging in any other activity. The frequent changes in sound, visuals, and products portrayed through electronic media reinforce a craving for novelty. Although a person's attention may be caught by a religious or spiritual personality or persona, a religious passage that can be recited daily or posted on a refrigerator door or a social media site, a meditative practice, or a product that is intended to create a spiritual environment, eventually the novelty wears off. The persona seems less profound and life changing, the passage seems to mean less, the practice or product that seemed to be making a difference at first is no longer appealing. People adapt to novelty more quickly when they have more choices.

Consumer desire is not about satisfying wants and needs, but about prolonging the sensation of desire (see Miller for an excellent discussion on this point). Increasingly, people crave the feeling of desire more than the satisfaction of desire (which can lead to disappointment). Commercial culture, of which modern religion in many of its guises is a part, is about buying new products and throwing away old products (unless the old product is very old and then it's exotic). Moreover, if the new persona, passage, practice, or product doesn't fulfill its promise, it is not about them or the world of goods, it is about us as individuals. Both New Age seekers and evangelicals think in terms of the culture's ideology of individualism (an atomistic view of the self).

Both assume that the way to change society is by changing people one person at a time. That is like saying people must love themselves before loving others. I believe that there is some truth to this, but as we have already discussed, loving others requires the acquisition of skills that cannot be learned solely by loving oneself. A person can consider the self a temple, and yet trample over other people who must also, by extension, be temples.

Religion in America today is not only materialistic and diverse, it is also highly syncretic. People cut and paste together a meaning system from a variety of religious beliefs, practices, and symbols. One person may wear a cross and hang a dream catcher from the rearview mirror in their car without realizing that they suggest contradictory meanings. The freedom that we have to create our own meaning can become a storehouse of contradictory beliefs about religious or spiritual phenomena. Miller states:

> [T]he bewildering task of constructing an identity . . . promises the freedom of constructing an identity of one's own that is not dependent on one's family of origin, ethnic background, or class. Even one's own past decisions recede in power as such identities seem endlessly revisable and replaceable should they fail or simply lose their appeal. Whatever the burdens that result . . . are accompanied by the ever-present promise of self-renewal. (p. 118)

The notion of the ongoing renewal of the self found among evangelicals and adherents of many forms of contemporary spirituality is a market-driven conception of the self based upon prolonging desire through the consumption of commodities. In the ancient world there was no concept of the individual as we understand it today. Ongoing renewal of the self first of all requires a social environment conducive to the notion of a detached self with multiple roles and options.

In order to sell megachurches or spiritual centers to a diversified mass of individualized consumers, religious leaders have to offer products that are consistent with what many people want to see and hear while not being a turn-off to those who are undecided about what they want. In order to do so, many megachurches today minimize references to Jesus and images of the cross, and spiritual centers tend to emphasize syncretism and ecumenism (Einstein; Moore).

The meaning and significance of religious personalities and symbols have always varied from one generation to the next, but the combination of what we now know about the past and our ability to fashion whatever images we want has created a plethora of contradictory notions. For example, when a person walks through the markets of Jerusalem, there are small signs indicating where Jesus actually walked. I would think that this would stimulate a kind of reverence for this place, but the people who live and work there do not seem to think about it in these terms. I suppose it could be due to adaptation; many people who see amazing sights on a regular basis lose that initial sense of awe. But I don't think adaptation is the issue in the markets of Jerusalem; I think instead that the people who live there have a context within which to think about religious personalities and images.

In order to get across to the reader the underlying point that I am making here, I would like to refer to a joke told by Joel Osteen. The joke goes something like this: Two men debate all their lives about the color of Jesus— white or black? The two men die on the same day and when they meet God they ask if Jesus is white or black. Just then Jesus approaches them and says, "Buenos dias" (cited in Einstein, p. 127). I would seriously suspect that when most Americans picture Jesus in their mind's eye, they see an Aryan figure (blue eyes, light complexion, and light colored hair) even though he was a member of Semitic-language-speaking people (who tend to be darker in color); they picture a person who espoused Christianity (even though Christianity didn't exist yet); and they imagine a successful person (even though he was crucified for his activities).

The fact of the matter is that the imagery that exists of Jesus is as diverse as the people of the world: some imagine Jesus as God, others as a healer and magician, others as caring and feminine, others as muscular and masculine. Some envision him as a rebel, while others picture a successful businessman, and then there are images of him as being of African descent, Native American descent, and so on. Some people say that Jesus can look these different ways because he is the son of God, and so he can appear differently to different people, but when he walked through the markets of Jerusalem can one imagine that his physical features would change like this? That he was that chameleon-like? I think what this is all about is that Jesus, divorced from context, frees the imagination to consider him in any way one wishes.

When people picture Jesus, or for that matter any important, historical religious figure, they usually do not or cannot envision that other person; rather, they see an image based upon their experiences and desires, and in a media-saturated environment, individual experience and desire are heavily overlaid with market-driven imagery. The United States is arguably the most market-driven society in the world, and Americans are the most religious people in the industrialized world—not in a literate way, but in an experiential way—in part because religious themes are an important part of the market. I emphasize experiential and not literate because Americans by and large do not actually read Scripture. Prothero points out that in surveys: "Only half of American adults can name even one of the four Gospels. Most Americans cannot name the first book of the Bible." And even among "born-again" Christians, less than half surveyed "correctly identified 'Blessed are the poor in spirit, for theirs is the kingdom of heaven' as a quote from the Sermon on the Mount" (pp. 30–31).

RELIGION AND MEMORY

In today's fast-paced, diverse, and crowded social environments, people are exposed to more bits of information and images on a daily basis than the human brain can possibly absorb. The result is that people tend to uncritically believe in one thing absolutely or uncritically believe in absolutely nothing. People tend to embrace a religious ideology that feels comfortable and familiar and refuse to seriously consider alternative religious worldviews. Others embrace elements of various faiths and ultimately come to believe that everything is relative—meaning is based upon a vague mishmash of ideas that are always subject to change, and perhaps, even meaning means nothing. In a thoughtful book called *Religion as a Chain of Memory*, Daniele Hervieu-Leger writes,

> Accelerated change . . . paradoxically gives rise to appeals to memory. They underpin the need to recover the past in the imagination without which collective identity, just as individual identity, is unable to operate. . . . [T]he impact of accelerated change cause[s] the demand for meaning on the part of society to proliferate in all directions. Reference to the past no longer supplies a system of meanings which afford an explanation for the imperfections of the world and the incoherence of experience . . . .Thus . . . continuity presents itself as an interlacing of shattered memories, memories that have also been worked upon and invented and constantly reshaped in response to the demands of a present which is increasingly subject to the pressures of change. The remark has been made that any tradition in its relationship to a past, given actuality in the present, always incorporates an imaginative strain. The memory it invokes is always, in part at least, a reinvention. This reinvention is most often effected through successive readjustments of memory . . . . The possibility of . . . change . . . requires the slackening of the tradition (of authorized memory) to have reached a sufficient degree for it to be possible to invent an alternative memory. (2000, pp. 141–145)

Some readers may find this quote rather dense, so I would like to break it down. Accelerated social change ruptures a sense of continuity between the present and the past. Indicative are comments like, "Things have changed so much since I was a kid." Concern about the rapid pace of social change has been a common refrain throughout recorded history. In this case, the truism is actually true—this pace builds on itself, and the necessity of adapting to newness is accelerating. As this break in the sense of continuity gives rise to increased desire for continuity with the past, "appeals to memory" increase. In a diverse culture with a minimum number of shared stories of the past, appeals to memory go in a variety of directions. Groups of people have different social histories that they are attempting to grasp. Moreover, appeals to remember the past are strongest during times when the past has already lost its authority over the present, and so people are going to take more liberties in remembering the past in the ways in which they want.

There is nothing particularly novel about this. People remember the past in terms of the needs of the present; people reconfigure the past in their imagination and apply it as reality in the present. Because memories of the past always include elements of the present, memories of the past are always changing, at least a little, over time.

To break it down even further, we can say that people do not preserve the past as it was; they preserve the beliefs about the past that the previous generation has maintained in terms of their needs. Every generation plays a role in acquiring memories, interpreting those memories in terms of present needs, and passing along the continuously reconstituted memories of the past as though they reflected the actual events of the past. People who spend little time studying the past usually fail to realize that history has a history—that people and events alter the collective memory of earlier people and events. The development of the notion of original sin exemplifies the point being made here.

The ideas of sinfulness, baptism, and redemption existed in early church writings, but not in the form of dogma. Tertullian was among the early church fathers who questioned infant baptism. In the second century he questioned the idea that infants are in need of the remission of sins. Tertullian's writings do not reject the importance of baptism, but they do suggest a refutation of inherited sin (Wiley 2002, pp. 6, 45). Contemporary theologian Ian McFarland notes, "Historical reviews of the many and various ways in which early Christians reflected on the theological significance of Genesis 2–3 testify to the long and often uneven course of development in the Christian doctrines of the fall and original sin before they took more definite form (at least in the Western churches) in the writings of Augustine" (2010, p. 29).

Augustine's writings on sin became official doctrine with the councils of Carthage in 411–418 C. E. and Orange in 529 C. E. Augustine did not invent the term "original sin" but it was his development of the concept that would influence church officials and Christian doctrine. Augustine's position that humankind inherited sin from Adam's fall received further sanction with the Council of Trent in 1545–1563. Trent spelled out Catholic dogma in response to the Reformation (Wiley, p. 88). Many people today believe that human beings are born sinful, but they do not realize that this belief acquired significance over time; they do not realize that "...the idea of original sin is a post-New Testament development" (Wiley, p. 37).

During the latter part of the twentieth century and into the twenty-first century, people felt that the continuity between present and past was fracturing, so they began to grasp at varying traditions in order to restore a sense of continuity and meaning. Religious liberals grasped onto one set of traditions, and religious conservatives onto a different set of traditions, and because of the strong desire for continuity and meaning, comments from one side challenging the legitimacy of the other side were met with intense emotional reactions. Yet, neither religious liberals nor religious conservatives, neither evangelical Christians nor adherents of contemporary spirituality, are engaged in a belief system rooted in ancient ideas; both are borrowing the accumulation of beliefs among generations of people with different religious ideas.

Left- and right-wing religious believers do not merely interpret ancient events differently. They have different interpretative histories that create and perpetuate different understandings of ancient events, yet one thing ties them together. Over the course of the past century, both groups have succumbed to market forces. Both are now so much entrenched in the marketplace that it is difficult to talk about faith other than in commodified form. This does not represent the end of religion; it represents what religion is now for most Americans. Ancients separated sacred and profane, but perhaps as a way of overcompensating for the legal separation of church and state, we have merged the two in terms of lifestyle practices that are affected significantly by income and market forces.

Today's religious right may be conservative in point of view, but they are not traditional in terms of practices. Today's religious left may be liberal in point of view, but they are just as tied in to the marketplace as religious conservatives.

RELIGION AND MENTAL HEALTH

Many years ago Georg Simmel ([1907] 1990) described how money and God have many of the same qualities: pervasive, powerful, intangible (money's value is not contained in the material in which it is made), meaning-making, and life-giving. Nothing seems to give people a greater sense of comfort than having money in the bank and/or God on their side (though a supportive relationship and having good health provide comfort so long as one does not take them for granted). As we have seen, it is among the more vulnerable that religion is strongest; so it is not a stretch to say that if people can't find or make money, they are much more likely to find God.

Anthropologist Bronislaw Malinowski (1948) observed many years ago that magic fills in gaps. Religion also fills in gaps. Religious thinking takes a person beyond the tangible, and thus requires the use of imagination. Through belief, a person can contemplate a range of possibilities. Will you, the reader, die today? If you are not in hospice care, then you are likely to say, "No, it is not likely that I will die today." But how do you know? We don't know when our time will come, and we can't sit around and think about it for too long without becoming paralyzed by the thought.

On some level, we all live with an "illusion of invulnerability." Psychologists Ronnie Janoff-Bulman and Irene Hanson Frieze state, "Our assumption of invulnerability rests, in part, on a basic belief that events in our world are comprehensible and orderly . . . . Our world 'makes sense,' for we have constructed social theories that enable us to account for specific occurrences. One way for us to make sense of our world is to regard what happens to us as controllable" (1983, p. 5). According to psychologists Bernard Spilka, Phillip Shaver, and Lee A. Kirkpatrick (1985, p. 3) people have a strong desire or need to perceive events as predictable and meaningful, and in a way that protects, maintains, and enhances one's sense of self.

Assumptions of control fit into different types of schemas. As we have already discussed, a schema is a cognitive framework for attributing meaning to events. Schemas are learned, and once internalized, people refer to them (as if they devised them) in order to make sense of events. Religious schemas offer explanations for events that defy what we would consider just and rational explanation. Statements coming from religious or spiritual schemas may include, "It happened for a reason." "What doesn't kill you, will make you stronger." "Go with the flow." "Every cloud has a silver lining." "Trust in God and everything will turn out fine." "God has a plan for me that I can't see yet." "The Lord works in mysteries ways." "God won't make you go through what you can't handle." "It was God's way of bringing me to Him." Religious schemas also provide a variety of procedures for enhancing a sense of control, such as prayer, meditation, lighting candles, and burning incense.

People use religious schemas as cognitive filters to interpret and internalize discordant information in a tolerable way (Taylor & Brown 1988, p. 201). People surround themselves with like-minded friends and groups in order to create a mutual filtering system; people depend upon significant others to create and maintain a social filter that reinforces each person's cognitive filter (Taylor & Brown, p. 202). The more the filtering system is used and depended upon, the more meaning a person derives from it and this creates a self-fulfilling prophecy regarding the validity or truth of the system. If the filtering system fails to fulfill expectations, revisions are made, new insights are garnered, and sometimes conversion to a different set of filters and friends is implemented. Because religious schemas, like ideologies, create meaning out of events (particularly if those events are stressful and resist rational explanation), individuals will, more often than not, vigorously defend them. Indeed, a person may only half believe in an idea and still act on it and defend it (Campbell 1996). When circumstances are ambiguous yet require action, when bad things happen that we believe should not have happened, we cope by referring to whatever we have available to us, and sometimes even notions that we only half believe in order to enable us to regain a sense of control. Acting on ideas even half believed in may feel like one is taking charge in a situation where outcomes are important and no control exists.

The key point is that religious or spiritual schemas serve as an important coping mechanism for people. According to historian Donald G. Mathews, "Religion as a lived experience is not merely about the ways in which beliefs that engage the meaning of the world shape daily life. It is also about how people find in a religious experience or the imagined dimensions of the transcendent a way to place everything in a perspective that salvages as much personal and communal dignity as possible" (2004, p. 182).

Like establishing a relationship with any being, people bring their socialization, wants, and needs into their relationship with the Divine. The Divine may be gentle and kind or authoritarian; white, black, or brown; speak in English, Arabic, Hebrew, or any other language known to humankind; be young or old, or male or female. The Divine may be represented as a single entity, tripartite being, be part of a cosmos of beings, exist in nature, exist as an infinite something or nothing, and so on. The Divine may have a son or favored prophet. Each representative of a given faith will describe that which is holy in a slightly different way. Some people do not believe in a divine being, but may use an obviously human endeavor, such as physics, ecology, constructivism, or economics in a way that mimics a religious schema. In each case, an endeavor becomes a worldview from which everything is interpreted or marginalized and like-minded people serve as mutual filters in order to make sense of the uncanny in a like-minded way.

Though particular schemas may be better suited for problem solving than others, all knowledge is, in one way or another, a distraction from the fact that human problem solving can't overcome its own indeterminate existence. One of the reasons why religion endures is because so many people derive a sense of mental health from it. Perhaps this is why the insane sometimes rant about religious themes: They are trying to get some peace of mind, an orientation, from religion and cannot.

RELIGION AND TODAY'S CHALLENGES

The surge in conservative and fundamentalist religions that occurred during the latter part of the twentieth century seems to have slowed down in the twenty-first century and what appears to be gaining widespread acceptance is personal spirituality. The question that we are going to address here is why the surge in religion occurred at the end of the twentieth century and why spirituality appears so popular in the twenty-first century. Some of the reasons have been already alluded to in the history section of this chapter, but there are economic factors that need to be addressed explicitly.

The latter part of the twentieth century involved the merging of the world's economies; economic and cultural conditions changed all over the world. As people from different cultures met for the first time, some reacted by grasping more firmly to their religion, others incorporated more and more elements of different religions into their faith, and some reacted with violence. The transformation of the economy, migration, and cultural differences resulted in the dislocation of millions of people.

In the United States, the world's capital of capitalism, identity depends upon income. Manufacturing jobs that once could be acquired without a college degree and that could support a family were replaced by service jobs. Today, people will change careers multiple times over the course of their lives. Flexibility is the key to finding and keeping a job. The American marketplace has seen a net loss in terms of adequate paying jobs and for those people who are able to keep their jobs, there is increased pressure to do more with less. What all of this means, is that a key piece of identity must live daily in flux and this translates into a relative lack of control.

Where control cannot be acquired in one place, it may be acquired someplace else: in the certainty of the Divine's love, in the hereafter where life is better, or in the flow of life where there is a natural course to the unveiling of events. Sociologists Matt Bradshaw and Christopher G. Ellison have observed in their research the buffering effect that religious attendance and belief in the afterlife has in reducing the distress brought on by financial hardship. Bradshaw and Ellison state

> Given these promises of future glory for the faithful, believers may be less prone to take current deprivations to heart, as threats to personal identity, or sense of self; rather, they may construct their "true" identity in religious or spiritual terms (e.g., as Christians, children of God, etc.). Service attendance and belief in an afterlife (and to a lesser extent, meditation) appear to function as significant emotional compensators . . . for persons who are experiencing real or perceived financial deprivation. (2010, p. 202)

Religious attendance provides a realm or filter of social and spiritual support.

Sociologist Timothy J. Nelson observed in his research that church goers believed that "supernatural agency" affected events in their everyday lives at work, home, and elsewhere. Nelson states, "[M]embers perceived the hand of God or the interference of Satan in the midst of such 'ordinary' events as getting or losing a job, becoming sick, or receiving some unexpected money to pay an overdue bill" (1997, p. 10). It should be emphasized here that what we are talking about is a means of coping and feeling in control.

Psychologists Fred Rothbaum, John R. Weisz, and Samuel S. Snyder argue that control involves two processes: If individuals fail in their attempts to change circumstances in order to fit their needs, what they call primary control, individuals will try to adapt to these circumstances or seek to obtain and maintain secondary control. Secondary control can involve the illusory conception that "chance is on my side" (1982, p. 8). Indeed, chance is chance because it is indeterminable, but under some circumstances aligning oneself with chance may provide a person with a semblance of control. Aligning oneself in a submissive way with someone who appears to be in control can also provide a person with some sense of control. For example, a well-dressed, affluent-looking religious leader can serve as a means for vicarious living; a member may be down-and-out, but s/he can bask in the success of the leader.

A third form of secondary control is interpreting or reinterpreting a problematic circumstance that one feels unable to change in such a way as to derive meaning from it (e.g., some of clichés we have already noted: "It happened for a reason," "What doesn't kill you, makes you stronger," "There's nothing else you can do but go with the flow," "God has some purpose in making this happen to me, it is part of God's plan for me").

These three forms of secondary control demonstrate attempts to acquire meaning and control in ways that a person feels left open to them. (Rothbaum, Weisz, & Snyder, p. 13). Rather than simply giving up, individuals may use secondary control strategies that include illusion and reconfiguring circumstances in order to avoid disappointment or preserve a sense of dignity (Rothbaum, Weisz, & Snyder, p. 24).

Whether it is about coming to terms with losing a job, a debilitating accident, or a terminal illness, people use a variety of strategies in order to help make sense of their circumstances and maintain a sense of power and control. Coping entails gaining some cognitive distance from one's circumstances so that the mind has some space to work out a strategy. However, if the source of the stress is persistent, always changing, and results in constant distress because the changes that may occur at any time can produce dire consequences, then adaptation becomes living in a state of tension or living in constant coping mode. Living in such a heightened state of tension then becomes normal; a person forgets that there are other ways of feeling, thinking, and reacting. Becoming accustomed to living with risk desensitizes people to its costs and undermines the ability to gain perspective on aspects of social life where risk could be reduced.

Popular or pop psychology, religion, and spirituality over the past forty years have focused more and more on how to change the self in order to make the best of one's circumstances. It may be fair to say that the following statement has become a social norm: "People interpret reality in different ways." However empowering to the self this statement may seem, it is often used because a person feels that they possess little primary control. In a social world where change or flexibility is required for survival or success, circumstances are never stable for long, and so a person is always playing catch-up or changing with the circumstances.

Ironically, the perception of constant change is produced by a fast moving, consumer society: there is a great deal to buy or experience. In a nutshell, people are creating a social environment that they are constantly trying to keep up with, but because they cannot see that they are the creators of their collective circumstances, and because they cannot get ahead of it, they are reduced to using secondary control.

Working conditions can either increase or decrease a person's sense of power and control; in recent years the gains that were made earlier in the twentieth century have eroded for more and more people. There are already many things that people have little control over, and the past forty years has entailed profound changes in the economy, profound changes in social roles, the demise of familial and social support systems, and making a virtue out of coping alone.

Modern forms of religion and spirituality (and the psychologies implicit in them) reflect the modern economy in not only being market and consumer driven, but they also reflect the modern economy in the ways in which they instruct people to cope with the modern economy. Rothbaum, Weisz, and Snyder state that "people reserve energy for activities that match the form of control they feel best able to exercise" (p. 20). As we discussed earlier in this book, people are cognitive misers. People can apply only so much energy in trying to reason things out; this is why people depend upon schemas and heuristics or mental short-cuts. The pervasive heuristic in the psychologies underpinning religion and spirituality today is since you can't change the situation, change yourself. Sociologists Scott Schieman, Kim Nguyen, and Diana Elliott similarly state, "By cultivating an interpretive framework [of secondary control] in which they develop a sense of meaning about their world and their place in it . . . people can use religious beliefs and practices to help solve problems and reduce a sense of uncertainty" (2003, p. 203).

The sense of relief that is gained here, however, comes with a cost. People who attribute to Divine forces what others attribute to individual effort may be relinquishing opportunities to acquire primary control. According to Schieman, Nguyen, and Elliott, "Religiosity may reduce mastery while concurrently relieving distressing conditions" (p. 204). Indeed, people who are stressed and perhaps spending a lot of their energy coping, seem to desire the feeling of control more than the acquisition of control (Friedland, Keinan, & Regev 1992). This is what Karl Marx was getting at when he described religion as "the opiate of the masses." Marx's point was not that religion per se is bad, but rather that poor people tend to turn to religion as a way of dealing with hardship. While religion helps people to feel better about their situation, it may do little in a practical way to help change the conditions that contribute to their hardship.

Religion has varying purposes for people of different social classes. While wealthy people tend to give to their religious institution of choice and talk publicly about the value of religion, they tend to be less "religious" than poor people in terms of emotional attachment to their faith, frequency of prayer, and reading Holy Scripture. People with money tend to attribute circumstances to their own efforts while people without money tend to attribute circumstances, both good and bad, to divine forces. Schieman, Nguyen, and Elliott add,

> Well-educated, wealthier people tend to possess personal, social, and economic resources that help them confront challenges and solve problems. For them, appeals to a divine being may yield a greater sense of personal efficacy because their advantage affords the concrete connections between their actions and desired outcomes. Moreover, religion may provide the upper classes with a sense of legitimacy and authority regarding their position. (p. 205)

Both wealthy and poor people turn to religion for support, but of different kinds; the wealthy want God to condone their position, while the poor want God to save them from their position. Max Weber presents an interesting argument in *The Protestant Ethic and the Spirit of Capitalism* that is relevant here. Weber argues that the followers of John Calvin could not accept his doctrine of predestination or the notion that God determines before a person is born whether or not they are saved or damned, and that nothing that a person did in their lifetime could change this. Weber goes on to say that people eventually sought clues as to whether they were among the elect or saved. Eventually, the accumulation of wealth became that sign. Of course, these ideas were transferred to America through the Puritans. It may not be an exaggeration to say that these ideas are still with us: Those who accumulate wealth are viewed as the blessed, while those who fail regardless of their efforts are viewed as the damned.

Psychologist Richard S. Lazarus (1983) makes an important distinction in his discussion of coping and denial. Lazarus states that in coping with situations people use "problem-focused coping" and "emotion-focused coping." Problem-focused coping deals with changing the relationship between person and environment, while emotion-focused coping deals with changing or regulating one's emotions in response to the environment. In a social world where people feel less in control of their economic destiny and where services or interactions with people represent the bulk of available work, a premium will be placed on getting in touch with one's feelings, but at the expense of doing things to make the social world a better place for everyone.

CONCLUSION

One of Weber's concerns about the rise of bureaucracy and technology was what he referred to as the disenchantment of the world. According to Weber,

> The increasing intellectualization and rationalization . . . means . . . the belief, that if one but wished one could learn it [knowledge of the conditions under which one lives] at any time. Hence, it means that principally there are no mysterious incalculable forces that come into play, but rather that one can, in principle, master all things by calculation. This means that the world is disenchanted. One need no longer have recourse to magical means in order to master or implore the spirits, as did the savage, for whom such mysterious powers existed. Technical means and calculations perform the service. (Weber, Gerth, & Mills 1946, p. 139)

What Weber is referring to here is the classic secularization thesis: Science and technology will make religion antiquated. However, despite, or perhaps because of science and technology, religion (increasingly in the form of personalized spirituality) appears to be doing just fine in the twenty-first century. I would say that as hope in science and technology to eliminate humankind's age-old problems declined over the course of the twentieth century, and as people realized that science and technology could actually make the world a more dangerous and confusing place to live, religion regained its footing.

The latest scientific discovery in today's news may contradict last week's latest discovery. People with nationalist sentiments want to buy American-made products but they may find that American products are made elsewhere and foreign products are made in the United States. People wanting to improve their strength or looks can see a doctor and increase the size of various body parts, wondering, "Is artificial as good as authentic if it gets you what you think you want?" Technology raises an interesting choice: simulation or real—and it turns out that if one engages in the world of simulation long enough, it becomes preferable to what is real. Indeed, reality is reduced to the personal, or even to the question: what is real anyway?

The point that I am making here is that rather than disenchanting the world as Weber predicted, science and technology have created new forms of mystery and enchantment. The inability to understand how our tools work, the inability to control some of the most important aspects of our lives (jobs, greed, corruption, media circus, intimacy), and the pure visual and auditory display of modern media to supplant the real world with human projections of its own imagination, have all served to reinvigorate mystery and magic on the one hand, and insecurity on the other. These are the vital ingredients of religion and spirituality, and hence perhaps, a key reason for its continued and widespread existence.

This is not intended as a critique of religion and its ongoing existence, for some of the world's greatest visionaries have been religious or spiritual. The problem, though, is confusion between religious enthusiasm and vision. Religious or spiritual enthusiasm at its best provides hope and support, while at its worst it masks ignorance and hatred. Too few people derive deep and penetrating vision from religion and spirituality. In this regard I agree with Greeley who notes that those with a highly developed capacity for the sacred have always been few in number (p. 169).

Yet, it doesn't require experience with the sacred to realize what is important and real in life. Ask nearly anyone who has come close to death and they will probably say that the experience changed their perspective. The perspective that they will describe is usually along the lines of realizing that what is important in life is accepting yourself, appreciating others, and appreciating the time that you're here. Acquiring perspective entails realizing that you've been living in some alternative state of consciousness for a long time.

FOR FURTHER READING

Einstein, M. (2007). *Brands of faith: Marketing religion in a commercial age.* New York: Routledge. A little challenging, but well worth the read because of its fine detail.

Gandhi, M. (1983). *The essential Gandhi: An anthology of his writings on his life, work, and ideas.* L. Fischer (Ed.). New York: Vintage Books. One of the best introductions to the thought of Gandhi in his own words.

Greeley, A. M. (1985). *Unsecular man: The persistence of religion.* New York: Schocken Books. A very readable book about the ongoing importance of religion in society.

Holmes, D. L. (2006). *The faiths of the founding fathers.* New York: Oxford University Press. A short and very readable book about the faiths of some of the Founders of the United States.

Lambert, F. (2006). *The founding fathers and the place of religion in America.* Princeton, NJ: Princeton University Press. A very thoughtful examination of religion in America beginning with the Founders.

Marsden, G. M. (1991). *Understanding fundamentalism and evangelicalism.* Grand Rapids, MI: Wm. B. Eerdmans Publishing Co. A very good introduction regarding the development and beliefs of Christian fundamentalists and evangelicals.

Moore, R. L. (1994). *Selling God: American religion in the marketplace of culture.* New York: Oxford University Press. A thoughtful and detailed study of the relationship between religion and commerce.

Noll, M. A., Marsden, G. M., & Hatch, N. O. (1989). *The search for Christian America.* Colorado Springs: Helmers & Howard. Another good book about the faith of the Founders.

Norris, P., & Inglehart, R. (2004). *Sacred and secular: Religion and politics worldwide.* New York: Cambridge University Press. A very good book about religion in global perspective.

Prothero, S. R. (2007). *Religious literacy: What every American needs to know—and doesn't.* New York: HarperOne. An informative book examining what Americans know about religion versus what they feel about religion.

Schmidt, L. E. (1995). *Consumer rites: The buying & selling of American holidays.* Princeton, NJ: Princeton University Press. An informative and fun read about the rise of popular religious holidays and consumerism in America.

Washington, J. M. (1991). *A testament of hope: The essential writings and speeches of Martin Luther King, Jr.* New York: HarperCollins Publishers. A very good compilation of the works of Martin Luther King, Jr., allowing the reader to get a much better sense of the man.

Chapter Eight

Education, Science, and the Informed Citizen

The story of education in America is one of many tensions. What is education for? Does it exist to ensure an informed citizenry (which, historically, has referred to people participating in enlightened self-government) or the ideal that only informed citizens can protect their liberties? Are we educated in order to be socialized into compliance with the prevailing culture? Should everyone have equal access to educational opportunities? If so, how can that be accomplished? Who pulls the strings in terms of what is taught and what information is made available to us? Should education and research be purely utilitarian, focusing on training and profits? Is knowledge for knowledge's sake a legitimate pursuit? We will look in some depth at the history and social role of education in American society to begin to examine these questions and how the answers have played out so far.

As the previous chapters have made clear, the relationships that make up society often produce results quite different from any superficial examination of them. What makes sociology deceptively subtle and powerful is that a sustained examination of the seemingly obvious usually requires that honest and thoughtful people reexamine the assumptions that sustain their identity. Becoming informed about one's society sometimes involves facing issues that a person would prefer to ignore and calls for taking responsibility in those matters. The point is well illustrated in a powerful little book by Theodore and Nancy Sizer (1999, p. 1), entitled *The Students Are Watching: Schools and the Moral Contract*. In this book they present the following scenario:

> "I've decided one thing, anyway," Dave says. "I don't want to be an American." Dave arrives early to social studies class, and while he seemingly

> throws these words into the air, he clearly intends for the teacher to pick them
> up. "Really? Why?" Ms. Santos's voice is calm, interested. "Oh, I don't know,
> all these problems. You know . . . we talk about them all the time in this class.
> Americans think they are so great. We think we have the answers to every-
> thing, that everyone should copy us. I don't want to live in a place that's only
> thought of as rich and powerful. Especially when it's not really a democracy.
> Other countries are better. I'll just go live in one of them." Dave is going
> through the First Disillusion, a rite of passage that history teachers [and sociol-
> ogists] learn to expect. [H]e is learning about how hard it has been for his
> country to live up to its ideals.

The cynicism and blind pride that we sometimes observe in our fellow citizens may be the result of trying to achieve and abide by the lofty goals
articulated in the Declaration of Independence and the United States Constitution. A part of the problem is that many of the Founders conceived of
liberty in a narrow way: the idea of an informed citizenry with freedoms of
liberty and property pertained to those white men who already possessed
them. When freedom of liberty began to expand to a wider population, the
idea of being informed became ideological: who should be educated and how
much? Let us look back to the days when the notion of informed citizenship
in America was taking root.

FROM ELITISM TO THE RISE OF COMMON SCHOOLS (1600–1900)

You have already been introduced to John Locke, the early intellectual leader
of liberalism. His ideas on liberty greatly influenced the Founders of the
United States. Locke stressed the importance of education for the well-being
and success of a nation. However, education was for gentlemen and not the
populace. The first colleges—Harvard in 1636, William and Mary in 1693,
Yale in 1701—were small institutions, and only a tiny proportion of the
population attended them. The primary functions of these colleges were
training clergy and certifying gentlemen. The intent of this education was not
about developing skills for a particular occupation or generating new knowledge, but rather about acquiring manners that projected status, preserving old
knowledge, and refining the reasoning skills necessary to participate in the
emerging market economy.

This is one of the reasons why education was not conceived to be for
everyone. As historian Richard Brown notes, "Because there was no place
for common men in public affairs, many believed that no useful purpose was
served by educating them beyond the level of the catechism and elementary
numeracy" (1996, p. 33). Moreover, the economy required the labor of everyone who could work. Children as young as six years old would care for
animals, garden, spin thread, and make candles; and those big enough to do
more labor intensive or skilled adult work did so (Hine 1999, p. 63). In New

England it was common for boys and girls to acquire additional skills by serving as apprentices for other families. During the seventeenth and eighteenth centuries work was primary, so the most common time for children to attend school was winter. Though the colonists were literate, the idea of an informed citizenry was elitist.

As the colonies grew in size, young people found it expedient to expand their horizons and seek out opportunities in newly emerging careers in the rapidly developing towns and cities. Reading materials became more abundant, particularly in the cities. By the middle of the eighteenth century, merchants, lawyers, and minor gentry were interested in providing their sons with a gentlemen's education. The notion of an informed citizenry expanded during the heady years preceding and following the American Revolution. Thomas Paine's pamphlet, entitled *Common Sense*, first appeared in Philadelphia in 1776. It addressed the politically interested everyday man and presented a strong case for revolution. Indeed, the popularity of the pamphlet helped to galvanize average young men to take up arms. By the time of the Revolution, political leaders such as John Adams and Thomas Jefferson were advocating education for the rising ranks. States varied, however, in their level of support for schools, and even in pro-education New England, outcomes did not always meet expectations (Brown, p. 75, Kaestle 1983, p. 9).

While America's leaders had a limited view of "the people," the average person had a limited view of education. Many people believed that calls for the expansion of education among political leaders meant government infringement on local matters, and they mistrusted government's handling of the collection of taxes for education. All of these factors undermined early attempts at state systems for free common schools.

As people gained distance from the time of the Revolution, their priorities shifted. The ideals that stirred people to action were slowly replaced with the practical details of getting on in life. In the early nineteenth century in the rural Northeast and Midwest, schools were maintained by small localities and funded by a combination of property taxes, tuition payments, and state aid. These district schools accommodated families dispersed in the surrounding area. Unlike the popular image of them, schoolhouses were not red, but rather log or unpainted wood siding (Kaestle, p. 13). In the South, schools were set up and maintained either by groups of parents or by itinerant schoolmasters who charged tuition for attendance (Kaestle, p. 13). The curriculum was the basic acquisition of reading, writing, and arithmetic. Oftentimes, children would recite in class from whatever books they brought to school from home. Not only did the reading differ from one child to the next, but children of different ages shared the same classroom. Education did not follow a particular pedagogy and teachers were untrained. At that time, teaching was not viewed as a profession. Wages for teaching were low and the school year was short. As a result, the turnover rate of teachers was high.

Most teachers were men who saw teaching as one of several ways to earn money or who saw teaching as a temporary means of achieving other ends.

While political leaders were engaged in nation building, average people were engaged in making ends meet. Most people saw value in literacy and acquiring basic arithmetic skills—they knew enough to know that ignorance can lead to the loss of independence—but how much information was it necessary to know? In small farming communities it did not seem that there was a lot more to know than what could be learned from family, church, and working the land.

Though cities in the early nineteenth century were small by contemporary standards, they shared with modern cities the problem of poverty. Urban leaders and philanthropists created charity schools for the poor, and while these schools did not provide the level of education received by students attending the better-funded independent and boarding schools, they laid the groundwork for public schooling (Kaestle, p. 57). Reformers were greatly aided in their outreach by incorporating the educational system devised by Joseph Lancaster. The Lancasterian system used older students to monitor and drill younger students. Though highly regimented, the system was an inexpensive way to educate large numbers of children, and it provided a steady flow of teachers.

Horace Mann, a lawyer and state legislator in Massachusetts, probably did more than anyone at the time to promote public schooling. Mann advanced the idea of a common school (primary education) that would serve the general educational needs of children of different religious beliefs and customs. The common school would offer reading, writing, and arithmetic at little or no direct cost. Mann led the way toward reforms that we recognize to this day: eight- or nine-month academic terms, systematic examinations, and training for teachers. He supported taxation for schools, argued that schooling was a public responsibility, and that schooling produced responsible citizenship, made workers more productive, and reduced social inequalities. After the Civil War many of the proposals that Mann and other like-minded reformers fought for gained acceptance. Indeed, among social historians of American education, the nineteenth century is referred to as the age of the common school. It was during the nineteenth century that basic educational opportunities became more readily available to the public.

The implementation of these reforms did not occur merely because of the efforts of reformers (though their efforts played an important role); American society itself was changing. More and more adults found work in factories and if their children were not working in the same factory, then they were probably in school. Increasingly, schools took on some of the functions of the home, particularly in what was referred to as character development. Such character training reflected changing circumstances: Home, school, and work were increasingly reflecting the values of the emerging market economy—efficiency, manipulation, and mastery (Kaestle, p. 69).

Common schools gained acceptance among people of varying classes (Kaestle, p. 101). Working class people recognized that their children probably would not be farmers and, like middle class people, saw value in obedient children and hard work. Affluent people felt little threat from the common schools; they sent their children to schools that certified their status, and they did not buy into the notion that schools represented *meritocracy*—people would settle into their stations in life.

Those able to afford to pay tuition for school had several options. Affluent families hired private tutors or sent their children to select boarding schools. Families in the economic middle sent their children to privately funded day schools if they could afford to do so. Perhaps the strongest resistance to the common schools came from religious groups, either because they did not like the nonsectarian nature of the education or because they believed that nonsectarian ultimately meant Protestant. By the end of the nineteenth century Catholics had successfully established parochial schools for their children.

Public schools experienced the most rapid growth in the Northeast. While the South and the Midwest were significantly more agricultural and less densely populated than the Northeast, by 1860 all of the Midwestern states had established publicly funded school systems while the Southern states lagged behind. According to educational historian Carl Kaestle (p. 216) the Midwest was more diverse both economically and ethnically than the South, and this helped to spur industry, which facilitated the assimilation of immigrants (i.e., public schools prepared immigrant children for work in America). However, there continued to be many inequalities of access to public education.

In the first half of the nineteenth century, educational opportunities for African Americans varied considerably by region. In the North, despite poverty and segregation, free blacks established schools for their communities. By the middle of the nineteenth century, a basic educational system for African Americans was in place, along with separate colleges. This educational system cultivated leaders who spoke out against slavery. In the segregated South, whites were typically unsupportive of schooling for blacks. Southern leaders were generally unsupportive of schooling for anyone who was not of the propertied class. At the time when common schools were gaining acceptance in the North and the Midwest, they had made little headway in the South.

Some peculiar statements in defense of slavery at this time had a bearing on sentiments regarding education. For example, proslavery lawyer William Harper argued that "The Creator did not intend that every individual human being should be highly cultivated . . . . It is better that a part should be fully and highly cultivated and the rest utterly ignorant" (cited in Kaestle, p. 206).

While the rise of common schools contributed to a more uniform delivery system of instruction, it did not produce the equality of opportunity that some reformers envisioned. Indeed, women and other minorities faced many obstacles in regard to education. Gender stereotyping worked both against and later for women receiving some level of formal schooling. Because women's primary role was viewed as bearing and raising children, many people did not see value in girls of any social class going to school. This idea would dominate throughout the colonies until the late eighteenth century (Kaestle, p. 28).

After the American Revolution the idea of "republican motherhood" gained momentum. Since women were responsible for raising young children, women needed to be educated with at least basic skills in reading, writing, and moral judgment. Women made inroads as teachers with the popularization of common schools, though for a familiar reason—women were viewed as being responsible for educating children. While women were paid less than their male counterparts, teaching became a means for young women to earn money (though her earnings usually went to support her parents and siblings).

In 1800 most teachers were men, but by 1900 most teachers were women (Kaestle, p. 125). By the late nineteenth century, women exceeded men in literacy and were not only working as teachers and in factories, but also as store clerks, sales, and record-keeping. Rury states, "[F]or those who had access to schooling, a transformation was underway. Women became active in public affairs and moved into new, higher status fields of employment" (2013, p. 111)

While women were pressed into a limited gender-defined mode of existence, and African Americans were pressed into slavery or abject poverty, Native Americans were nearly pressed out of existence. Rury states, "By the end of the nineteenth century . . . battered by almost constant conflict . . . and steadily losing land and resources, the Native American population in the United States had dropped from perhaps 2 million in 1800 to about 250,000" (p. 123). Many Native American children were sent to boarding schools away from their families and were not allowed to speak their native languages. Ultimately this system was abandoned as many returned to the reservations from which they had come.

COLLEGES, UNIVERSITIES, AND THE SCIENCES (1700–1930)

Colleges in colonial America were founded to serve the small, wealthy class of people who dominated the budding nation. However, as commerce, science, and middle-class ambitions grew, and as competition for students increased, colleges diversified their curriculum and showed greater tolerance of religious differences. Curricular changes, shaped by practical changes within America and the growing influence of Enlightenment thought from Europe, included less in the way of theology, literature, and classical languages and more focus on philosophical and scientific studies. Enlightenment thought was more scientific than religious, more skeptical than faithful. It focused more on discovering new knowledge than on preserving old knowledge, and it saw human beings as the shapers of society. (We see here some of the roots of sociology.) The new curriculum would influence greatly the young men who attended the colleges at this time and it would influence their decision to lead the colonies to independence in 1776: John Adams went to Harvard, Thomas Jefferson attended William and Mary, and James Madison went to Princeton.

Partly in resistance to a focus on Enlightenment thought and largely due to denominational rivalry, the number of independent colleges grew tremendously after 1800. Small religious schools dotted the American landscape. According to historian Richard Hofstadter, "The evidence is overwhelming that during the denominational era a great proportion of the schools in the United States that called themselves 'colleges' were in fact not colleges at all, but glorified . . . academies that presumed to offer degrees" ([1955] 1996, p. 223). Nevertheless, the competition for students produced by these schools left many of the older institutions of higher education struggling to survive financially. This prevented the growth of a stable environment conducive to new discoveries. As a result, more science was still being done outside of the colleges than inside them, and American colleges could not keep up with the new discoveries coming out of their European counterparts.

The Civil War divided scientists as much as it did everyone else. The colleges tended to either support abolition or espouse a proslavery position; academic freedom had not yet been established and so faculty members were either muted or supportive of the prevailing ideology. In the North and Midwest, some of the colleges—such as Berea in Kentucky, Oberlin in Ohio, and New York College—unequivocally supported abolition; however, most of the colleges and their faculties did not engage in serious efforts to assuage the issues leading to secession. In the South, any faculty opposition to slavery was suppressed.

This schism between American scholars contributed to the burgeoning notion that the scientific method would produce results without bias. Mathematician and philosopher of science Chauncey Wright said that science comes into its own "when it ceases to be associated with our fears, our respects, our aspirations; when it ceases to prompt questions as to what relates to our personal destiny, our ambitions, our moral worth; when it ceases to have man, his personal and social nature, as its central and control-

ling objects" (cited in Metzger, 1961, p. 80). While the pursuit of this idealis-
tic notion of overcoming personal bias in order to maintain a neutral or
disinterested stand obscured how difficult a goal that is to achieve, there was
some benefit to at least aspiring toward an objective science that might
transcend ideology and profit. (We will return to this issue later in the chapter.)

Following the Civil War, the older colleges and state universities acquired
new revenue streams and an energized new direction. Innovations in science
and technology widened people's views of what seemed possible. The federal government invested in technology in order to support a more sophisticated defense. Congress began appropriating federal aid annually for state and
university research. This contributed to the rise of observatories, a national
weather service, geological surveys, national parks, marine science, and other innovations (Bruce 1987, pp. 317–324). More and more American scientists traveled to Germany to study at their universities, considered at the time
to be the model of higher education, and returned home ambitious to emulate
those universities on American soil. Industrial growth led men of commerce
to see benefit in research, so their contributions to higher education increased
in scale.

As industrial development invigorated the idea of new discoveries, religious fervor about focusing on knowledge of the past dimmed. Darwinism
also came to America around this time and stimulated much discussion about
science. Debates about evolution were raging in Europe and in the United
States by the late nineteenth century. The debates about Darwin's theory of
evolution not only centered on humankind's origins and purpose, but also
methodology: Careful observation of the natural world would reveal knowledge that faith in past knowledge could not. Historian Walter Metzger states,

> There had been a time when the only systematic professional training in Amer-
> ica had been for ministry. Lawyers and doctors had learned their trades as
> apprentices, and scientists had practically trained themselves. By the 1880s the
> universities were taking over the professional and pre-professional training of
> doctors and lawyers, and a trend toward specialized training in the sciences
> was going on apace. (1961, p. 76)

At early American colleges, the president of the school was the teacher and
there were a few tutors to supplement training. Gradually professors replaced
tutors, and, rather than the trustees or president, professors began to govern
the curriculum, textbook selections, the hiring of colleagues, and other facul-
ty-related matters. Additional changes during this time period included the
replacement of recitation (i.e., the memorization and reproduction of a text)
with lecture and discussion, and the rise of a diversity of electives—changes
that reflected the German university model. Johns Hopkins University was
established in 1876 and was the first research institution modeled after the

German university. Another significant import from the German university was the idea of academic freedom, which held that an institution of higher learning was a place that was safe for independence of mind and free inquiry.

The development of the American university mirrored and benefitted from the growth of American industry. The connection between education and industry was facilitated by the passage of the Morrill Land Grant Act in 1862. Introduced by Representative Justin Morrill of Vermont and supported by Lincoln and Congress, the legislation "offered every state thirty thousand acres of public land per senator and representative for endowment of 'colleges for the benefit of agriculture and the mechanic arts . . . without excluding other scientific or classical studies'" (Bruce, p. 302). The Morrill Act facilitated the growth of private and state colleges and universities, agricultural colleges, and technological institutions. It fostered trained engineers who could depend upon scientific principles, rather than hunches acquired from experience, to build the nation's growing infrastructure. While success based upon experience and intuition had contributed to the mystique of American ingenuity, engineers realized that there were better options than learning from their mistakes to effect improvements on their structures (Bruce, p. 159). The rise of technological institutions fostered the growing interdependence of technology and science. The most successful of these institutions was the establishment of the Massachusetts Institute of Technology (MIT) in 1861.

The role of education and science in the United States would be twofold: The larger role would be geared toward practical application, while the subsidiary role would be toward pure science or investigation without immediate application. The value placed on practical application was also reflected in the rise of undergraduate and graduate schools of business. These schools reflected the changing times. Businessmen anxious to pass along their success to their sons found that higher education added influence to their already advantaged position (Hofstadter & Hardy 1954, p. 91). The founding of the Wharton School in 1881 at the University of Pennsylvania was the first of many business schools to open their doors during the late nineteenth and early twentieth centuries. By the turn of the century more and more young executives were being recruited out of these schools (Hofstadter 1963, p. 261).

The tension between practical application and pure science in higher education was not lost on many scientists. While scientists wanted freedom from restraint in the pursuit of knowledge, they recognized that economically driven interest groups were replacing religiously driven interest groups in attempting to define the meaning of "educated," the limits of knowledge, and the direction of scientific investigation.

During the late nineteenth and early twentieth centuries the American university acquired its basic modern identity of offering a variety of undergraduate courses, graduate specialization, and an emphasis on research. As the twentieth century would progress, the basic modern university would diversify further by incorporating and sometimes stressing courses in the humanities and by offering a wider range of pre-professional and professional programs.

THE RISE OF HIGH SCHOOLS, STANDARDIZATION OF EDUCATION, AND THE NEW ECONOMY (1865–1930)

Though colleges and universities grew in numbers, size, and scope, they served only a minority of the nation's population until well into the twentieth century. Apprenticing to learn a trade had died out, and for the growing number of children from the managerial and professional classes, high school became the route to receive training. High school was not necessarily preparation for college, but it was preparation for work in one of the professions (e.g., business, law, medicine).

Northern victory in the Civil War not only facilitated industrial growth, but it also led to a massive shift of people into the nation's cities. A wide gulf opened up between a minority of wealthy industrialists and a majority seeking work. The United States went into an economic depression that lasted from 1873 to about 1879. This led to a major railroad strike in 1877. The United States went into another economic depression in 1893 that lasted until 1897 and this contributed to another series of strikes.

A further reaction to these events was the rise of the Populists, a political movement comprised of hard-pressed farmers in the Midwest and South. Working sometimes in cooperation with labor unions, the Populists formed a powerful, though short-lived, coalition against the industrialists and urbanization. Members of these and other groups expressed concern that concentrated wealth and private interests were corrupting government and threatening democracy. The Populists were the latest expression of folk Americana: surviving on your wits as a frontiersman, cowboy, or independent, small property owner.

Between the 1880s and the 1920s the idea of "rugged individualism" would be forged into its modern guise. As Frederick Jackson Turner wrote about the closing of the American frontier, new frontiers were being dreamt up by men such as Horatio Alger who popularized the story of "rags to riches" and James Truslow Adams who popularized the idea of the American Dream. While the majority of people did not get to experience it, no one had ever seen such a concentration of wealth, influence, and glamour in the hands of a minority of citizens. The way of life of a few was transformed into a romantic myth of hard work, financial success, and the consumption of goods. At the same time, the notion of individualism was transformed from meaning "self-sufficient" to meaning "financially capable and influential." This period of time became known as the Gilded Age.

By 1920 the majority of Americans were no longer growing up on farms but rather in or near cities. Urbanization and industrialization created the need for trained workers who could carry out specialized tasks. A new group of reformers called Progressives (with greater ambitions than the earlier group of Populists) debated amongst themselves and with other interest groups (e.g., industrialists and politicians) about how best to structure education under these changing demographic and economic conditions.

John Dewey was a leading voice among one group of reformers. Following in the footsteps of Horace Mann in some respects, Dewey stressed the importance of schooling for the well-being of individuals and for the nation. Emphasizing a pragmatic and experiential approach to learning, Dewey argued that an informed citizenry was the key to social order, prosperity, and democracy. According to Dewey, "[Society] must have a type of education which gives individuals a personal interest in social relationships and control, and the habits of mind which secure social changes without introducing disorder" (cited in Hofstadter 1963, p. 378). In other words, education should include enough lessons in civics so that individuals can understand the society of which they are a part. Like the title of one of his books, *Democracy and Education* go hand in hand. Dewey was reminding Americans of what Thomas Jefferson had said many years prior: "If a nation expects to be ignorant and free in a state of civilization, it expects what never was and never will be" (cited in Hofstadter 1963, p. 300).

Other reformers, realizing that many people, perhaps the majority, are motivated more by a clear and relatively quick path to a concrete goal rather than coming to an understanding of the abstract factors that link together work and politics, focused more on training people for jobs that needed to be filled in the new economy. These reformers saw high school as the road on which young people could acquire the needed skills and aspire to a middle-class life (Rury 152).

The popularization of public secondary education was slow in coming. Indeed, public secondary education trailed behind the development of both common schools and post-secondary education. The first high school opened in Boston in 1821, but it was not until the twentieth century that attending high school became a social norm. By 1900 advances in technology required the use of fewer, more skilled workers. Young and inexperienced workers were becoming less cost effective. Consider that by the end of the nineteenth century innovations in the uses of electricity and the combustion engine were transforming people's relationships with technology and with each other.

The split in vision among reformers and other interest groups displayed wide disagreement about the goals and the curriculum of public secondary education. The issue came to a head with the Depression. In order to keep jobs available for adults with families, the federal government enacted regulations barring or obstructing teen employment (Hine, p. 204). Many young people found themselves in school or wandering the streets. During the Depression, high school enrollment increased by nearly 50 percent (Hine, p. 215). The reformers who stressed the importance of practical training and work had won the day—at least temporarily. Secondary education was to be about fortifying the three R's, character development, citizenship, and vocation (Hofstadter 1963, p. 335). The curriculum for boys and girls, which had been the same in the late 1800s, would increasingly become divided into gendered roles—boys would acquire skills for a practical trade and girls would acquire the skills necessary to manage the home (Rury p. 166). According to educational historian John Rury, "[T]he term social efficiency . . . represented the ability of schools to provide students with appropriate knowledge and skills, and to sort them according to achievement. This was a new form of efficiency . . . . It referred to the degree that schools . . . contributed to the growing number of roles and economic functions people would play in the social order" (p. 153).

While education had once been elitist, it would now become about consumption and conformity—a far cry from what George Washington may have intended in his Farewell Address when he urged the promotion of "institutions for the general diffusion of knowledge" (Hofstadter 1963, pp. 299, 344). Education would reinforce existing trends in gender bias and racial and ethnic discrimination, but one thing was new: as it became fixed in many people's minds that schooling was important for the success of the individual and for the functioning and growth of society, education became a part of the institutional landscape of America.

As primary and secondary education coalesced into a standardized system during the early decades of the twentieth century, their role of socializing youth became more important. High schools would broaden their curriculum and become the mainstream way of processing young people into the labor market.

THE RISE OF THE SOCIAL SCIENCES (1900–1945)

Conflicting events and changes, along with the rise of universities and specialized academic training, led to the growth and development of the social sciences in America. It was during these years that sociologist William Graham Sumner popularized Herbert Spencer's interpretation of society as the "survival of the fittest." In many people's minds, the idea that only the most fit in society could thrive went hand-in-hand with the romantic myth of individual success.

Other social scientists expressed more critical views of the times. Economist Thorstein Veblen was one of the earliest social critics of the rise of consumer society, noting how business values and consumption were coming to dominate all other values. Historian Dorothy Ross notes that Veblen observed, "In the class society America had become in the Gilded Age, democracy did not destroy classes, only widened the field of emulation, thereby strengthening upper-class hegemony" (2004, p. 209) In other words, by making business values the dominant values or the values of hegemonic status, all individual goals would be tailored toward meeting the values of the dominant business class (i.e., if education is not about tailoring people to fit into corporately defined bureaucratic roles, then education is of little value).

During the early years of the twentieth century American social science slowly acquired a voice of its own. C. W. A. Veditz, Lester Ward, William Sumner, Franklin Giddings, Albion Small, and others formed the American Sociological Society in 1905. Small also developed a strong sociology department at the University of Chicago. Along with George Herbert Mead, W. I. Thomas, Robert Park, and others, Small would go on to found "Chicago sociology," uniquely combining field work, urban issues, and sociological concepts. Meanwhile, at Columbia University, Giddings developed a strong sociology department that emphasized statistical methods.

These two approaches to examining social issues would become the pillars of sociology in the United States: one being a more qualitative and activist approach, the other being a more quantitative and disinterested approach. The former also was the place where the philosophy of pragmatism and sociology came together and would become known as symbolic interactionism (a school of thought that would influence more and more sociologists as the twentieth century progressed).

Another group of social scientists formed the American Association of University Professors. Their development of the "Declaration of Principles on Academic Freedom and Academic Tenure" in 1915 helped to establish the members of the growing professorate as a professional class, independent from the domination of hegemonic trends. The codification of academic freedom at the universities was advanced because of the point of view that knowledge and innovation can only occur in an environment of free inquiry. If a society seeks to further its interests through education, then it must support the institution without seeking to limit its scope: Without free inquiry, open debate, and responsible, broadminded, and forward-thinking support, new knowledge cannot be obtained.

The development of the social sciences in higher education, the growth of professional academic organizations, the participation of scientists of all kinds in the government and military, and the rise of polling and marketing research all took shape during the early decades of the twentieth century. These outlets would become the paths on which the social sciences would expand and influence society for decades to come. However, these influences would be in ways not foreseen by many of the early proponents of sociology and psychology.

Since the time of Isaac Newton's publication of the *Principia* in 1687, in which he devised a mathematical formulation of the workings of the universe, most scientists in nearly all fields of study have embraced the ideal of objectivity in their pursuit to understand phenomena. In sociology, August Comte, the man who coined the term, argued that he was advancing the scientific study of society. In psychology Sigmund Freud argued that psychoanalysis was the scientific study of the mind. In order to establish their fields of inquiry, both Comte and Freud embraced the ideal of objectivity. At the time in which sociology and psychology were becoming established, the ideal of objectivity and empirical investigation was associated with scientific inquiry, with the view that such inquiry would enable investigators to bypass subjective judgment and derive objective information about the phenomena under study, including the workings of society and the workings of the mind. Nevertheless, the argument can be made that they, like all contemporaries, failed to see the bigger picture of how everyday practical pressures associated with economic, social, and political shifts were changing the times in which they lived and the nature of their studies.

The acceptance and expansion of science and higher education in America was not only due to the efforts of scientists who believed in what they were doing, but also in large measure was because of government and corporate investment in projects that might yield quick military and economic benefits. For a variety of reasons the United States has always been a mobile and practical society. American scientists always have been more keenly aware of the ideal of objectivity in research design and methodology than of the ideal of objectivity in terms of culture's influences on the community of scientists. As scientists of all types acquired social legitimation, the notion that academic freedom serves as a precursor to innovation and societal progress collided with America's orientation of practical application and quick fixes. Economic benefits during the early years of the twentieth century did not simply mean developing new and better products; it also meant training people for different roles in the new industrial economy as well as taming those who encouraged labor unrest. In time, industries and government would call on psychologists and sociologists in order to achieve these goals.

Psychologists Hugo Munsterberg and Walter Dill Scott developed the first psychological tests used by industry and government. Tests of intelligence and general ability devised by Scott were used by the military during World War I. After the war, former army psychologists saw opportunities to work as consultants for industry. Industrial leaders realized "that a careful study of this 'human factor' pays in dollars and cents, that 'it is admittedly good business to consider the psychological side'" (Baritz 1960, p. 35).

In the 1920s a group of researchers led by Elton Mayo conducted pioneering work in the social scientific study of productivity in the workplace. The research was carried out at an old manufacturing plant called Hawthorne Works of the Western Electric Company. The purpose of the Hawthorne experiments was to learn how to increase the motivation of employees in order to increase production. The most significant finding from this research was that workers form social bonds that regulate their productivity: the workers put social pressure on each other in order to arrive at a mutually comfortable or tolerable level of output. Employees formed social bonds in order to maintain a collective as well as individual sense of dignity and independence in the face of social pressures stemming from management's attempts to regulate their behavior. Another significant finding from these studies came when the researchers interviewed employees: They discovered that nondirective interviews gave employees a sense of recognition.

The Hawthorne experiments awakened industry to the importance of interpersonal processes. Industry realized that social and psychological factors could be regulated to increase productivity. Hofstadter and Hardy make the point that "in a society in which raw, forceful modes of self-assertion were giving way to more subtle ways of personal manipulation—a society obsessed with its 'personnel problems' and its 'interpersonal relations'—sensitivity and humane culture became valuable properties even in a paradoxically crass and utilitarian sense" (1954, p. 59). Creating personnel offices that included counseling enabled employees to express their feelings, making the employee feel better while not disrupting business practices. Management also discovered that by giving employees a voice (however superficial) in the operations of the company and encouraging employees to work in teams, individual behavior could be regulated through social processes to enhance productivity. The fact that the members of management as well as the group of researchers formed social bonds—which influenced their behavior—to deal with the social pressures impinging upon them was not addressed by these studies (Baritz, p. 142).

While productivity increased the supply of goods, it did not address the problem of maintaining sales and combating negative press and public recalcitrance. To deal with these issues, business leaders were once again aided by psychologists and social scientists. The goal was not only to manage the behavior of employees, but also to manage the behavior of potential customers (the transition in categorization from citizen to consumer was only one part of a hard-won campaign). It was during the Gilded Age that government and business leaders realized the importance of impression management.

The government got into monitoring and attempting to shape public opinion when Woodrow Wilson established the Committee on Public Information to mobilize public support during World War I (Cutlip, Center, & Broom 2006, p. 102). Edward Bernays, sometimes referred to as the "father of spin" was a leader in forging impression management into a lucrative profession. Bernays took advantage of his association with his famous uncle, Sigmund Freud. (Freud was married to Martha Bernays, and Sigmund's sister, Anna, was married to Martha's brother Eli. Edward Bernays was the son of Eli and Anna.) According to Sheldon Rampton and John Stauber, "Bernays used Freudianism's scientific claims as a sort of marketing hook with which to sell his services to anxious corporate executives" (2001, p. 41).

As education became institutionalized in America, its purposes would be molded to fit in with the more dominant institutions (i.e., education would be a soft institution in relation to its economic and political hard institution counterparts). Increasingly, education and research would be channeled into shifting political visions of expediency, the creation of an aimless and bloated weapons industry, and the mass marketing of business values and consumption.

ADDRESSING THE STRATIFICATION OF EDUCATION (1945 TO THE PRESENT)

Debates among progressive educators and their critics raged on before and after the Second World War. After the war more children than ever before were going to school. A baby boom, greater emphasis on education, liberal trends, and prosperity during the postwar boom years led to a series of government policy initiatives in education. The 1954 Supreme Court ruling in *Brown vs. Board of Education* officially ended segregation in the schools. In 1965 President Lyndon Johnson oversaw the passage of the Elementary and Secondary Education Act and the founding of the Head Start program, both of which were created to increase equality of opportunity in education. In 1972 an amendment referred to as Title IX was passed as part of federal education legislation. Title IX challenged discrimination on the basis of sex in education. Title IX eventually led to greater equality of opportunity for women in collegiate sports. The Education for All Handicapped Children Act was signed into law by President Gerald Ford in 1975; this required schools to provide educational opportunities for students with special needs.

Federal funding for education, the focus on civil rights, and other liberal trends led to experimentation in instructional methods in the late 1960s and 1970s; in particular, "open education" attracted a lot of attention at this time. Open education, like progressive education earlier in the twentieth century, emphasized experiential learning.

While many people applauded nontraditional courses of study and flexible scheduling, concerns about falling scores on standardized tests produced a backlash call for schools to return to "the basics." By the 1980s the postwar boom years were over, liberalism had run its course, and a different approach to reforming education was underway. In 1983 a report issued by the Department of Education, entitled *A Nation at Risk*, expressed concern that a lack of sufficient content in education was denying students the tools necessary to have a fair chance. The report focused on matters such as curriculum, graduation requirements, teacher preparation, and the textbooks in use (Ravitch 2010, p. 25). To address these issues, leaders in both political parties called for national standards and testing. Federal oversight went to the states, and local legislatures devised various definitions and procedures for assessing and meeting educational standards. A program was finally put into place shortly after the presidential election of George W. Bush in 2000. The federal program, called No Child Left Behind, mandates that every child in grades three through eight be tested annually, that poorly performing schools take corrective measures, that children in poorly performing schools have the choice to transfer to another school, and that every state take responsibility for implementing these policies in whatever way they see fit. Student performance on tests and teacher accountability on assessment reports measure whether or not standards are improving.

The program, however, has run into a number of difficulties. For one, because proficiency varies per state, children who meet standards in one state can find themselves failing to meet standards if their family moves to another state. In addition, while schools that show proficiency are rewarded, in many cases struggling schools continue to lack the resources necessary to take corrective action. As a result, some schools have engaged in questionable and unscrupulous practices in order to appear proficient and receive federal dollars. Some school districts have been found surreptitiously lowering their standards in order to meet proficiency and then reporting improved standards (Ravitch 2010, p. 158). By the end of Bush's second term, nearly 36 percent of all public schools were failing to make adequate yearly progress (Ravitch, p. 105).

It was in this environment that charter schools, magnet schools, and home schooling became popular options. Charter schools are privately managed institutions that receive public funding. Magnet schools are publicly funded institutions with specialized curricula (in areas such as engineering, the humanities, and so on). The problem with charter and magnet schools is that enrollment is based upon a lottery. If families want their children to go to a better school than the one they attend, then they must win the lottery, move to another district, or have the resources for private or home schooling. The other problem with charter and magnet schools is that they vary greatly in quality. They offer no promise of providing a superior education to public schooling, yet they drain funds away from standard public schools, where the vast majority of children are educated.

Of those children who remain in a failing school, if the school closes, the children are funneled into a school that likely has been accumulating students who lack adequate academic preparation from other schools that have closed; the result is a larger aggregate of students who lack adequate academic preparation, which in turn, increases the difficulty of reaching and teaching each child. Since Barack Obama has been president, his version of No Child Left Behind, entitled Race to the Top, has done little of substantive value to correct the problems outlined here.

In the 1980s and 1990s, as the world's economies merged and global processes facilitated the transformation of the United States economy from manufacturing to services, the role of education became more important just as funding and vision for education were dissipating. Ironically, as the managerial bureaucracy for schooling got bigger, resources for teachers and students got smaller. The result was that schools had to do more with less, and confidence in public education eroded. States and local districts took greater responsibility for determining education, and leaders, not knowing where to go for solutions, turned to what leaders since the Gilded Age have resorted to—business models and marketing. Although education had been viewed as a means to an economic end for decades, this notion now buried from view (with some individual exceptions) the centuries-old connection between education and informed citizenship. For the majority of students, the battle of education as vocational training versus training in the liberal arts appeared to be over.

Yet despite, or perhaps because of, the victory of education as vocational training, by the 1980s schools were once again appearing segregated by income, race, and ethnicity. Moreover, the nature of vocational training had changed. During the postwar boom years, vocational training meant the acquisition of skills necessary for a job in manufacturing. Such training could be acquired in high school, and the job a young man could get with this training would support the needs of a family. By the 1980s, the opportunity for transition from high school vocational training to a reasonably paying manufacturing job was gone. Today, people with a high school degree will earn much less money over the course of their lives than people with a college degree. In today's service economy, vocational training means, minimally, the acquisition of social and technical skills.

In the current global economy—of which our service economy is a part— every unique skill can make one applicant stand out from the crowd. By the end of the twentieth century some form of post-secondary education was required in order to gain an economic advantage. As the nineteenth century was the age of the common school; and the early twentieth century, the age of the high school; the latter part of the twentieth century would be the age of post-secondary education.

In order to take advantage of post-secondary education, a child needs to be prepared adequately. However, without vision and funding, preparation for college is a rigged game. Within this framework of the new service economy, parents who understand the new rules in education begin to prepare their children for college starting in kindergarten. Parents in the know and with resources understand that education is now, more than ever before, not only an investment, but a series of connections linking together the right kindergarten and primary school with the right secondary school, the right college or university, and then a higher paying entry-level job.

Over the past thirty years getting an elite education has become increasingly important in getting an edge over the competition for higher paying status positions. What the elite schools offer is, in many ways, the opposite of what is offered in many public schools. While pressures on the public schools have led them to focus almost exclusively on reading, math, and test-taking, the elite schools include music, theater, literature, and critical thinking along with their focus on reading, math, and test-taking. This additional training provides learners with skills and opportunities that set them apart from the majority. In this growing system of educational inequality, the marketing of meritocracy and of the American Dream has become more pronounced. Rather than investing in the public schools and aligning them with the demands of today's challenges, leaders over the past thirty years have taken the easier path of investing in the marketing of ideals that do not remedy the circumstances.

With a lack of vision, people look to the past for guidance rather than toward the future. The old vision—which did not last very long—was a working dad, a stay-at-home mom, and a high school education that would prepare the young for entry into the workforce. In today's global economy and with America's divorce rate hovering around 50 percent, reality makes that vision obsolete for most people, though many still hold onto that vision because a new one has not taken hold. As Thomas Hine states,

> [F]amilies in middle- and lower-income ranges have been suffering from a squeeze, one that helps explain their inability to spend as much time with their children as middle-class norms have traditionally required. What contemporary American families are attempting—providing prolonged, protected period of childhood and youthful preparation for our offspring while both parents work outside the household—is novel. In the past, when both parents worked, their children did so as well. And when schooling became the job of the young, it was usually supported by a nonworking mother maintaining a household that explicitly supported educational values. Today the only constant presence in the household is the television set . . . . What the television set conveys is an unrealistic view of the linkages associating family and education with financial success. (p. 285)

Over the past thirty years, researchers have learned much about the factors that perpetuate educational inequality (though this research has not really had an impact on public policy). Arguably the individual who has had the greatest impact in recent years in this area is French sociologist Pierre Bourdieu. In his landmark book (published in 1979), entitled *Distinction: A Social Critique of the Judgment of Taste*, Bourdieu laid out a new vocabulary for understanding the subtle processes that perpetuate inequality. Bourdieu discusses four types of capital: *cultural capital* refers to social skills, language skills, mannerisms, and the like; *social capital* refers to social networks; *symbolic capital* refers to authority and power; and *economic capital* refers to financial resources. He refers to the first three factors as capital because they all contribute to the acquisition of the fourth factor (resulting in economic gain).

These forms of capital are acquired in the family and through education and they culminate in what Bourdieu calls *habitus*. Cultural capital, in particular, molds an individual's personal disposition in ways that either open up or shut down opportunities. According to Bourdieu, these dynamics operate on what he calls a *field*. A classroom, a baseball diamond, and a rough urban street represent different fields, and each requires a different habitus in order for a person to be successful.

Our upbringing prepares us for some fields better than others. A kid who dreams of being a baseball player and spends all of his/her free time practicing and playing ball will come to feel very comfortable on a baseball diamond, but s/he may feel less comfortable in a classroom or a rough urban street. A kid who grows up in an academic home is more likely to feel comfortable in a classroom than the kid who spends most of his/her time engaged in a sport or a kid who grows up in poverty. This feeling of comfort is a part of one's habitus and it conveys to others whether or not a person belongs on a given field. A student who feels comfortable in the classroom and knows how to communicate with his/her teachers is more likely to get the attention s/he needs in order to advance on that field.

In the United States today, young people are told that they need to finish high school and go on to college in order to be successful. However, young people are equipped with varying amounts and forms of habitus that may or may not prepare them to excel on that field. While the majority of young people today begin college at a two-year or four-year public, private, or for-profit institution, most never finish. According to the United States Department of Education, the number of Americans who obtain a bachelor's degree hovers around 30 percent.

Sociologists refer to the processes described by Bourdieu as *social reproduction*. People with economic capital invest in their children's future success by providing them with the habitus they need in order to acquire a competitive edge. As a result, they send their kids to private schools, have them participate in competitive sport, dance, and so on, and encourage them to network with others. The goal is to raise children who are articulate, able-bodied, and confident on the fields that yield economic benefits. While this may be the ultimate goal of most parents, many do not know how to increase the likelihood of this result.

Most researchers agree that parental education and family income are the best predictors of academic outcomes among youth (Grace & Thompson 2003; Roksa et al. 2007). Habitus contributes to structural inequalities. To remedy the situation, young people either need to be prepared better for being successful in today's service and knowledge-based economy, or the structure of the United States economy needs to be reshaped so that a wider range of occupations lead to modern standards of maintaining a livelihood. Current research shows that neither educational expansion nor specific public policies to-date have altered the effects of socioeconomic background on educational attainment. Josipa Roksa, Eric Grodsky, Richard Arum, and Adam Gamoran state,

> While postsecondary education became open to virtually all high-school grad-uates by the end of the twentieth century, solidification of an educational hierarchy and a split between elite and mass forms of education constrained student opportunities. The mass sector developed a diversified range of lower-status academic institutions and vocationally oriented programs, while the elite institutions maintained academic focus and selectivity, resulting in a highly stratified system. (p. 168)

The for-profit educational industry has taken the most advantage of young people inexperienced in education by making false promises of a bright future with their degree while their students have racked up huge debts from educational loans. Even though the United States needs a more highly trained workforce than ever before, government aid for higher education has not kept pace with the costs of earning a post-secondary degree. As a result, more young people are incurring greater school debt than ever before. This harms society in many ways. First of all, it delays the ability of young people to become established. Second, it produces psychological and sociological ten-sions because the means of achieving society's commercialized view of suc-cess is undercut. Finally, it demonstrates little regard for the future of soci-ety—there is no real understanding of how society is maintained across gen-erations.

PUBLIC POLICY AND THE PUSH TOWARD UTILITARIAN
EDUCATION (1945 TO THE PRESENT)

During the Second World War Franklin Roosevelt tapped an engineer by the name of Vannevar Bush to mobilize scientists and engineers for the war effort. Bush organized a federal grant system that enabled scientists working at universities, research institutes, and industrial laboratories to follow through on their lines of investigation. The coordination of these efforts led to the atomic bomb, advanced radar systems, advances in computer technology, and breakthroughs in medicine and treatment. The mix of science, technology, and defense proved to be a powerful and innovative combination.

After the war Bush and a panel of experts wrote an influential document, entitled *Science: The Endless Frontier*. Bush did not want to lose ground on scientific research and innovation during peace time. The document recognized a division of labor between scientists in industry and scientists at research universities.

Working under commercial pressures, industrial scientists focus on research projects that may be developed and earn a return on their investment relatively quickly. University researchers tend to focus on projects that take time to develop and may or may not see a fruitful return. The difference represents research for utilitarian purposes and pure research. Both are needed for innovation. For example, the laser was developed before it had a practical use. Today, lasers are used in retail stores, hospitals, and defense.

The document proposed increasing federal funding of military research and development (R & D), greater support of medical R & D, and more support of basic research at the universities. All three of these proposals were implemented over time (though military R & D received the most support) and constituted what was sometimes referred to as the "military-industrial-academic complex." Universities received federal funding through the National Science Foundation, and greater support of medical R & D occurred by way of the National Institutes of Health. Meanwhile, the university-military connection remained vital. Rapid growth and development in research occurred from the 1950s until the early 1980s. Throughout this period the United States was the world's frontrunner in most fields of science (Rosenberg & Nelson 1993, p. 335).

Government support of education and science was evident in many ways. The Serviceman's Readjustment Act created the GI Bill providing assistance to veterans seeking to further their education after wartime service. The ties established during the war between behavioral and social scientists and many branches of the government continued after the war. The Kennedy and Johnson administrations turned to behavioral and social scientists to acquire a better understanding of the social upheavals occurring in society at that time and to devise social policies to address them. In hindsight, the variety of views expressed by different behavioral and social scientists and expectations for quick results led to disillusionment among many government leaders and members of the public about what psychologists and sociologists could actually do to ameliorate psychological and social ills. Many professionals were also unaware of the amount of time and effort it takes for social institutions to change. By and large, institutional leaders resist change even when they express public support for it.

In the 1970s, with the decline of economic growth and corporations on the defensive due to social welfare groups' and government regulators' charges of corporate misuse of power, business leaders took to the offensive. By the 1980s and thereafter, behavioral and social scientists would see the effects of their efforts being used less in the public sector and more in the private sector. Scientists in all fields increasingly saw the results of their research being used by policy makers and business leaders in order to "sell" an ideology or a product.

While the economy was strong during the postwar years, many Americans felt more comfortable sharing the wealth and exploring the connections between existential well-being and everyday real life. However, in the 1980s as the schools returned to "the basics," opportunities for work became more challenging, and business leaders popularized corporate values, courses in the arts and sciences began to decline in both the public high schools and second-tier universities. While the liberal arts enjoyed popularity during the postwar years, by the 1980s the pendulum had swung back in the utilitarian direction of occupational and professional programs. Rury observes that "[t]he years following Ronald Reagan's election in 1980 marked a rather dramatic shift in the way Americans thought about education. Concerns about equity gave way to an abiding interest in schooling as a tool for economic development, and for individual advancement" (p. 213). The graduating class of 1970 was the last year in which a majority of students from four-year colleges and universities graduated with a degree in the arts and sciences (Brint 2002, p. 232).

People, young and old, completing college today are most likely to earn a degree in business, information technology, health care, or corrections. The fields out of the arts and sciences that remain popular are life sciences and psychology (in part because of their links to occupational and professional fields). While more people are attending college today than in the past, enrollments are down in the humanities, social sciences, physical sciences, and mathematics. These shifts in enrollment exemplify how social factors affect individual decision-making. When asked why an individual is pursuing a degree in a particular field, they may say that it's because they love the subject area, but most likely they will say that they have conducted some type of cost/benefit analysis in their mind, and have determined that their area of study is most likely to lead to a high-paying job. This is another way of saying that most individuals choose among a list of options made available to them by social circumstances that seem (if one is aware of them) beyond control.

As noted earlier, the rise of the service economy during the latter part of the twentieth century created more higher paying, skilled labor jobs than did the manufacturing-based economy, but it produced fewer jobs overall, particularly in unskilled labor. Reforms in education since the 1980s have attempted to meet, with varying degrees of success, the demands of a service economy in a global marketplace. Rury sums it up well,

> The point of systemic reform was to make schooling productive in terms of specific curricula, and most of the attention . . . was focused on mathematics, science, and reading. These were the subject areas most frequently linked to the new service and professional sectors of the economy . . . . Standardized tests simply were a form of technology well suited to the task of identifying individuals who had developed these abilities . . . . Making a school accountable for producing more such skilled individuals was thus a strategy for strengthening the national capacity for economic growth and . . . improving the productivity and earning power of individual Americans. In other words, education was increasingly seen as just another factor of production, subject to measurement and improvement like . . . new machinery . . . . [S]chools appear to have been made subsidiary to their economic function, at least as regards national policy. (pp. 228–229)

Education had always served a utilitarian function, but under economic pressures, national concerns, and a corporate ideology, education as a means of maintaining an informed citizenry was thrust further into the background. Since the 1980s, the norm in education has stressed that learning is a means to an economic end and not an end in itself. The new popular fields of study reinforce self-interest and acquisition as normal and proper goals in life, and while self-interest and acquisition have their place, the times have twisted these values into the goals of life, the road to happiness, and human nature.

As generations of youth have been educated with these new priorities, the results are predictable: a population of self-interested consumers. Unfortunately, utilitarian values, while practical, are not always realistic in solving individual and societal problems. For one, human beings are social creatures, so to promote self-interest as a norm contradicts how we as a species function and thrive. Second, consumption is a self-limiting means of acquiring happiness. Past a certain point, consumption does not bring happiness (Myers 1993; Frey and Stutzer 2001). Happiness is a byproduct of meaningful action and interaction. Third, while many schools and colleges have marginalized the liberal arts in order to satisfy consumer demand and pay their bills, it is from the liberal arts that one acquires the skills to engage in critical thinking, exploration, and the development of new ideas.

The fact of the matter is that people in the occupation and professional fields depend upon individuals who have received training in the arts and sciences. Art, literature, psychology, chemistry, biology, physics, and so forth, are basic requirements for people in many applied fields who realize that training in the liberal arts is perhaps the best way of getting innovation out of technical proficiency. The nations that lead the world in education do not strip down their curricula in order to produce more engineers and scientists; they enrich their curricula so that young people come to realize that education makes one more thoughtful. In a global marketplace, of which the United States is a part, language requirements should be on the rise rather than in decline.

The most dangerous thing about superficial mass education may be that it produces people with credentials who believe that they know more than they do. And those who recognize this and shun formal education (rather than working through the educational system and getting the most out of the experience) wind up like their counterparts, believing that they know more than they actually do. One of the hallmarks of a thoughtful person is to be able to look at an engrained and unexamined assumption and say, "I don't know why I believe that."

PRIVATIZATION OF SCIENTIFIC KNOWLEDGE (1970 TO THE PRESENT)

The desire to maintain economic dominance and be globally competitive led many in government, industry, and academe to assume that the best way to achieve those goals was to emphasize a utilitarian approach in research (i.e., scientific investigations should yield a quick return on their investment). The differences between pure research at the universities and applied research in industry were blurred.

The convergence of these streams of research began in earnest after 1973 when Stanley Cohen, a geneticist at Stanford University, and Herbert Boyer, a biochemist at the University of California at San Francisco (UCSF), engaged in the first successful series of experiments to engineer the replication of genes, or cloning. Up until this time, university research was usually considered to be a public good. Universities received federal grants to conduct their investigations and the notion of restricting access to health-related discoveries was viewed by many in academe to be antithetical to their mission. For example, when Jonas Salk developed the polio vaccine, he did not patent his discovery; when asked who owned the vaccine, he is known to have replied, "The people."

By the 1970s federal support for university research was on the decline, and university administrators were on the lookout for new sources of generating revenue. The Cohen-Boyer gene-splicing technique was nonexclusively licensed. This meant that anyone could use the technology for a price. The scientists, Stanford, and UCSF profited from the discovery. Several years later Boyer founded a biotech firm called Genentech. When the company went public in 1980, Boyer and his investors made millions of dollars. Thereafter, venture capitalists and the pharmaceutical industry began to invest more in university-based research projects. University researchers began to establish privately owned biotech firms.

All of this was facilitated by the University Small Business Patent Procedures Act of 1980. This legislation, usually referred to as the Bayh-Dole Act, created a patent policy that enabled universities and businesses to have automatic ownership rights to federally funded research. Legislation subsequent to Bayh-Dole extended licensing agreements to government labs and corporations. According to Jennifer Washburn, "The collective effect was a dramatic increase in the overall amount of publicly financed research now subject to proprietary commercial control" (2005, p. 69). In essence, people were now paying (through tax-dollars) for the research to be done, and paying market prices to receive the product.

By 2000, every research university in the United States had its own patenting and licensing office. Applied research began to replace pure research. In order to get the funding necessary to conduct their research, scientists have become inclined to allow the funder to decide the nature of the investigation. For example, in exchange for funding Stanford University's Global Climate and Energy Project, ExxonMobil and other corporate sponsors decide on the academic projects (Washburn, p. 83). Corporations such as IBM and Kodak pay annual fees that allow them to designate topics of investigation at Carnegie Mellon's Magnetic Technology Center (p. 139).

Because the latest discovery might be worth millions, scientists at universities, in government, and biotech firms have become less willing to share their research. Moreover, contractual arrangements between public and private sector scientists and private sector funders usually forbid such disclosure. When researchers at the University of Pennsylvania were studying the links between two genes and breast cancer, they were threatened with a lawsuit by the biotech firm Myriad Genetics for patent infringement (Krimsky 2003, p. 67). The privatizing of health-related research has made the human genome into a lucrative commodity that, like all products, may be monopolized.

Contractual agreements can also determine how findings are disclosed. In a survey of engineers working in major university-industrial research centers, it was found that 35 percent would allow corporate sponsors to delete information from papers prior to publication (Washburn, p. 75). In a survey of thirty-two hundred American scientists, 15 percent admitted to changing the design, methodology, or results of their investigation because of pressures from the funder (McGarity & Wagner 2008, p. 65). Manipulating research designs and methods to get satisfactory results has been found among drug manufacturers who enroll young subjects for clinical trials with drugs intended for older people as well as testing a drug in people who are healthier than the subjects taking the competing drug (McGarity & Wagner, pp. 68–69).

Some scientists never get to see the results of their research. For example, in 2002 Aubrey Blumsohn signed a contract with Proctor and Gamble to head a three-year study that involved thousands of women taking the company's drug for osteoporosis. The researchers were conducting a double-blind study so neither the investigators nor the participants knew who was taking the drug. When the results were in, Proctor and Gamble declined to show the analysis to the primary investigator, Dr. Blumsohn, and the study was written up by a hired writer for publication in a scientific journal with Blumsohn's name on it (McGarity & Wagner, p. 73). In fact a lucrative ghostwriting industry exists in science and medicine. For example, Excerpta Medica is a medical publishing company that provides scientific articles placed in leading medical journals for a price (Krimsky, p. 115).

If a company sponsors a study, should they have the right to package the results as they see fit? Under current law, "trade secrets" are broadly interpreted so that privately funded research that yields damaging results can escape disclosure. Scientists who feel tempted to disclose damaging information may be bound by contract from revealing it or face legal charges.

The subjugation of knowledge also exists, of course, in government. Political leaders have always been dependent on scientists to some degree for their expert advice on a wide range of issues (e.g., defense, agriculture, public safety, and so forth). Such dependence increased after World War II as relations between government and university research increased and as government regulations increased. Hundreds of advisory panels exist throughout the government. These panels (which may or may not include scientists) are comprised of experts whose job it is to advise policy makers and government agencies.

Oftentimes agencies are charged with opposing interests. For example, the Department of Energy may propose policies based upon expert recommendations that contradict policies based upon experts advising the Environmental Protection Agency. Whether it pertains to energy, defense, food and drugs, environmental policy and so on, advisory panels are usually occupied by people who have an interest in the outcome (see, for example, Krimsky, p. 96). Once science enters into debates of public policy, various interest groups attempt to control what the research means and manipulate how it is to be perceived and used. To achieve their aims, interest groups emphasize the evidence that supports their claims while minimizing damaging evidence; they may attempt to disrupt the work of independent scientists whose research points in another direction; they may recruit scientists from the best universities to critique detrimental independent research; and they may attempt to distort the prevailing evidence in order to affect public perceptions and change the debate.

American science and education has always had an applied bent, the logic being that applied research is ultimately more rational than pure research because it contributes more to private profitability and the public good. But is this the case? Is our utilitarian approach rational? To answer this question, let us look at biotechnology, pharmacology, and public health.

Life expectancy in the United States is ranked fiftieth in the world according to the *CIA World Factbook*. The infant mortality rate is amongst the highest in the industrialized world. The United States has the most sophisticated medical technologies in the world, but most Americans have limited access to them. According to Otis Brawley (2011), the chief medical and scientific officer of the American Cancer Society, if a patient can afford a medical service, s/he will receive it whether or not it is really helpful. In other words, people without resources do not get the treatments they need, and people with resources get treatments they do not need. Pharmaceuticals are one of the most lucrative industries in the world. They used to rely on university-based research, but in recent years they have invested in their own labs. This has given rise to what some scientists call *funding bias* or the *funding effect*. A comprehensive review article summarizing over one thousand biomedical studies found that "industry-sponsored studies were significantly more likely to reach conclusions that were favorable to the sponsor than were nonindustry studies" (McGarity & Wagner, p. 96; Krimsky, p. 146). Despite the pharmaceutical industry's investment in research, it actually spends more on product development, which includes marketing. Drug commercials are among the most common advertisements on television. They not only market their products directly to consumers, but offer physicians incentives for using their drugs. Manufacturers give volume discounts to private practitioners so that the more they prescribe a particular drug, the greater the return on that practice's investment. Brawley and Goldberg state that these problems are not due to a failing system because "[i]t's functioning exactly as designed" (2011, p. 280).

The same comment can be made about higher education in America: "It's functioning exactly as designed." As tuition rates have been on the rise, full-time faculty employment has been on the decline. Fewer faculty members are expected to do more and part-time adjuncts take up the slack in terms of teaching. Because part-time instructor positions are partly based upon student evaluations, there is a temptation to engage in grade inflation. While this makes the courses easier to pass, and makes everyone, temporarily at least, happy, consider the consequences on society of graduating more and more college students who have simply skated through the system. Young people graduate from college ill prepared for the world of work and even less pre-pared to recognize manipulations of informed citizenship. Michael Crow, former executive of technology-transfer operations at Columbia University sums up a bleak scenario, "[T]he emergence of universities that are basically 'job shops.' They just become marginal, industrially driven, technology-transfer-driven enterprises. [As such, they] won't be a university" (quoted in Washburn, p. 188). Graduate students, particularly in biotechnology and the life sciences, are increasingly finding themselves under pressure to work on preconceived, privately funded lines of research rather than developing something new.

The problem with the increasing privatization and manipulation of re-search and the encroachment of corporate values in education is that market rules, politics, and ideology tend to trump the best practices in science and education. These concerns are not new. In 1918 economist Thorstein Veblen described the tensions between academic and market values in his book, *The Higher Learning in America*, detailing how market values infiltrate and over-take all competing values, not only trivializing the meaning of informed citizenship, but leading to irrational and detrimental consequences. Human knowledge is not geared to solving social problems, humankind's problems, but rather to maximizing a profit in the short term. Krimsky states,

> The mission behind corporate funding of occupational disease is to defend the safety of a product. Occupational health science is primarily public-interest oriented because the questions investigated are connected to preventing dis-ease. Public-interest science asks how knowledge can contribute to ameliorat-ing social, technological, or environmental problems. Private-interest science asks how knowledge can produce a profitable product or defend a corporate client, whether or not it has social benefits. (p. 181)

Today, many of the best minds in America work on missile systems, fossil fuels, drugs, and entertainment. Any dissension is subject to labeling as heretical and may threaten one's livelihood. With academic freedom on the ropes, new ideas, new technologies, different ways of doing things are inhib-ited. Despite innovations in technology over the past sixty years, we are still benefitting from the collective efforts of scientists from World War II. Our devices are smaller and faster but not truly innovative. Market forces (the so-called engine of America), left to their own devices lead to monopolization, which hinders innovation. Much of this is condoned or passively accepted by consumers whose educational system has failed to teach them critical think-ing and the duties of citizenship.

So far, we have discussed the relationship between the market, biotech-nology, and the life sciences, but the behavioral and social sciences played an important role in establishing as well as maintaining the kinds of relation-ships that exist among business, engineering, and the physical and life sciences. We were introduced earlier to Sigmund Freud's nephew Edward Bernays. Freud's theories influenced generations of psychiatrists, psychologists, and various other sorts of intellectuals. But he also had a great impact on his nephew who devised ways of using psychology to promote the interests of his clients.

Bernays offered corporate leaders defensive and offensive public relations strategies for protecting their interests. For example, he developed the "third party technique." A supposedly disinterested or independent group (that has ties to the business under fire) announces its support or denounces the charges against the business under attack by another group (e.g., union, newspaper, government agency). The appearance of independence of the third party tends to quell some of the antagonism, especially among the public, against the business. Bernays sold his talents as a shaper of public opinion and he enjoyed a long and successful career.

As noted above, the times (1920s–1930s) in which Bernays and other public relations men like John Hill (who, with Don Knowlton would establish one of the most successful PR firms in the industry) came into prominence was a period in which government and corporate leaders discovered and utilized more than ever before, psychological and sociological theories and methods in order to facilitate compliance and social order. This trend would continue during and after World War II. Baritz states,

> The use of social scientists by every branch of the armed services contributed to the rising prestige of psychologists and sociologists. In this war, the government used social scientists to improve personnel selection techniques, maintain military and civilian morale, analyze propaganda, develop campaigns to sell war bonds, study and report on the social and psychological characteristics of the enemy, and train personnel to deal with many different peoples and cultures. (p. 143)

After the war, thousands of people sought to implement their psychological or sociological skills in the private sector, and many in top management agreed that judging, and if possible influencing the behavior of people was an important ingredient of success. Psychological and behavioral tests would now be utilized in the workplace.

Through various forms of assessment, managers, PR consultants, and behavioral and social scientists sought to realize the benefits of a controlled workforce. The history of the control of workers is long and sometimes sordid, but the scientific attempt to control labor dates back only about a hundred years. In 1911 Frederick Taylor developed what he called the principles of *Scientific Management*. Taylor observed craftsmen in the process of manufacturing a product. He then broke down each aspect of the manufacturing process into discrete tasks that would be performed (and timed) by a particular worker (Henry Ford would refine the process by adding assembly-line production).

Scientific Management increased production by decreasing the amount of control the workers could exercise in making products—they lost the ability to control the process of production. Sue Newell, Maxine Robertson, Harry Scarbrough, and Jacky Swan state,

> [W]ith the craft system the knowledge required to carry out work had resided in the "head and the hands" of the workers, with the new system of Scientific Management engineer-managers would extract and capture this knowledge by systematic observation. They would then use these observations to redesign the work process that workers would then follow. In short, managers would be the heads, and workers the hands, of the organization. (2009, p. 19)

The human element that both management and social scientists focused on was motivation. Research in the behavioral and social sciences showed that individuals succumb to group pressures. Managing group relations could be used to get workers to monitor their own actions, and have them be consistent with managerial expectations.

John Hill and Don Knowlton's (H & K) PR firm established many of the practices used today to assist business leaders with staying in control of situations and achieving their goals. H & K worked for a variety of clients in government and business, but their most celebrated or notorious campaign (depending upon your point of view) was for clients in the tobacco industry. As funding for medical research increased after the war, evidence mounted that tobacco was linked to cancer. As sales of tobacco products declined, industry leaders turned to H & K, the largest PR firm at the time. Using the third party technique, H & K and tobacco manufacturers created the Tobacco Industry Research Committee (TIRC) to promote the impression that the research on tobacco and cancer was mixed. H & K's strategy was that if doubt could be raised in the public's mind about the link between tobacco and cancer, then sales might hold steady, or it would at least buy time for the industry. Sympathetic or unconcerned scientists were hired and paid millions of dollars in order to write reports critiquing the evidence. Karen Miller states,

> In its first six months of existence, the [TIRC] issued eleven press releases, built a library of information on the scientific case for and against smoking, assisted at least two dozen reporters with stories and editorials, published several brochures, monitored press coverage, established personal contacts with doctors, medical organizations, and science writers, created mailing lists, attended or covered state, national, and international medical scientific meetings, and began to work through its international offices to coordinate information gathering. (1999, p. 131)

H & K developed the scheme of using front groups with legitimate sounding names and filling them with well-paid experts who would represent their clients' interests. Front groups produce documents denouncing the science of damaging reports, attempt to tarnish the reputation of scientists producing detrimental reports, engage in lobbying, and make sure that their "talking points" get media attention. Today, there are thousands of front groups such as The Advancement of Sound Science Coalition (created by tobacco giant Philip Morris) and the American Council on Science and Health (supported by petrochemical companies and other industries).

In the popular text, *Effective Public Relations*, considered by some to be "the bible of public relations," Cutlip, Center, and Broom state, "Public relations counselors monitor public opinion, social change, political movements, cultural shifts, technological developments, and even the natural environment. They then interpret these environmental factors and work with management to develop strategic plans of organizational change and responsiveness" (p. 175).

In some respects reading this text and management texts such as Newell, Robertson, Scarbrough, and Swan's *Managing Knowledge Work and Innovation*, is like reading texts in sociology. They discuss individuals and concepts noted in this and other sociology books. The difference between the two fields though is that in PR and management, sociological concepts are applied in ways that are consistent with the business culture that pervades the nation.

The United States, and particularly its politics, is not merely a collection of competing interest groups vying for power. These interest groups must have wealth and organization to exert their will, and such groups utilize PR firms that have adapted the tools of psychology and sociology to do the business that is the business of America. As Cutlip, Center, and Broom state, "In the final analysis, public relations practitioners are applied social and behavioral scientists working as part of a strategic plan. . . . [P]ublic relations professionals are agents and managers of change, both inside and outside their organizations" (pp. 190–191). Effective PR requires not only strategy, but a plan of action. Cutlip, Center, and Broom suggest specifying the outcomes to be achieved, measuring the rate of change over time, and establishing a date for achieving outcome goals (p. 324). They note, "Continuity is required in communication. So is repetition of a consistent message in simple form . . . and a variety of media that converge on the audience from several avenues" (p. 345).

Finally, Cutlip, Center, and Broom emphasize the importance of framing and semantics (pp. 345–348). Behavioral, social, and linguistic research shows that how a message is expressed or framed influences how it is received. For example, it is better public relations to use the term "rightsizing" rather than "downsizing" or "cutbacks." PR consultants help their clients in industry and government to script responses to probing questions. Scripted responses convey concern without admitting responsibility and they attempt to draw attention away from the central topic. "Talking points" are repeated whenever possible; utterances supposedly intended to convey detail are ultimately vague. Bad occurrences are due to someone else's failings, result from the actions of someone who exercised poor judgment but deserves a second chance, were based on wrong information or ignorance of such outcomes, or stem from circumstances still under investigation.

Software packages are also available to assist people in learning how to script or frame their messages. One such package is called Outrage, and it allows users to develop strategies to "deflect, defer, dismiss, or defeat" (Rampton & Stauber, p. 105).

Most Americans are probably familiar with the script that says something like, "Please listen carefully to the following menu; our options have changed in order to better serve you." Scripts that convey convenience may require more of the caller's time than had s/he been able to speak to a person right away. Recorded scripts enable downsizing and contribute to the degradation of language and meaning.

Using words to convey a particular meaning in order to soften the blow for what is actually happening undermines the meaning of words. While words are the product of social relations and these relations can change the meaning of words, such changes lead to either the clarification of meaning and improved communication or the breakdown of meaning and communication. Words are like money: If a series of exchanges do not presume some degree of trust in value or meaning, then their symbolic value and practical use diminish.

The eradication of derogatory words eliminates some of the fuel that adds to the fire of hatred and discrimination. On the other hand, when the word "honest" acquires various meanings, what the meaning of the word represents loses its social significance. As the word becomes loose in meaning, so does the phenomenon of which it represents. Changes in the meaning of words can have dramatic consequences for either the better or the worse.

Given today's service economy and greater reliance on technical specialists, information is more of a commodity than ever before. Many services involve the acquisition of information or the time of people with specialized knowledge. This is partly why the late twentieth and early twenty-first centuries have been referred to as the "Information Age."

Some knowledge specialists possess information and skills that are difficult for most people, including managers, to understand. As a result, management has developed models of control based upon types of knowledge work. For example, work in a science lab requires people with specialized knowledge and skills. Their work is not just technical, but highly cognitive. This is referred to as *embrained knowledge* (Blackler 1995). Other people work in fast food, and the knowledge work there is in routinized activities; knowledge is embedded in the routines so that meals basically taste the same at every franchise. This is referred to as *embedded knowledge* (Blackler 1995). In order to maximize efficiency, workers in these two environments must be managed differently.

Scientists working in a lab tend to engage in their own routinized work, so external pressure from managers to stay on routine is usually unnecessary, and if exerted may decrease efficiency if it causes conflict. However, knowledge workers in a lab or a university may need reminding that, in order to remain solvent, a series of activities that may seem unrelated to one's work must be completed on a regular basis (e.g. assessment reports, progress reports, assessment of assessment and progress reports).

Social scientists refer to these different working environments as *knowledge cultures*, where different working environments—through the nature of the work and the interactions of the persons involved in the work—produce different norms and values. For example, working environments vary in their emphasis on speed versus skill, strength versus beauty, aggression versus compromise, action versus communication, self-interest versus community, and so on. By using insights from sociology about how people negotiate and construct their working environments, successful managers facilitate productivity with or without the workers' awareness of the process.

Of course, management also works within a knowledge culture, not only in terms of feeling pressure to meet quotas, maintain budgets, and manage people, but also in terms of tending to generalize from their knowledge culture about how people are and what the world is like. For example, a person flipping burgers or working in the garment industry, a prostitute, a state senator, a professional athlete, a computer programmer, and a social scientist are going to be influenced by their line of work and the knowledge culture it produces about the pros and cons of "human nature." Even if one's work involves contact with others primarily through technology, a knowledge culture exists.

FINAL THOUGHTS AND RECOMMENDATIONS (FOR THE PRESENT AND THE FUTURE)

Throughout this book, I have emphasized certain topics and perspectives that I believe are important, and in this way I must admit bias. But at the same time I have tried to present these topics and perspectives as they are currently understood by scholars and not necessarily by me, and in this way I have tried to avoid bias. In this final section of the chapter and book, I must acknowledge to the reader that I will be taking greater liberties in wittingly expressing my own views—some views shared and some contested by other scholars.

Human beings have come a long way because of our ability to work together, problem-solve, develop sophisticated technologies, and create a powerful storehouse of knowledge. Yet, it would be an understatement to assert that we do not always use our knowledge well. Indeed, the downside to the progress that has been made over the course of the twentieth century may be the very technological advances that could be used to eliminate age-old problems of human suffering, such as mass starvation and certain diseases. While it used to be a lack of technology and know-how that prevented us from resolving some of our greatest challenges, today it is due to the lack of will—something that we exert a lot of social and psychological energy to deny (e.g., this may explain, in part, why we invest so much of our time and money on entertainment).

Alvin Weinberg (1963) wrote in a seminal essay, entitled *Criteria for Scientific Choice,* that because of limited resources, humankind must consider the types of science worthy of investment. He suggested three broad categories for consideration: technological merit, scientific merit, and social merit. Moreover, social merit ought to be considered in light of technological and scientific merit. In other words, Weinberg suggests that we ask ourselves, "Are the social goals attained, if the technology succeeds . . . worthwhile?" (p. 164). He argues that social goals that seem to have "rather uncontroversial" merit are adequate defense, more food, and less sickness (p. 166). But is this the case? In light of the discussion above, it would appear that while defense has support as a social goal, more food and less sickness does not. Rather, sickness is sometimes an externality or unfortunate consequence of our investments.

Science is a powerful tool. Sometimes it tells people what they would rather not know or think about. Some people would rather discount modern education and science altogether. In some ways, I don't blame them. Scientists, like politicians, preachers, and millionaires, oftentimes talk about subjects of which they know very little. It's amazing to me to see a chemist go off on politics as assuredly as a political scientist; yet, the chemist would not expect the political scientist to understand his/her business better than s/he does.

Some subjects feel like common sense because we are exposed to them more, but this is really where we have to be careful lest we expose our ignorance. People today depend upon science and technology more than ever before. Some people may not like what modern education and science tells them, but they depend upon the device that science and technology has developed in order for them to get their information. If science were not a powerful tool, people would not use scientifically named front groups to manipulate public opinion. McGarity and Wagner state,

> [S]cientific processes are contaminated by determined advocates who under-
> stand the power of supportive science in legal and policy proceedings (p.
> 5). . . . From a theoretical perspective . . . bending science is not surprising. . . .
> [I]f the scientific research can be manipulated in ways that benefit the interests
> of a party . . . that party will invest in manipulating the research up to the point
> at which the last dollar expended just equals the expected benefits of the
> manipulation. The value of science may not figure into the accounting. (p. 22)

This is reminiscent of industries that continuously pollute the air or water because the fine for doing so is less than the profits reaped by failing to do so. Science itself becomes an externality, a casualty of the business of America. Rampton and Stauber state,

> The public today is bombarded with scientific information regarding the safety
> and efficacy of everything from drugs to seat belts to children's toys. Eating
> garlic bread brings families closer together, says research sponsored by Peppe-
> ridge Farms bakeries . . . . Eating oat bran lowers cholesterol, according to
> research sponsored by Quaker Oats. Eating chocolate may *prevent* cavities,
> says Princeton Dental Resource Center, which is financed by the M&M/Mars
> candy company and is not a part of Princeton University. Sometimes the
> contradictions reflect genuine disagreements, but often they simply mirror the
> opposing interests of different companies and industries. (pp. 220–221)

The result is that people do not know what to believe, and this adds to the consumption of unhealthy goods and the consumption of fantasy as fact. The relativity of beliefs today is celebrated by some and condemned by others. In either case, the relativity of beliefs (or the social acceptance of believing in what you want) is said to reflect our value in individuality. But I don't think the relativity of beliefs reflects individuality; rather I think it reflects a lack of investment in education. Science has become absorbed into politically based ideological battles. Scientists themselves are complicit, complacent, oblivi-ous, or politically too weak to alter the circumstances. Because of ignorance or fear, people believe the science and information they want to see and hear, and this fuels investment in propaganda, reinforces all sorts of superstitions, and draws people away from each other.

Postmodernism, which celebrates the relative while acknowledging its dangers, tends to draw strength from social constructivist theories much the way in which economists draw strength from rational choice and game theo-ries. Social constructivism emphasizes how people create and maintain their social worlds; rational choice and game theories emphasize self-interest. While all of these theories have value for understanding human behavior, their advocates tend to enthusiastically rely upon them to explain literally everything.

Theories become a world-view like a religion, and as such their adherents do not face the possibility that these popular theories do not so much explain social life and human motivation as reflect the times in which we live. For example, while there is much to be learned from a social constructivist point of view, many of its adherents seem to maintain that once people see how reality is the product of the interactions of the members of groups, they will realize how they produce the social factors that affect them as individuals. Yet, in a culture that emphasizes individualism, people tend to turn social theories into psychological theories: Social constructivism becomes psychological constructivism and another rationale for self-interest.

Science lacking disinterestedness cannot gain sufficient distance to adequately explain its subject matter. While objectivity in science may be rightfully challenged, the elimination of even aspiring to disinterestedness contributes to the degradation of science (i.e., there is little difference between opinion and views derived from scientific investigation).

Robert Merton (1968) wrote a number of important essays on the sociology of science. While some social scientists may view his arguments as passé, also merely reflections of the times in which he wrote them, I believe there is enduring value in what he described as the ethos of science (see below for elaboration). Some of what Merton argues has already been mentioned: For example, science must not become subservient to the institutional values of religion, economy, or government. In the hands of these institutions science becomes limited and destructive. While Merton sees value in research as an end in itself, rather than just a means to an applied end, he warns against scientists being ignorant of the possible applications and social repercussions of their research (p. 598). In elaborating on what he calls *the imperious immediacy of interest*, Merton states,

> Concern with the primary goal, the furtherance of knowledge, coupled with a disregard of those consequences which lie outside the area of immediate interest . . . may be rational in the sense that it may be expected to lead to the satisfaction of the immediate interest. But it is irrational in the sense that it defeats other values which are not, at the moment, paramount but which are none the less an integral part of the social scale of values. (p. 599)

By the ethos of science, Merton is referring to the norms and values that typically make up a part of scientific training. According to Merton four imperatives make up this ethos: universalism, communism, disinterestedness, and organized skepticism (p. 607). Scientists should not allow personal and cultural biases to taint their scientific claims. Just as it was wrong for leaders in the mid-nineteenth century to justify bigotry in the name of religion, it was wrong for leaders in the early years of the twentieth century to justify bigotry in the name of science (see, for example, eugenics). Personal and cultural assumptions should not be the tail that wags the dog (science).

This is the meaning of universalism. Science is not egocentric or ethnocentric. Communism here does not refer to Marxism; it is intended to convey the fact that scientific knowledge is cumulative. According to Merton, "secrecy is the antithesis of this norm" (p. 611).

Science is historical and social. Scientific discovery is unending—this is why some people really like science (i.e., there is always something new to learn). Science is tolerant of ambiguity. Disinterestedness refers to professionalism and preserving the integrity of the scientific enterprise. Scientific claims should not be tainted by conflicts of interest (i.e., making claims because of payoffs). Science is about furthering understanding and human capacities whether or not such knowledge reaps financial gains. While science benefits from private investments, scientific outcomes are better when they concern the public over the long term. Finally, science involves organized skepticism. Science asks, "What?" "How?" and "Why?" about everything. Science is inquisitive and reflective.

Merton argues, "Conflict becomes accentuated whenever science extends its research to new areas toward which there are institutionalized attitudes or whenever other institutions extend their area of control" (p. 615). As science continues to place in the hands of people the power of a god, some people attempt to use that power for self-gain and call it rational, while others turn to their God because they fear what humankind may do with such power, and while using some of this power against those they fear, call their actions moral. There is really nothing new about this, as Woodhouse and Sarewitz state, "The history of science policy is very much a history of interests vying for power and influence over resources and agendas" (2007, p. 141).

The blurring of the lines separating science from government and industry in recent years is causing harm in multiple ways. For one, it has provided justification for scientists, physicians, and educators to place convenience and profit above professionalism. Certainly there have always been charlatans, but it would be nice to think that we have advanced beyond the fellow selling his tonic on a wagon.

I would like to end this chapter and book with a few recommendations.

1. Recognize the distinction between university-based science and industry-based science. In a study, Rosenberg and Nelson found that scientists in industry depend upon the pure science they learned in school. Rosenberg and Nelson state that academic researchers primarily create the knowledge that industry researchers use to develop and improve upon their products (p. 344). In order to be innovative, the university needs to function as an autonomous institution that protects academic freedom. While some scientists take advantage of academic freedom and do not contribute much to the storehouse of knowledge, the threat of eliminating academic freedom is a recipe for further degradation.

2. Approaches to medicine should be preventive rather than oriented toward treatment and profit making. The former could be a whole new

growth industry, while we know that the latter is wasteful in terms of lives and money.

3. There needs to be greater investment in clean energy and green chemistry. The United States' dependence on foreign supplies of oil kills Americans and turns American values into a contradictory knot. Green chemistry develops products less hazardous or innocuous to humans and environments. Alternative forms of United States-based energy and green chemistry are promising new growth industries.

4. Develop budgets for research and development that are inclusive of cost to poor people. The development of medical technologies and medicines that serve less than 10 percent of the world's population should not only be a cause of concern in and of itself, but it leads to resentment and violence, as well (Woodhouse & Sarewitz, p.140).

5. Develop budgets for research and development that acknowledge the relationships among environment, lifestyle, and physical and mental health. If people were not influenced by their environments, then public relations would not be a lucrative industry. Applications of recommendations four and five applied to food and medicine would decrease mass starvation and health-related epidemics.

6. Acknowledge what Hofstadter and Hardy wisely observed, "A college curriculum is significant chiefly for two things: it reveals the educated community's conception of what knowledge is most worth transmitting to . . . its youth, and it reveals what kind of mind and character an education is expected to produce" (Hofstadter & Hardy 1954, p. 11). Today, we do not impart to our youth knowledge that is useful to society nor beneficial for producing a happy life. Young people are inundated with messages that claim that they are always one purchase away from happiness. This is a great message for the business of America, but an inaccurate message for the psychology of Americans.

My hope is that readers of this book have learned to see society, their relationships, and themselves through a sociological perspective. Such a perspective is cognizant of the historical factors that shape contemporary beliefs, is able to distinguish ideology and knowledge, understands how economic conditions affect real lives and decision-making, and realizes that while pleasure can be bought, happiness cannot. Then again, how often does a single book change attitudes and behavior?

Therefore, though I make these recommendations I do not expect the fulfillment of any of them. This is not because of cynicism; it is because after teaching for twenty years and living for over fifty years, I have learned that most people are financially dependent upon what is wrong with America. Indeed, when many people leave their homes in the morning, they enter into a rat race that involves slowly killing other people in order to make a living.

Moreover, I have learned that the more outside influences entangle themselves in education in the name of accountability, the process of accountability becomes like public relations: impression management rather than improving pedagogy.

For many years I have heard people say that the classroom should be made more relevant to the real world. There is a degree to which I believe this is important, but when the real world becomes more about appearances, this means removing the rigor and strain of learning from the classroom. As a result, we acquire more people with degrees and more people passive to the conditions that make up the real world.

Perhaps, instead, we should strive to make the real world relevant to an inquisitive classroom. Then we might see a real world based upon inquiry and judgment based upon such inquiry—one in which conflicts of interest are recognized and kept in check. Perhaps then we would move a little closer to creating the kind of world that many say they want.

Perhaps everything I have said since the discussion of the ethos of science is nothing more than idealism. I am always taken by the ideals expressed in this quote:

> Wisdom and knowledge, as well as virtue, diffused generally among the body of the people, being necessary for the preservation of their rights and liberties; and as these depend on spreading the opportunities and advantages of education in the various parts of the country . . . it shall be the duty of legislatures and magistrates, in all future periods of the Commonwealth, to cherish the interests of literature and sciences . . . ; to encourage private societies and public institutions . . . for the promotion of agriculture, arts, sciences, commerce, trades, manufactures, and a natural history of the country. (cited in Brown 1996, pp. 80–81)

These words were expressed by John Adams, the second president of the United States. The difference, I believe, between the first generation of leaders and the leaders of today is that they were forward looking and not backward looking. Even a leader today who is forward looking is held back by the fearful, who usually constitute a loud minority. It is as though people, from top to bottom on the economic ladder, feel too insecure or rapacious to be brave enough to live authentically. Without ideals to help us look forward, people look backward. And when ideals are continuously dashed by daily life, people do not live; they endure: they hurt others or themselves, or they escape psychologically, which relieves the pressure to be socially accountable for their actions.

How do you want to live *your* life? Do you really want to be true to yourself? If people want to achieve their ideals, then those ideals cannot be based upon illusion. A careful reading of our past suggests that the only way to make ideals real is by living authentically.

FOR FURTHER READING

Baritz, L. (1960). *The servants of power: A history of the use of social science in American industry*. Middletown, CT: Wesleyan University Press. A very good and readable social history of the corporate use of psychological and sociological research during the early years of the twentieth century. Unfortunately, out of print.

Hine, T. (1999). *The rise and fall of the American teenager: A new history of the American adolescent experience* (1st ed.). New York: HarperCollins Publishers. A very good and readable social history of the conception of teenager.

Hofstadter, R. (1963). *Anti-intellectualism in American life*. New York: Vintage Books. A classic book on anti-intellectualism in American culture. A bit challenging but well worth the effort.

Hofstadter, R., & Hardy, C. D. (1954). *The development and scope of higher education in the United States*. New York: Columbia University Press. A very good and readable social history on the development of higher education in America. Unfortunately, out of print.

Kaestle, C. F. (1983). *Pillars of the republic: Common schools and American society, 1780–1860*. New York: Hill and Wang. A good and reasonably detailed history of the development of common schools in the United States.

McGarity, T. O., & Wagner, W. E. (2008). *Bending science: How special interest groups corrupt public health research*. Cambridge, MA: Harvard University Press. Excellent examination of how special interest groups are undermining the integrity of academic research. Challenging but worth the effort.

Ravitch, D. (2010). *The death and life of the great American school system: How testing and choice are undermining education*. New York: Basic Books. A very good and readable analysis of recent trends in primary and secondary education.

Swartz, D. (1998). *Culture and power: The sociology of Pierre Bourdieu*. Chicago, IL: University of Chicago Press. One of the more accessible books on the sociology of Bourdieu.

Bibliography

Adams, J. T. (2012). *The epic of America.* Piscataway, NJ: Transaction Publishers. (Original work published 1931)

Adler, N. E., & Conner Snibbe, A. (2003). The role of psychosocial processes in explaining the gradient between socioeconomic status and health. *Current Directions in Psychological Science, 12*(4), 119–123.

Adolphs, R. (2003). Cognitive neuroscience of human social behaviour. *Nature Reviews Neuroscience, 4*(3), 165–178.

Allred, R. (1996). Catharsis, revision, and re-enactment: Negotiating the meaning of the American Civil War. *The Journal of American Culture, 19*(4), 1–13.

Anderson, B. (2006). *Imagined communities: Reflections on the origin and spread of nationalism.* London: Verso.

Anderson, C. J., & Prentice, N. M. (1994). Encounter with reality: Children's reactions on discovering the Santa Claus myth. *Child Psychiatry and Human Development, 25*(2), 67–84.

Aneshensel, C. S. (1992). Social stress: Theory and research. *Annual Review of Sociology, 18,* 15–38.

Bader, C. D., Mencken, F. C., & Baker, J. O. (2010). *Paranormal America: Ghost encounters, UFO sightings, Bigfoot hunts and other curiosities in religion and culture.* New York: New York University Press.

Baker, J. (2008). Who believes in religious evil? An investigation of sociological patterns of belief in Satan, hell, and demons. *Review of Religious Research, 50*(2), 206–220.

Bales, K. (1999). *Disposable people: New slavery in the global economy.* Berkeley: University of California Press.

Barber, B. R. (1995). *Jihad vs. McWorld: How globalism and terrorism are reshaping the world.* New York: Ballantine Books.

Bargh, J. A. (1999). The cognitive monster: The case against controllability of automatic stereotype effects. In S. Chaiken & Y. Trope (Eds.), *Dual process theories in social psychology* (pp. 361–382). New York: The Guilford Press.

Bargh, J. A., & Chartrand, T. L. (1999). The unbearable automaticity of being. *American Psychologist, 54*(7), 462–479.

Bargh, J. A., Chen, M., & Burrows, L. (1996). Automaticity of social behavior: Direct effects of trait construct and stereotype activation on action. *Journal of Personality and Social Psychology, 71*(2), 230–244.

Baritz, L. (1960). *The servants of power: A history of the use of social science in American industry.* Middletown, CT: Wesleyan University Press.

Barnet, R. J., & Cavanaugh, J. (1994). *Global dreams: Imperial corporations and the new world order.* New York: Simon & Schuster.

259

Barnett, J. H. (1954). *The American Christmas: A study in national culture.* New York: The Macmillan Company.

Barton, B. (1987). *The man nobody knows.* New York: Collier Books. (Original work published 1925)

Bateson, M. C. (1975). Mother-infant exchanges: The epigenesis of conversational interaction. *Annals of the New York Academy of Sciences, 263,* 101–113.

Bauman, Z. (2000). *Liquid modernity.* Cambridge: Polity Press.

Baumeister, R. F., Bratslavsky, E., Muraven, M., & Tice, D. M. (1998). Ego depletion: Is the active self a limited resource? *Journal of Personality and Social Psychology, 74*(5), 1252–1265.

Bavelas, J. B., Black, A., Lemery, C. R., & Mullett, J. (1986). "I *show* how you feel": Motor mimicry as a communicative act. *Journal of Personality and Social Psychology, 50*(2), 322–329.

Becker, E. (1973). *The denial of death.* New York: The Free Press.

Belk, R. W. (1987). A child's Christmas in America: Santa Claus as deity, consumption as religion. *Journal of American Culture, 10*(1), 87–100.

Belk, R. W. (1988). Possessions and the extended self. *Journal of Consumer Research, 15*(2), 139–168.

Belk, R. W., Bahn, K. D., & Mayer, R. N. (1982). Developmental recognition of consumption symbolism. *Journal of Consumer Research, 9*(1), 4–17.

Belk, R. W., & Costa, J. A. (1998). The mountain man myth: A contemporary consuming fantasy. *Journal of Consumer Research, 25*(3), 218–240.

Bellah, R., Madsen, R., Sullivan, W. M., Swidler, A., & Tipton, S. M. (1985). *Habits of the heart: Individualism and commitment in American life.* New York: Harper & Row.

Berger, P. L. (1963). *Invitation to sociology: A humanistic perspective.* New York: Anchor.

Berger, P. L. (1969). *The sacred canopy: Elements of a sociological theory of religion.* New York: Anchor.

Berger, P. L., & Luckmann, T. (1967). *Social construction of reality.* Garden City, NY: Anchor Books.

Berlin, I. (1990). *Four essays on liberty.* New York: Oxford University Press.

Best, S. (1989). The commodification of reality and the reality of commodification: Jean Baudrillard and post-modernism. *Current Perspectives in Social Theory, 9,* 23–51.

Blackler, F. (1995). Knowledge, knowledge work and organizations: An overview and interpretation. *Organization Studies, 16*(6), 1021–1046.

Bodenmann, G., Atkins, D. C., Schär, M., & Poffet, V. (2010). The association between daily stress and sexual activity. *Journal of Family Psychology, 24*(3), 271.

Bodenmann, G., Ledermann, T., & Bradbury, T. N. (2007). Stress, sex, and satisfaction in marriage. *Personal Relationships, 14*(4), 551–569.

Bodenmann, G., Meuwly, N., & Kayser, K. (2011). Two conceptualizations of dyadic coping and their potential for predicting relationship quality and individual well-being: A comparison. *European Psychologist, 16*(4), 255–266.

Bodrova, E., & Leong, D. J. (2007). *Tools of the mind: The Vygotskian approach to early childhood education* (2nd ed.). Upper Saddle River, NJ: Pearson.

Boorstin, D. J. ([1961]1982). *The image: A guide to pseudo-events in America.* New York: Atheneum.

Bourdieu, P. (1984). *Distinction: A social critique of the judgment of taste* (R. Nice, Trans.). Cambridge, MA: Harvard University Press.

Bozeman, B., & Sarewitz, D. (2005). Valuing S&T activities: Public values and public failure in US science policy. *Science and Public Policy, 32*(2), 119–136.

Bradbury, T. N., & Karney, B. R. (2004). Understanding and altering the longitudinal course of marriage. *Journal of Marriage & Family, 66*(4), 862–879.

Bradshaw, M., & Ellison, C. G. (2010). Financial hardship and psychological distress: Exploring the buffering effects of religion. *Social Science and Medicine, 71*(1), 196–204.

Brady, D. W., & Han, H. C. (2006). Polarization then and now: A historical perspective. In P. Nivola & D. Brady (Eds.), *Red and blue nation: Characteristics and causes of America's polarized politics* (pp. 119–151). Stanford, CA : Hoover Institution on War, Revolution and Peace, Stanford University.

Brawley, O. W., & Goldberg, P. (2011). *How we do harm: A doctor breaks ranks about being sick in America*. New York: St. Martin's Griffin.

Breen, T. H. (2004). *The marketplace of revolution: How consumer politics shaped American independence*. Oxford: Oxford University Press.

Brint, S. (2002). The rise of the "practical arts". In S. Brint (Ed.), *The future of the city of intellect: The changing American university* (pp. 231–259). Stanford, CA: Stanford University Press.

Brown, R. D. (1996). *The strength of a people: The idea of an informed citizenry in America 1650–1870*. Chapel Hill: The University of North Carolina Press.

Bruce, R. V. (1987). *The launching of modern American science*. Ithaca, NY: Cornell University Press.

Bruce, S. (2002). *God is dead: Secularization in the West*. Malden, MA: Blackwell Publishing.

Bruner, J. (1987). Life as narrative. *Social Research, 54*(1), 11–32.

Buchanan, M. (2003). *Nexus: Small worlds and the groundbreaking theory of networks*. New York: W. W. Norton & Company.

Buchmann, M. (1989). *The script of life in modern society: Entry into adulthood in a changing world*. Chicago, IL: The University of Chicago Press.

Bulman, R. J. R., & Wortman, C. B. C. (1977). Attributions of blame and coping in the "real world": Severe accident victims react to their lot. *Journal of Personality and Social Psychology, 35*(5), 351–363.

Bulmer, M. (2001). Knowledge for the public good: The emergence of social sciences and social reform in late-nineteenth- and early-twentieth-century America, 1880–1940. In D. L. Featherman & M. A. Vinovskis (Eds.), *Social science and policy-making: A search for relevance in the twentieth century* (pp. 16–39). Ann Arbor: The University of Michigan Press.

Burke, E., & Mitchell, L. G. (Ed.). (2009). *Reflections on the revolution in France*. New York: Oxford University Press. (Original work published 1790)

Cacioppo, J., & Patrick, W. (2008). *Loneliness: Human nature and the need for social connection*. New York: W. W. Norton & Company.

Campbell, C. (1996). Half-belief and the paradox of ritual instrumental activism: A theory of modern superstition. *The British Journal of Sociology, 47*(1), 151–166.

Carlson, D. S., & Kacmar, K. M. (2000). Work-family conflict in the organization: Do life role values make a difference? *Journal of Management, 26*(5), 1031–1054.

Caughey, J. L. (1984). *Imaginary social worlds: A cultural approach*. Lincoln: University of Nebraska Press.

Central Intelligence Agency. (2013, December 19). *The world factbook*. Retrieved from https://www.cia.gov/library/publications/the-world-factbook/rankorder/2172rank.html

Chartrand, T. L., & Bargh, J. A. (1999). The chameleon effect: The perception-behavior link and social interaction. *Journal of Personality and Social Psychology, 76*(6), 893–910.

Chaudhuri, A. (2006). *Emotion and reason in consumer behavior*. Boston, MA: Elsevier Butterworth-Heinemann.

Chen, M., & Bargh, J. A. (1997). Nonconscious behavioral confirmation processes: The self-fulfilling consequences of automatic stereotype activation. *Journal of Experimental Social Psychology, 33*, 541–560.

Cherlin, A. J. (2009). *The marriage-go-round: The state of marriage and the family in America today*. New York: Alfred A. Knopf.

Christiano, K. J., Swatos, W. H., & Kivisto, P. (2008). *Sociology of religion: Contemporary developments* (2nd ed.). Lanham, MD: Rowman & Littlefield Publishers.

Cohen, T. F. (2001). *Men and masculinity: A text reader*. Belmont, CA: Wadsworth Thomson Learning.

Cooley, C. H. (1902). *Human nature and the social order*. New York: Charles Scribner's Sons.

Coontz, S. (1992). *The way we never were: American families and the nostalgia trap*. New York: Basic Books.

Cushman, P. (1996). *Constructing the self, constructing America: A cultural history of psychotherapy*. New York: Da Capo Press.

Cutlip, S. M., Center, A. H., & Broom, G. H. (2006). *Effective public relations* (9th ed.). Upper Saddle River, NJ: Pearson Prentice Hall.

Dahl, R. A. (2000). *On democracy*. New Haven, CT: Yale University Press.

D'Andrade, R. G. (1984). Cultural meaning systems. In R. A. Shweder & R. A. LeVine (Eds.), *Culture theory: Essays on mind, self, and emotion*. Cambridge: Cambridge University Press.

Darwin, C. ([1859] 1988). *On the origin of species*. Washington Square, NY: New York University Press.

Davis, G. F., Yoo, M., & Baker, W. E. (2003). The small world of the American corporate elite, 1982–2001. *Strategic Organization, 1*(3), 301–326.

Davison, W. P. (1983). The third-person effect in communication. *Public Opinion Quarterly, 47*(1), 1–15.

Deighton, J. (1992). The consumption of performance. *Journal of Consumer Research, 19*(3), 362–372.

Deighton, J., Romer, D., & McQueen, J. (1989). Using drama to persuade. *Journal of Consumer Research, 16*, 335–343.

Delli Carpini, M. X., & Keeter, S. (1996). *What Americans know about politics and why it matters*. New Haven, CT: Yale University Press.

D'Emilio, J., & Freedman, E. B. (1997). *Intimate matters: A history of sexuality in America* (2nd ed.). Chicago, IL: The University of Chicago Press.

Devine, P. G. (1989). Stereotypes and prejudice: Their automatic and controlled components. *Journal of Personality and Social Psychology, 56*(1), 5–18.

Dijksterhuis, A., & van Knippenberg, A. (1998). The relation between perception and behavior; or how to win a game of Trivial Pursuit. *Journal of Personality and Social Psychology, 74*(4), 865–877.

DiMaggio, P. (1997). Culture and cognition. *Annual Review of Sociology, 23*, 263–287.

Domhoff, G. W. (2006). *Who rules America?: Power and politics, and social change* (5th ed.). New York: McGraw-Hill.

Dull, V. T., & Skokan, L. A. (1995). A cognitive model of religion's influence on health. *Journal of Social Issues, 51*(2), 49–64.

Dunbar, R. I. M. (2009). The social brain hypothesis and its implications for social evolution. *Annals of Human Biology , 36* (5), 562–572.

Durkheim, E. (1984). *The division of labor in society*. New York: The Free Press. (Original work published 1933)

Durkheim, E. ([1897]1997). *Suicide: A study in sociology*. New York: Free Press.

Easterbrook, G. (2003). *The progress paradox: How life gets better while people feel worse*. New York: Random House.

Einstein, M. (2007). *Brands of faith: Marketing religion in a commercial age*. New York: Routledge.

Ellis, J. J. (2001). *Founding brothers: The revolutionary generation*. New York: Alfred A. Knopf.

Ellison, C. G. (1991). Religious involvement and subjective well-being. *Journal of Health and Social Behavior, 32*(1), 80–99.

Ellison, C. G., Boardman, J. D., Williams, D. R., & Jackson, J. S. (2001). Religious involvement, stress, and mental health: Findings from the 1995 Detroit area study. *Social Forces, 80*(1), 215–249.

Ericson, D. F. (1993). *The shaping of American liberalism: The debates over ratification, nullification, and slavery*. Chicago, IL: The University of Chicago Press.

Escalas, J. E., & Bettman, J. R. (2000). Using narratives to discern self-identity related consumer goals and motivations. In S. Ratneshwar, D. G. Mick, & C. Huffman (Eds.), *The why of consumption: Contemporary perspectives on consumer motives, goals, and desires*. New York: Routledge.

Escalas, J. E., & Bettman, J. R. (2005). Self-construal, reference groups, and brand meaning. *Journal of Consumer Research, 32*(3), 378–389.

Evans, W. F. (1869). *The mental cure: Illustrating the influence of the mind on the body, both in health and disease, and the psychological method of treatment.* London: Houlston & Sons.

Farah, G. (2004). *No debate: How the Republican and Democratic Parties secretly control the presidential debates.* New York: Seven Stories Press.

Farberman, H. A. (1980). Fantasy in everyday life: Some aspects of the intersection between social psychology and political-economy. *Symbolic Interaction, 3*(1), 9–22.

Fazio, R. H., Jackson, J. R., Dunton, B. C., & Williams, C. J. (1995). Variability in automatic activation as an unobtrusive measure of racial attitudes: A bona fide pipeline? *Journal of Personality and Social Psychology, 69*(6), 1013–1027.

Featherman, D. L., & Vinovskis, M. A. (2001). Growth and use of social and behavioral science in the federal government since World War II. In D. L. Featherman & M. A. Vinosvskis (Eds.), *Social science and policy-making: A search for relevance in the twentieth century* (pp. 40–82). Ann Arbor: The University of Michigan Press.

Fein, G. (1981). Pretend play in childhood: An integrative review. *Child Development, 52*(4), 1095–1118.

Fenigstein, A. (1984). Self-consciousness and the overperception of self as a target. *Journal of Personality and Social Psychology, 47*(4), 860–870.

Finke, R. (1990). Religious deregulation: Origins and consequences. *Journal of Church & State, 32*(3), 609–627.

Finkelman, P. (2003). *Defending slavery, proslavery thought in the Old South: A brief history with documents.* Boston: Bedford/St. Martin's.

Finkin, M. W., & Post, R. C. (2009). *For the common good: Principles of American academic freedom.* New Haven, CT: Yale University Press.

Fiorina, M. P., Abrams, S. J., & Pope, J. (2011). *Culture war: The myth of a polarized America* (3rd ed.). Boston: Longman Publishing Group.

Fisher, H. E. (1992). *Anatomy of love: The natural history of monogamy, adultery, and divorce* (1st ed.). New York: W. W. Norton & Company.

Fogel, R. W. (2000). *The fourth great awakening & the future of egalitarianism.* Chicago, IL: The University of Chicago Press.

Fournier, S. (1998). Consumers and their brands: Developing relationship theory in consumer research. *Journal of Consumer Research, 24*(4), 343–373.

Freud, S. (1975). *Group psychology and the analysis of the ego.* (J. Strachey, Trans.). New York: W. W. Norton & Company. (Original work published 1922)

Frey, B. S. (2008). *Happiness: A revolution in economics.* Cambridge, MA: The MIT Press.

Frey, B. S., & Stutzer, A. (2001). *Happiness and economics: How the economy and institutions affect well-being.* Princeton, NJ: Princeton University Press.

Friedan, B. (1963). *The feminine mystique.* New York: W. W. Norton & Company.

Friedland, N., Keinan, G., & Regev, Y. (1992). Controlling the uncontrollable: Effects of stress on illusory perceptions of controllability. *Journal of Personality and Social Psychology, 63*(6), 923–931.

Frith, C. (2009). Role of facial expressions in social interactions. *Philosophical Transactions of the Royal Society of London, B: Biological Sciences, 364*(1535), 3453–3458.

Fromm, E. (1974). *The art of loving.* New York: Harper & Row.

Fundamentals, The. (1910–1915). Chicago: Testimony Publishing Company.

Gandhi, M., & Fischer, L. (Ed.). (1983). *The essential Gandhi: An anthology of his writings on his life, work, and ideas.* New York: Vintage Books.

Geertz, C. (1973). *The interpretation of cultures: Selected essays.* New York: Basic Books.

Geiger, R. L. (2004). *Knowledge & money: Research universities and the paradox of the marketplace.* Stanford, CA: Stanford University Press.

Geldard, R. G. (2005). *The essential transcendentalists.* New York: J. P. Tarcher/Penguin.

Gelman, A. (2008). *Red state, blue state, rich state, poor state: Why Americans vote the way they do.* Princeton, NJ: Princeton University Press.

Gerbner, G. (1990). Epilogue: Advancing on the path of righteousness (maybe). In N. Signorielli & M. Morgan (Eds.), *Cultivation analysis: New directions in media effects research* (pp. 249–262). Thousand Oaks, CA: Sage Publications.

Gerbner, G. (1998). Cultivation analysis: An overview. *Mass Communication & Society*, *1*(3/4), 175–194.

Gilbert, D. T., & Jones, E. E. (1986). Perceiver-induced constraint: Interpretations of self-generated reality. *Journal of Personality and Social Psychology*, *50*(2), 269–280.

Gilbert, D. T., Krull, D. S., & Pelham, B. W. (1988). Of thoughts unspoken: Social inference and the self-regulation of behavior. *Journal of Personality and Social Psychology*, *55*(5), 685–694.

Gilbert, D. T., & Malone, P. S. (1995). The correspondence bias. *Psychological Bulletin*, *117*(1), 21–38.

Gilbert, D. T., Pelham, B. W., & Krull, D. S. (1988). On cognitive busyness: When person perceivers meet persons perceived. *Journal of Personality and Social Psychology*, *54*(5), 733–740.

Gilovich, T., Medvec, V. H., & Savitsky, K. (1998). The illusion of transparency: Biased assessments of others' ability to read one's emotional states. *Journal of Personality and Social Psychology*, *75*(2), 332–345.

Goffman, E. (1974). *Frame analysis: An essay on the organization of experience*. Cambridge, MA: Harvard University Press.

Golomb, C., & Kuersten, R. (1996). On the transition from pretence play to reality: What are the rules of the game?. *British Journal of Developmental Psychology*, *14*(2), 203–217.

Gottlieb, B. (1993). *The family in the Western world: From the Black Death to the Industrial Age*. New York: Oxford University Press

Graber, D. A. (2005). *Mass media and American politics*. Washington, DC: CQ Press.

Grace, K. & Thompson, J. S. Thompson (2003). Racial and ethnic stratification in educational achievement and attainment. *Annual Review of Sociology*, 29, 417–442.

Granovetter, M. S. (1973). The strength of weak ties. *American Journal of Sociology*, *78*(6), 1360–1380.

Greeley, A. M. (1985). *Unsecular man: The persistence of religion*. New York: Schocken Books.

Gurevitch, Z. D. (1990). Being other: On otherness in the dialogue of the self. *Studies in Symbolic Interaction*, *11*, 285–307.

Hall, D. (1994). Civil War reenactors and the postmodern sense of history. *Journal of American Culture*, *17*(3), 7–11.

Hall, S. (1980). Encoding/decoding. In S. Hall (Ed.), *Culture, media, language: Working papers in cultural studies, 1972–1979* (pp. 128–138). London: Hutchinson; Birmingham, West Midlands: Centre for Contemporary Cultural Studies, University of Birmingham.

Hamilton, D. L., Sherman, S. J., & Ruvolo, C. M. (1990). Stereotype-based expectancies: Effects on information processing and social behavior. *Journal of Social Issues*, *46*(2), 35–60.

Harris, P. L. (2000). *The work of the imagination*. Malden, MA: Blackwell Publishers.

Harris, P. L., Brown, E., Marriott, C., Whittall, S., & Harmer, S. (1991). Monsters, ghosts and witches: Testing the limits of the fantasy-reality distinction in young children. *British Journal of Developmental Psychology*, *9*(1), 105–123.

Harris, R. (2003). *Political corruption: In and beyond the nation state*. London: Routledge.

Hartz, L. (1991). *The liberal tradition in America: An interpretation of American political thought since the revolution* (2nd ed.). New York: Harcourt Brace.

Hayek, F. A. (1960). *The constitution of liberty*. Chicago, IL: The University of Chicago Press.

Haynes, J. L., Burts, D. C., & Dukes, A. (1993). Consumer socialization of preschoolers and kindergartners as related to clothing consumption. *Psychology & Marketing*, *10*(2), 151–166.

Helson, H. (1964). *Adaptation-level theory*. New York: Harper & Row, Publishers.

Herberg, W. (1960). *Protestant, Catholic, Jew: An essay in American religious sociology* (rev. ed.). Garden City, NY: Anchor Books.

Heritage, J. (1984). *Garfinkel and ethnomethodology*. Cambridge: Polity Press.

Hervieu-Leger, D. (2000). *Religion as a chain of memory*. New Brunswick, NJ: Rutgers University Press.

Hine, T. (1999). *The rise and fall of the American teenager: A new history of the American adolescent experience* (1st ed.). New York: HarperCollins Publishers.

Hirschman, E. C. (1994). Consumers and their animal companions. *Journal of Consumer Research, 20*(4), 616–632.

Hirschman, E. C., & Thompson, C. J. (1997). Why media matter: Toward a richer understanding of consumers' relationships with advertising and mass media. *Journal of Advertising, 26*(1), 43–60.

Hochschild, A. (1983). *The managed heart: Commercialization of human feeling.* Berkeley: University of California Press.

Hofstadter, R. (1963). *Anti-intellectualism in American life.* New York: Vintage Books.

Hofstadter, R. (1996). *Academic freedom in the age of the college.* New Brunswick, NJ: Transaction Publishers. (Original work published 1955)

Hofstadter, R., & Hardy, C. D. (1954). *The development and scope of higher education in the United States.* New York: Columbia University Press.

Holbrook, M. B., Chestnut, R. W., Oliva, T. A., & Greenleaf, E. A. (1984). Play as a consumption experience: The roles of emotions, performance, and personality in the enjoyment of games. *Journal of Consumer Research, 11*(2), 728–739.

Holbrook, M. B., & Hirschman, E. C. (1982). The experiential aspects of consumption: Consumer fantasies, feelings, and fun. *Journal of Consumer Research, 9*(2), 132–140.

Holmes, D. L. (2006). *The faiths of the founding fathers.* New York: Oxford University Press.

Horwitz, A. V. (2003). *Creating mental illness.* Chicago, IL: The University of Chicago Press.

Huizinga, J. (1955). *Homo ludens: A study of the play-element in culture.* Boston, MA: Beacon Press.

Huntington, S. P. (1981). *American politics: The promise of disharmony.* Cambridge, MA: Harvard University Press.

Huntington, S. P. (1996). *The clash of civilizations and the remaking of world order.* New York: Simon & Schuster.

Huxley, A. (1954). *The doors of perception.* New York: Harper & Brothers, Publishers.

Iacoboni, M. (2009). Imitation, empathy, and mirror neurons. *Annual Review of Psychology, 60*, 653–670.

Iannaccone, L. R. (1994). Why strict churches are strong. *The American Journal of Sociology, 99*(5), 1180–1211.

Illouz, E. (2007). *Cold intimacies: The making of emotional capitalism.* Cambridge: Polity Press.

Jacobson, N. S., Follette, W. C., & McDonald, D. W. (1982). Reactivity to positive and negative behavior in distressed and nondistressed married couples. *Journal of Consulting and Clinical Psychology, 50*(5), 706–714.

James, W. (1890). *The principles of psychology, in two volumes.* London: Macmillan.

Janoff-Bulman, R., & Frieze, I. H. (1983). A theoretical perspective for understanding reactions to victimization. *Journal of Social Issues, 39*(2), 1–17.

Jeffery, K., & Mischel, W. (1979). Effects of purpose on the organization and recall of information in person perception. *Journal of Personality, 47*(3), 397–419.

John, D. R. (1999). Consumer socialization of children: A retrospective look at twenty-five years of research. *Journal of Consumer Research, 26*(3), 183–213.

Johnson, M. K., Hashtroudi, S., & Lindsay, D. S. (1993). Source monitoring. *Psychological Bulletin, 114*(1), 3–28.

Kaczynski, T. J. (1995, September 22). Industrial society and its future. *The Washington Post*, supplement.

Kaestle, C. F. (1983). *Pillars of the republic: Common schools and American society, 1780–1860.* New York: Hill and Wang.

Kahneman, D., & Deaton, A. (2010). High income improves evaluation of life but not emotional well-being. *Proceedings of the National Academy of Sciences of the United States of America, 107*(38), 16489–16493.

Kahneman, D., Slovic, P., & Tversky, A. (2007). *Judgment under uncertainty: Heuristics and biases.* Cambridge: Cambridge University Press.

Kao, G., & Thompson, J. S. (2003). Racial and ethnic stratification in educational achievement and attainment. *Annual Review of Sociology, 29*, 417–442.

Karney, B. R., & Bradbury, T. N. (1995). The longitudinal course of marital quality and stability: A review of theory, method, and research. *Psychological Bulletin, 118*(1), 3–34.

Keenan, M., & Bailett, S. D. (1980). Memory for personally and socially significant events. In R. S. Nickerson (Ed.), *Attention and performance VIII* (pp. 651–670). Hillsdale, NJ: Lawrence Erlbaum Associates.

King, D. C. (1997). The polarization of American parties and mistrust of government. In J. S. Nye, P. D. Zelikow, & D. C. King (Eds.), *Why people don't trust government* (pp. 155–178). Cambridge, MA: Harvard University Press.

Klatch, R. E. (1999). *A generation divided: The new left, the new right, and the 1960s.* Berkeley: University of California Press.

Kleinman, D. L., & Vallas, S. P. (2006). Contradiction in convergence: Universities and industry in the biotechnology field. In S. Frickel & K. Moore (Eds.), *The new political sociology of science* (pp. 35–59). Madison: University of Wisconsin Press.

Korgen, K. O., & White, J. M. (2007). *The engaged sociologist: Connecting the classroom to the community.* Thousand Oaks, CA: Sage Publications.

Krimsky, S. (2003). *Science in the private interest: Has the lure of profits corrupted biomedical research?* Lanham, MD: Rowman & Littlefield Publishers.

Kronenwetter, M. (1984). *Are you a liberal? Are you a conservative?.* New York: F. Watts.

Kubey, R., & Csikszentmihalyi, M. (1990). *Television and the quality of life: How viewing shapes everyday experience.* Hillsdale, NJ: L. Erlbaum Associates.

Kubey, R., & Csikszentmihalyi, M. (2002). Television addiction is no mere metaphor. *Scientific American, 286*(2), 74–80.

Kyle, D., & Koslowski, R. (Eds.). (2001). *Global human smuggling: Comparative perspectives.* Baltimore, MD: The Johns Hopkins University Press.

LaFeber, W. (1999). *Michael Jordan and the new global capitalism.* New York: W. W. Norton & Company.

Lambert, F. (2006). *The founding fathers and the place of religion in America.* Princeton, NJ: Princeton University Press.

Lambert, L. (2009). *Spirituality, Inc.: Religion in the American workplace.* New York: New York University Press.

Lamott, A. (1995). *Bird by bird: Some instructions on writing and life.* New York: Anchor Books.

Langer, E. J. (1975). The illusion of control. *Journal of Personality and Social Psychology, 32*(2), 311–328.

Lashley, K. S. (1951). The problem of serial order in behavior. In L. A. Jefress (Ed.), *Cerebral mechanisms in behavior.* New York: Wiley.

Lawrence, R. Z. (1997). Is it really the economy, stupid?. In J. S. Nye, P. D. Zelikow, & D. C. King (Eds.), *Why people don't trust government* (pp. 111–132). Cambridge, MA: Harvard University Press.

Lazarus, R. S. (1983). The costs and benefits of denial. In S. Breznitz (Ed.), *The denial of stress* (pp. 1–30). New York: International Universities Press.

Lennon, M. C., & Rosenfield, S. (1992). Women and mental health: The interaction of job and family conditions. *Journal of Health and Social Behavior, 33*(4), 316–327.

Leslie, A. M. (1987). Pretense and representation: The origins of "theory of mind." *Psychological Review, 94*(4), 412–426.

Lewis, C., & The Center for Public Integrity. (2000). *The buying of the president 2000.* New York: Avon Books.

Lewis, C., & The Center for Public Integrity. (2004). *The buying of the president 2004: Who's really bankrolling Bush and his democratic challengers—and what they expect in return.* New York: Avon Books.

Lindstrom, M., & Seybold, P. B. (2004). *Brand child: Remarkable insights into the minds of today's global kids and their relationships with brands* (rev. ed.). London: Kogan Page.

Lippmann, W. (1922). *Public opinion.* New York: Macmillan.

Locke, J. (2010). *Two treatises of government: In the former, the false principles and foundation of Sir Robert Filmer, and his followers are detected and overthrown; the latter is an essay concerning the true original, extent, and end of civil-government.* Clark, NJ: Lawbook Exchange. (Original work published 1690)

Love, N. S. (2006). *Understanding dogmas and dreams: A text.* Washington, DC: CQ Press.

Macpherson, C. B. (1972). *The real world of democracy.* New York: Oxford University Press.

Maddox, W. S., & Lilie, S. A. (1984). *Beyond liberal and conservative: Reassessing the political spectrum.* Washington, DC: Cato Institute.

Madrick, J. G. (1997). *The end of affluence: The causes and consequences of America's economic dilemma.* New York: Random House.

Malinowski, B. (1948). *Magic, science and religion and other essays.* Boston: Beacon Press.

Mark, M., & Pearson, C. (2001). *The hero & the outlaw: Building extraordinary brands through the power of archetypes.* New York: McGraw-Hill.

Marsden, G. M. (1991). *Understanding fundamentalism and evangelicalism.* Grand Rapids, MI: Wm. B. Eerdmans Publishing Co.

Mathews, D. G. (2004). Lynching is part of the religion of our people. In B. B. Schweiger & D. G. Mathews (Eds.), *Religion in the American South: Protestants and others in history and culture* (pp. 153–194). Chapel Hill: The University of North Carolina Press.

May, E. R. (1997). The evolving scope of government. In J. S. Nye, P. D. Zelikow, & D. C. King (Eds.), *Why people don't trust government* (pp. 21–54). Cambridge, MA: Harvard University Press.

McCarty, N., Poole, K., & Rosenthal, H. (2006). *Polarized America: The dance of ideology and unequal riches* (1st ed.). Cambridge, MA: The MIT Press.

McCombs, M. E. (2004). *Setting the agenda: The mass media and public opinion.* Malden, MA: Polity Press.

McCracken, G. (1986). Culture and consumption: A theoretical account of the structure and movement of the cultural meaning of consumer goods. *Journal of Consumer Research, 13*(1), 71–84.

McEwen, B. S. (2005). Stressed or stressed out: What is the difference?. *Journal of Psychiatry & Neuroscience, 30*(5), 315–318.

McFarland, I. A. (2010). *In Adam's fall: A meditation on the Christian doctrine of original sin.* Chichester: Wiley-Blackwell.

McGarity, T. O., & Wagner, W. E. (2008). *Bending science: How special interest groups corrupt public health research.* Cambridge, MA: Harvard University Press.

McIntosh, D. (1995). Religion-as-schema, with implications for the relation between religion and coping. *The International Journal for the Psychology of Religion, 5*(1), 1–16.

McLoughlin, W. G. (1978). *Revivals, awakenings, and reform, an essay on religion and social change in America, 1607–1977.* Chicago, IL: The University of Chicago Press.

McNeal, J. U., & Yeh, C-H. (1993). Born to shop. *American Demographics, 15*(6), 34–40.

McNulty, J. K., & Karney, B. R. (2001). Attributions in marriage: Integrating specific and global evaluations of a relationship. *Personality and Social Psychology Bulletin, 27*(8), 943–955.

Mead, G. H., & Deegan, M. J. (Ed.). (2006). *Play, school, and society.* New York: Peter Lang.

Merton, R. K. (1968). *Social theory and social structure.* New York: The Free Press.

Metzger, W. P. (1961). *Academic freedom in the age of the university.* New York: Columbia University Press.

Meyer, F. S. (1968). Conservatism. In R. A. Goldwin (Ed.), *Left, right and center: Essays on liberalism and conservatism in the United States.* Chicago, IL: Rand McNally.

Michaels, D. (2008). *Doubt is their product: How industry's assault on science threatens your health.* New York: Oxford University Press.

Micklethwait, J., & Wooldridge, A. (2004). *The right nation: Conservative power in America.* New York: Penguin Press.

Miller, D. T., & McFarland, C. (1987). Pluralistic ignorance: When similarity is interpreted as dissimilarity. *Journal of Personality and Social Psychology, 53*(2), 298–305.

Miller, D. T., & Prentice, D. A. (1994). Collective errors and errors about the collective. *Personality and Social Psychology Bulletin, 20*(5), 541–550.

Miller, J. (1997). *Seminar studies in history: The glorious revolution* (2nd ed.). London: Longman.

Miller, K. S. (1999). *The voice of business: Hill & Knowlton and postwar public relations.* Chapel Hill: The University of North Carolina Press.

Miller, V. J. (2005). *Consuming religion: Christian faith and practice in a consumer religion.* London: Continuum.

Mills, C. W. (1956). *The power elite.* New York: Oxford University Press.

Mills, C. W. (1972). *The sociological imagination.* New York: Oxford University Press.

Mintz, S., & Kellogg, S. (1988). *Domestic revolutions: A social history of American family life.* New York: The Free Press.

Mitchell, S. A. (2002). *Can love last?: The fate of romance over time.* New York: W. W. Norton & Company.

Moore, R. L. (1994). *Selling God: American religion in the marketplace of culture.* New York: Oxford University Press.

Muraven, M., & Baumeister, R. F. (2000). Self-regulation and depletion of limited resources: Does self-control resemble a muscle? *Psychological Bulletin, 126*(2), 247–259.

Muraven, M., Tice, D. M., & Baumeister, R. F. (1998). Self-control as limited resource: Regulatory depletion patterns. *Journal of Personality and Social Psychology, 74*(3), 774–789.

Myers, D. G. (1993). *The pursuit of happiness: Discovering the pathway to fulfillment, well-being, and enduring personal joy.* New York: Quill.

Napoleoni, L. (2003). *Modern jihad: Tracing the dollars behind the terror networks.* London: Pluto Press.

Napoleoni, L. (2005). *Terror incorporated: Tracing the dollars behind the terror networks.* New York: Seven Stories Press.

Neff, L. A., & Karney, B. R. (2004). How does context affect intimate relationships?: Linking external stress and cognitive processes within marriage. *Personality and Social Psychology Bulletin, 30*(2), 134–148.

Neff, L. A., & Karney, B. R. (2009). Stress and reactivity to daily relationship experiences: How stress hinders adaptive processes in marriage. *Journal of Personality and Social Psychology, 97*(3), 435–450.

Nelson, T. J. (1997). He made a way out of no way: Religious experience in an African-American congregation. *Review of Religious Research, 39*(1), 5–26.

Newell, S., Robertson, M., Scarbrough, H., & Swan, J. (2009). *Managing knowledge work and innovation* (2nd ed.). New York: Palgrave Macmillan.

Noll, M. A., Marsden, G. M., & Hatch, N. O. (1989). *The search for Christian America.* Colorado Springs: Helmers & Howard.

Norris, P., & Inglehart, R. (2004). *Sacred and secular: Religion and politics worldwide.* New York: Cambridge University Press.

Oatley, K. (1999). Why fiction may be twice as true as fact: Fiction as cognitive and emotional simulation. *Review of General Psychology, 3*(2), 101–117.

O'Guinn, T. C., & Shrum, L. J. (1997). The role of television in the construction of consumer reality. *Journal of Consumer Research, 23*(4), 278–294.

Orren, G. (1997). Fall from grace: The public's loss of faith in government. In J. S. Nye, P. D. Zelikow, & D. C. King (Eds.), *Why people don't trust government* (pp. 77–107). Cambridge, MA: Harvard University Press.

Otnes, C., Kim, Y. C., & Kim, K. (1994). All I want for Christmas: An analysis of children's brand requests to Santa Claus. *The Journal of Popular Culture, 27*(4), 183–194.

Otnes, C., & Scott, L. M. (1996). Something old, something new: Exploring the interaction between ritual and advertising. *The Journal of Advertising, 25*(1), 33–50.

Packard, V. (1957). *The hidden persuaders.* New York: Pocket Books.

Paley, V. G. (2004). *A child's work: The importance of fantasy play.* Chicago, IL: The University of Chicago Press.

Pargament, K. I., & Park, C. L. (1995). Merely a defense? The variety of religious means and ends. *Journal of Social Issues, 51*(2), 13–32.

Patterson, J. T. (1996). *Grand expectations: The United States, 1945–1974*. New York: Oxford University Press.

Peale, N. V. (1952). *The power of positive thinking*. New York: Prentice-Hall.

Pew Forum on Religion & Public Life. (2008). *U.S. religious landscape survey, 2008*. Washington, DC: Pew Research Center.

Phillips, K. (2002). *Wealth and democracy: A political history of the American rich*. New York: Broadway Books.

Pickering, M. (1993). *Auguste Comte: An intellectual biography, volume I*. Cambridge: Cambridge University Press.

Pileggi, M. S., Grabe, M. E., Holderman, L. B., & de Montigny, M. (2000). Business as usual: The American dream in Hollywood business films. *Mass Communication & Society, 3*(2 & 3), 207–228.

Polkinghorne, D. E. (1991). Narrative and self-concept. *Journal of Narrative and Life History, 1*(2 & 3), 135–153.

Pollner, M. (1989). Divine relations, social relations, and well-being. *Journal of Health and Social Behavior, 30*(1), 92–104.

Powers, S. P., Rothman, D. J., & Rothman, S. (1992). Hollywood's class act. *Society, 29*(2), 57–64.

Prentice, D. A., & Gerrig, R. J. (1999). Exploring the boundary between fiction and reality. In S. Chaiken & Y. Trope (Eds.), *Dual-process theories in social psychology*. New York: The Guilford Press.

Prentice, N. M., Manosevitz, M., & Hubbs, L. (1978). Imaginary figures of early childhood: Santa Claus, Easter bunny, and the tooth fairy. *American Journal of Orthopsychiatry, 48*(4), 618–628.

Price, R. H., Choi, J. N., & Vinokur, A. D. (2002). Links in the chain of adversity following job loss: How financial strain and loss of personal control lead to depression, impaired functioning, and poor health. *Journal of Occupational Health Psychology, 7*(4), 302–312.

Promislo, M. D., Deckop, J. R., Giacalone, R. A., & Jurkiewicz, C. L. (2010). Valuing money more than people: The effects of materialism on work-family conflict. *Journal of Occupational and Organizational Psychology, 83*(4), 935–953.

Pronin, E., Gilovich, T., & Ross, L. (2004). Objectivity in the eye of the beholder: Divergent perceptions of bias in self versus others. *Psychological Review, 111*(3), 781–799.

Pronin, E., Lin, D. Y., & Ross, L. (2002). The bias blind spot: Perceptions of bias in self versus others. *Personality and Social Psychology Bulletin, 28*(5), 369–381.

Prothero, S. R. (2007). *Religious literacy: What every American needs to know—and doesn't*. New York: HarperOne.

Putnam, R. (2000). *Bowling alone*. New York: Simon and Schuster Paperbacks.

Rampton, S., & Stauber, J. (2001). *Trust us, we're experts!: How industry manipulates science and gambles with your future*. New York: Jeremy P. Tarcher / Putnam.

Randall, A. K., & Bodenmann, G. G. (2009). The role of stress on close relationships and marital satisfaction. *Clinical Psychology Review, 29*(2), 105–115.

Ravitch, D. (1983). *The troubled crusade: American education 1945–1980*. New York: Basic Books.

Ravitch, D. (2010). *The death and life of the great American school system: How testing and choice are undermining education*. New York: Basic Books.

Reichley, J. (1992). *The life of the parties: A history of American political parties*. New York: The Free Press.

Reising, R. (2006). *ChurchMarketing 101: Preparing your church for greater growth*. Grand Rapids, MI: Baker Books.

Remondet, J. H., & Hansson, R. O. (1991). Job-related threats to control among older employees. *Journal of Social Issues, 47*(4), 129–141.

Rice, T. W. (2003). Believe it or not: Religious and other paranormal beliefs in the United States. *Journal for the Scientific Study of Religion, 42*(1), 95–106.

Ricoeur, P. (1984). *Time and narrative, volume 1* (K. McLaughlin & D. Pellauer, Trans.). Chicago, IL: The University of Chicago Press.

Ridley, M. (1996) *The origins of virtue*. New York: Viking.

Riesman, D., Glazer, N., & Denney, R. (1950). *The lonely crowd.* New York: Doubleday & Company.

Rizzolatti, G., & Craighero, L. (2004). The mirror-neuron system. *Annual Review of Neuroscience, 27,* 169–192.

Rokeach, M. (1965). The paradoxes of religious belief. *Society, 2*(2), 9–12.

Roksa, J., Grodsky, E., Arum, R., & Gamoran, A. (2007). United States: Changes in higher education and social stratification. In Y. Shavit, R. Arum, & A. Gamoran (Eds.), *Stratification in higher education: A comparative study* (pp. 165–191). Stanford, CA: Stanford University Press.

Rose-Ackerman, S. (1999). *Corruption and government: Causes, consequences, and reform.* Cambridge: Cambridge University Press.

Rosenberg, N., & Nelson, R. R. (1993). American universities and technical advance in industry. *Research Policy, 23*(3), 323–348.

Rosenfeld, E., Huesmann, L. H., Eron, L. D., & Torney-Purta, J. V. (1982). Measuring patterns of fantasy behavior in children. *Journal of Personality and Social Psychology, 42*(2), 347–366.

Rosengren, K. S., Johnson, C. N., & Harris, P. L. (Eds.). (2000). *Imagining the possible: Magical, scientific, and religious thinking in children.* Cambridge: Cambridge University Press.

Ross, C. E., Mirowsky, J., & Goldsteen, K. (1990). The impact of the family on health: The decade in review. *Journal of Marriage & Family, 52*(4), 1059–1078.

Ross, C. E., Reynolds, J. R., & Geis, K. J. (2000). The contingent meaning of neighborhood stability for residents' psychological well-being. *American Sociological Review, 65*(4), 581–597.

Ross, D. (2004). *The origins of American social science.* New York: Cambridge University Press.

Rothbaum, F., Weisz, J. R., & Snyder, S. S. (1982). Changing the world and changing the self: A two-process model of perceived control. *Journal of Personality and Social Psychology, 42*(1), 5–37.

Rozin, P., Millman, L., & Nemeroff, C. (1986). Operation of the laws of sympathetic magic in disgust and other domains. *Journal of Personality and Social Psychology, 50*(4), 703–712.

Rury, J. L. (2013). *Education and social change: Contours in the history of American schooling* (4th ed.). New York; London: Routledge.

Sarewitz, D. (2010). Normal science and limits on knowledge: What we seek to know, what we choose not to know, what we don't bother knowing. *Social Research, 77*(3), 997–1009.

Schanck, R. L. (1932). A study of community and its group institutions conceived of as behavior of individuals. *Psychological Monographs, 43*(2), 1–133.

Schenk, C. T., & Holman, R. H. (1980). A sociological approach to brand choice: The concept of situational self image. *Advances in Consumer Research, 7,* 610–614.

Schieman, S., Nguyen, K., & Elliott, D. (2003). Religiosity, socioeconomic status, and the sense of mastery. *Social Psychology Quarterly, 66*(3), 202–221.

Schmidt, L. E. (1995). *Consumer rites: The buying & selling of American holidays.* Princeton, NJ: Princeton University Press.

Schneider, D. M. (1973). Notes toward a theory of culture. In K. H. Basso & H. A. Selby, (Eds.), *Meaning in anthropology* (pp. 197–220). Albuquerque: University of New Mexico Press.

Schudson, M. (1984). *Advertising, the uneasy persuasion: Its dubious impact on American society.* New York: Basic Books.

Schuster, J. H., & Finkelstein, M. J. (2006). *The American faculty: The restructuring of academic work and careers.* Baltimore. MD: The Johns Hopkins University Press.

Sheldon, C. (1896). *In his steps: What would Jesus do?.* New York: George Monroe's Sons.

Shelton, J. N., & Richeson, J. A. (2005). Intergroup contact and pluralistic ignorance. *Journal of Personality and Social Psychology, 88*(1), 91–107.

Silverstein, M. (1973). Shifters, linguistic categories, and cultural description. In K. H. Basso & H. A. Selby (Eds.), *Meaning in anthropology* (pp. 11–54). Albuquerque: University of New Mexico Press.

Simmel, G., & Frisby, D. (Ed.). (1990). *The philosophy of money* (T. Bottomore & D. Frisby, Trans.). New York: Routledge. (Original work published 1907)

Simmel, G., & Wolff, K. H. (Ed.). (1964). *The sociology of Georg Simmel* (K. H. Wolff, Trans.). New York: The Free Press.

Sinclair, B. (2006). *Party wars: Polarization and the politics of national policy making*. Norman: University of Oklahoma Press.

Singer, D. G., & Singer, J. L. (1986). Family experiences and television viewing as predictors of children's imagination, restlessness, and aggression. *Journal of Social Issues, 42*(3), 107–124.

Singer, D. G., & Singer, J. L. (1990). *The house of make-believe: Children's play and the developing imagination*. Cambridge, MA: Harvard University Press.

Sizer, T. R., & Sizer, N. F. (1999). *The students are watching: Schools and the moral contract*. Boston: Beacon Press.

Smith, A. (2000). *The wealth of nations*. New York: Modern Library. (Original work published 1791)

Smith, C. (2002). *Christian America? What evangelicals really want*. Berkeley: University of California Press.

Solomon, M. R. (1983). The role of products as social stimuli: A symbolic interactionism perspective. *Journal of Consumer Research, 10*(3), 319–329.

Spilka, B., Shaver, P., & Kirkpatrick, L. A. (1985). A general attribution theory for the psychology of religion. *Journal for the Scientific Study of Religion, 24*(1), 1–20.

Stampfl, R. W., Moschis, G., & Lawton, J. T. (1978). Consumer education and the preschool child. *The Journal of Consumer Affairs, 12*(1), 12–29.

Stark, R., & Bainbridge, W. S. (1985). *The future of religion: Secularization, revival, and cult formation*. Berkeley: University of California Press.

Steele, C. M. (1997). A threat in the air. *American Psychologist, 52*(6), 613–629.

Stern, D. N. (1984). *The interpersonal world of the infant: A view from psychoanalysis and developmental psychology*. New York: Basic Books.

Sternberg, R. J. (1986). A triangular theory of love. *Psychological Review, 93*(2), 119–135.

Sternberg, R. J. (1996). Love stories. *Personal Relationships, 3*(1), 59–79.

Stiglitz, J. E. (2003). *The roaring nineties: A new history of the world's most prosperous decade*. New York: W. W. Norton & Company.

Stiglitz, J. E., & Bilmes, L. J. (2008). *The three trillion dollar war: The true cost of the Iraq conflict*. New York: W. W. Norton & Company.

Story, L. B., & Bradbury, T. N. (2004). Understanding marriage and stress: Essential questions and challenges. *Clinical Psychology Review, 23*(8), 1139–1162.

Strange, J., & Leung, C. (1999). How anecdotal accounts in news and fiction can influence judgments of a social problem's urgency, causes, and cures. *Personality and Social Psychology Bulletin, 25*(4), 436–449.

Sverke, M., & Hellgren, J. (2002). The nature of job insecurity: Understanding employment uncertainty on the brink of a new millennium. *Applied Psychology: An International Review, 51*(1), 23–42.

Swartz, D. (1998). *Culture and power: The sociology of Pierre Bourdieu*. Chicago, IL: The University of Chicago Press.

Swidler, A. (1980). Love and adulthood in American culture. In N. J. Smelser & E. H. Erikson (Eds.), *Themes of work and love in adulthood* (pp. 120–147). Cambridge, MA: Harvard University Press.

Symonds, W. C., Grow, B., & Cady, J. (2005). Earthly empires. *Bloomberg Businessweek,* (3934), 78–88.

Symons, D. (1979). *The evolution of human sexuality*. New York: Oxford University Press.

Taylor, E. (1999). *Shadow culture: Psychology and spirituality in America* (1st print ed.). Washington, DC: Counterpoint.

Taylor, S. E. (1983). Adjustment to threatening events: A theory of cognitive adaptation. *American Psychologist, 38*(11), 1161–1173.

Taylor, S. E., & Brown, J. D. (1988). Illusion and well-being: A social psychological perspective on mental health. *Psychological Bulletin, 103*(2), 193–210.

Thomas, W. I., & Thomas, D. T. (1928). *The child in America: Behavior problems and programs.* New York: A. A. Knopf.

Thompson, S. C., Armstrong, W., & Thomas, C. (1998). Illusions of control, underestimations, and accuracy: A control heuristic explanation. *Psychological Bulletin, 123*(2), 143–161.

Trenchard, J., & Gordon, T. (1971). *Cato's letters: Essays on liberty, civil and religious, and other important subjects.* New York: Da Capo Press. (Original work published 1755)

Trevarthen, C. (1993). The self born in intersubjectivity: The psychology of an infant communicating. In U. Neisser (Ed.), *The Perceived self: Ecological and interpersonal sources of self-knowledge* (pp. 121–173). Cambridge: Cambridge University Press.

Turner, R. (1990). Bloodless battles: The Civil War reenacted. *The Drama Review, 34*(4), 123–136.

Turner, R. J., Wheaton, B., & Lloyd, D. A. (1995). The epidemiology of social stress. *American Sociological Review, 60*(1), 104–125.

Valkenburg, P. M. (2001). Television and the child's developing imagination. In D. G. Singer & J. L. Singer (Eds.), *Handbook of children and the media.* Thousand Oaks, CA: Sage Publications.

Veblen, T. (1899). *Theory of the leisure class: An economic study in the evolution of institutions.* New York: Macmillan.

Vinden, P. (1998). Imagination and true belief: A cross-cultural perspective. In J. de Rivera & T. R. Sarbin (Eds.). *Believed-in imaginings: The narrative construction of reality.* Washington, DC: American Psychological Association.

Vinokur, A. D., Price, R. H., & Caplan, R. D. (1996). Hard times and hurtful partners: How financial strain affects depression and relationship satisfaction of unemployed persons and their spouses. *Journal of Personality and Social Psychology, 71*(1), 166–179.

Vygotsky, L., & Cole, M. (1978). *Mind in society: The development of higher psychological processes.* Cambridge, MA: Harvard University Press.

Wallbott, H. G. (1991). The robustness of communication of emotion via facial expression: Emotion recognition from photographs with deteriorated pictorial quality. *European Journal of Social Psychology, 21*(1), 89–98.

Washburn, J. (2005). *University, Inc.: The corporate corruption of American higher education.* New York: Basic Books.

Washington, J. M. (1991). *A testament of hope: The essential writings and speeches of Martin Luther King, Jr.* New York: HarperCollins Publishers.

Weber , M. (2001). *The protestant ethic and the spirit of capitalism.* London: Routledge. (Original work published 1904)

Weber, M., Gerth, H. H. (Ed.), & Mills, C. W. (Ed.). (1946). *From Max Weber: Essays in sociology.* New York: Oxford University Press.

Weber, M., Roth, G. (Ed.), & Wittich, C. (Ed.). (1978). *Economy and society: An outline of interpretive sociology* (E. Fischoff, H. Gerth, A. M. Henderson, F. Kolegar, C. W. Mills, T. Parsons, . . . C. Wittich, Trans., Vol. 2). Berkeley: University of California Press.

Weedon, C., Tolson, A., & Mort, F. (1980). Theories of language and subjectivity. In S. Hall (Ed.), *Culture, media, language: Working papers in cultural studies, 1972–1979* (pp. 194–216). London: Hutchinson.

Weinberg, A. M. (1963). Criteria for scientific choice. *Minerva, 1*(2), 158–171.

Wells, W. D. (1989). Lectures and dramas. In P. Cafferata & A. Tybout (Eds.), *Cognitive and affective responses to advertising.* Lexington, MA: Lexington Books.

Whitfield, S. J. (1992). *The culture of the cold war.* Baltimore, MD: The Johns Hopkins University Press.

Wiley, T. (2002). *Original sin: Origins, developments, contemporary meanings.* New York: Paulist Press.

Williams, J. D., & Qualls, W. J. (1989). Middle-class black consumers and intensity of ethnic identification. *Psychology & Marketing, 6*(4), 263–286.

Williams, R. (1997). *Problems in materialism and culture: Selected essays.* London: Verso.

Wilson, C. (1963). *The outsider.* London: Pan Books.

Wood, G. (1991). *The radicalism of the American Revolution* (1st ed.). New York: Vintage Books.

Woodhouse, E., Hess, D., Breyman, S., & Martin, B. (2002). Science studies and activism: Possibilities and problems for reconstructivist agendas. *Social Studies of Science, 32*(2), 297–319.

Woodhouse, E., & Sarewitz, D. (2007). Science policies for reducing societal inequities. *Science and Public Policy, 34*(3), 139–150.

Woolley, J. D. (1997). Thinking about fantasy: Are children fundamentally different thinkers and believers from adults? *Child Development, 68*(6), 991–1011.

Wright, J. C., Huston, A. C., Truglio, R., Fitch, M., Smith, E., & Piemyat, S. (1995). Occupational portrayals on television: Children's role schemata, career aspirations, and perceptions of reality. *Child Development, 66*(6), 1706–1718.

Wuthnow, R. (1988). *The restructuring of American religion: Society and faith since World War II*. Princeton, NJ: Princeton University Press.

Zajonc, R. B. (1980). Feeling and thinking: Preferences need no inferences. *American Psychologist, 35*(2), 151–175.

Zerubavel, E. (1991). *The fine line: Making distinctions in everyday life*. New York: The Free Press.

Zweigenhaft, R. L., & Domhoff, G. W. (1998). *Diversity in the power elite: Have women and minorities reached the top?*. New Haven, CT: Yale University Press.

Index

About the Author

Nathan Rousseau is professor of sociology at Jacksonville University. He also serves as commissioner on the Jacksonville Human Rights Commission. Previous publications include his edited book *Self, Symbols, and Society: Classic Readings in Social Psychology* and articles on human rights as well as religion. Rousseau's research interests include social theories of individualism, East-West comparative religions, and human rights issues concerning race relations in the United States and ethnic relations in the Middle East.